D0284131

NEW YORK STREETSCAPES

NEW YORK STREETSCAPES

TALES OF MANHATTAN'S SIGNIFICANT BUILDINGS AND LANDMARKS

Christopher Gray

RESEARCH BY
Suzanne Braley

HARRY N. ABRAMS, INC., PUBLISHERS

DEDICATION

To Erin

CONTENTS

INTRODUCTION

MY PERSONAL INTRODUCTION TO NEW YORK HISTORY was like shock treatment. At age nine, I was moved (over my protests) from a quiet little streetcar suburb of Kansas City, Missouri, to East 56th Street near the East River in New York. Every day I walked to the Browning School at 62nd Street and Park Avenue through a landscape that bore little relation to what I had left: it was a jagged cross-section of the typical New York jumble of tenements, brownstones, white brick apartment houses, mansions, fancy co-ops, and stores. It piqued in me the ambition to explain (if only to myself) how this train wreck of a city was assembled. Thus, from an early age I was interested not simply in the major landmarks of New York but also in the day-to-day architecture of the streets. This need to order my environment grew as I got older. As a taxi driver, I learned the best routes around the city. (The most important rule: Take the narrow east-west streets; only the boring and cautious take the broad ones.) And as a post office truck driver, I saw the invisible network of routes, relay boxes, drop points and other logistical systems that go into our astonishingly efficient mail service. I saw that telephone repairmen, UPS drivers, dog walkers, mortgage lenders, and everyone else had their own unique ways of mapping the city. I decided I would map the city by its history.

This casually chosen ambition was fueled by a life-long annoyance with the blissful acceptance of ignorance, a common condition in New York, as in, "Nobody knows the name of the architect—all the records were burned in a fire." (There was no such fire.) Or, even worse, "Oh, yeah, it was built for the three Vanderbilt sisters by Stanford White." (It wasn't built for them, and it wasn't built by him.)

My day-to-day walks through the city are a whirl of half-baked story ideas, which I usually reject because of some negative thought. No, there's no good old photograph of that structure. Or, no, that's such a boring building, like dry toast! Or, no, the story is too arcane. For newspaper purposes there has to be an angle to every story—a building is being restored, not being restored, being ignored, being...anything, as far as I can tell. Editors believe their readers cannot just revel in peculiar arcana. But generally, I am much more interested in minor-league, oddball structures than in tour-bus monuments like the Woolworth Building, which are either much gone over or (here is my particular heresy) much ado about the obvious.

Once the news-angle requirement is satisfied when I'm developing a column, the next item of business is identifying a historic photograph, preferably a sharp image full of street life, showing not only the subject building in a virginal state but also the adjacent buildings in awful desuetude. This contrast—between the fresh and the fetid—is one of the things I find most pleasurable. It is the changing, constantly aging face of the city that is most delicious to me: the sense of thousands of feet wearing down the front steps of a tenement, or a multitude of hands burnishing an oak subway handrail, or the weather smoothing a bluestone flag to an ancient, feathery silver. And that is why most "restorations" leave me cold—very, very few restored buildings retain a sense of the place's history.

Next I focus on the people with interesting stories, whether they are millionaires or sweatshop workers. Their stories are found in census returns, directories, tax and building records, and newspaper stories. To riff on Luc Sante's *The Unknown Soldier,* they are "everywhere under your feet." What human suffering and endurance is presented by the bare, factual census return for 1910 of the Lower East Side family of fifty-three-year-old Max Goldstein, a fish dealer, who came to the United States from Russia in 1890. He came with his son Nathan, then only ten. Goldstein had to leave behind his wife, Zlote, and the rest of his family. However, in 1896 Zlote came to America with Goldstein's younger children including Morris, who was five years old in 1890, and Sophie, then still unborn. How they all must have pined for each other during the separation and rejoiced as they were reunited in their cramped quarters in the New World. Also consider the poignancy of the entry "9, 4" in the 1910 census record for Zlote Goldstein—meaning "9 children born, 4 living." (If you're interested in such stories, a guide to researching New York City buildings is posted at www.nysoclib.org.)

New York, especially Manhattan, is a particularly gratifying place for this type of research for several reasons. First, the sheer number of people coming through the city assures that almost every building will have an interesting tale. Second, the anonymity of the city means that most information is lost to local memory far sooner than in a suburban or rural environment. Where I spent my first nine years, people could commonly recount neighborhood events from fifty or seventy-five years ago—in New York that's like asking people when the last woolly mammoth came through.

This book, which Abrams' former publisher Mark Magowan first envisioned and editor Elisa Urbanelli first nurtured, includes about two hundred of the "Streetscapes" columns originally published in the Sunday *New York Times* Real Estate Section. The column originated in 1987, when it was edited by the late Michael Sterne, and has been edited since 1992 by Michael Leahy. Shortening the columns by half, as they are here, eliminates most of the "news" and focuses instead on my favorite parts, the old: the anarchist architect John Edelmann; the butler Ernest Vernon, who was dressed in black and weeping into a handkerchief at his master's funeral; Dr. Louise Robinovitch, who threw away her medical career to help her swindler brother, defying her parents to do so. New York's buildings are much too often described simply in dry architectural terms, empty of the human condition. Sure, I'm an architectural historian, but in New York "Architecture" has little to do with it.

CHRISTOPHER GRAY

RESEARCHER'S NOTE

While I was at the Municipal Archives doing research for one of the articles included in this book, someone searching for information on his family asked me what I was doing. I answered that I was examining tax records, building permits, and directories to trace information about a building, rather than a family. "I've got it. You're a building genealogist," he said. From cranking microfilms of nineteenth-century New York City newspapers through readers at the New York Public Library years ago to conducting online searches through newspaper archives today, the life of a researcher has changed over the period these "Streetscapes" articles were written. Facilities have closed and reopened, have moved and been remodeled, have added new materials and new technologies, and, unfortunately, have sometimes misplaced items or limited access. Through it all, the dedicated staffs at the Municipal Archives, the New York Public Library, the New-York Historical Society, and Columbia University Libraries have unfailingly provided assistance whenever asked. They must know the joy that finding the answer to a question, or the answer that leads to another question, can bring to a "building genealogist."

SUZANNE BRALEY

LOWER MANHATTAN

THE AMERICAN SURETY BUILDING

PINE STREET AND BROADWAY

THE AMERICAN SURETY BUILDING, at the southeast corner of Pine Street and Broadway, was the Seagram Building of the 1890s, the apotheosis of sensitive office-building design at a time when new skyscrapers were widely criticized. In 1894 the American Surety Company, established in 1884 to guarantee corporate and legal obligations, paid almost $1.5 million for a squarish plot at Broadway and Pine, measuring only 85 feet on a side. The architect Bruce Price won a competition for a new twenty-one-story skyscraper.

The American Surety Building came at a time when the new crop of tall buildings was shocking New Yorkers. In 1894 the *Real Estate Record and Guide* said the incipient generation of twenty-story buildings "evokes only one feeling, that of horror." The Chamber of Commerce proposed restrictions on tall buildings, and most architects agreed with a bill introduced in Albany to restrict heights. Their objections involved increased sewage, congestion, and fire danger, and the shutting off of light and air to adjacent buildings.

There was also the question of aesthetics: In the magazine *Architectural Record* the critic Russell Sturgis decried the "inconceivably ugly back walls and side walls . . . hardly justifiable even in the rear wall of a cheap brick three-story dwelling house." Perhaps because of the controversy the new American Surety Building was unlike any previously built. In basic quality it was almost public in character. Built entirely of Maine granite, it presented Broadway with a giant Ionic entry portico surmounted by standing female figures representing honesty, fidelity, self-denial, and other virtues, by the sculptor J. Massey Rhind.

Above, the relation between the raised banding and the width of the shaft worked with particular harmony, and the upper floors and attic were sumptuously carved. But the most distinctive elements were the lot-line walls: they were fully detailed, all the way around the building, something not even done on Fifth Avenue mansions. The writer Barr Ferree, writing in *Stone* magazine, praised the American Surety Company and predicted "the heartfelt thanks of all art lovers for its wise and generous action."

But it turned out that the American Surety Company was being generous with the property of another: John Jacob Astor IV. Astor owned the L-shaped parcel around the new building, and the American Surety Building's cornices, banding, and other elements projected up to three feet over the low buildings on Astor's lot. Astor protested in mid-construction and was rebuffed.

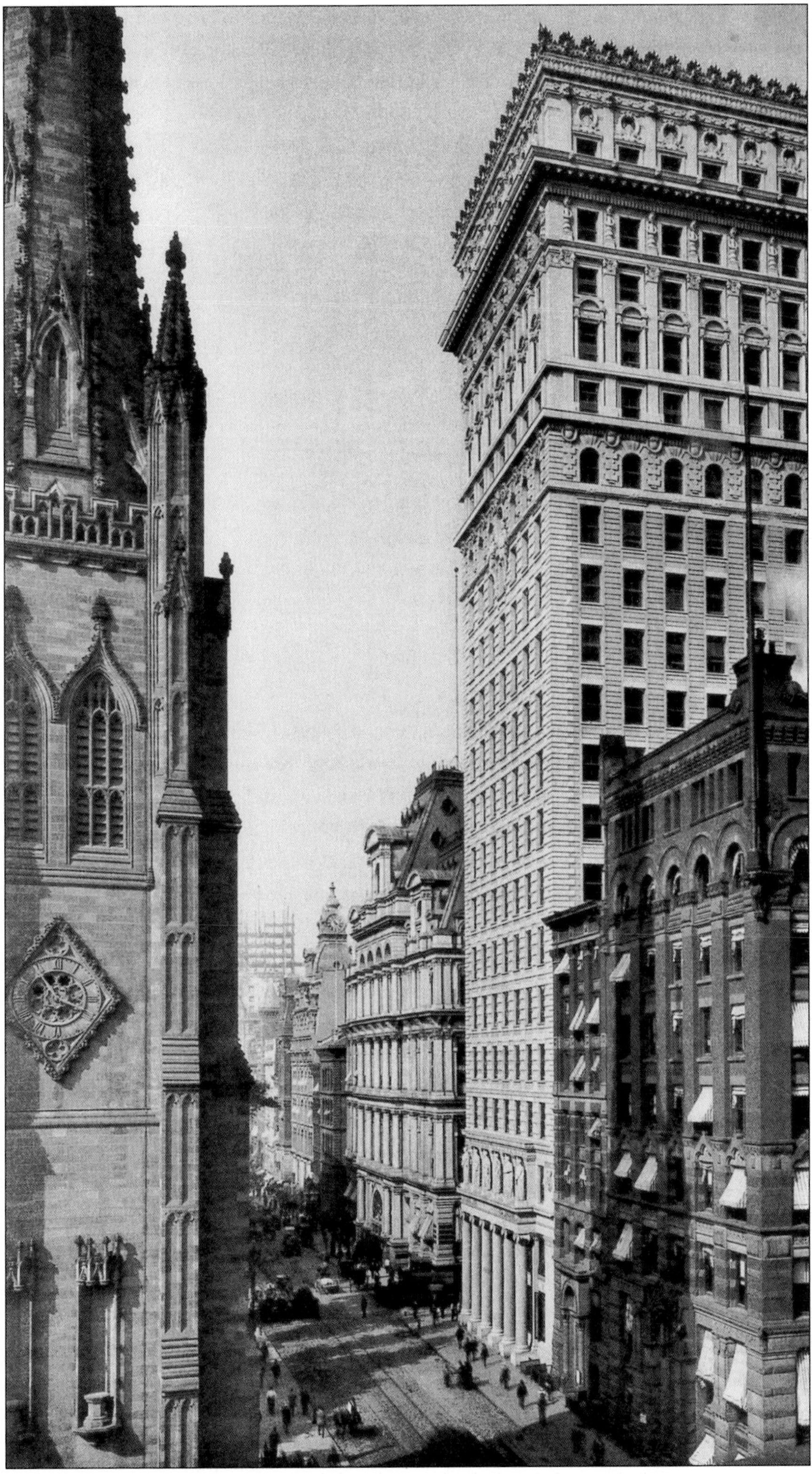

FIG 1.1

THE TWENTY-ONE-STORY AMERICAN SURETY BUILDING, *completed in 1896.*
COURTESY OFFICE FOR METROPOLITAN HISTORY

In May 1896 he had his engineers, Purdy & Henderson, file plans for a new twenty-one-story building on his land that would not only shear off much of Bruce Price's decoration but block up the two-hundred-odd windows that overlooked Astor's property. Within a few weeks the American Surety Company had agreed to lease Astor's property for $75,000 a year, about $900 for each office it was protecting.

The American Surety Building remained a point of reference for critics and architects long after its construction, even after the 1916 zoning law placed the first regulation on office heights.

40 WALL STREET

IN 1929, THE 1913 WOOLWORTH BUILDING, at 792 feet, was the world's tallest. Early that year, George L. Ohrstrom, a young investment banker, filed plans for a forty-seven-story office building at 40 Wall Street. He then amended his plan to sixty stories, still short of the Woolworth and the projected 808-foot-high Chrysler Building, announced in 1928. But in April his architect, H. Craig Severance, drew new plans, for a sixty-seven-story, 840-foot building, edging out the Woolworth by 48 feet and the Chrysler by 32.

Severance had made a name designing unusual Modernist commercial buildings in the early '20s with William Van Alen, and he may have found satisfaction in the new plan for 40 Wall Street—Van Alen was the architect of the Chrysler Building. In July 1929 a gold rivet was driven into the steelwork at 40 Wall and work proceeded at a furious pace. But in the fall, as the stock market crashed and the final steelwork was going into place, it was clear that something was afoot at the Chrysler Building.

Severance got a permit for a huge lantern at the top of 40 Wall Street, increasing the height to 875 feet, plus a 50-foot flagpole, and settled on a total height of 925 feet. But Van Alen had designed a 175-foot-high "vertex"—a spire—that was built secretly inside the Chrysler Building and hoisted into place in November, after changes to 40 Wall were impossible, making the Chrysler Building 1,030 feet high.

Accounts of the exact stages of the race—and the degree of rivalry between the former partners—are incomplete and contradictory, but it was an indisputable competition, one that Severance lost. However, he won in critical opinion, as most serious writers considered the Chrysler Building a commercial stunt whereas they liked the reserved, French Renaissance style of 40 Wall.

40 WALL STREET *with the Cities Service Tower in the background in 1938.* COURTESY OFFICE FOR METROPOLITAN HISTORY

Van Alen was the subject of many interviews and articles, but no one, it seems, interviewed Severance, the second-place finisher, as to his thoughts. His nephew, Malcolm Severance, remembers him as "a commanding, inspiring presence," kind but also tough: In a tennis game, his uncle once advised him, "when you get a guy down, don't let him up."

According to Leonard Levinson's history, *Wall Street*, published in 1961, some of the leases signed in 1929 for 40 Wall Street at $8 per square foot were made by companies that were bankrupt by 1930. The building was half empty and other space rented for $3 per square foot, but foreclosure came only in 1940.

In 1946 a military transport plane crashed into the fifty-eighth floor, killing four on board but no one in the building.

THE BRIDGE CAFE

NEW YORK'S OLDEST SURVIVING BAR AT 279 WATER STREET

UNTIL 1995, MCSORLEY'S OLD ALE HOUSE claimed the title of the oldest surviving saloon in New York, giving its opening date as 1854, based on casual research. But 1995 research by Richard McDermott, an amateur researcher, gave the title to the Bridge Cafe, in the sagging wooden building at 279 Water Street, which he has dated to 1847—and he's still working backward.

Mr. McDermott, a retired John Adams High School science teacher, began researching the Bridge Cafe as part of a larger project, and found a reference to a famous brothel at 279 Water Street "filled with river pirates and Water Street hags" run by a Tom Norton. He found Norton's bar listed in city directories from 1880 back to 1861. "Then it occurred to me that this might have been around even before McSorley's," he said.

So he first constructed a chain of title back to the early nineteenth century, and checked those names in city directories. That added only one listing, Maurice Hyland, who owned and ran the place from 1888 to 1890. In 1888, Hyland extended the old, two-and-a-half-story wooden building with a peaked roof into the present flat-topped three-story structure, with new wooden facades designed by Kurtzer & Rohl. He had established that the McCormacks took over the bar in 1922, and one day, he just happened to meet a habitué who remembered the operator prior to 1922—Peter J. Boyle. Mr. McDermott documented Boyle's bar at 279 Water Street back to 1910.

Mr. McDermott then worked the bar back to 1847, when business directories list Henry Williams operating a "porter house" in the building. At first he was told the business directories ended in 1860. But he discovered a later run, giving him enough names to fill in the period of 1847 to the present, except for 1892–1909. With dread, Mr.

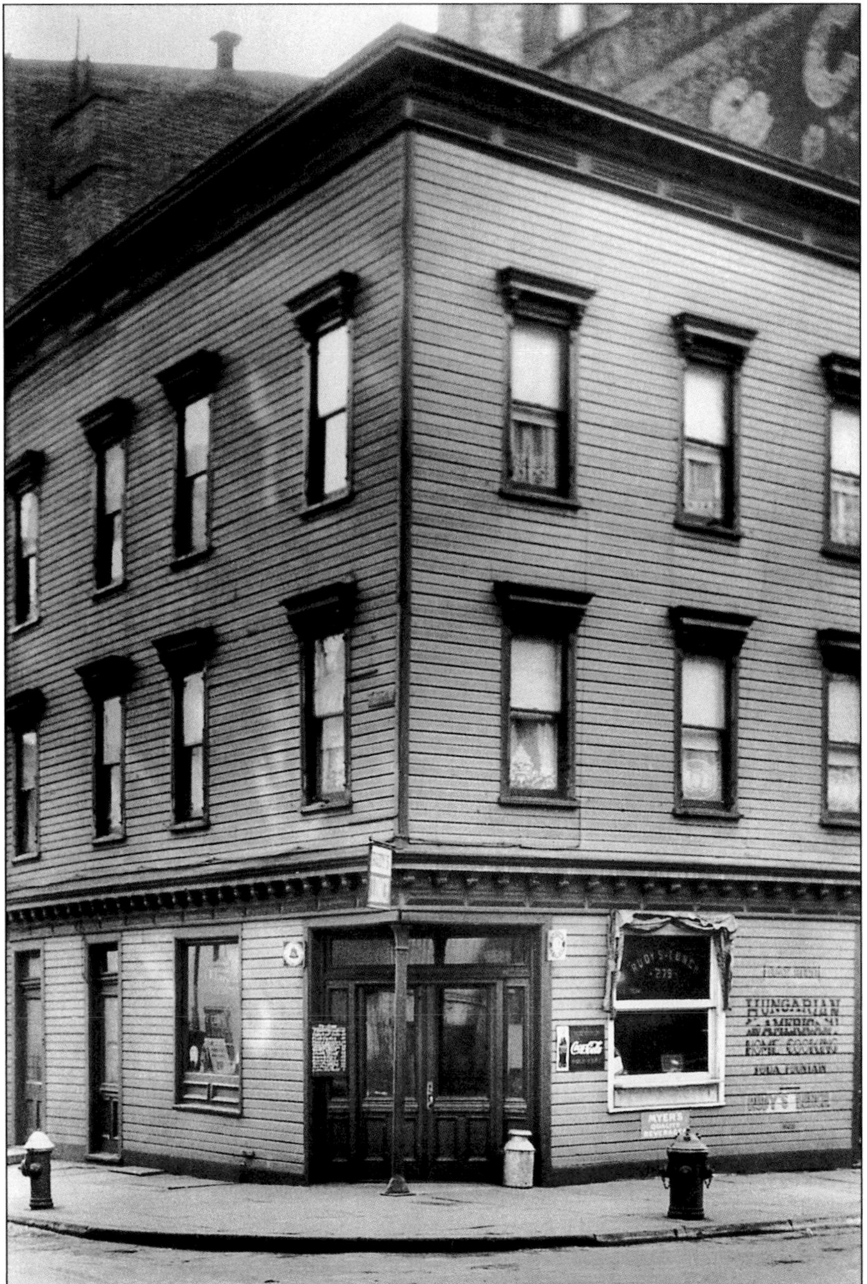

THE BAR AND RESTAURANT *at 279 Water Street in 1932.* COURTESY MUSEUM OF THE CITY OF NEW YORK

McDermott contemplated trying to catch an odd saloon operator by just reading through the regular, alphabetical city directories in that period; they are one thousand to two thousand pages long, with tiny print.

At the Municipal Archives, Leonora Gidlund, deputy director, produced, from an unprocessed collection, an elaborately printed license to sell liquor in "quantities less than five gallons at a time." The license was issued to Jeremiah Cronin and dated 1896—the archives has fewer than one hundred, and only for that year. Luckily for Mr.

McDermott, Jeremiah J. Cronin, an alderman from 1898 to 1901, operated the bar at 279 Water Street for the entire missing period, from 1892 to 1909. It was at that point that Mr. McDermott, to his satisfaction, unseated McSorley's as the oldest drinking establishment in New York.

At the time there were dark suggestions of legal action from McSorley's partisans. However, nothing came of it, perhaps because its own hallowed date of 1854 may need some more research of its own: John McSorley first appeared in city directories in 1862, and the building his bar occupies was built no earlier than 1858.

Then, too, the census taker who visited the Irish-born McSorley in 1900 recorded the year the founder of the pub at 15 East Seventh Street first arrived in the United States: 1855.

SEPTEMBER 16, 1920

A BOMB THAT ROCKED NEW YORK'S FINANCIAL DISTRICT

THE BOMB WENT OFF ON THURSDAY, SEPTEMBER 16, 1920, on Wall Street outside the headquarters of J. P. Morgan & Company, which still bears the scars. The Morgan bank had been finished in 1914 at the southeast corner of Broad and Wall Streets, "a rival to the Parthenon," said the *Real Estate Record and Guide.*

Since the rise of labor troubles in the late nineteenth century, the symbols of wealth and capitalism had been occasional targets of terrorist attacks. The *New York Times* quoted an unnamed Associated Press reporter who was standing nearby: "I first felt, rather than heard the explosion . . . with a concussion of air . . . sufficient to all but throw me off my balance. A mushroom-shaped cloud of yellowish green smoke mounted to the height of more than 100 feet, the smoke being licked by darting tongues of flames . . . . From the Morgan Building there was belching forth through the broken windows clouds of dust and white vapor. Almost in front of the steps leading up to the Morgan bank was the mutilated body of a man.

"Other bodies, most of them silent in death, lay nearby. As I gazed, horror-stricken at the sight, one of these forms, half-naked and seared with burns, started to rise. It struggled, then toppled and fell lifeless into the gutter. On the opposite side of the street were other forms. One of them was that of a young woman. It was moving, not in an effort to rise, but in the agony of death."

Of the thirty people killed, most were clerks, stenographers, and other such employees. The only person actually in the bank to die in the explosion was William A. Joyce, a twenty-four-year-old clerk who was filling in on the Wall Street side of J. P. Morgan for another worker.

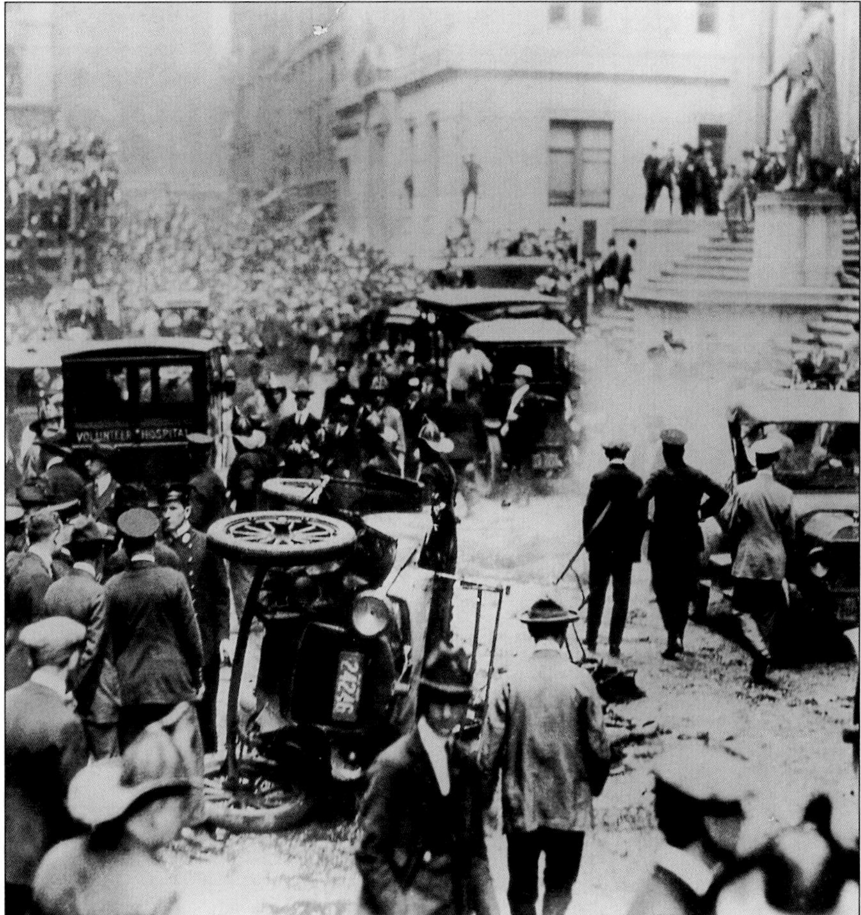

THE SCENE OUTSIDE J. P. MORGAN & COMPANY'S *headquarters on Wall Street on September 16, 1920, after a bomb in a parked horse-drawn wagon exploded at noontime.* COURTESY MUSEUM OF THE CITY OF NEW YORK

Broken sash weights that had been placed as shrapnel around the explosives flew up as high as thirty stories, and at least one landed five blocks away on John Street off Broadway.

Although rumors of an explosives wagon, a construction accident, and a labor dispute were widely discussed, the general suspicion was that the bomb was the work of foreign terrorists—Italian, German, or Russian. In the days after the blast, the police questioned hundreds of suspects and found a farrier who had recently reshod the horse that had drawn the wagon with the bomb.

By 1922, the reward money was up to $80,000, and the remains of the harness had been taken to every harness manufacturer in the United States, without result. No one was ever actually charged with the crime, and indeed the exact nature of the bomb was never firmly established: identification at that time was on the basis of the color, smell, and sound of the blast.

The fist-sized holes in the marble Wall Street facade of J. P. Morgan were never repaired. They are a textbook illustration of the damage caused by antipersonnel bombs, an inadvertent monument to the dead and wounded that can bring a chill to any spine. The person who carved it must have died long ago.

AT&T HEADQUARTERS

195 BROADWAY

THE OLD AT&T BUILDING, AT 195 BROADWAY, owes its existence to Theodore N. Vail. When Vail became the general manager of the nascent Bell Telephone Company, he moved it to New York and extended its reach into long distance and telephone manufacturing, organizing the American Telephone and Telegraph Company to oversee its growing empire. Vail became the president of AT&T in 1907 and of Western Union in 1909, when AT&T acquired it, promising important economies of scale.

To house this new enterprise, Vail planned a new twenty-nine-story headquarters at 195 Broadway in 1912, to be built in two parts along the full blockfront from Dey to Fulton Streets. The first part, at the Dey Street corner with an L-shaped wing connecting to Fulton Street, was not completed until 1916. So in 1915, when Alexander Graham Bell completed the first cross-country telephone call, he had to do it from another telephone-company building on the south side of Dey Street. In that call, Bell repeated his famous words of 1876—"Mr. Watson, come here, I want you"—to Thomas A. Watson in San Francisco.

While the building was going up, AT&T spun off Western Union in 1913, amid antitrust allegations. About this time, AT&T had commissioned Evelyn Beatrice Longman, a sculptor, to design an appropriate statue for its new building. The statue was a 24-foot winged male figure in gilded bronze, standing atop a globe, encircled by cables and holding electric bolts in one hand. She called the finished work *Genius of Telegraphy*, later renamed *Genius of Electricity*. The official name was changed once more, in the 1930s, to *Spirit of Communication*, reflecting the company's evolution. But it was the "Golden Boy" nickname that stuck.

World War I delayed the Fulton Street half of the AT&T Building, which was finally completed in 1922. It presented a massive neoclassical rebuke to the Beaux-Arts froufrou of earlier downtown skyscrapers. Layer upon layer of Doric and Ionic columns in cool gray granite rose up like an ancient monument. William Welles Bosworth, its architect, designed the lobby as a forest of forty-three giant marble columns, notable in their Doric simplicity, one of the great commercial interiors of the city. *American Architect* magazine noted that this emphasis on simplicity extended to the smallest details: "There are no manufacturers' names to be seen anywhere in the building, not even in the elevators. It is a relief to the tired brain, not to be forced to read lettering on all the fixtures, as has been so universally customary in this country. One sees no name placarded on the exterior of this building. It needs none."

FIG 5.1

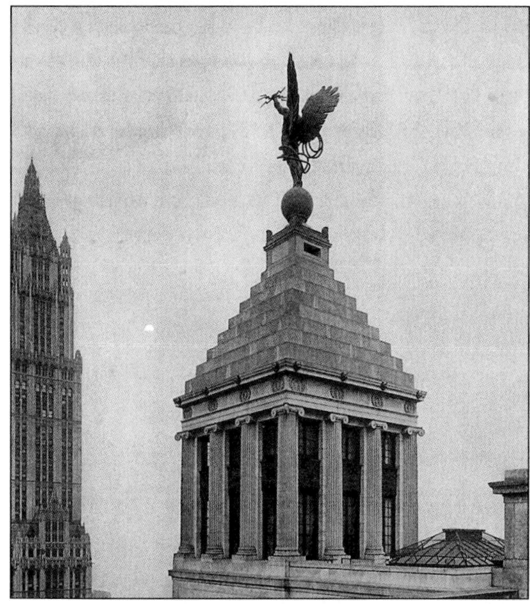

THE ORIGINAL STATUE, *Spirit of Communication.* COURTESY OFFICE FOR METROPOLITAN HISTORY

FIG 5.2

THE FIRST HALF OF THE AT&T BUILDING *completed in 1916, the L-shaped building, at left in 1920, began at Broadway and Dey Street and wrapped around to Fulton Street.* COURTESY OFFICE FOR METROPOLITAN HISTORY

Bosworth worked extensively for the Rockefeller family—he designed Kykuit, their Westchester estate—and in 1924 moved to France to supervise the Rockefeller-financed restoration of Versailles. Although the first cross-country call was placed from another building, the first transatlantic call, to London in 1927, was made from 195 Broadway, says Dr. Sheldon Hochheiser, AT&T's corporate historian.

The astonishing hall of this building is worth a trip, but look up no longer for "Golden Boy"—it is now at AT&T headquarters in Basking Ridge, New Jersey.

OLD CITIES SERVICE TOWER

70 PINE STREET

THE SIXTY-SIX-STORY BUILDING AT 70 PINE was the accomplishment of a grade-school dropout, Henry L. Doherty. Born in 1870 in Ohio, Doherty left school at age ten to sell newspapers in saloons. At twelve he was an office boy in a gas company office; he rose quickly as a manager and engineer, came to New York, and at forty founded the Cities Service Company, which both explored oil and gas fields and supplied local users.

Doherty lived on top of an office building at State and Bridge Streets—where 1 Battery Park Plaza is now—with a gym, squash court, and motorized bed that slid out onto the terrace. He bought several downtown sites for redevelopment but was hindered by recurrent bouts of arthritis. Doherty almost died in 1927 from complications of the disease—causing Cities Service stock to plunge—but recovered with the help of a family friend, Grace Eames, whom he wed in December 1928. She was a widow; it was his first marriage.

In 1930 Doherty filed plans for what became Wall Street's last jazz-age skyscraper. Designed by Clinton & Russell, Holton & George, the new building took the street address 70 Pine Street but, by an aerial bridge connection with 60 Wall Street, initially took the name 60 Wall Tower for cachet.

For a sixty-six-story building it was a tight plot, only 120 feet wide on Pearl. Engineers estimated that the economic height of the building was forty-eight stories—

THE TOWER AT 70 PINE STREET, *known as the Cities Service Building in 1938.* COURTESY MUSEUM OF THE CITY OF NEW YORK

FIG. 6.1

THE OBSERVATION ROOM *at 70 Pine Street in the early 1930s.*
COURTESY MUSEUM OF THE CITY OF NEW YORK

beyond that the service core of plumbing, stairs, and, especially, elevators, took up too much space relative to rentable area.

But in January 1930 D. L. Lundquist, chief engineer for Otis Elevator, had been interviewed by the *New York Sun* on the limiting factor for tall buildings and had predicted that double-deck elevators—two connected cabs using the same shaft—could solve the problem.

Doherty adopted the Otis plan, and the resulting design provided sixty floors of rentable offices, plus six smaller floors, including a kitchen and a mechanical floor, in the tower served by a separate small elevator from the sixtieth floor. A 1932 article in *Engineering News-Record* stated that eight shafts with double-deck cabs saved $200,000 in construction costs over fourteen regular elevators, and freed up 40,000 square feet. At the time $3.50 a square foot was a typical annual rent for such office space.

Unless the cab stopped without opening its door—a sign that the other cab was opening on another floor—passengers were not particularly aware of the double-deck operation. Perhaps they were still recovering from the lobby, an eye-burning Art Deco symphony of figured marble in high colors and sinuous metalwork.

On the outside the architects created a tapering shaft of simple streamlined design with sophisticated touches—in the corners at the upper floors, every third brick is rounded instead of squared, giving animation to the tower. The topmost floor, an observation deck, is a greenhouse-aerie, perhaps 30 by 20 feet square, with 360-degree views. It's in near-original shape, a glass jewel box at the top of the world. It has tiny outside balconies; a dizzying look down at 950 feet of upward streamlining can make one appreciate the view from street level.

FEDERAL RESERVE BANK

33 LIBERTY STREET

BUILT IN 1924, THE FLORENTINE-STYLE FEDERAL RESERVE BANK at 33 Liberty Street had long ago acquired an ancient-looking patina of black crust on its noble stones. When a yearlong facade cleaning was completed in the summer of 2001, it revealed a fascinating variety of coloration and pattern in the huge blocks of stone.

The Federal Reserve Bank, with its twelve regional divisions, was established in 1913 by a Congress wary of the growing concentration of giant banking interests. Benjamin Strong was selected to head the new Federal Reserve Bank of New York, which because of geography already held a leadership role in the system.

FIG 7.1

THE EXTERIOR OF THE FEDERAL RESERVE BANK *of New York in 1924.* COURTESY OFFICE FOR METROPOLITAN HISTORY

The bank had been using rented quarters, but in 1919 it held a competition for a new fourteen-story headquarters on the block bounded by Maiden Lane and Nassau, Liberty, and William Streets. The *Real Estate Record and Guide* said that "no sensational type of building would be entertained by the bank." York & Sawyer's design for the new Federal Reserve Bank of New York recalled the fortified Florentine palazzi of the Medici period in the Renaissance, with a deeply rusticated stone base banded by barred windows within pointed Florentine arches.

In 1929 the magazine *Architecture* quoted a young American who had come back from Europe marveling at

DETAIL OF THE FEDERAL RESERVE BANK *of New York in 1924.*
COURTESY OFFICE FOR METROPOLITAN HISTORY

everything he had seen except for one city. "Well, Florence didn't astound me so much," the anonymous American said jokingly. "Everywhere I looked I saw a building by York & Sawyer." York & Sawyer also carefully mixed the stone on the facade, using both the traditional Indiana limestone and a richly mottled Ohio sandstone. The walls' meeting point with the sidewalk rises and falls on the irregular, hilly site like a ship on a pitching ocean; each wall is alive with texture and movement.

On the interior, the three-level gold vault was cut into raw stone, which itself was below the waterline, making a robbery attempt by tunneling unlikely; the vault doors each weighed 230 tons. The $500 million in gold then on deposit was also protected with listening devices to detect any drilling or cutting. In 1929 a writer for the *Saturday Evening Post* asked a guard outside the building what time it was; the guard grabbed the handle of his gun, directed the writer to a nearby sidewalk clock, and instructed him to move on.

Strong died in 1928, leaving a power vacuum at the Federal Reserve. Although President Herbert Hoover blamed the severity of the Great Depression in part on Strong's aggressive efforts for European recovery in the 1920s, some analysts say that the depression would not have lasted as long had Strong been alive to direct Federal Reserve efforts.

By the 1960s, airborne soil had given the building a striking checkerboard look. The Ohio sandstone, more porous than the limestone, became blackened, making the building appear almost black and white. It was cleaned in the summer of 2001, freeing the stone of its black shroud, and revealing exuberant whorls and eddies, swirling lines of whiskey-brown in a matrix the color of heavy cream, as sensual as some exotic cheese.

THE OLD DELMONICO'S

56 BEAVER STREET

JOHN AND PETER DELMONICO, SWISS IMMIGRANTS, began a restaurant in lower Manhattan in 1827 and ten years later built a new one on the triangular lot at Beaver and South William Streets. An 1838 menu, "Carte du Restaurant Français de Frères Delmonico" runs eleven pages, with forty-seven kinds of veal, twelve kinds of boiled beef, fifty fish dishes, and twenty-one red Bordeaux—but only one kind of coffee.

FIG 8.1

CHARLES CRIST DELMONICO
DELMONICO'S
CATERER AND RESTAURATEUR

CHARLES CRIST DELMONICO. COURTESY OFFICE FOR METROPOLITAN HISTORY

By midcentury, Delmonico's was one of the most important restaurants in New York. According to Gale Harris, a historian with the Landmarks Preservation Commission, Charles Ranhofer, the chef of Delmonico's, created baked Alaska and lobster Newburg.

In 1884 ownership of the restaurant descended to the family of Rosa Delmonico Crist and her son, Charles, who changed their last name to Delmonico as a condition of the inheritance. In 1890 Charles Crist Delmonico filed plans for a new building on the site, designed by James Brown Lord.

"Now You May Dine Again," read a headline in the *World* on July 8, 1891, when the new eight-story building opened. "If you wanted to see a money broker, a stock broker, a produce broker, or any kind of a broker who has an office downtown, it was a ten to one shot that you would find him, after noon yesterday, at Charley Delmonico's," the accompanying article said.

The new Renaissance-style building had dining rooms on the first and second floor and a kitchen on the eighth floor, connected to the serving areas by pneumatic tubes and hydraulic elevators. The intermediate floors were leased out as offices. Lord's Renaissance design was sophisticated for a period of often-clunky Victoriana. At the ground floor, two marble columns and a cornice are sheltered inside the entryway; these were salvaged from the original building.

AND
HIGGINS
DELMONICO'S

DELMONICO'S BUILDING IN 1893. COURTESY OFFICE FOR METROPOLITAN HISTORY

In 1893 Delmonico's was found guilty of serving woodcock out of season. Delmonico at first said that they were other, legal birds prepared to deceive the customers. But after being presented with scientific testimony that they were indeed woodcock he told the *New York Times* that it was "his duty as a restaurateur to serve his customers with whatever viands they desired" even if they wanted "hummingbirds or bumblebees." The fine was $350—$25 for each of ten birds—plus $100 in costs.

Delmonico's also operated a succession of other restaurants on Broadway, 14th Street, and then Madison Square. The downtown building evolved into a daytime lunch operation, but the branches were the scenes of many society dinners and parties.

In the same year as the woodcock fine, the waiters at the Madison Square Delmonico's walked off the job just before dinner, demanding $35 a month, the privilege of wearing mustaches, and a day off every two weeks. Delmonico refused them, breaking the strike with waiters from the Beaver Street restaurant.

Charles Crist Delmonico died in 1901, and the company was saddled with increasing debt and family disagreements. In 1917 the Delmonico family sold the Beaver Street building and closed the restaurant, and the same happened with their other locations.

THE BENNETT BUILDING

87 NASSAU STREET

NOW IT IS LOST AMONG THE RETAIL PANDEMONIUM of upper Nassau Street. But the Bennett Building, on the west side of Nassau between Fulton and Ann Streets, was once one of New York's notable skyscrapers and is perhaps the tallest cast-iron building in the world.

In the late 1860s James Gordon Bennett Jr. took over the management of the *New York Herald* from his father, who had founded it on a shoestring in 1835. The newspaper had recently vacated its old location at the northwest corner of Nassau and Fulton Streets for a new building on Broadway, and in 1872 the younger Bennett filed plans for a new structure on the old site, seven stories capped by a mansard roof.

Completed in 1873, it was not the tallest building in the city. But the size of the operation—292 front feet on three streets—made it one of the most prominent.

Designed by Arthur D. Gilman, the facade is heavy with repetition, like most other cast-iron buildings of its period, although the architect avoided the column-on-top-of-column format common at the time.

The Bennett Building had two large stairways and two elevators. It is known that upper-floor space in walk-up buildings rented for substantially less money than that on

FIG 9.1

A HIGH VIEW *of the Bennett Building in 1883.* COURTESY THE NEW-YORK HISTORICAL SOCIETY, NEW YORK CITY

lower floors, but architecture historians are not clear on what happened when the elevator made all floors relatively equal.

The *Herald* published a figure of $125,000 for the yearly rent roll in the Bennett Building: $22,500 for the ground floor; $40,000 for the main floor (designed for a banking office); $20,000 for the second floor; $15,000 for the third floor; $12,500 for the fourth floor; $10,000 for fifth floor; and $5,000 for the sixth floor, the one enclosed by the mansard. Apparently the elevator did not instantly erase the prejudice against height.

FIG 9.2

THE BENNETT BUILDING *after three floors were added in 1895.* COURTESY OFFICE FOR METROPOLITAN HISTORY

Bennett was flamboyant and unpredictable in his personal and professional life. Just before he built the Bennett Building, he financed Henry Stanley's expedition to Africa in search of David Livingston, and he was active in the worlds of yachting, trap shooting, and polo.

Early in 1877, engaged to Caroline May, he committed some indiscretion while inebriated (by some accounts, urinating into the fireplace of the Union Club) and subsequently survived a duel with her brother, Frederick, over the matter. Unmarried, Bennett moved to France, where he started a Paris edition of the *Herald*, which survives today as the *International Herald Tribune*.

Bennett sold the structure in 1889, and in the 1890s a new owner first added three floors and then a matching, 25-foot-wide bay on Ann Street, all in cast iron. The rebuilt structure is ten full floors.

THE TWEED COURTHOUSE

52 CHAMBERS STREET

IT HAS BEEN ONE OF THE MOST REVILED BUILDINGS in the city's history, denounced as an eyesore and officially slated for demolition for three-quarters of a century until it was declared a landmark in 1984. But, after an extensive restoration, the Tweed Courthouse, at 52 Chambers Street, is prime space. It was the scene of a recent contest between a plan developed by former Mayor Rudolph Giuliani for reuse by the Museum of the City of New York and the idea of his successor, Mayor Michael Bloomberg, to give it over to the Board of Education.

William M. Tweed got his start in politics in the 1840s in the volunteer fire department and by 1857 had won appointment to the New York County Board of Supervisors. The board was given control over a projected county courthouse north of City Hall and during its prolonged construction the Tweed Ring—reaching even the mayor's office—inflated what should have been a $1 million project into nearly $12 million.

FIG 10.1

WILLIAM M. TWEED. COURTESY OFFICE FOR METROPOLITAN HISTORY

Tweed bought a quarry in Sheffield, Massachusetts, to supply marble for the exterior. Others also profited: Andrew Garvey, the "prince of plasterers," got $133,187 for two days' work, and George S. Miller, a carpenter, received $360,751 for his work in the month of June 1870 on a building with practically no woodwork.

The Tweed Ring began to disintegrate in 1871 after the *New York Times* published lists of fraudulent invoices, and work on the courthouse ended, although the building, designed by John Kellum, was incomplete.

The marble walls, in the Anglo-Italianate style, were up but the north and south porticoes and their grand stairs were unbuilt. Many of the rooms were completed—rich confections of Renaissance Revival styling—but the central rotunda was unfinished.

THE TWEED COURTHOUSE *at 52 Chambers Street near City Hall in 1929.* COURTESY DEPARTMENT OF GENERAL SERVICES

Kellum died in 1871, and in 1876 Leopold Eidlitz was retained to complete the building. He finished the grand portico and stair to Chamber Street, but built a medieval-style wing, beautiful but curiously out of place, where a matching southern entrance had been originally planned.

In the 1880s, pressure grew for more government buildings, and siting proved to be politically sensitive. The easiest thing was to build a huge complex in City Hall Park along the south side of Chambers Street—on the site of the Tweed Courthouse.

But there was strong sentiment in favor of ridding City Hall Park of any structures except City Hall; Mayor Hugh Grant supported demolition of the Tweed Courthouse in the early 1890s. The factions seesawed back and forth, with the incidental result that the courthouse survived, even though successive plans for a new Civic Center called for its removal right up through 1974.

The first defense of the building on historic grounds may have been by the architectural historian Henry Hope Reed, who promoted it in walking tours in the late 1950s. But in 1974, the Abraham D. Beame administration proposed demolition, and a Committee to Save the Tweed was formed, and it was later designated a landmark.

THE YOUNG MEN'S INSTITUTE

222 BOWERY

IN 1884 THE REAL ESTATE RECORD AND GUIDE predicted a rosy future for the Bowery, saying that it was "destined to be the great retail mart of the central and eastern portion of the city," even though it was lined with beer gardens and saloons and surrounded by tenements and lodging houses. But the officers of the Young Men's Christian Association (YMCA) focused on the saloons, because a year later they built their first branch, the Young Men's Institute, at 222 Bowery, between Spring and Prince Streets, to try to counteract the forces of dissipation.

The YMCA had been established in 1852 for the mental, social, and physical improvement of young men in a Christian environment; its central building was at 23rd Street and Fourth Avenue, now Park Avenue South. But most of the members of the Young Men's Institute were not active Christians, and the institute did not seek to proselytize but only to provide healthful alternatives to the Bowery's dance halls and liquor joints. For dues of $4 a year, an institute member got access to the five-story building's library, gymnasium, reading room, bowling alleys, and classes, including penmanship, bookkeeping, and architectural drawing. Inside and out, the new building was designed by Bradford Lee Gilbert in the Queen Anne style, and a review in the *Record and Guide* in 1885 praised it as "spirited and picturesque."

In 1887 what the *New York Tribune* termed "a rather delicate question" arose with an applicant, Wiltshire Payne. Requirements for admission were only that the candidate be of good moral character and between seventeen and thirty-five years old. Payne, who ran or worked in a restaurant, met those conditions, and sought to join the institute to take a mechanical-drawing course, a subject in which he had already received a bronze medal elsewhere. A member of St. Philip's Episcopal Church, he lived at 116 Macdougal Street.

What was "delicate" was that Payne, thirty-three, was black (the *Tribune* said he was "of light skin and good manners"). The institute finally refused Payne's request for admission, saying that the existing membership in the Bowery building was so prejudiced that many would resign, jeopardizing the good work already in progress. "You do not know how sorry I am that any restriction is made," Robert Ross McBurney, the YMCA's general secretary, wrote in a letter to Payne. McBurney offered Payne membership at the main branch at 23rd Street, which had similar classes and whose constituents were apparently not as prejudiced—it had other black members, although they did not use the gym. The *Tribune* reported only that Payne was indignant. Later directories continued to list him as a restaurant worker.

By 1891 the institute had 659 members studying vocal music, typewriting, engineering, and electricity. The next year it built a rooftop platform for chess and reading, "a pleasant, lofty perch on a hot evening," according to the *New York Times*, with bunting, lanterns, and a downwind bench for smokers. Membership had dropped to 444 by 1915, when the institute tore out the old gymnasium in the rear and put in a pool, but it finally left the building in 1932, when the area had become in part a symbol of drunkenness and dissipation.

FIG 11.1

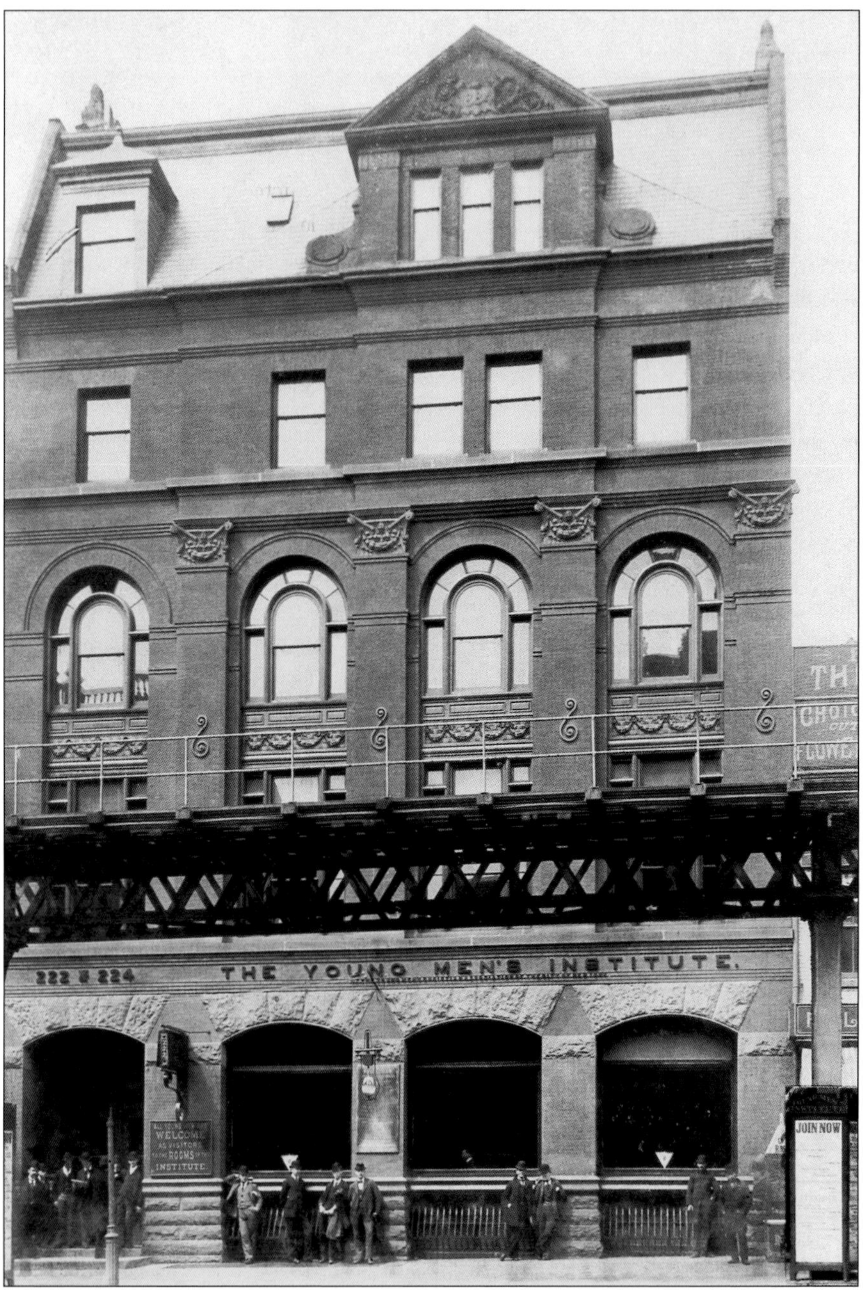

THE YOUNG MEN'S INSTITUTE IN 1886. COURTESY ARCHIVES, YMCA OF GREATER NEW YORK

MANHATTAN BRIDGE PLAZA

CANAL STREET AND THE BOWERY

FLYING TO EUROPE THIS SUMMER TO PONDER the ruins of ancient cultures? Take the subway instead, because over at Canal Street and the Bowery we've got a neat classical monument that looks like the barbarians had a great time—demolition, graffiti, fires, the works. Only in this case, the 1916 colonnade at the Manhattan Bridge Plaza is a city landmark, and the barbarians are . . . well, as Pogo observed, "We have met the enemy, and he is us."

No project ever realized the concept of the entire city as an integrated work of art more successfully than the plaza of the Manhattan Bridge, completed in 1916. The bridge had a complex history, but was ultimately designed by Carrère & Hastings and completed in 1909.

For the bridge plaza, a rectangle 400 by 750 feet bounded by the Bowery, Canal, Bayard, and Forsyth Streets was cleared. Over one thousand families were evicted for what the *New York Times* said, in 1912, would be "a complete, dignified and monumental ensemble, worthy of one of the principal gateways of a great modern city."

Granite retaining walls with ornamental balustrades bounded the entire area, and they enclosed large park spaces at opposite corners of the rectangle. The plaza itself was dominated by a great oval plaza similar to Bernini's for St. Peter's in Rome, with colored mosaic walkways and granite colonnade, centered on a triumphal arch modeled after the one at Porte Saint-Denis in Paris.

The sculptural decoration unites American and classical traditions. On the sides of the arch, C. A. Heber designed large sculptural panels, obelisk shaped, with allegorical figures. At the top a frieze of Native Americans hunting buffalo was designed by Carl Rumsey.

Early drawings for the plaza show sparse traffic, as if in a stately minuet around the center, which had a small island with poles for flags or banners. But later photographs show a more frenzied dance, as automobile speeds radically remade the city and its streets.

Modernizations during a half century of growing auto traffic have nibbled away most of the outer landscaping and balustrades. In 1968 the Department of Parks gave up the parkland to the south for what was built as Confucius Plaza.

Today the plaza of the Manhattan Bridge evokes not the City Beautiful but the sack of Rome. About one hundred parking spaces have been turned over to the Fifth Precinct for personal cars, putting Detroit metal on an even standing with Beaux-Arts sculpture.

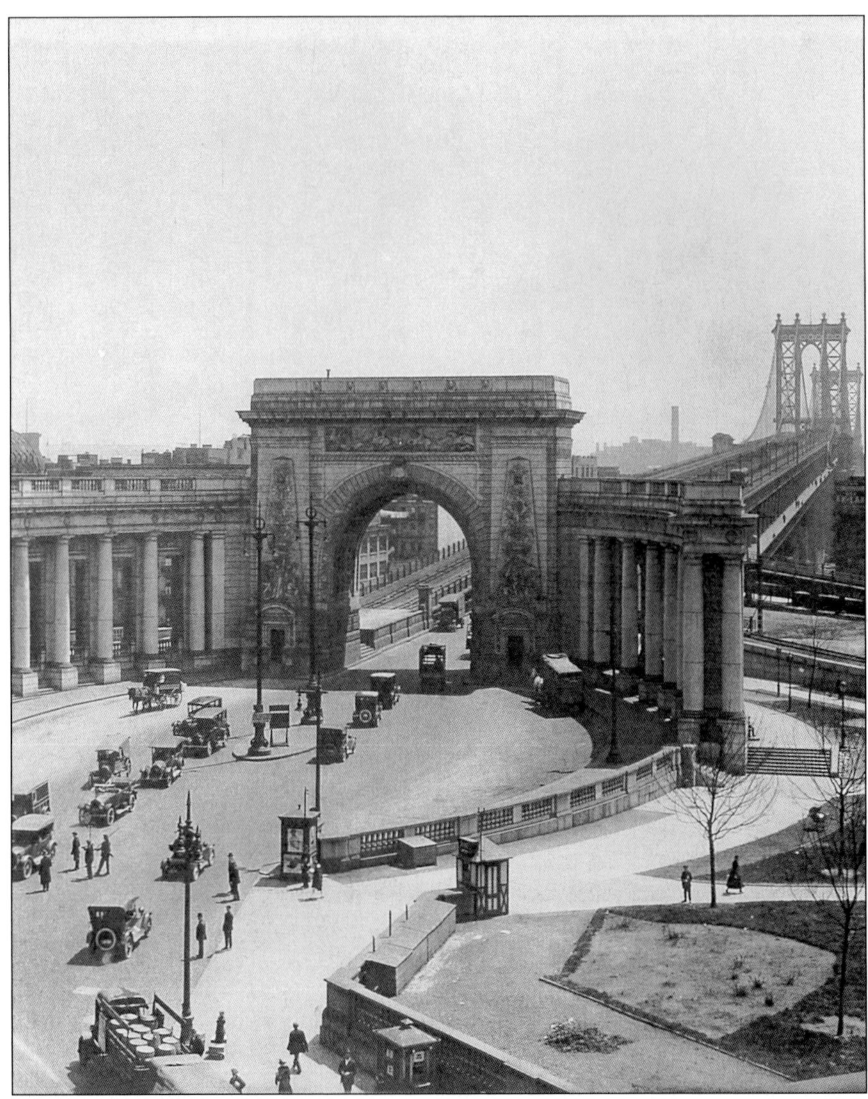

THE CLASSICALLY DESIGNED *Manhattan Bridge Plaza about 1920.* COURTESY OFFICE FOR METROPOLITAN HISTORY

The stonework of the colonnade and arch, although cleaned perhaps ten or twenty years ago, has wide-open mortar joints, with bushes and even small trees growing at the top. They are covered with graffiti and scarred by indifference. Sand and gravel piled against one side were removed with a front-end loader—which left giant gouges in the granite.

Although Robert Schulman, a spokesman for the Department of Transportation, said that department engineers assure him that there is no fire damage on any part of the colonnade or arch, the bonfires in one bay have spalled off more stone than that which remains.

Each bay of the half-encircling colonnade has a stone bench, and it is still ennobling to sit there, as the trucks thunder past, and contemplate the original design—it awakens a sense of citizenship, of being part of an ambitious and glorious undertaking.

ELDRIDGE STREET SYNAGOGUE

12–16 ELDRIDGE STREET

IF YOU HAVEN'T VISITED THE 1887 ELDRIDGE STREET SYNAGOGUE, you have missed one of New York's great interiors, a majestic collage of psychedelic polychromy and ruinous (but stabilized) decay.

Although the Lower East Side teemed with immigrants in tenement houses, it wasn't all poverty. Sender Jarmulowsky, a banker who was the synagogue's president, lived at 201 Henry Street, and Nathan Hutkoff, a trustee who was in the glass business, lived at 205 East Broadway.

Their architects, the Herter Brothers, produced a nice but not exceptional design for the exterior, a Moorish-style facade of brick and terra-cotta with a central gable.

Although the synagogue's organizers were all established Americans, the area was in the middle of a flood tide of newer arrivals, especially poor Eastern European Jews, who were often considered, even by their fellow Jews, unwashed, uneducated, and potentially un-American.

Thus, the account of the opening services in the *American Israelite* of September 16, 1887, concentrated on inappropriate behavior by those who attended. The article recounted a violent dispute, cigar smoking, talking out loud, walking around, and foot-tapping, all during the opening ceremonies, despite the attempts of the trustees to maintain order. In 1901 the congregation bought four dozen spittoons.

But Richard Wheatley, visiting in 1891 for the *Century* magazine, called the congregation "courteous," adding: "lawyers, merchants, artisans, clerks, peddlers and laborers compose the dense and changeful throng." By the 1910s many of the original incorporators had moved away: Jarmulowsky and Hutkoff both had moved to Upper East Side brownstones. In the 1930s, the congregation began to struggle for members—or perhaps, prosperous members.

In the 1950s, the congregation closed off the upper sanctuary and began worshippng in the basement, but a preservation group now offers tours. What greets the visitor now is a large, cubic space ringed by a gallery and heavy with dust and moldy air. Light streams through the large windows on four sides to illuminate a tangled litter of pews, fallen plasterwork, and original mural decoration, now dark with age. Even though the main floor has been tidied up, there is still the sense that you have entered a secret place.

AN 1886 WATERCOLOR DRAWING *of Eldridge Street Synagogue, completed the next year.* COURTESY MUSEUM OF THE CITY OF NEW YORK

Lines of construction lights are strung from the underside of the gallery and from the ancient gas jets that ring the columns. On the left of the ark a patch of mural—an illustionistic painting of windows overlooking Jerusalem—has recently been restored to its original brilliant colors. On the right is a matching portion, unrestored and darkened with age, adjacent to a large white slash of raw plaster.

The view from the upper gallery is like seeing a different building. From the sanctuary floor, you look up as if from the bottom of a pit, slightly blinded by the glare through the windows.

But on the gallery level the light is all around, even under you, and you can see the dreamy, fantastical decoration of the upper walls and ceiling: a quilted William Morris–type design on the walls, the deep azure with gold stars on the domes, and the wild Byzantine tracery on the middle wall. But there are also large areas of peeling paint and man-sized holes in the plaster. It is an astonishing place.

THE JARMULOWSKY BANK BUILDING

54–58 CANAL STREET

THE INDUSTRY OF THE WAVES OF IMMIGRANTS ARRIVING in New York at the turn of the twentieth century was matched by the rise of scores of banks catering to ethnic groups with different degrees of formality. "There is a bank in Mott Street," reported the *New York Tribune* in 1903, "where patrons receive no acknowledgment whatever for their deposits," leading to confusion and fraud.

Sender Jarmulowsky's bank was more conventional. He arrived in the United States from Russia in the early 1870s and by 1878 had established a bank in an existing building at the southwest corner of Canal and Orchard Streets, already an immigrant district. In 1886, 1890, 1893, and 1901, he experienced various bank runs but proudly paid one hundred cents on the dollar to each panicky depositor.

All four of his sons followed him into banking, with Meyer and Louis opening their own bank in an exotic, Moorish-style building—designed by Meyer himself—at 165 East Broadway in 1903. When the father decided to rebuild at the southwest corner of Canal and Orchard, he chose neither Meyer nor a showy design. In 1912, with the architects Rouse & Goldstone, he put up a reserved, twelve-story loft building with a bank on the ground floor at the same corner where he had established himself thirty years earlier.

It was, with its rusticated limestone lower section and a terra-cotta upper part, no bare-bones loft building. The entrance to the ground-floor bank at the curved corner is surmounted by two reclining figures in classical style flanking a clock. Period photographs of the banking floor show a conventional work of marble and bronze; it could have been any well-known uptown bank.

These touches aside, it did not have much to set it apart from most other loft buildings—except at the rounded corner of the roof. At that point a giant, circular *tempietto*—a roofed screen of columns—rose perhaps 50 feet to a dome ringed by eagles. Viewed down Orchard Street, across Canal, or from any other distant place, it was an instantly recognizable point of reference.

Sender Jarmulowsky died in 1912 as his building neared completion; the *Times* noted he left "only $501,053" as an estate, apparently expecting much more. His sons Harry and Louis continued the business. In 1914, the East Broadway bank was closed by the state, and Meyer Jarmulowsky was attacked by a depositor with a knife.

In 1917, as depositors withdrew nearly $3 million to send to overseas relatives caught in the war, the State Banking Department took over Sender Jarmulowsky's bank too. It had

RESTAURANT
BOSTON
RESTAURANT

FIG 14.1 THE JARMULOWSKY BANK BUILDING IN 1945. COURTESY OFFICE FOR METROPOLITAN HISTORY

liabilities of $1.25 million and assets of only $600,000. Over five thousand depositors crowded around the branch, and Harry and Louis Jarmulowsky were indicted for banking fraud later in the year. The bank never reopened, and the building was sold at a bankruptcy auction in 1920.

In 1990 the owner demolished the circular *tempietto*. When that happened, the building was instantly reduced from the exceptional to the ordinary—and the area's skyline lost one of it signature elements.

THE ROUSS BUILDING

555 BROADWAY

THE NINETEENTH-CENTURY MERCHANT CHARLES BALTZELL ROUSS liked Broadway so much he adopted it as his middle name—and ran the words "Charles Broadway Rouss" across the front of the two-part store he built at 555 Broadway, between Prince and Spring Streets.

Born in the 1830s, Charles Rouss grew up in Virginia but vowed to get rich in New York, and—after a term in New York's debtor's prison—he developed a specialty of buying distressed and auctioned merchandise for resale. In 1889, he put up his own building, a ten-story cast-iron and stone structure at 549–553 Broadway, designed by Alfred Zucker.

It must have been about the time of his new store that Rouss changed his name, for he put it in raised letters across the third floor; the store itself was called Charles Broadway Rouss.

Rouss summarized his goals for the *New York Evening Post*: "We shall keep everything calculated to make a man fashionable, a lady irresistible, and a family comfortable." Trade directories and advertisements indicate that the ten-story building was divided into departments: carpets, jewelry, Japanese goods, corsets, parasols, and the like.

One 1895 advertisement declared that the store had branches in Paris, Berlin, Nottingham, Vienna, Yokohama, and Chemnitz.

In that same year, Rouss went blind. Against the advice of doctors, he offered $1 million to anyone who could cure his blindness. Overwhelmed with offers, he hired a stand-in, James J. Martin, to undergo likely cures.

In 1899, *National Magazine* described Rouss as the only one of New York's 1,200 millionaires who was blind, and photographed him in his office with his reading assistant. The article noted that Mr. Rouss's hair was often messy because of his nervous habit of combing it with his fingers.

FIG 15.1

CHARLES BROADWAY ROUSS *in 1899.* COURTESY OFFICE FOR METROPOLITAN HISTORY

FIG 15.2

THE ROUSS BUILDING IN 1945. COURTESY OFFICE FOR METROPOLITAN HISTORY

In 1900, Rouss had the architect William J. Dilthey expand his building one bay to the north; the entire building was given the address 555 Broadway. The spaces between the letters of Charles Broadway Rouss at the third floor were enlarged to allow for the increased width. The meeting point between the original building and the addition is evident to the careful observer.

Dilthey expanded the store at the rear and also added two small triangular rooftop structures at either end of the Broadway facade. They are curious details, especially on what is otherwise a straightforward commercial building. Perhaps they were added because Rouss could easily feel them in an architectural model. The town house of Joseph Pulitzer at 11 East 73rd Street is deeply modeled, supposedly because the near-blind publisher reviewed the design in three dimensions.

When Charles Rouss died in 1902, his death certificate gave Broadway as his middle name. He left his business to his children, who continued it until 1929, after which they sold the building—even though the name remains.

THE CABLE BUILDING

611 BROADWAY

CABLE CARS WERE FIRST INSTALLED IN NEW YORK in the mid-1880s, a promising advance over the slower and dirtier horse-drawn cars. But the city was divided into many surface-transit franchises, and the smaller companies did not have the financing to install cable mechanisms, so cable expansion lagged, especially in the congested city center, where construction issues also impeded progress.

So it took something like the giant Metropolitan Traction Company—a syndicate that included a former city corporation counsel, William C. Whitney, a financier; Thomas Fortune Ryan; and John D. Crimmins, a Tammany contractor—to raise the kind of money it took for a comprehensive change. In 1892 Metropolitan filed plans for a new eight-story office and loft building at the northwest corner of Houston and Broadway, stretching back to Mercer Street.

The upper floors were designed for offices, but the basement was given over to a series of steam engines and winding wheels—26 feet in diameter—that moved one-and-a-half-inch steel cables just under the surface of Broadway from Bowling Green to 36th Street.

The cables moved at a constant speed, reported as thirty miles an hour; car operators clamped on or off and used ancillary brakes. The cables weighed forty tons each and drew up to sixty cars at once. The company expanded the service as it bought more and more lines. By 1897 it controlled most surface transit lines in Manhattan.

RHIND'S SCULPTURE
at the doorway in 1894.
COURTESY OFFICE FOR METROPOLITAN HISTORY

The building's architects, McKim, Mead & White, collaborated with the sculptor J. Massey Rhind, who designed two colossal female figures flanking the doorway—commissioned sculpture is also unusual on commercial buildings. The *Real Estate Record and Guide* called the new Cable Building "the highest achievement of the art" and remarked that, with its example, "no excuse remains for building cheaply or meanly on any New York City property."

The theory of cable power was not completely borne out. The cables moved at a constant speed, so conductors had to be careful to release the cable nearing a tight corner, like the one at 14th Street and Broadway. But conductors were forgetful, there were many accidents, and the bend earned the name "Dead Man's Curve."

It took only one problem to interrupt service on the entire line. During rush hour on October 9, 1900, a cable broke in the basement of the Cable Building, shutting the system down for four hours during a heavy rainstorm.

These shortcomings were magnified as Metropolitan expanded its system. Only two years after the building was completed the *New York Tribune* reported that, for its eighteen million car-miles annually, the company could save $2 million a year if a good electric system could be developed. Electric propulsion was also much smoother.

So on May 25, 1901, the last cable car left Houston Street for the Battery, and the line switched to electricity. The Cable Building retained its name, but the machinery stood silent and was later removed.

FIG 16.2

THE CABLE BUILDING IN 1910. COURTESY OFFICE FOR METROPOLITAN HISTORY

THE SCHEPP BUILDING

165 DUANE STREET

17.1 FIG

LEOPOLD SCHEPP
COCOANUT IMPORTER AND MANUFACTURER
"SCHEPP'S DESICCATED COCOANUT"

LEOPOLD SCHEPP. COURTESY OFFICE FOR METROPOLITAN HISTORY

LEOPOLD SCHEPP WAS BORN IN NEW YORK City in 1841 and by the age of ten was supervising a crew of boys selling goods on Third Avenue railroad cars. Seven years later he was in the spice business, and in 1873 he entered and soon concentrated on the field of dried coconut. He had a loft at 178 Duane Street, between Hudson and Greenwich Streets, in the emerging commodities district.

Schepp's successful techniques in preserving what had been a perishable item from the tropics brought him a fortune, and in 1880 he began work on a large manufacturing building at 165 Duane Street, designed by Stephen D. Hatch.

The Schepp Building tends toward the Romanesque, with round-arched windows, blackened bricks, and an emphasis on virtuoso brickwork rather than carved stone detailing. The little triangle of Duane Park at its base gives it a commanding presence.

Some tenants have heard that the building once was New York's tallest. But Kevin Bone, an architect who has worked on the facade, said that it measures 145 feet to the base of the mansard tower, which would have added about 20 feet more.

Research by Dr. Sarah Landau, the architectural historian, indicates that both the Tribune and Western Union buildings of 1873 far exceeded this, at 260 and 230 feet, respectively. Trinity Church's spire's height is generally given as 280 feet.

It appears that the Schepp Building was used principally for coconut processing and packaging, and millions of coconuts flowed through the building yearly. Schepp himself became active in the stock market and, according to the *New York Times* in 1887, had "a temper that would make the North Pole melt."

What the newspaper termed "unparliamentary language" led to several fracases at the Stock Exchange and at least one suspension for Schepp.

In 1925, at a time when Schepp's sales of preserved coconut averaged $1 million a year, he began to give away his fortune, making gifts of $500 to $5,000 to his employees.

FIG 17.2

THE SCHEPP BUILDING *at Duane and Hudson streets, circa 1900.* COURTESY THE NEW-YORK HISTORICAL SOCIETY, NEW YORK CITY

In the same year, he established the Leopold Schepp Foundation with a gift of $2.5 million to assist boys who pledged "to abstain from bad habits."

He also asked for other suggestions from the public. In the next day's mail he got two thousand begging letters, and crowds gathered outside his ground-floor office. According to the *Times*, Schepp had to "decamp from office to escape besiegers for help." Ultimately, Schepp expanded his philanthropy to include girls. He died at his residence at the old San Remo Apartments in 1926.

According to the *Times*, the "Coconut King" had already given away $7 million and still left over $1 million. The Leopold Schepp Foundation awarded about two hundred partial scholarships in 1990.

SIGNS
PAINTING
ENGRAVING
SIGNS
SIGNS

THE FIRST ARTISTS' LOFT IN SOHO

80 WOOSTER STREET

EVEN IN THE LAST QUARTER CENTURY OF PROFOUND CHANGE, no neighborhood in Manhattan has been as utterly transformed as Soho. If this rags-to-riches saga started anywhere, it was with George Maciunas's 1967 conversion of 80 Wooster Street.

In the 1880s and 1890s, Soho was experiencing a revival as dramatic as that in our own time. Scores of early-nineteenth-century brick houses—by that time converted to boarding or bawdy houses—were being demolished for new loft and factory buildings.

In 1895, the real estate firm of Boehm & Coon put up a seven-story warehouse at 80 Wooster Street, a grand, Renaissance-style work designed by Gilbert Schellenger.

Boehm & Coon put their initials in a shield at the seventh floor, but there is no reason to believe the building was used for anything different from others in what was becoming New York's newest area of light industry.

By 1931, the building was occupied by the Miller Paper Company, which remained there until 1967. In that time, Soho saw little change. But artists began occupying lofts in increasing numbers all over the city, some in the huge, inexpensive spaces in Soho. Living in a district zoned for manufacturing was illegal, so they jerry-rigged plumbing, avoided doorbells, and blocked out windows to cover their presence.

This changed in a big way in 1967 when Mr. Maciunas, a designer and artist, bought 80 Wooster Street from the Miller family. Mr. Maciunas had founded the Fluxus Group with Yoko Ono and other artists, and his idea was in the service not of real estate but of art. He envisioned an invasion of Soho by artists through the communal purchase of buildings. With the help of a grant from the J. M. Kaplan Foundation, he initiated it at 80 Wooster Street, taking title as Fluxhouse Cooperative II.

It appears that an earlier venture was not completed, and by all accounts this was the first such effort in Soho.

Charles Ross, a sculptor who still lives in Soho, was one of the group that bought into the 50-by-100-foot building at $8,000 a floor. An informal allocation of shares and floors "sorted itself out nicely," he said.

But it was too casual for some. Mr. Maciunas, who lived in the basement of the co-op while organizing others, ultimately embedded blades in his door so that no one could pound on it. He operated largely without permits and once chased a building inspector into the street with a samurai sword, said Mr. Ross. He also commingled

80 WOOSTER STREET IN 1920. COURTESY OFFICE FOR METROPOLITAN HISTORY

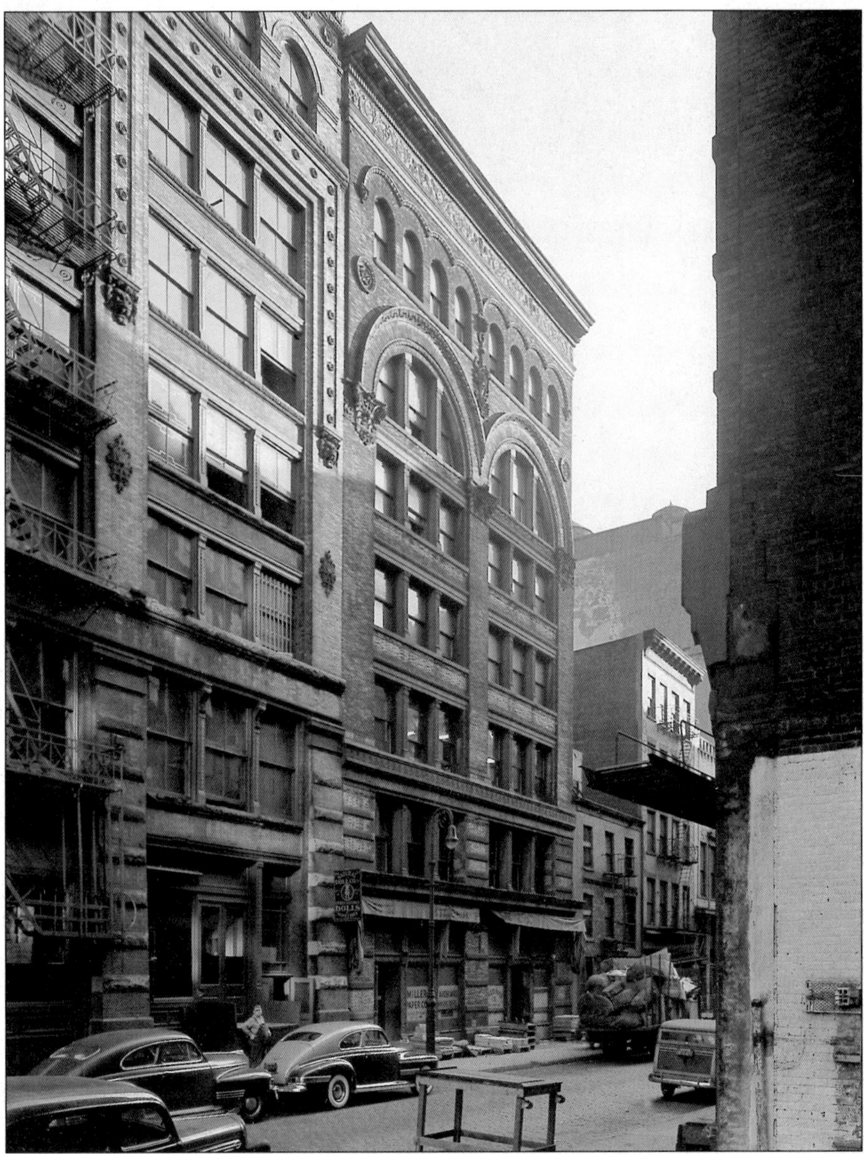

80 WOOSTER STREET *about 1945.* COURTESY OFFICE FOR METROPOLITAN HISTORY

funds from the accounts of various nascent informal co-ops not, it is largely agreed, for his own pocket, but to help establish other struggling buildings. He was really the father of Soho.

In 1971, the city legalized residential use of Soho lofts, but for most early Soho residents, 1973 was when urban frontier became tourist attraction, especially after a *New York* magazine cover story late that year.

Soho quickly became "a boutique zone," said P. Adams Sitney, professor of film history at Princeton University, who knew Mr. Maciunas. "Now it's just a tourist zone—lots of purple hair."

Mr. Maciunas was hard to deal with, and continuing problems with disgruntled co-op buyers caused him to leave Soho and the city in disgust. He died in Massachusetts in 1978.

ST. LUKE'S PLACE

LARGE PARTS OF TRIBECA AND THE WEST VILLAGE rest on land once owned by Trinity Church, which gradually sold or leased its properties as New York City grew. In 1812 it established St. John's Cemetery on the south side of Leroy Street east of Hudson Street, when the area was just developing. In 1851 Trinity began to sell off the north side of Leroy Street east of Hudson as house lots.

It was apparently Trinity that renamed this stretch of Leroy Street St. Luke's Place—it was a common fashion to rename certain blocks, for the cachet of a separate numbering system. The house sites were sold off singly to people like William M. Wilson, a commission merchant; John Romer, a flour dealer; and Charles Olmsted, a grocer. The resulting houses are handsome, a notch or two above the typical mid-nineteenth-century house in design and execution. When completed, their position

FIG 19.1

11–13 **ST. LUKE'S PLACE**, *circa 1900*. COURTESY MUSEUM OF THE CITY OF NEW YORK

facing the open green of the cemetery must have recalled "the row" on the north side of Washington Square, the cynosure of private house development of the 1830s.

Wilson, who usually described himself as "gentleman" in census records, was the last of the original settlers to remain on St. Luke's; he left his house at No. 7 by 1890. By 1910 the census recorded the eight-person McEntee family at No. 8 along with eleven boarders. By that time the cemetery had been turned into a public park, now known as James J. Walker Park.

Shortly afterward St. Luke's Place partook of the bohemian revival of the village. In 1920 Max Eastman, who edited the revolutionary journal the *Masses* until it was suppressed in 1917, lived at 11 St. Luke's Place. Theodore Dreiser began *An American Tragedy* in his room at 16 St. Luke's Place in 1923; that was where he lamented the state of American literature to the *New York Times*, saying "We have no substance today."

Marianne Moore, the late poet, lived at No. 14 in the 1920s while editing the *Dial* and working at the branch library across the street, and the flamboyant James J. Walker was elected mayor in 1926 while living at No. 6. The painter Paul Cadmus was living at No. 5 in 1934 when the lascivious sailors in his *The Fleet's In* generated a nationwide controversy.

Today St. Luke's Place is a quiet little enclave, the angled turn of the narrow street from Seventh Avenue South keeping out all but the most knowledgeable drivers. If residents are bothered by anything, it's walking tours and sight-seeing buses, which often bring nosy visitors at eye level with the parlor floors.

For privacy's sake, Sara-Jane Roszak keeps her second-floor windows dirty in her family's building at the northeast corner of St. Luke's Place and Hudson Street, and counts "hundreds of them—they're relentless." She and other residents can hear the guides on the top of the buses inform—and misinform.

"One guide said that Herman Melville wrote *Moby Dick* in my building, and said that the old desk in the Anglers & Writers restaurant downstairs was where he wrote it."

Moby Dick was published in 1851, before No. 1 was even built, and as for the desk, "my husband, Bruce Porter, sold them that desk eight years ago," says Ms. Roszak.

75½ BEDFORD STREET

TAX RECORDS FIRST SPECIFICALLY REFER TO the 9½-foot-wide structure at 75½ Bedford Street in 1873, but the assessed value of the entire parcel did not change, suggesting that the house had been built before then but simply not noted. Evidence from land maps is contradictory, but a 1922 photograph at the

New-York Historical Society shows a house with the simple Italianate styling common to the 1850s.

In 1880, Martha Banta, a confectioner, occupied 75½ Bedford, and Thomas Newett, a shipper, followed her in the 1890s. By the turn of the century the West Village was a modest neighborhood, cut off from the rest of New York by its bizarre street system—at that time neither Seventh nor Sixth Avenue had been extended south.

The 1920 census shows that the area around Bedford and Commerce had become a largely Italian community—Victor Ponchione, a cooper in a vineyard, lived in 75½ Bedford with his wife and two children. (The census did not indicate the location of the vineyard.) They had all arrived in the United States in 1916.

In 1923 a syndicate of artists and actors headed by Spalding Hall leased 73–77 Bedford and 34–44 Commerce Street from the Hendricks/Gomez heirs. They established the Cherry Lane Theater at 38 Commerce Street and renovated the other buildings for rental, all with a common garden in the back; it was typical of the artistic improvement schemes then flowering in the Village.

They made a coup with 75½ Bedford Street, renting it to Edna St. Vincent Millay, who had that year received the Pulitzer Prize for poetry. According to Regina Kellerman, who has studied the neighborhood, Millay had just married Eugen Jan Boissevain, a coffee importer, and to alter the house they hired Ferdinand Savignano, who was active in Village alteration work. Savignano put in a skylight to make the top floor into a studio, and gave the front a stepped gable; Ms. Kellerman believes this was probably in deference to Mr. Boissevain's Dutch heritage.

FIG 20.1

75 ½ BEDFORD STREET, *with the stepped gable roof, circa 1940.* COURTESY THE NEW-YORK HISTORICAL SOCIETY, NEW YORK CITY

Millay and her husband lived in the house from early 1924 until mid-1925, later moving to a seven-hundred-acre farm in Austerlitz, New York. Jean Gould's 1969 biography of Millay, *The Poet and Her Book*, quotes her as saying that she wanted more nature than she heard from the "noisy chirping of urchin sparrows" in the Village.

Ms. Kellerman has discovered that the house was occupied in the 1930s by the cartoonist William Steig, his wife, Elizabeth, and her sister, the anthropologist Margaret Mead. Ms. Mead's pioneering book *Coming of Age in Samoa* had been published in 1928.

THE MISSING CORNER OF 61 GROVE STREET

THE WEST VILLAGE'S IRREGULAR NETWORK OF STREETS was the last to be plotted before the grid plan of 1811. By the 1850s the area was largely built up. In 1890 the builder Philip Goerlitz bought a mid-block site on Grove Street, between Bleecker Street on the west and West Fourth Street on the east, then a block of aging houses. Goerlitz built two apartment buildings, 61 and 63 Grove Street, both stretching about 90 feet back to Christopher Street.

Goerlitz's architect, Frederick Baylies, designed a small but robust five-story building at 61 Grove Street and, presumably, a matching building at 63 Grove, no longer standing. The first tenants included Vernon Burgar, a musician; Edwin S. Payne, a seaman; and Abraham Webb, a lawyer. These and other early known tenants moved from other buildings within a four-block radius, suggesting that the area was an insular community, attracting few outsiders.

In the 1890s the West Village was isolated from the rest of Manhattan—Seventh Avenue started its northward trek at 11th Street—and in 1915 the *Real Estate Record and Guide* wrote: "This section of Manhattan, owing to its peculiar street system . . . preserves to this day the traditions, habits, and quaintness of old New York."

But Village real estate agents became concerned that the West Village would decay because there was no main north-south thoroughfare. In the early 1900s Charles C. Hickok, a village real estate agent, began to make a case for extending Seventh Avenue south of 11th Street through eleven solidly built blocks and connecting it at Carmine and Clarkson Streets with Varick Street. Such a visionary scheme seemed unlikely, and things did not begin to move until the privately held Interborough Rapid Transit Company, which operated the city's first subway on Broadway north of 42nd Street, planned a southerly extension along Seventh Avenue to Pennsylvania Station and beyond. In 1913, in part to make subway construction easier, the city decided to extend Seventh Avenue

FIG 21.1

61 GROVE STREET *on July 24, 1914, with its southeast corner cut off.* COURTESY THE NEW-YORK HISTORICAL SOCIETY, NEW YORK CITY

FIG 22.1

ROBERT BLUM'S CHRYSANTHEMUM *mural in his dining room at 90 Grove Street.* COURTESY LIBRARY OF CONGRESS

to the south, clear-cutting a 100-foot-wide swath through the West Village. It also widened Varick Street by slicing off the easterly side; in 1914 the project destroyed 194 buildings that housed several thousand residential tenants and hundreds of businesses.

The cut sliced off the southern half of 63 Grove Street, and the owner simply demolished the remains. But 61 Grove Street lost only its extreme southeast corner, a triangle perhaps 10 feet on a side. By this time the building was owned by Jennie Messing of French Lick Springs, Indiana, and she hired the architects Wortmann & Braun to rebuild the corner.

Their design salvaged the stone, brick, terra-cotta, and metalwork to rebuild the corner with projecting oriel windows as if it had always been that way. Only the five A-line apartments at 61 Grove Street were affected, and those tenants apparently had to move out.

88 AND 90 GROVE STREET

IN 1827, AS GREENWICH VILLAGE WAS EMERGING as a popular outlying section of New York, two masons, Henry Halsey and William Banks, built 88 and 90 Grove Street, just east of Seventh Avenue South, for their own occupancy.

In 1862, Thomas A. Wilmurt bought 88 Grove and perhaps it was he who added the mansard roof with dormer windows and lacy iron trim, which still survive. Wilmurt, a frame maker, lived at 88 with his wife, Ann, and eight children, and he often worked for Tiffany & Company.

In 1893, the painter Robert Blum bought 90 Grove Street and hired Carrère & Hastings, later designers of the New York Public Library on Fifth Avenue, as his architects. The peaked roof was removed, making the second floor into a double-height studio space for the artist, who was well known as an illustrator. According to Bruce Weber, director of research and exhibitions at Berry-Hill Galleries and an expert on Blum, the artist had been living in the old Benedick studio building on Washington Square East, but learned a new building would cut off his light. This is something that could not happen with a house like 90 Grove, which faces what is now Grove Park. Mr. Weber says that Blum's patron, Alfred Corning Clark, who owned the Dakota, helped him with the purchase of 90 Grove.

A visit to Japan increased Blum's interest in the artistic techniques of that country, and he painted a mural of chrysanthemums in his dining room and decorated parts of the house in Japanese style. An account from the *Cincinnati Enquirer* in 1900 said that, with the "pale yellow front" and studio window, the house "never fails to arrest the passerby."

90 GROVE STREET, *left, with partial view of 88 Grove Street, right, circa 1900.* COURTESY CINCINNATI MUSEUM ARCHIVES

"The oiled floors are covered with Japanese mats and the old time mantle is enclosed in blue Chinese tiles," the article noted. Silks, prints, and ceramics completed the effect. The 1900 census taker recorded Blum, forty-three, as living in the house with Senta Kato, twenty-two, his Japanese servant, who had been in this country ten years.

Blum died at 90 Grove in 1903 just as he was finishing the Art Nouveau–style mural above the proscenium arch in the New Amsterdam Theater, which he worked on with Albert Wenzel. Blum's estate sold 90 Grove Street to Jules Guerin, a painter who also decorated the old Pennsylvania Station; Guerin added shutters but changed little else.

In 1908 Guerin sold 90 Grove to the painter Helen Olivia Phelps Stokes, a member of a prominent family who was active in trade-union causes. She would often appear in court to pay the fines of pickets who had been arrested. A year later the landscape architect Ferruccio Vitale bought 88 Grove, where he lived until 1915 when Helen Stokes's brother, James Graham Phelps Stokes, bought it and moved in.

James Stokes, a millionaire railroad investor, had served with the elite Squadron A cavalry in the Spanish-American War. He also ran for several city posts on the Socialist ticket, and in 1905 had married Rose Pastor, a cigar-factory worker also active in Socialist causes. While the Stokeses lived at 88 Grove, Rose Stokes risked arrest by passing out birth-control literature at Carnegie Hall in 1916 and was convicted in 1918 of federal espionage charges for antiwar statements, although her ten-year sentence was set aside.

Rose and James Stokes were divorced in 1925, and James remained in the house and remarried the former Lettice Sands in 1926. Around this time Helen Stokes created additional studio space in the rear, and at some point multiple doors were cut between 88 and 90 Grove. Mr. Weber says that the Stokeses also covered over Blum's chrysanthemum mural.

Helen Stokes died in 1945, and her brother James died in 1960. Lettice Stokes kept both buildings and remained in 88 Grove until her death in 1988.

In 1996, Howard Reed, a dealer in contemporary art, was living with his wife, Katia, and two daughters in a loft in the Flatiron district, hoping to move to the Village, where his daughters were at Grace Church School. But he says they were looking for something "with scale," not the typical small Village house.

So when he saw 90 Grove Street in 1996—almost completely intact, with its large studio and sophisticated detailing—he was sold. But No. 90 was being offered for $2 million as a package with No. 88, so he and his wife approached another Grace Church School family, with one daughter.

The wife in that family, who would speak only on condition of anonymity, said that "it took about ten minutes" for them to make up their mind to buy 88 Grove Street, which is also almost completely intact, with high-style Victorian moldings and mantles, probably from the same 1860s alteration that produced the mansard.

The families simplified things by using the same architect, Kathryn McGraw Berry. But the buildings now have quite different characters. The Reeds' house is a sleek, spare showpiece with works of art and top-notch plastering and painting. They have uncovered one ragged swath of the Blum mural in the dining room, but the rest was too damaged to restore.

The house at No. 88 seems more lived in, with a vintage wooden back porch looking out over the large backyard toward an ancient wooden shed. But although they share a yard and some other common elements, both families say they haven't yet had any noticeable disagreements—perhaps because, as one of their first projects, they sealed up the doors connecting the buildings.

MINETTA LANE AND MINETTA STREET

BY THE TURN OF THE TWENTIETH CENTURY the West Village was a dense spiderweb of tiny streets crowded with aging buildings. Sixth Avenue only went as far south as Minetta Lane; Seventh Avenue dead-ended at 12th Street. The tiny clutch of houses at the corner of Minetta Lane and Minetta Street was a backwater.

The 1920 census recorded a rich mix of tenants on Minetta Lane. The house at 1 Minetta Lane had five households, including Mary Davis, forty-seven, of Irish extraction, with her nephew, Robert Davis, twenty-one, a longshoreman. Other tenants

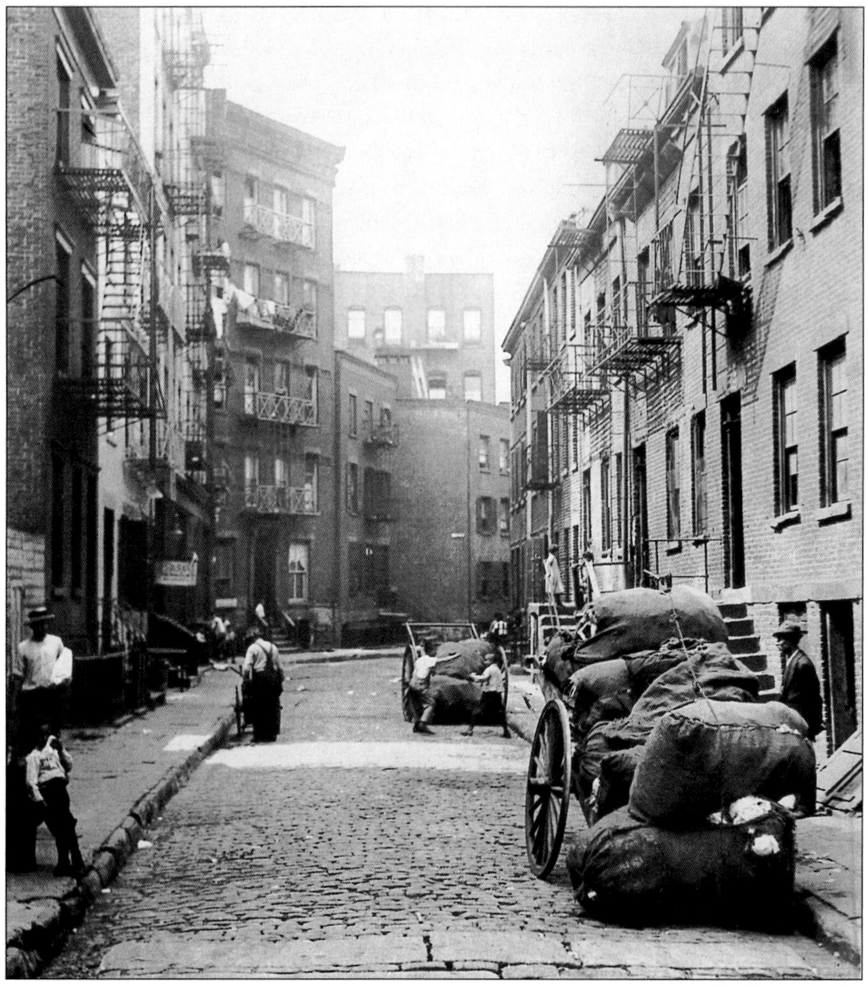

SOUTH ON MINETTA STREET *from Minetta Lane, circa 1920.* COURTESY LIBRARY OF CONGRESS

included the family of a Swiss barber, an Italian hotel porter, a Swiss baker, and a German butcher. The three households in 3 Minetta Lane included a chauffeur, a trucker, and a hotel clerk; all members were born in New York or New Jersey.

The house at 5 Minetta Lane included blacks and whites born variously in Mexico, Georgia, New York, South Carolina, and Virginia. One tenant there was Lewis Bellano, twenty-eight, born in Italy, in the United States since 1893, married to Mabel Bellano, black, twenty-two, born in New York, and their sons, Edward and Lewis, five and six. Lewis Bellano was a garage mechanic; Mabel Bellano was a dishwasher in a tearoom, many of which were emerging as popular tourist spots for those curious about the Village, seen as a bohemian enclave. Another member of the household was Mabel Bellano's mother, Bella Jackson, sixty-nine, a scrubwoman born in Virginia.

In the 1910s, Vincent Pepe became convinced that the picturesque parts of the Village were ripe for metamorphosis and saw that single renovations could not affect a whole community. Beginning in the late 1910s he bought up, on his own account and acting for others, houses and tenements on both sides of Minetta Street for comprehensive redevelopment as what he called "the Minettas."

On the west side of Minetta Street Pepe was able to combine a group of thirteen buildings and make their rear yards into a common garden with a back entrance. "The artist, the writer, the creator of beauty in any medium—these are the men for whom the Minettas should be preserved," he said in a promotional brochure.

On the east side of Minetta Street, at the southeast corner of Minetta Lane, Pepe acquired, with partners, 1, 3, and 5 Minetta Lane and 17 Minetta Street. Existing tenants either moved or were evicted, and in 1924 he gave the buildings the same rear-yard treatment, although the garden area was less generous. The architect Richard Berger divided up the houses into small studio apartments.

Writers waxed poetic over the change in the tiny district. In 1926, *House Beautiful* noted its "comforting charm. . . which you would not exchange for Long Island, New Jersey, or all of Murray Hill." Despite Pepe's stated goal of housing artists, it appears that the existing residents were not evicted solely for culture, but also for commerce—the 1925 census taker recorded a decorator, a painter, and an artist, but also a tire salesman, an advertising manager, and an auto salesman.

THE LITTLE RED SCHOOL HOUSE

196 BLEECKER STREET

IN 1920 THE FIRST PRESBYTERIAN CHURCH, at 12th Street and Fifth Avenue, put up a new building at 196–198 Bleecker Street as a settlement house and church for the area, which had become a working-class and poor district. It had two names—the Church of the Gospel, which served Italians, and, for English speakers, the Bethlehem Chapel, which it was more commonly called.

Designed by George B. Post & Sons, the new building was of rough pink stucco trimmed with irregular brick and a rooftop pergola. *Architectural Forum* praised the building and said that it "suggests some old quarter of a city in the homeland" and that, for the immigrants, "the psychological effect is tremendous."

For some reason Bethlehem Chapel closed down around 1930, which proved fortunate for the educator-reformer Elisabeth Irwin. Born in Brooklyn, she attended Packer Collegiate Institute and Smith College, class of 1903. Dissatisfied with traditional teaching methods, she began an experimental school in the early '20s in the red-painted annex of P.S. 61 at 535 East 16th Street.

She started with some first-graders and emphasized learning by doing; her first-graders received no academic work of any kind until the middle of second grade. Later the school moved into space at P.S. 41, then on Greenwich Avenue between 10th and 11th Streets.

FIG 24.1 BETHLEHEM CHAPEL IN 1923. COURTESY LIBRARY OF CONGRESS

In 1932 the Board of Education announced it would stop supporting Miss Irwin's school. In an article at the time in the *New York Times*, Miss Irwin defended her program, where field trips took precedence over classroom work, and where "grades and marks, merits and demerits . . . have no part at all in the progressive scheme."

Miss Irwin's supporters rallied around and financed the school privately. The First Presbyterian Church lent the Bethlehem Chapel for classroom space, and the Little Red School House opened at 196 Bleecker Street in September 1932 with 138 students in six grades. Advisers and supporters included educators such as Professor John Dewey and prominent citizens like Eleanor Morgenthau, wife of Henry Morgenthau Jr.

There were some scholarships, but most families paid the $150 per year; at the time, typical private school tuition was $600. The pupils went to see the Coney Island lighthouse keeper, fishermen in Sheepshead Bay, storekeepers, street sweepers, and others.

Dr. James Keck of Andover, Massachusetts, recalls trips to milk plants and the Fulton Fish Market with relish. "With the emphasis on extracurricular activities," he says, "I really thrived. One year we devoted an entire year to making a relief map of the United States. We drew the boundaries, then put on the clay, the mountain ranges, and painted it to correspond to the desert, the prairies, and the forests. Then we put on the first thirteen colonies, then the Louisiana Purchase, then the Lewis and Clark expedition—by the end of the year we had all the forty-eight states, and we had been all through the history and geography of the United States."

THE OLD WHITNEY MUSEUM

8–12 WEST EIGHTH STREET

THE WHITNEY MUSEUM, NOW ON MADISON AVENUE AT 75TH STREET, was founded by Gertrude Vanderbilt Whitney. Though her grandfather was Commodore Cornelius Vanderbilt and her husband was the playboy-financier Harry Payne Whitney, she did more than just bounce around the New York–Newport society circuit.

According to Avis Berman, author of the 1990 *Rebels on Eighth Street*, within a few years of her marriage in 1896, Gertrude Whitney discovered that her husband was unfaithful, and she decided to become a sculptor. She took up with a group of artists who formed the Ashcan School—Robert Henri, John Sloan, William Glackens, and others. They were fighting to establish artistic realism in a conservative atmosphere of society portraits and soothing landscapes.

In 1907 she took a studio on Macdougal Alley, a street of stables serving the flanking rows of houses on Washington Square North and Eighth Street. She proved to have

WHITNEY MUSEUM IN 1931. COLLECTION WHITNEY MUSEUM OF AMERICAN ART, NEW YORK

only moderate talent as a sculptor but excelled as an organizer. In 1914 she took over the adjacent row house at West Eighth Street for a meeting place and gallery for other artists on the outs with the establishment.

Gradually, she added the houses at 10, 12, and 14 West Eighth Street—as well as their corresponding stables on Macdougal Alley—and what had become the Whitney Studio Club became a center of advanced thinking in American art.

John Sloan and Reginald Marsh had their first one-man shows there, and in 1924 the club mounted the first exhibit of American folk art, a complete reversal of the old-master theory of collecting that had dominated the nineteenth century.

Mrs. Whitney also directly supported artists with gifts, loans, and purchases, and by the late 1920s she had amassed a collection of about five hundred works by Hopper, Bellows, Prendergast, Sloan, and others.

In 1929 she offered these to the Metropolitan Museum of Art along with $5 million for a new wing. The Met, long criticized for collecting dead artists but ignoring the living, rejected the offer, and, says Ms. Berman, Mrs. Whitney and her assistant, Juliana Force, concocted the idea of their own museum, specifically to serve American artists while they were still alive.

Mrs. Whitney retained the architects Noel & Miller, who in 1931 rebuilt 8, 10, and 12 West Eighth Street with a coating of salmon-colored stucco and a modernistic entranceway. The stucco veneer was by then a standard solution for redoing old houses, but the doorway shouted out with the novelty of a brave new post-crash architecture.

Severe white marble columns support a giant entablature, itself topped by an eagle in white metal designed by Karl Free, a painter and curator at the new museum.

25.2 FIG

THE 1932 BIENNIAL. COLLECTION WHITNEY MUSEUM OF AMERICAN ART, NEW YORK

25.3 FIG

PEGGY BACON (1895–1987), *The Whitney Studio Club*, 1925, drypoint. COLLECTION WHITNEY MUSEUM OF AMERICAN ART, NEW YORK, GIFT OF GERTRUDE VANDERBILT WHITNEY 31.596

Aluminum strips are bundled into giant, reedlike columns, and the sidewalk is in diaper-shaped sections of pink and gray tints. Aluminum outer doors, with American-flag stars and Art Moderne details set in red Numidian marble, were removed when the Whitney left the building in 1954.

The interior, designed by the decorator Bruce Buttfield with the architects, began with a striking, almost surreal, vestibule with a vibrant terrazzo floor, a double staircase with strange, tendril-like balusters, and sculpture niches with starkly realistic figures of nymphs.

It is difficult to document, but the rest of the interior changed repeatedly over the next decade. The changes showed how architects and designers were starting from scratch with the advent of modern design.

Baseboards have a strange, angular top molding. The mahogany handrail on a stairway ends in a supremely exaggerated curlicue. Rectangular light fixtures mix the Federal-era symbols of five-pointed stars with blue glass and metal casing recalling several periods.

Indeed, the controlling personality of the museum building is its furious mixture of styles and periods. A nineteenth-century pier mirror faces a nightclub-modern restroom entrance.

Italianate door and room moldings co-exist with sophisticated 1930s gallery lighting. Ancient wooden stair balusters run past Art Moderne doorways.

The old Whitney is rich with the presence of artists. To close off a hidden staircase, the artist Robert Locher painted a trompe l'oeil door imitating a staircase. A fragment of Thomas Hart Benton's mural series on American arts survives in the original library—an arc with the words "She'll Be Wearin' Red Pajamas."

And Gertrude Whitney's studio, on Macdougal Alley, is eye-popping, one of the great unknown interiors in New York, designed by Robert Chanler. In a high, whitewashed space of plain brick walls, a blaze of sculptured flame encases a chimney. As it reaches the ceiling, the flame changes into waves and clouds, spreading out over a ceiling sea of fantastic figures—dragons, sea horses, demons, mermaids, angels, and octopi.

The Whitney Museum opened in 1931 with George Bellows's *Dempsey and Firpo* painting of a boxing match as a centerpiece symbolizing its challenging stance. "There may be pictures here that you do not like, but they are here to stay, so you may as well get used to them," Mrs. Force declared at the opening.

In 1932 came the first of the Whitney's Biennial exhibitions, pilloried in the press, according to *Rebels on Eighth Street*. The museum—for another decade largely reflecting the personalities of Gertrude Whitney and Juliana Force—continued to join in controversy without reservation.

Active in helping unemployed artists during the depression, it got criticism that larger (and less helpful) institutions were spared. Mrs. Whitney died in 1942 and Mrs. Force in 1948. In 1954 the Whitney moved up to West 54th Street, behind the Museum of Modern Art, finally relocating to its present site at 75th Street and Madison Avenue in 1966.

The old building remained, however, and was bought by the New York Studio School in 1967. It is now a picturesque gaggle of studio spaces, with ancient linoleum coming up off even more ancient pine floors and with puddles of clay, paint, and other materials everywhere.

1 FIFTH AVENUE

BY THE 1920S, THE LITERARY AND POLITICAL REVIVAL of Greenwich Village had changed it from a picturesque but declining quarter to one that was attractive to developers. Sailors' Snug Harbor, a charitable institution, owned much of the land in the area of Washington Square, and in 1926, one developer, Joseph G. Siegel, took a long-term lease on the southeast corner of Eighth Street and Fifth Avenue.

He announced plans to build a skyscraper apartment tower looming over the red-brick houses and marble arch of Washington Square.

This was not a conventional apartment house but an apartment hotel of two- and three-room units, each with a serving pantry for food brought up by service elevator from a central restaurant on the ground floor. In fact, the apartment hotel was a widespread fiction of the period; "non-housekeeping" residential buildings could be built taller and deeper than regular multiple dwellings because they were considered commercial buildings—tenants in fact usually set up full kitchens in the serving pantries.

In prior operations, Joseph Siegel had worked with the architects Sugarman & Berger, who produced standard-issue architecture. But for 1 Fifth Avenue Siegel brought in Harvey Wiley Corbett as design architect, perhaps because Corbett's firm, Helme & Corbett, had already designed numerous buildings for Sailors' Snug Harbor. (In the case of a long-term leasehold, it is common for the fee owner to exercise some control over the nature of any building erected.)

Corbett was a freethinker in the matter of architecture, an advocate of skyscrapers who ridiculed slavish historicism. Although 1 Fifth Avenue has a vaguely Venetian or Gothic cast, it is atypical, more "tall building" than anything else.

Even so, Corbett used historical details to make references to well-known structures of the area.

According to Luther Harris, who has done extensive research on the history of Greenwich Village, certain isolated details on 1 Fifth Avenue are taken from other buildings. He says that, among other items, the paneling in the lobby recalls that in the prior Greek Revival house on the site, and the Gothic-style quatrefoil designs on the lanterns at the main entrance refer to the Church of the Ascension nearby.

But the most interesting of Corbett's devices is the shaded brick. He gave the four turretlike corners a false projection—darker vertical bands of brick look like shadows cast against the main wall. The vertical paired white-and-black brick stripes convincingly imitate angled masonry projections rising between the windows.

THE TWENTY-SEVEN-STORY APARTMENT BUILDING *at 1 Fifth Avenue in 1930.*
COLLECTION LUTHER HARRIS

The effect of shading brick dark at the base but using lighter colors as the building rises—as at the Art Deco–style 55 Central Park West—is fairly well known in New York, but Corbett's fakery at 1 Fifth was the type of thing that made serious architects nervous. So it is little seen in New York and thus all the more refreshing.

If you think Corbett is trying to fool you, then you are likely to be annoyed; but if you see it as a witty aside for all to appreciate, then you will smile each time you pass it.

THE BENEDICK

80 WASHINGTON SQUARE EAST

THE BUILDING AT 80 WASHINGTON SQUARE EAST was designed by the firm of McKim, Mead & Bigelow just months before Stanford White replaced William B. Bigelow. In early 1879 a successful iron merchant named Lucius Tuckerman asked the firm to design a new kind of building on the east side of Washington Square.

Tuckerman had in mind an apartment house exclusively for bachelors, a group viewed with suspicion by boardinghouse operators and apartment builders alike. He named it the Benedick, after the confirmed bachelor in *Much Ado About Nothing*.

The six-story Benedick opened in the fall of 1879 with thirty-three apartments and, on the sixth floor, four artists' studios; rents ranged from $350 to $550 a year. Its facade is of simple red brick, much of it molded and shaped, with touches of light stone trim and, as originally built, large iron window bays on the third to fifth floors. The sunburst design in the third-floor balcony appears in other works by the firm in the period.

FIG 27.1

AN APARTMENT IN THE BENEDICK, *circa 1880.*
COURTESY JOHN PRESTON.

Shortly before its opening, the *New York Tribune* said the building had "considerable pretensions to architectural dignity and quaintness" and reported that the tenants

FIG 27.2

THE BENEDICK ABOUT 1925. COURTESY NEW YORK UNIVERSITY ARCHIVES

would not have sinks, but would have to make do with bowls and pitchers "for the sake of keeping out sewer gas."

A janitor living in the basement furnished breakfast, and maid service and bootblacking were offered, along with an elevator to run night and day for the bachelors "whose hours are naturally somewhat irregular."

Before the Benedick, the two principal artists' studio buildings in New York were the University Building, one block north on Washington Square East, and the Tenth Street Studio, at 51 West 10th Street.

But the Benedick's accommodations were attractive, and the 1880 census lists the sculptor Olin Levi Warner; the painters Winslow Homer, J. Alden Weir, George W.

Maynard, and Albert Ryder; the architect William R. Mead; and the artist John LaFarge. Ryder, Weir, and Warner were close friends and often posed for each other.

In 1881, one writer for the *Tribune* reported on one of Ryder's typically moody canvases on display in his studio, noting its "vivid moonrise . . . contrasting with the dark old house and a shadowy lane, overhung with trees."

Homer was equally famous for his Civil War sketches and Americana paintings like his *Snap the Whip* of 1872. Gordon Hendricks, in his 1979 book, *The Life and Work of Winslow Homer*, offers an account of Homer splashing models with water on the roof of the Benedick as preparation for his 1886 painting *Undertow*.

In *Stanny*, his 1989 biography of Stanford White, Paul R. Baker describes another presence in the Benedick—the "Sewer Club." The group was formed by White, the sculptor Augustus Saint-Gaudens, and others. Its activities are not recorded, but some historians have speculated that they included sexual encounters. White took a room for the Sewer Club in the Benedick for 1888 and 1889.

THE OLD ASTOR LIBRARY

425 LAFAYETTE STREET

BEFORE HE DIED IN 1848, THE FINANCIER JOHN JACOB ASTOR had worked with the book collector and librarian Joseph Green Cogswell to lay the groundwork for a great public library, with a gift of $400,000. The site chosen was on the east side of Lafayette Street, then still a distinguished residential address.

The first building—the southern third of what is now the Public Theater—opened in 1854 with more than 80,000 books. The architect, Alexander Saeltzer, developed a wonderfully open, two-story-high hall surrounded by gilded balconies and books arranged in double-height alcoves. But patrons had to apply to the librarians for access to any titles, and in a letter Cogswell reflected on his decision in favor of closed stacks: "It would have crazed me to have seen a crowd ranging lawlessly among the books, and throwing everything into confusion."

In another letter he said the library was getting about two hundred visitors a day of whom he said, "they read excellent books, except the young fry, who employ all the hours they are out of school in reading the trashy, as Scott, Cooper, Dickens, Punch, and the *Illustrated News*." The building was extended to the north (the present center section of the Public Theater) in 1859 and northward again in 1881.

Astor's good deed did not go unpunished, and there were early and frequent complaints often directed at the family, about library policies. It was open only during daylight hours, and Frank H. Norton, writing in the magazine *Galaxy* in 1869, said that this excluded the working class and poor: "The picture I have seen drawn by enthusiastic

THE ASTOR LIBRARY ABOUT 1870. COURTESY THE NEW-YORK HISTORICAL SOCIETY, NEW YORK CITY

newspaper hacks of the rich capitalist and the mechanic sitting here side by side in honorable community of thought is agreeable, but also entirely fanciful."

And the library policy of closed stacks and no loans was also much lamented. Those who favored tight controls pointed to patrons like the writer Richard Boyle Davy, who in 1872 tore ninety-eight pages from an old volume of *Revue de Paris* magazine to cover his plagiarism of one of its stories.

In 1894, even after the library put some basic reference books on open shelves, and granted some researchers stack access, the *New York Daily Tribune* noted that the reader felt like "an interloper and intruder" against the librarians' longstanding "reputation for churlishness and indifference."

This sentiment was evoked again in 1897 when Jacob Friedman, a Rivington Street student at City College, removed nine books surreptitiously. He got the sympathy of Magistrate Henry A. Brann by saying he took them temporarily for class work, because his parents were too poor to buy them. Magistrate Brann repeatedly implored the library to drop its complaint, saying a conviction would ruin the boy's life, but the library conformed to expectations and was intransigent. However, it soon developed that the boy had given a false name and torn out the title pages with the library's stamp on them; it is not clear how his case ended.

The Astor Library relocated to the new, central library, at 42nd and Fifth Avenue, and since 1965 the Public Theater, at 425 Lafayette Street, has operated the structure, although with little attention to architectural detail. But even in its abused state, the interior contains some of New York's most remarkable Victorian spaces.

THE OTTENDORFER LIBRARY

135 SECOND AVENUE

IN 1884 OSWALD AND ANNA OTTENDORFER BUILT AND ENDOWED a new building at 137 Second Avenue for the German Dispensary, which was established in 1857 to offer health services for German Americans in the neighborhood. The Ottendorfers, who ran the German-language newspaper *Staats-Zeitung*, had more land than they needed for the three-story dispensary, and Mrs. Ottendorfer had the idea of building a branch for the Free Circulating Library on the extra plot. The dispensary retained ownership of the library land and building.

She died in May 1884 while the Ottendorfer Library was in construction, designed by the German-born William Schickel. At the dedication that December, the remarks of Carl Schurz, the German-American political leader, reflected contemporary views of the effects of libraries, both good and bad. Schurz acknowledged that "some boys and girls had been led astray" by reading fiction, and that "not much learning was derived from novels," but that even working people deserved "rest and relaxation."

FIG 29.1

OSWALD OTTENDORFER, LL.D.
PRESIDENT AND EDITOR "NEW YORKER STAATS ZEITUNG"
FOUNDER ISABELLA HEIMATH AND OTTENDORFER LIBRARY

OSWALD OTTENDORFER. COURTESY OFFICE FOR METROPOLITAN HISTORY

The *Staats-Zeitung* described the red brick and terra-cotta exterior as "early Italian Renaissance" and noted that anyone twelve or older, with references, could borrow one book per visit. Librarians retrieved any of the eight thousand books from closed stacks on the ground floor behind the protection of the main desk, with English on one side and German on the other. Patrons could borrow books or consult them in a reading room on the second floor.

A writer for the *Real Estate Record and Guide* was not impressed by either the dispensary or the library, calling them both "entirely commonplace," especially the decorative terra-cotta work, and particularly criticizing the "ugly and fashionable three-centered arch" on the library.

The movement to expand city libraries kept growing, and in 1886 the first proposal for what became the New York Public Library included a series of branches. The board of the Free Circulating Library—including Oswald Ottendorfer—saw the movement as poaching on its territory and successfully opposed it. The board had been lobbying for the city's support and got it in 1887.

Schickel designed a rear extension for the Ottendorfer Library in 1897 that included a new system for open stack access, a double gallery of iron book stacks with thick glass flooring, and a central light well.

The New York Public Library proposal gained strength in the 1890s, and the Free Circulating Library's trustees began discussing possible merger terms. Four years later

FIG 29.2

OTTENDORFER LIBRARY *and part of the German Dispensary, at right, in 1899.*
COURTESY THE NEW-YORK HISTORICAL SOCIETY, NEW YORK CITY

they ratified an agreement with the New York Public Library system to combine the Free Circulating Library's eleven buildings with the sixty-five branches to be built by the $5 million gift of Andrew Carnegie.

Although the German-American community gradually left the Lower East Side, the Ottendorfer branch was reinvigorated in the 1930s with German-speaking refugees from Europe. The librarian, Charlotte Hubach, invited patrons to listen to a series of opera concerts on a donated radio on the second floor. She also began a lecture series, "Literature in Exile."

Recently renovated, the library is a treat for any book-lover, especially the glass-floored stacks in the rear.

THE LOCKWOOD DE FOREST HOUSE

7 EAST 10TH STREET

LOCKWOOD DE FOREST WAS BORN INTO A SOCIALLY PROMINENT FAMILY that had made its money in South American and Caribbean shipping. He studied with Frederic Church and had a moderate success as a painter. But he was also interested in decoration and architecture, and in 1879 he joined Louis Comfort Tiffany and others to found Associated Artists.

Their firm was one of the most influential decorating companies in the nineteenth century, at the forefront of the Aesthetic Movement, which emphasized handwork, intricate color and texture, and tasteful but exotic schemes. Associated Artists broke up in 1883, but by that time de Forest had taken a wedding trip to India and established a woodworking factory at Ahmadabad to make Indian pieces for export to America.

In 1887 de Forest bought two lots, 7 and 9 East 10th Street. He sold No. 9 for development with a small apartment house, then had the architect Van Campen Taylor design a single house for himself. The basic house is as plain as can be; it is what de Forest added that is so striking—intricately carved teak elements made in India, interspersed on the exterior from top to bottom.

The casing of the main and service doorways is in teak carved in low relief, and a small window on the second floor has a teak fence. The windows on the upper floors have perforated, arched teak screens and the cornice is of the same material, all in the Indian style.

These features alone are remarkable, but it is the projecting oriel window on the second floor that is astounding: a giant box of intricate filigree, covered with relief carvings of birds, flowers, beaks, elephant forms, crescent moons, and other details.

What is equally astonishing is that the wood is so crisp, so undamaged. In New York, even the best hardwoods rot after a decade exposed to the weather; this carving is in even better condition than stone, terra-cotta, metal, or other carving of equal vintage. Only the slow darkening of the wood gives away its age.

In 1900 a writer for *House Beautiful* visited what a headline dubbed "The Most Indian House in America" and described the interiors: large expanses of teak paneling and screens, some carved and some plain; Indian-style furniture and trim details like red sandstone from Agra, deep blue tiles from Damascus, and a patterned brass ceiling in the parlor, the room with the oriel window.

De Forest kept up his connection with the Tiffany firm, which sent him to India in 1892 to acquire jewelry and other artifacts, and he expanded his Ahmadabad factory.

He also continued his decorating practice, with commissions like the library and bedroom at the Andrew Carnegie house, now the Cooper-Hewitt National Design Museum.

De Forest met Rudyard Kipling in India and the writer visited 7 East 10th Street on at least one American trip. But with a declining market for exotic interiors after 1900, de Forest began to pay more attention to painting and built a house in Santa Barbara, California, in the 1910s. He sold 7 East 10th Street in 1922, and the building was divided into apartments sometime after 1930.

FIG 30.1

THE LOCKWOOD DE FOREST HOUSE, *interior (above) and exterior (opposite), 7 East 10th Street, circa 1900.* COURTESY ARCHIVES OF AMERICAN ART, SMITHSONIAN INSTITUTION

FIG 30.2

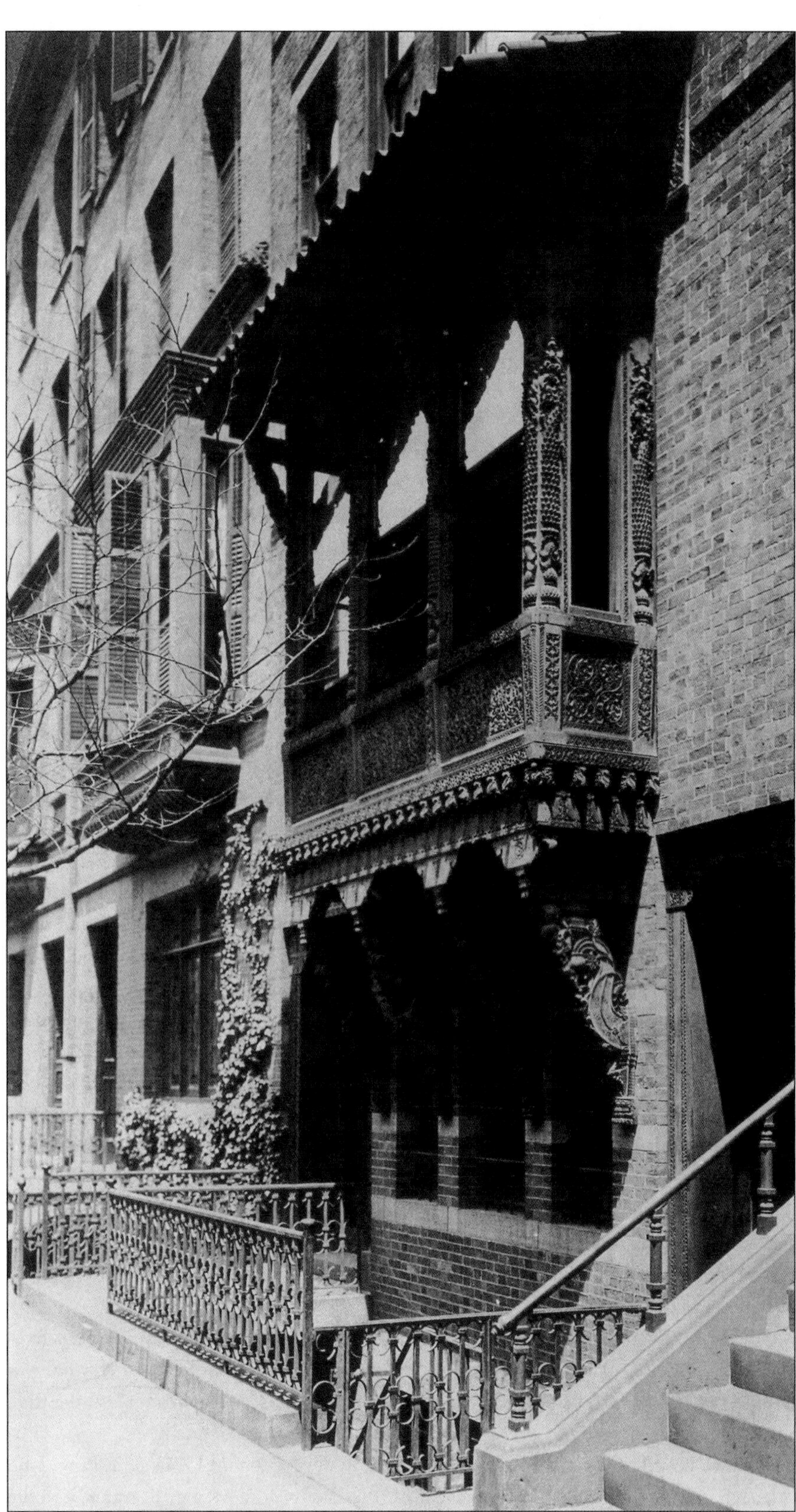

THE AVA

9 EAST 10TH STREET

NEXT DOOR TO DE FOREST'S HOUSE WAS THE AVA, at 9 East 10th Street, built by architect William H. Russell in 1888. Russell, who lived a block away at 21 West 10th Street, built the Ava, a five-story apartment house designed by his firm, Renwick, Aspinwall & Russell. For reasons that are not clear, Russell decided to use teak decoration on his building too, and the cornice and first-floor trim are in teak carved in a fashion extremely similar to that on the de Forest house—the work must also have been from de Forest's factory.

On the ground floor of the Ava, the door and window casing is in teak carved in low, sinuous relief; above this runs a more heavily modeled cornice, across the entire front. To the right of the door is a large plaque with the building's name, Ava, surrounded by more Indian-style decoration and two triplet groups of elephants, also in teak. The roof cornice is also teak. Inside, the vestibule appears mostly intact, but the door and sidelights carry panes of glass unusually large for this period in such a location. Closer inspection indicates pin mounts at the top and locking devices at the bottom, as if some sort of rigid screen had been locked into place; tenants report that there has been nothing there for at least thirty years. There isn't enough depth in the frame for something made of iron; more likely it was some sort of wood that could be easily worked into a thin screen—perhaps teak?

In 1890 Russell sold the building to Christian Tietjen, a banker and lard manufacturer, and there is no indication that the Ava was anything but a standard rental apartment house built on speculation. The earliest tenants were people like John Beavor-Webb, yacht designer and intimate of J. P. Morgan. Beavor-Webb designed Morgan's yacht *Corsair*. Another resident was Dr. Alexis Carrel, who won a Nobel Prize in 1912 for his work in organ transplants and surgical techniques. Later, as Greenwich Village became an artists' colony, it attracted people like Helen Dryden, who was described in the *New York Times* in 1956 as once having been the highest-paid female artist in the country. Dryden designed covers for *Vogue* and other journals and did interiors for Studebaker automobiles.

The 1925 census recorded her living at 9 East 10th Street with her twenty-five-year-old Philippine-born cook and butler, Ricardo Lampitok. But by 1956 Dryden was living in a $10-a-week hotel room paid for by the city's Welfare Department; at the time she referred nostalgically to her "$200 a month" 10th Street apartment.

Dawn Powell was another artistic resident, in the 1930s and 1940s. Tim Page, who has been involved in five books on the prolific diarist and author, said, "it was where she lived when her writing was strongest, where she finished books like *Angels on Toast*." Mr. Page said that "in a letter dated September 16, 1931, Powell described the building as 'calm, spacious—one's soul breathes deep breaths in it and feels at rest.' "

FIG 31.1

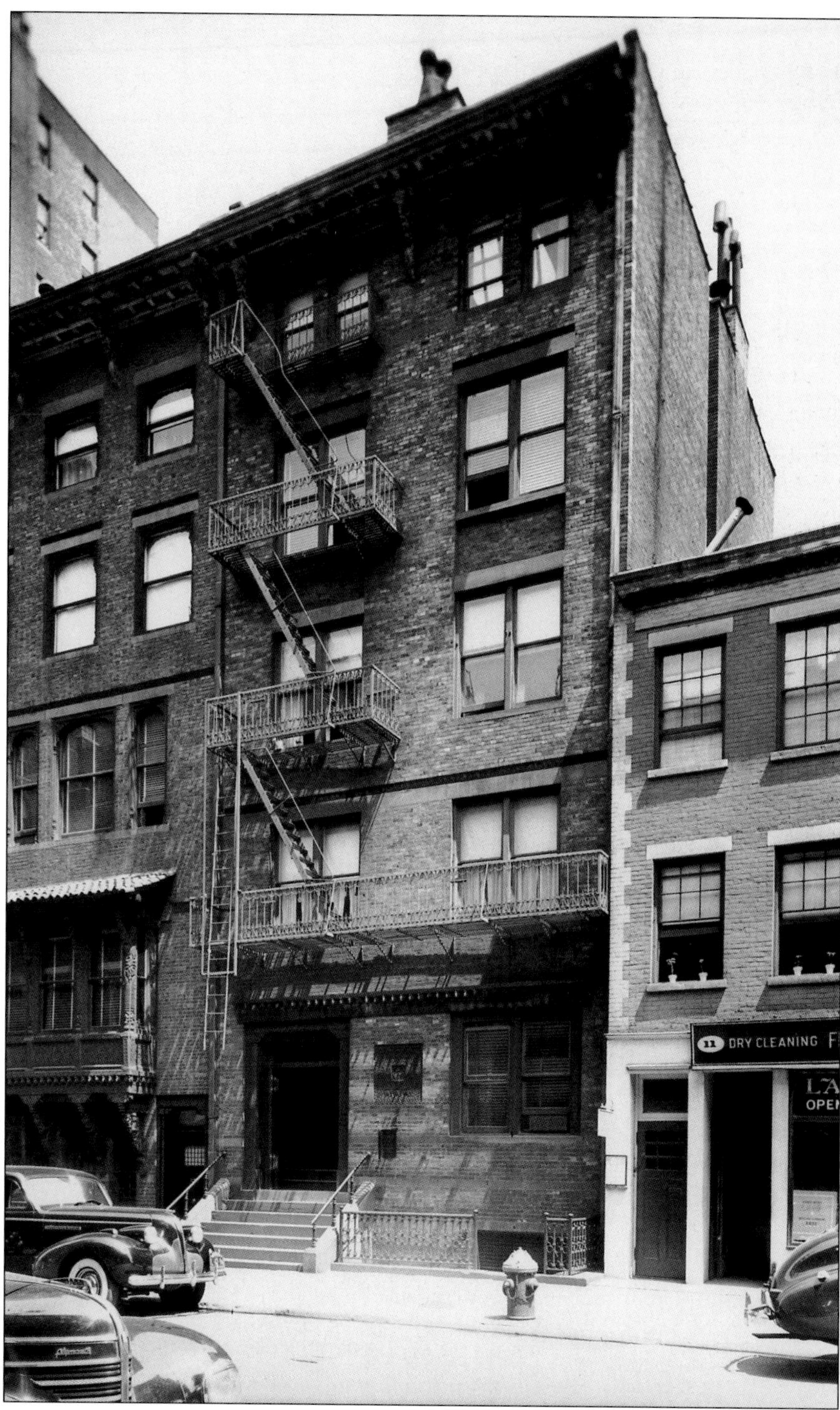

THE AVA, CIRCA 1941. COURTESY OFFICE FOR METROPOLITAN HISTORY

THE JEFFERSON MARKET COURTHOUSE

425 SIXTH AVENUE

THE JEFFERSON MARKET COURTHOUSE, AT WEST 10TH STREET and Avenue of the Americas, is a delicious fantasy of turrets, gables, lookouts, and stone carving, but it was also the object of New York's earliest major struggle for historic preservation, one in which a band of Greenwich Villagers saved one of the city's greatest structures before there was a landmarks law.

The Jefferson Market Courthouse began life in the early 1870s as another graft effort by the circle of William M. (Boss) Tweed. The Tweed scheme stalled—he was arrested in 1871—but a revised courthouse project went ahead.

Designed in 1874 by Frederick Withers, an established academic architect, the new Third Judicial District Courthouse at its completion in 1877 was "a delight to the eye," according to the *New York Tribune*.

The delicate polychromed corner tower rises up in successive shapes—octagonal, round, square—to a four-faced clock and fire-lookout post. Its prison that stretched out to the west was demolished long ago, but the main building facing the Avenue of the Americas—then called Sixth Avenue—still survives, a vigorous, complicated series of masses, all in deep red Philadelphia brick and soft, buff-colored Ohio stone.

In his design, Withers consciously imported up-to-the-minute ideas from London, where High Victorian Gothic was the most sophisticated style Europe could offer. When the churchlike building was completed the *Tribune* hoped for quick action by "the reforming influence of its elegant outlines" on the vagrants and drunkards who were brought to justice there.

But the *New York Times*, while praising the architecture, said that "the lowest criminals, the most trivial cases, are here housed within one of the most ornate structures in the city."

The paper, which had been instrumental in exposing the waste of the Tweed ring, estimated that a suitable building could have been built for less than half the cost—$550,000—and that the disreputable surroundings made the courthouse nothing more than "a jewel in a swine's snout."

There was general speculation as to whether the building had been a "job," that is, a large source of graft, and one contractor so accused Withers. But there were no formal charges, and perhaps all the money was indeed spent properly, even if it was too much to start with.

THE JEFFERSON MARKET COURTHOUSE *on West 10th Street and Sixth Avenue in 1906.* COURTESY LIBRARY OF CONGRESS

By 1906, when Harry Thaw was tried at the courthouse for the murder of Stanford White, most Victorian buildings had become objects of derision. But the Jefferson Market Courthouse continued to hold the esteem of critics; the 1939 *WPA Guide to New York City* called it "an exceptionally interesting work of its period."

In the 1950s the city slated the entire block for sale for private development. Margot Gayle, a Democratic district leader living at 44 West Ninth Street, remembers a fateful discussion at a cocktail party at the apartment of Robert Ratner, at 51 Fifth Avenue, before Christmas of 1959. Everyone in her circle agreed it would be a shame to lose the building. She and others hit on a campaign to restore the clock, which had long been stuck at 3:20, and expanded that small campaign into renovating the interior for a branch library.

THE VERMEER

77 SEVENTH AVENUE

THE REPUTATION OF THE WHITE-BRICK, MODERN APARTMENT HOUSE is at a low ebb, and even developers now use "white brick" as epithet rather than advertisement. Yet thirty years ago, when the age of white brick was at its peak, it was considered a premium material carrying a premium cost. But in recent years white brick has been reconsidered, as a failure-prone material, especially considering the sloppy construction practices of the 1960s. An outstanding example is the 1964 Vermeer, a 352-unit co-op at 77 Seventh Avenue, between 14th and 15th Streets, which in 1992 spent $3 million to replace the white brick.

The late Philip Birnbaum was one of the most active apartment-house designers in New York in the '50s and '60s. He said white brick came into use because "in the midst of an old block you put up a bright, new building, like a woman going out and buying a new dress.

"The public liked the idea," he said. Normal unglazed red brick cost about $45 for one thousand, he said, and white brick double that.

The developers of the Vermeer, Hyman and Irving Shapiro, filed plans for the building in 1961 along with other developers rushing to build before a new zoning law became effective that year. Their architects, Herbert and Clarence Lilien of New York City,

33.1 FIG

THE VERMEER, *the 352-unit co-op at 77 Seventh Avenue between 14th and 15th Streets, as it was under construction, in white brick in 1963.* COURTESY OFFICE FOR METROPOLITAN HISTORY

designed a twenty-one-story, $4.6 million building with studios and one- and two-bedroom apartments along 5-foot-wide, 240-foot-long windowless corridors. No apartment had a dining room.

When Hyman Shapiro was interviewed in the *New York Times* in 1974 he said: "Architectural amenities are sheer nonsense. Zoning determines architecture."

The original brochure, in the collection of the architectural historian Andrew Alpern, called the building's facade "imposing," with "quiet elegance and charm."

But in the 1980s real problems developed in the facade, with lines of bulging brickwork every floor or so. One panel of the 15th Street corner pushed out so far that the Department of Buildings issued a violation.

The Vermeer's restoration architect, Walter Melvin of New York, said the bulging is caused by a slight shrinkage of the reinforced concrete frame that occurred within a few years of construction.

The exterior brickwork—only four inches deep—was supported independently at each floor by steel shelf angles bolted to the concrete frame. As the frame settled, the brick panels rested not on the shelf angles, but on each other, resulting in a brick wall four inches wide and twenty stories high only loosely attached to the building and beginning to crush the ground-floor storefronts.

Complicating this were many construction flaws. Mr. Melvin examined twenty-seven shelf angle connections at the ninth floor and found only four sound. Others were broken, had never been attached, or were entirely missing.

With Mr. Melvin's advice, the co-op did what had become fairly common: replacing its entire facade, up to the beginning of the first setback, of 350,000 bricks. According to Carol Sendar, the board president, the shareholders, choosing among three alternatives, opted for a taupe color. Red brick finished second and white "a poor third," she said.

HENRY SIEGEL AND THE 14TH STREET STORE

14TH STREET AND SIXTH AVENUE

HENRY SIEGEL'S TURN-OF-THE-CENTURY RETAILING OPERATIONS rose and fell like Internet stocks. His 14th Street Store, opened in 1904 on Sixth Avenue between 13th and 14th Streets, was one of his biggest projects, and it fell apart a decade after he put it up.

Siegel came from Germany to America in 1867 and ultimately controlled large department stores in Chicago and Boston as well as New York. In the book *Great Merchants of Early New York* Joseph Devorkin calls him "the Napoleon of the Department Store industry." He is best known for his gigantic Siegel-Cooper store, which he built with his associate Frank Cooper in 1896 at Sixth Avenue and 18th Street.

Siegel-Cooper was one of a half dozen large stores that went up on Sixth Avenue between 14th and 23rd Streets, expanding beyond the retail successes of stores on West 14th like Hearn's, which was between Fifth and Sixth Avenues, and Macy's, established in 1858 on the east side of Sixth Avenue between 13th and 14th Streets.

Macy's initially occupied a small structure facing Sixth, but in the 1890s built a wide

THE 14TH STREET STORE *in 1904.* COURTESY LIBRARY OF CONGRESS

nine-story building at 55 West 13th Street, east of Sixth Avenue, and a narrow nine-story building at 56 West 14th.

In 1902, Macy's leapfrogged Siegel-Cooper and its neighbors by building its present store at 34th Street and Sixth Avenue. Macy's sold its previous site to Siegel, who saw opportunity where the Sixth Avenue Elevated intersected with one of New York's busiest crosstown streets.

Siegel had the architects Cady, Berg & See work out a design for the whole Sixth Avenue blockfront, from 13th to 14th, not as grand as the Siegel-Cooper store—the new 14th Street Store was to offer lower-priced merchandise. To compete with the hulking Elevated structure, the new ten-story building carried huge electric signs with "6th Avenue's busy corner" in script, and giant limestone portals as entrances on 14th, Sixth, and 13th. The ancillary Macy's structures at 55 West 13th and 56 West 14th were left intact.

In 1904 the *New York Times* quoted Siegel as saying that the success of his new store would depend on absolute fair dealing and avoiding even the most "trifling deception" in any of the seventy departments. In the same year the *New York Tribune* reported that

Siegel was selling stock in a $10 million corporation that would own the 14th Street Store, the Simpson-Crawford store on Sixth Avenue between 19th and 20th Streets, and his other retailing operations.

But while Siegel was finishing his new store, he had to sell his interest in the Siegel-Cooper Store to Joseph B. Greenhut, another retailer, to cover his expenses. Greenhut said later that Siegel cried as he signed over the 1896 store for $500,000.

In 1914 Siegel was tried on fraud charges for falsifying data to secure further credit, and the 14th Street Store closed. Many of the nine-hundred-plus employees lost their savings, leading to angry protests at the store. Siegel was sentenced to ten months in jail; the *Times* reported that "tears rolled down the cheeks" of the man who had once been one of the most powerful retailers in New York.

In 1916 Siegel opened a short-lived cloak and suit company on Broadway, and in 1921 he opened a haberdashery in Hackensack, New Jersey, where he lived in a boardinghouse. He died in Hackensack in 1930.

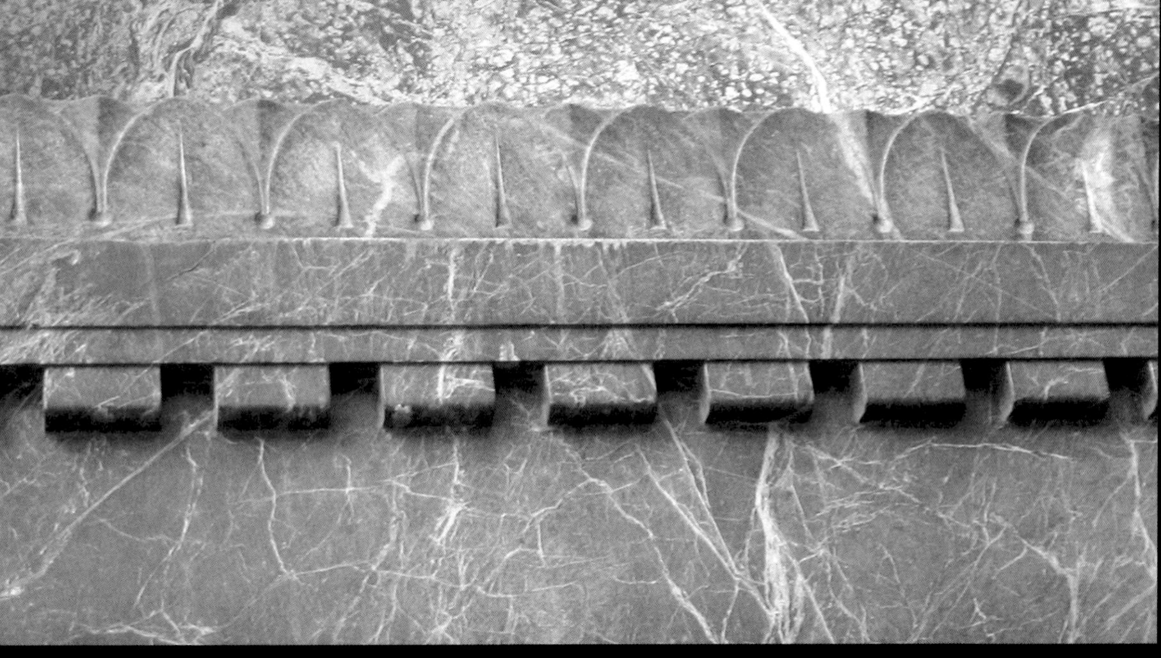

MIDTOWN

GRAMERCY PARK

FLATIRON

CHELSEA

MURRAY HILL

HEARALD SQUARE

GRAND CENTRAL

TIMES SQUARE

THE PLAZA AREA

THE "WASHINGTON IRVING HOUSE"

49 IRVING PLACE

ONE MAY HAVE FAITH THAT TRUTH WILL TRIUMPH OVER FRAUD and still believe that myth is stronger than both. In the case of the famously misidentified "Washington Irving House" at 49 Irving Place, the southwest corner of 17th Street, the Irving myth is tenacious.

Washington Irving was one of the preeminent cultural figures of early-nineteenth-century New York, author of *The Legend of Sleepy Hollow* and *Rip Van Winkle*, and influential in the creation of Central Park. In the 1840s he began spending most of his time at Sunnyside, his country seat in Tarrytown, New York, where he died in 1859.

He never had any observable connection to the three-story Italianate-style house at 49 Irving Place, which was built in 1844—the street was named after Irving in 1833. The first several decades of occupants at 49 Irving Place included an insurance agent, a merchant, and a banker—but not Washington Irving.

In the early 1890s, 49 Irving Place was rented to two women, Elsie de Wolfe, a chic and stylish actress, and Elisabeth Marbury, a powerful literary agent who represented authors like Oscar Wilde and George Bernard Shaw. The two women met in the 1880s and were, by most accounts, the most famous lesbian couple in Victorian New York, often and happily in the public eye.

The 1905 census listed the forty-two-year-old literary agent as head of household and the actress, who was thirty-five, as her "partner." They established a famous salon in their house, one that mixed old money and new talent, from the Astors to Sarah Bernhardt to Bernard Berenson.

De Wolfe is generally credited with inventing the profession of interior decorator, which she took up around 1905. One of her first commissions was for Stanford White, architect of the Colony Club on Madison near 29th Street, the first elite social club for women in New York.

It was while the publicity-friendly de Wolfe was living at 49 Irving Place that the Washington Irving story first appears, in 1897 in the *New York Times*. It was an enthusiastic article about the Irving Place house and, especially, the wonderful talents of Elsie de Wolfe. The anonymous writer inexplicably quoted Irving in great detail about the exact design of "his house," but without any source. The author clearly relied on de Wolfe for most of the other material in the story.

The Irving question came to the fore with a fund-raising effort in 1927 to create a museum. There was a great hue and cry, including letters from Irving's nieces and

FIG 35.1

"WASHINGTON IRVING HOUSE" *on Irving Place at 17th Street, circa 1900, then rented by Elsie de Wolfe.* COURTESY BYRON, MUSEUM OF THE CITY OF NEW YORK

FIG 35.2

ELSIE DE WOLFE, *the actress, at the house in 1898.* COURTESY BYRON, MUSEUM OF THE CITY OF NEW YORK

nephews stating that he "never crossed the front door" of the corner house, though he may have stayed at times with a relative at 120 East 17th Street.

But for some reason, through all this great controversy Elsie de Wolfe remained most curiously silent. The Washington Irving story is remarkably durable and appears in many books published in the last twenty years; despite the facts, it may be here to stay.

129 EAST 19TH STREET

IN 1855 JAMES COUPER LORD, an iron merchant and philanthropist who lived on Gramercy Park, built the two-story stable at 129 East 19th Street in 1861.

The first account of its nineteenth-century occupancy is a 1903 article in the *New York Times*, which attributed its diamond-paned leaded-glass windows to an unidentified glassworker who occupied it for some time in the 1890s.

Indeed, classified directories show that Craig F. R. Drake, "stained-glass maker," leased and occupied the building for a year in 1899.

FIG 36.1

EXTERIOR OF 129 EAST 19TH STREET IN 1904. COURTESY MUSEUM OF THE CITY OF NEW YORK

INTERIOR OF 129 EAST 19TH STREET IN 1904. COURTESY MUSEUM OF THE CITY OF NEW YORK

In 1903, a new lessee, F. Berkeley Smith, filed plans to convert what was described as a studio into a residence. Smith was trained as an architect but was apparently independently wealthy—he summered in Paris and wrote *The Real Latin Quarter, How Paris Amuses Itself,* and other books. He had worked with the architect R. H. Robertson, and a Robertson employee, August Pauli, designed extensive interior alterations for the 19th Street house.

Smith installed fireplaces for heat—a bohemian touch in a time when a furnace was considered civilized—two bedrooms, a boudoir for Mrs. Smith, and a trunk room, all furnished with wood wainscoting, antique metal lamps, furniture, and artwork.

A photograph taken by Joseph Byron in 1904 shows a brick stable with neo-Gothic trim, window moldings, bottle-end stained glass, and other artistic touches. In 1903, the *Times* wrote that there was "no more picturesque exterior" in the whole city, "none so riotously gay in color" with window boxes of geraniums, evergreen shrubs, bright brass hardware, green painted brick, and white trim—"an exterior that attracts the attention of the least observant passerby."

The building seems to be a mid-nineteenth-century Gothic revival work, but it is a bit late for that style. The moldings above the windows conflict with and partially obscure curved, segmental brick arches. Are they original or alterations? Did the stained-glass maker put them on in 1899 or did Smith in 1903—or someone else in an entirely different time? If the moldings are an alteration, what about the decorative frieze panel under the cornice, and the Gothic-style projecting doorway? If the Gothic trim is original, conflicting with the brickwork, was the brick originally painted or left bare?

Unfortunately, a "restoration" undertaken in 1992—with the blessings of the Landmarks Preservation Commission—has almost certainly destroyed the physical evidence that would have answered these questions. The facade was stripped of all paint, and some of the wood trim was replaced.

Chemical and microscopic testing of the successive paint layers, comparing those on the exposed brick, the surface of the trim, the brick underneath the trim, the window sash, and other locations, would at least give educated guesses as to the changes in appearance of the house from construction until the 1904 photograph. A limited analysis was undertaken, but nothing so extensive, and now that evidence has been removed.

The building is still a marvel. What a pity that the curiosity it provokes is never to be satisfied.

NATIONAL ARTS CLUB, THE FORMER SAMUEL TILDEN HOUSE

15 GRAMERCY PARK SOUTH

SAMUEL TILDEN BECAME RICH AS A CORPORATION LAWYER in the 1850s and then became interested in Democratic politics. Although he later opposed the corrupt ring of William M. Tweed, initially he had to get along with Tammany Hall, which had a chokehold on the party.

Tilden bought the Gothic Revival–style house at 15 Gramercy Park South in 1863. Elected governor of New York State in 1874, he ran for president in 1876 against Rutherford B. Hayes. He was in his Gramercy Park house on election night, and the early returns appeared to indicate his certain election, both in popular and electoral votes. But returns in Florida, South Carolina, and Louisiana were challenged by the Republicans, with some backing from disaffected Democrats, amid shady actions by both sides. Finally, an electoral commission decided Tilden had won the popular vote but lost the electoral vote by one, 185 to 184.

At a rally in front of his house in October 1877 Tilden declared that the commission's decision was "a robbery of the dearest rights of American citizens." In 1880 Tammany Democrats blocked his renomination for president, and he basically retired from political life.

The next year he retained Calvert Vaux, who had designed Central Park with Frederick Law Olmsted, to merge Nos. 15 and 14 Gramercy Park South behind a new facade. In 1882 the *Tribune* said the reason for the expansion was that "Tilden's library was growing so rapidly that there had to be some place to hold it." The newspaper estimated the cost at $200,000.

Vaux's highly colored facade of brownstone trimmed with dark granite and large sections of red Carlisle stone from Scotland is in line with the original buildings of the Metropolitan Museum of Art and the American Museum of Natural History, which he had also designed.

FIG 37.1

INTERIOR OF THE TILDEN HOUSE *in 1876.* COURTESY THE NEW-YORK HISTORICAL SOCIETY, NEW YORK CITY

FIG 37.2

EXTERIOR OF THE TILDEN HOUSE *in 1905.* COURTESY THE NEW-YORK HISTORICAL SOCIETY, NEW YORK CITY

Vaux had extensive carving carried out over the whole front. Most memorable is a panel with five heads modeled in brownstone that "represents the literary idea which is the foundation of the whole new structure," according to the *Tribune*. Represented are Shakespeare, Milton, Goethe, Dante, and, in the center, Benjamin Franklin.

Completed in 1884, the new house had two entries, on the left for residential visitors and on the right for political or literary guests. The literary and political folk entered under a bust of Michelangelo.

In 1886 Tilden died and left the bulk of his $5 million estate to begin a public library for New York—the consensus was that he had intended his house to be converted to make his collection open to the public.

But Tilden made no special provisions for his house in his will, and the Tilden collection was later combined with the Astor and Lenox Libraries for what was built as the New York Public Library, at Fifth Avenue and 42nd Street. In 1905 the house was purchased by the National Arts Club, which has been careful to maintain the interiors, which remain some of the most sumptuous residential work in New York.

THE DECKER BUILDING

33 UNION SQUARE WEST

NOT MANY BUILDINGS ARE DESIGNED BY ANARCHIST ARCHITECTS. That is a good enough reason to look up at John Edelmann's fanciful, Islamic sliver that is the Decker Building, at 33 Union Square West.

In 1893 the Decker Brothers piano company built a new headquarters. Eleven stories high but only 30 feet wide, the new Decker Building jumped up above the surrounding shop buildings as if it were spring-loaded.

Just as startling was the styling, a combination of Islamic and Venetian, culminating in a tiled roof and domed minaret. The entire facade of the building is still alive with ornament, an architectural ant-swarm of ogees, sunflowers, arches, filigree, arabesques, and other elements.

The *Real Estate Record and Guide* praised the Decker Building's "highly artistic exterior." It noted that it had a site with the unusual advantage of a broad vista, "an inspiration to the architect, Alfred Zucker, for he has made the most that was possible of it." Zucker had an active commercial practice in the 1880s and 1890s and is known for his unusual and fluid ornament.

THE DECKER BUILDING, *topped by a minaret, on Union Square in 1893.* COURTESY THE NEW-YORK HISTORICAL SOCIETY, NEW YORK CITY

BRENTANO'S
TO LET
DECKER BUILDING

But it appears that there was another architect—John H. Edelmann—according to Paul Sprague, a professor of architectural history at the University of Wisconsin at Milwaukee. An authority on the architect Louis H. Sullivan, Professor Sprague began studying Edelmann in the 1960s because Sullivan credited Edelmann with the idea for his maxim, "form follows function."

Sullivan admired Edelmann tremendously, and Edelmann helped Sullivan throughout his career, though Edelmann did not meet with the same success.

Professor Sprague said Edelmann's children and some surviving sketches confirmed that it was Edelmann, in the employ of Zucker, who was responsible for the design of the Decker Building.

Edelmann had worked for the Chicago architects William LeBaron Jenney and Dankmar Adler, to whom he introduced the young Sullivan.

Research by the late Professor Donald Egbert, a Princeton art historian, indicates that Edelmann became active in radical politics in the 1870s. He came to New York in 1886 to work in the mayoral campaign of the single-taxer Henry George, working for Zucker from 1891 to 1893.

During that period Edelmann was expelled from the Socialist Labor Party for his increasing tilt toward anarchism, and in 1893 he and other radicals published and edited the anarchist journal *Solidarity*. He was also a friend of the prominent American anarchist and writer Emma Goldman.

In 1897 the Russian anarchist Prince Peter Kropotkin stayed with Edelmann on a trip to the United States. During most of this period Edelmann remained in close touch with Sullivan.

Edelmann died during a heat wave in July 1900. The Decker Building is his only known structure still standing in New York. As for Zucker, he moved to the Decker Building, where he may have occupied the eleventh floor, which includes a tiny room up a flight of stairs at the base of the tower. A decade ago, this room still had fragments of a remarkable red, black, and gold stenciling scheme.

THE SIEGEL-COOPER BUILDING

632 SIXTH AVENUE

IN THE 1870S, THE AVENUE OF THE AMERICAS—then called Sixth Avenue—began developing as a department store area with the B. Altman and Hugh O'Neill stores on the west side of the avenue, at 19th and 21st Streets. These huge stores, soon served by the new Sixth Avenue Elevated, attracted a broader crowd than the more elite shops running up Broadway from Union Square, two blocks east.

The 1890s brought more construction of giant buildings on Sixth, of which the most ambitious was surely the Siegel-Cooper.

Henry Siegel and Frank Cooper had established a successful department store in Chicago. To penetrate the New York market, they acquired a full blockfront plot distinguished by its great depth, running 460 feet east toward Fifth Avenue.

FIG 39.1

SIEGEL-COOPER DEPARTMENT STORE *on Sixth Avenue between 18th and 19th Streets in 1895.* COURTESY OFFICE FOR METROPOLITAN HISTORY

Their architects, DeLemos & Cordes, designed what was claimed to be the largest store in the world—750,000 square feet spread over a florid six-story Renaissance-style structure with a tall central tower and grand entrance.

"The Big Store" it was called, and the New York Times wrote that it carried "all that is between a tenpenny nail and a roast rib of beef to a diamond bracelet and a velvet cape." It opened in September 1896 in a near riot as a crowd of 150,000 tried to squeeze into a store that could accommodate only 35,000. According to the New York Tribune, even Frank Cooper could not get in.

The attractions included not only goods in elaborate display—the bicycle department had its own track—but also ancillary services: a bank, a post office, a hospital, a nursery, an aviary, a florist, a dentist, a pharmacy, a ticket office, and a servants' employment agency.

The store did well even as change crept past it. In 1902, the New York Tribune said that it served 180,000 people each day and used 40 million square feet of wrapping paper each year but also that the main shopping district now began at 18th Street, reaching up to the new Macy's store at 34th Street.

B. Altman began its new store on Fifth Avenue and 34th Street in 1904, but no others made the leap eastward.

SIEGEL-COOPER DEPARTMENT STORE *on Sixth Avenue between 18th and 19th Streets in 1955.* COURTESY OFFICE FOR METROPOLITAN HISTORY

In the same year, Joseph B. Greenhut bought out Siegel's share of the store—later saying that Siegel wept at parting with his interest for only $500,000—and took over.

But in 1915, the Greenhut operation failed, a result in part of the decline in its mail-order business, cut in half by World War I.

The store reorganized and reopened but closed again in 1918—the last of the big stores to survive below 23rd Street. Joseph Greenhut was quoted then as saying that closings had given the neighborhood a "black eye."

The Siegel-Cooper Building next served as a military hospital but soon was used for loft space—just like its neighbors. What had been a five-block-long shoppers' paradise had lasted less than a generation.

In 1937, the distinctive central tower was cut down, giving the building a stumpy look, but it otherwise has remained largely intact. Now thanks to cleaning and a general revival in the area, the building has recaptured some of its original ambition.

THE FLATIRON BUILDING
175 FIFTH AVENUE

IT IS ONE OF NEW YORK'S MOST BELOVED STORIES: that cocky, disdainful New Yorkers caustically labeled the triangular 1902 structure at 23rd and Fifth Avenue the "Flatiron," foiling the attempts of the huge Fuller Company to name it after itself. This is anything but the truth, but the twenty-story building has enough real history without needing to invent any.

In 1901, a syndicate including Chicago's George A. Fuller Construction Company filed plans for a twenty-story building on the triangular plot bounded by 22nd and 23rd Streets, Broadway, and Fifth Avenue. The building was never the city's tallest, but its location in what was then the main shopping district made it one of the most famous. The facade itself is handsome but not exceptional for its time: horizontal rusticated courses of

FIG 40.1

THE FLATIRON SITE IN 1884. COURTESY THE NEW-YORK HISTORICAL SOCIETY, NEW YORK CITY

RENDERING OF DANIEL BURNHAM'S *"Flat-Iron," 1902.* COURTESY OFFICE FOR METROPOLITAN HISTORY limestone, brick, and terra-cotta of intricate design, with occasional classically styled medallions of female faces and other elements. It was designed by the firm of Daniel H. Burnham—who often worked for out-of-town interests.

But what was most dramatic about the building had less to do with art than commerce: it made full use of the small, oddly shaped lot, rising straight up, directly and bluntly, from its wedge-shaped site without the setbacks, turrets, towers, or domes that characterized the tall buildings then being designed by New York architects.

Indeed *Architectural Record* in 1902 sounded disappointed. The site "clamored for an original and unconventional solution," it said, whereas Burnham "has simply drawn three elevations of its three fronts," approaching the design as merely three connected facades rather than as a sculpted space.

But what was to a professional journal simply a "conventional skyscraper" attracted crowds, "sometimes one hundred or more," said the New York Tribune in 1902. They looked up "with their heads bent back until a general breakage of necks seems imminent."

But stories of the wind effects of the building are apparently true. In February of 1903, a gust magnified by the great triangle blew John McTaggart, a fourteen-year-old messenger, out into Fifth Avenue where he was killed by a passing automobile.

Newspapers ran many articles on the wind problem, among them a 1903 story in the *New York Herald* headlined "Whirling Winds Play Havoc with Women at the Flatiron." And in the same year Gibson N. Vincent, a store owner across Broadway, sued for $5,000 to cover the replacement cost of plate glass broken, he said, by gusts caused by the new building.

Anyone who wants to believe the conventional story must first deal with the fact that the triangular site—not the building—was well known as the "Flat-Iron" long before the Fuller Company rolled into town. And then they should inspect Burnham's original specifications for the Fuller Company: they labeled it "Flat-Iron Building."

THE CHELSEA HOTEL

222 WEST 23RD STREET

THE ELEVEN-STORY CHELSEA HOTEL AT 222 WEST 23RD STREET was completed in 1884 in the middle of New York's first luxury apartment boom, when at least eight other big apartment houses had already risen.

News accounts and city records do not absolutely clarify who conceived of the Chelsea, which was built as an apartment house. The building application was taken in the name of George M. Smith, a building-materials dealer—but he may have acted for someone else. In 1884, the *New York Tribune* said that "some fifty people of means" had cooperatively organized the project, but that might have been a promoter's smokescreen to give it cachet.

The idea of the Chelsea is often attributed to Philip Hubert, a French-born architect whose firm, Hubert & Pirsson, designed the Chelsea and many other such buildings. Hubert is sometimes credited with originating the co-op in New York, as well as the duplex apartment concept. For most of the early 1880s he lived in Connecticut; in 1885, he moved to the Chelsea.

The original Chelsea had a barbershop, restaurant, top-floor artists' studios, a roof garden, maid service, and about one hundred apartments, seventy owned by stockholders and thirty rented out. In 1885, the *Real Estate Record and Guide* said that many of the apartments were owned by tradesmen and suppliers on the project "who were persuaded" to take them in lieu of money—apparently under duress. *Carpentry and Building* magazine said the apartments cost from $7,000 to $12,000 each; there are only vague accounts of maintenance fees.

Early residents included lawyers and businessmen, but also more artistic types—Rufus Zogbaum, an artist who later covered the Spanish-American War for *Harper's* magazine, and Henry Abbey, a theatrical producer.

The bloom of the co-op movement wilted in 1885 as several failed, and new legislation severely restricted construction of tall apartment houses. At some point the Chelsea's original co-op corporation was dissolved, and around 1900 the building began to shift toward transient occupancy—the writer O. Henry stayed there for a short time in 1907. In 1912, *Titanic* survivors with second-cabin-class tickets stayed at the Chelsea for a few days.

FIG 41.1

CHELSEA HOTEL IN 1912. COURTESY THE NEW-YORK HISTORICAL SOCIETY, NEW YORK CITY

In 1921, the Knott Hotels Corporation acquired the Chelsea. Knott tussled with the manager, Jerry Gagin, in 1934 over restaurant decorations. Gagin had hired the artist John McKiernan to paint satirical murals showing the contemporary political figures Alfred E. Smith, Huey Long, and James A. Farley. The one of Senator Long showed him overburdening a donkey and holding a drum and a rifle. Knott ordered the murals covered.

But in 1942 an investment group, including David Bard, bought the hotel after a foreclosure sale, and they were more art friendly. In 1953 the hard-drinking poet Dylan Thomas, thirty-nine, collapsed in his room at the Chelsea, and later died at St. Vincent's Hospital. An article in *Life* in 1964 listed recent or current tenants as the playwright Arthur Miller, the painter John Sloan, and Elizabeth Gurley Flynn, chairman of the Communist Party in the United States.

THE DONAC

402 WEST 20TH STREET

IN THE EARLY 1830S DON ALONZO CUSHMAN bought a large plot in Chelsea at the southeast corner of 21st Street and Ninth Avenue, opposite the General Theological Seminary, and built a large freestanding house numbered 9 Chelsea Square.

The early settlers, in naming the street, had envisioned that an enclave of private houses would surround the green block of the seminary. Cushman worked with Clement Clarke Moore to build up the neighborhood and soon bought from Moore the land at 406–418 West 20th Street. In 1840 Cushman improved this plot with one of the most elegant Greek Revival rows in New York, a group of four-story brick houses with iron fencing. Cushman and Moore had agreed in 1834 to a 10-foot setback in the front yard to create a garden effect that gave the houses an even greater presence.

FIG 42.1

DON ALONZO CUSHMAN

MRS. D. A. CUSHMAN

DON ALONZO CUSHMAN *and Mrs. Cushman in 1870.* COURTESY OFFICE FOR METROPOLITAN HISTORY

Cushman retired from the dry-goods business in 1855 but continued to survey his real estate from an office in his big brick house at 21st and Ninth, which was surrounded by gardens. At least seven of his children lived within a block or two of the family house, among them his daughter Angelica Faber, who lived at 430 West 20th Street. *Cushman Chronicles—A Tale of Old Chelsea*, a 1932 book by Pauline Sainsbury, Cushman's granddaughter, describes a close clan, united by singing parties, European trips, and activities at St. Peter's Church, at 346 West 20th Street.

When Cushman died in 1875 his estate was estimated at $3.5 million. Later press accounts indicate that the estate was run jointly for the benefit of the Cushman children but that the land was divided among the family members in the 1890s. The division spurred a small building boom: the Cushman Building, at the northeast corner of Maiden Lane and Broadway (now occupied by Barthman, the jeweler with the clock in the sidewalk); a commercial building at 240 West 23rd Street; the Chelsea Court apartment building on the site of the old homestead at 21st and Ninth; and, in 1898, the Donac. All were designed by C. P. H. Gilbert, the mansion specialist, whose buildings included the Warburg mansion at Fifth Avenue and 92nd Street, which now houses the Jewish Museum.

Although the Donac was not subject to the original setback restriction, Gilbert curved the facade to match the setback line and put a convex oriel window within the bay. The word "Donac" is incised in the terra-cotta over the door. Angelica Faber, his sixth child, was the owner of record—at the time of construction, she was still living in her West 20th Street house and the family was still gathering weekly at St. Peter's Church. But now, a century later, all the Cushmans have long moved away from Chelsea.

FIG 42.2

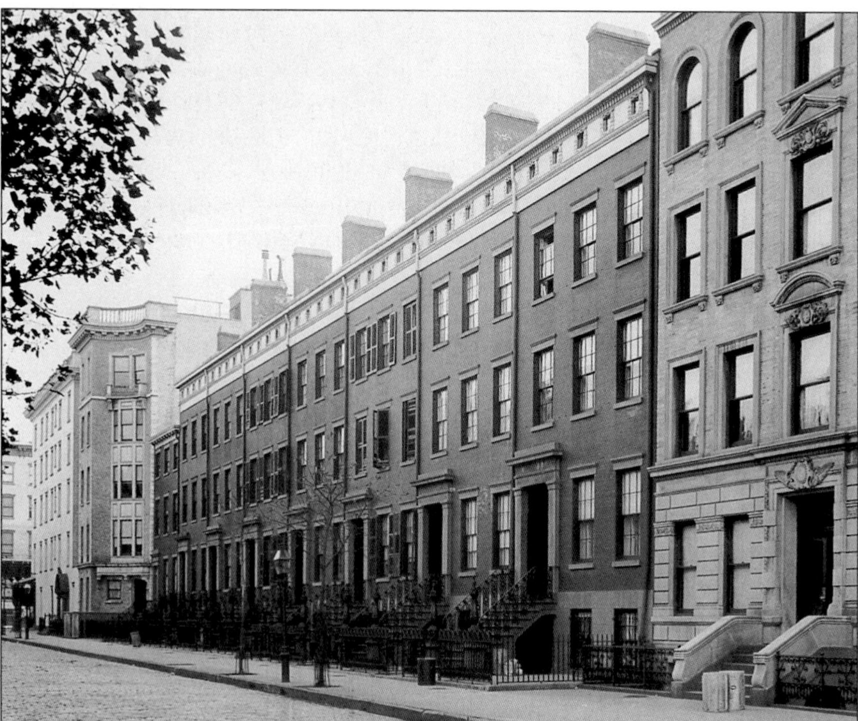

GREEK REVIVAL ROW HOUSES *built by Don Alonzo Cushman in 1840 at 406–418 West 20th Street, with the curved-front Donac in the distance, 1905.* COURTESY THE NEW-YORK HISTORICAL SOCIETY, NEW YORK CITY

STARRETT-LEHIGH BUILDING

WEST 26TH–27TH STREETS, ELEVENTH TO TWELFTH AVENUES

BY THE 1920S, NEW YORK BUSINESSES WERE REGULARLY LAMENTING the cost of traffic delays, but matching the forms of nineteenth-century buildings to the modern city of truck, railroad, and barge transport was hard to achieve. In 1930 William A. Starrett, a prominent financier-builder, leased the block bounded by 26th and 27th Streets and Eleventh and Twelfth Avenues from the Lehigh Valley Railroad, which operated an open-air freight yard on the site served by car floats docking at Pier 66 across Twelfth Avenue.

The Starrett-Lehigh Building was completed in 1932; the railroad retained the ground floor as a vast freight yard, and the nineteen-story, 1.8 million-square-foot building directly above it provided the railroad with a large pool of potential customers.

Trucks pulled into driveways from 27th Street, descended to a bay of three giant elevators in the basement, and were carried to particular floors for deliveries or pickups. On the way out, they were brought down and exited at grade level to 26th Street.

Inside, the floors were wide open—long forests of mushroom columns recessed from the perimeter, an eight-foot-high strip of steel casement sash. On the outside, the architects Cory & Cory made the simplest possible statement: ribbon windows alternating with plain brick bands. The engineers for the Starrett-Lehigh Building were Purdy & Henderson.

Lewis Mumford, writing in his "Skyline" column in the *New Yorker* in late 1931, called the Starrett-Lehigh Building "a victory for engineering" and said that "the contrast between the long, continuous red-brick bands and the green-framed windows, with sapphire reflections or depths, is as sound a use of color as one can see about the city."

Mumford objected only to the "rabble of water tanks" on the roof and to the central bay, expressed with the vertical line of a traditional skyscraper, which he said spoiled "the noble severity" of the facade.

Early Manhattan address-telephone directories list as tenants in the building the types of businesses that might need boxcar-size shipments: Standard Pressed Steel, the Il Duce Wine Company, and the Wheeling Tire Company. They also list Buckminster Fuller—at the time he was experimenting with mass-produced kitchen/bathroom combinations.

Starrett died in March 1932, and the Lehigh Valley Railroad bought the building that June. In 1935 the railroad reported to the Interstate Commerce Commission that the building had been losing money, more than $300,000 in 1933.

STARRETT-LEHIGH BUILDING IN 1932. COURTESY LIBRARY OF CONGRESS

Thomas Flagg, an industrial archeologist, said that by 1943 the building was 100 percent occupied. But, he said, rail freight served by car floats "could not compete with the tax-supported public roads" in the 1950s. In 1966 the railroad gave up its ground floor, and the tracks were torn out for a trucking operation.

THE 30TH STREET STATION HOUSE

138 WEST 30TH STREET

WHEN THE 30TH STREET STATION HOUSE WAS BUILT in 1908 at 138 West 30th, the area was the heart of the Tenderloin district, where the police were reputed to make small fortunes off New York's heaviest concentration of gambling and prostitution.

Most accounts agree that it was Alexander Williams who coined the Tenderloin name. In 1876 he was transferred from the Lower East Side to command the station house, then across the street at 139 West 30th Street, and the *New York Times* reported in

FIG 44.1

THE 30TH STREET STATION HOUSE IN 1911. COURTESY OFFICE FOR METROPOLITAN HISTORY

a 1906 article that he exclaimed: "Ah fine, my boy, fine. It's been chuck steak for me; it'll be tenderloin now."

The *Times* also reported in 1906 that, responding to an 1890s city inquiry into his surprising wealth, he stated that he made it in real estate investments in Tokyo, knowing that details would be impossible to trace.

By 1900 the existing precinct house was in terrible shape, both for the police and the prisoners. A few years later, the Board of Health condemned it as unfit for human habitation. The architect R. Thomas Short was hired in 1903 to design a replacement.

Completed in 1908, the medieval-style building of granite and orange brick was described as a "model police station" by *Architects and Builders* magazine in the same year.

It had cells for forty-two prisoners, and the cells were furnished with toilets that could be flushed by the keeper from outside the bars. On the three upper floors were nine dormitories holding eighteen officers each, plus extra sleeping rooms for plainclothes detectives. In those days the police, like firefighters, served multiday shifts.

The building has a square central courtyard and a vehicular entrance so that criminals could be driven into the station house by patrol wagon instead of walked up the steps. The *Times* indicated that the "perp walk" of the 1900s was different from today's, noting that the police often "even up scores" by dragging a prisoner up the stone stairs.

But the design also received negative criticism. Montgomery Schuyler, writing in the *Architectural Record* in 1911, called it "hilarious," with "a fort at the bottom and a lodging house at the top. Why all this pother of warlike parade?" Schuyler asked, adding that the designer should be condemned "to the deepest donjon beneath the station house moat."

Commissioner Bingham was known for an abrupt manner that offended many, and he was relieved of duty in 1909. The *Times* praised his inflexible courage but noted that he was "a bluff soldier, unaware that discretion is sometimes the better part of valor." Bingham later served as a city engineer and returned to the army in World War I.

Newcomers to 30th Street still stop and stare at this peculiar castle, a fitting compliment to its designer.

THE OFFICES OF THE ASTOR ESTATE

21–23 WEST 26TH STREET

JOHN JACOB ASTOR, WHO ARRIVED IN THE UNITED STATES from London in 1784, amassed a fortune of $20 million, most of it in real estate, by his death in 1848. His son, William Backhouse Astor, retained his father's Doric-style, temple-fronted office at 81 Prince Street.

By the time William died in 1875, the fortune exceeded $100 million, and it went to his two sons, John Jacob Astor III and William Astor. In 1881, they demolished the Prince Street office for the present office at 575 Broadway, and the two brothers built a pair of matching buildings at 21 and 23 West 26th Street.

Thomas Stent, the family's regular architect at the time, designed two-story buildings as close as New York ever got to the work of the great Philadelphia architect Frank Furness. Above the ground floor—barred like a treasure house—rises a facade of brick, granite, and terra-cotta.

In approved Victorian fashion, materials, colors, and finishes fight and strain against each other: polished gray granite, raw orange terra-cotta, and curved red brick. Above this the cornice is corbeled out on brickwork, but the attic pediment slopes back in ribbons of granite. Heavy lintels, like droopy eyebrows, weigh down the second-floor windows and ostensibly protect a richly carved terra-cotta panel—which needs no protection at all.

Some carved ornament seems to imitate Chinese sculpture, but most is patterned after the naturalistic designs of William Morris. The whole building has the blocky, brusque quality of Frank Furness's 1879 masterpiece, the Provident Life and Trust Company in Philadelphia.

FIG 45.1

NO. 21 (RIGHT) AND 23 WEST 26TH STREET IN 1940. COURTESY THE MUNICIPAL ARCHIVES

John Jacob Astor III occupied No. 21 and William occupied No. 23; from these buildings issued the most sustained record of private architectural patronage ever seen in New York.

From 21 West 26th Street, the John Jacob Astor III line built the old Waldorf, Netherland, and Astor Hotels (all now demolished) and the Graham Court and Apthorp apartments. From 23 West 26th, the William Astor line built the St. Regis and Knickerbocker Hotels, and, under Vincent Astor, the Astor Court apartments at 90th Street and Broadway, the old Astor Market at 95th Street and Broadway, and 120 East End Avenue.

Along with these came scores of other works—a 1905 account in *McClure's* magazine estimated the estate's income at $10 million a year.

In 1922, Vincent Astor hired Peabody, Wilson & Brown to redo the facade of No. 23 in a chaste, neo-Federal style, but No. 21 has remained untouched. Both were sold by the Astors after 1940, by which time their real estate interests were winding down. Today the buildings are surrounded by tall loft buildings, which makes them a particularly piquant surprise on the art gallery of the New York streets.

METROPOLITAN LIFE TOWER

1 MADISON AVENUE

IN 1905 METROPOLITAN LIFE BOUGHT THE SOUTHEAST CORNER of 24th Street and Madison Avenue and announced plans for a 560-foot tower, designed by the LeBrun firm. One of the architects, probably Pierre LeBrun, told the *New York Tribune* that it would probably be the tallest in the world. But, he added, the record was "not the object"; the height was purely for "architectural effect."

Perhaps that was the case, but Metropolitan Life was also attempting to catch up to older and more established companies like Home Life and New York Life—and owning the tallest building couldn't hurt.

By 1907, as the Metropolitan tower was under construction, a new building for the Singer Sewing Machine Company was nearing completion at 149 Broadway; it would rise to 612 feet. In that year Metropolitan Life revised its plans to produce a 700-foot tower—the tallest in the world.

The completed tower, based on St. Mark's Campanile in Venice, was all white Tuckahoe marble, with a giant four-faced clock and a beacon at the top. From the summit the company calculated that one-sixteenth of all of the nation's homes could be seen. And the white shaft and beacon were clearly visible miles away.

THE 700-FOOT METROPOLITAN LIFE TOWER *near its completion in 1908.*
COURTESY OFFICE FOR METROPOLITAN HISTORY

A critic writing in the magazine *Architecture* in 1908 said the decoration was fussy but thought that the diamond pattern on the pyramidal roof was "extremely excellent."

No scholar has yet analyzed the costs, but purely as commercial real estate, the tower must have been ridiculous; plans show that its typical floors lost more than 25 percent of their space to common elements such as bathrooms and elevators.

Indeed, for much of its life the highest areas in the tower have been used for storage. But as an advertisement the tower succeeded, even after it was topped by the 792-foot Woolworth Building in 1913.

In the early '50s Metropolitan Life began a renovation campaign for its headquarters. All of the buildings except the tower were demolished and replaced with a single new, mildly Art Moderne limestone structure. This new structure was much more efficient: it housed half again as many employees, with better lighting, elevators, and mechanical services. For the tower, the company mounted a massive renovation campaign from 1960 to 1964 that dealt not with function, but with aesthetics. The outside of the tower was stripped of its marble quoining, arcades, brackets, balconies, and other decorative details.

On the tower itself, only the decorative rim of the clock remained; the pyramidal roof and cupola were rebuilt in a simplified imitation of the original. At a distance, the tower does not appear dramatically changed, but close-up it looks like any plain 1960s office building.

According to a 1962 article in the *New York Times* the company contended that the "ornamental details make the structure look much smaller than its actual height." Other publications indicated a desire to have the tower "match" the modern building on 23rd Street.

This occurred when the preservation movement in New York was just forming, and Henry Hope Reed, the classicist and architectural historian, remembers the work as "a disaster—but the stupidity current at the time."

APPELLATE DIVISION

25TH STREET AND MADISON AVENUE

THE COURTHOUSE OF THE APPELLATE DIVISION, First Department, of the New York State Supreme Court, was in rented quarters on Fifth Avenue and 19th Street in 1896 when plans were filed for a new building facing Madison Square. Responding to the City Beautiful movement, legislators required that a large percentage of the construction budget be devoted to decoration. In the end, about 25 percent of the $700,000 cost was spent on sculpture alone. *American Architect and Building News* predicted that "the rest of the country will envy New York the possession of this building."

The architect James Brown Lord selected the cream of the American art establishment, including Henry Siddons Mowbray and Kenyon Cox, for the interior decorative work, and Daniel Chester French and Karl Bitter for the sculptural work on the exterior.

FIG 47.1

THE COURTHOUSE IN 1900. COURTESY OFFICE FOR METROPOLITAN HISTORY

On the inside, the result is an elaborate entrance hall and dome-topped courtroom covered with paneling, stained glass, gilding, and painted friezes, one of the most sumptuous interiors in New York.

On the exterior, the sculpture program was generous enough for a building five or ten times the size. On the 25th Street front a giant pedimental group, *Triumph of Law* by Charles H. Niehaus, rests on a screen of six Corinthian columns, rising from several groups of allegorical sculpture. On the Madison Avenue front, at the third-floor level, a screen of female caryatids by Thomas Shields Clarke represents the seasons—*Summer,* for instance, holds a sickle and a sheaf of wheat.

Ten other sculptors designed a ring of ten other larger-than-life-size figures at the roof level on the north and south ends of the Madison Avenue front, representing famous lawgivers like Confucius and Moses.

In 1900 the *New York Tribune* reported that there had been behind-the-scenes maneuvering by Tammany Hall insiders to include the living as well as the dead. But the newspaper said that artists opposed modern figures because they would result "in a number of pants statues, which at a distance would have looked alike." The *Tribune* also ridiculed the idea of a gallery of portly Tammany bosses.

In 1952 Frederick Zurmuhlen, the city's Public Works commissioner, said that he was afraid the statues were so deteriorated they might fall, and that they had been offered to every museum in the city—with no takers. He said the cost to restore them was prohibitive—even in a $1 million-plus construction budget—and, he told the *New York Times*, "they have to go."

But after protests, he announced that the statuary would be repaired—at a cost of $8,500. At the same time, the statue of Mohammed originally at the western end of the 25th Street side was removed at the request of the governments of Indonesia, Egypt, and Pakistan—Islam prohibits such human portraiture. The other statues on 25th Street were each moved one spot to the west, leaving an empty position at the easterly end.

TIFFANY BUILDING

25TH STREET AND PARK AVENUE SOUTH

CHARLES LEWIS TIFFANY ESTABLISHED HIS SILVER AND JEWELRY FIRM in 1837. A quarter-century later he had become so successful that his son, Louis Comfort Tiffany, did not need to work for a living—he studied painting in Europe in the 1860s and became convinced that he could reach people more effectively as a decorative artist.

In 1881 he moved his growing decorating company to a pair of buildings at the southeast corner of 25th Street and Park Avenue South—then Fourth Avenue—taking over an unusual High Victorian Gothic studio building designed in 1875 by J. C. Markham.

It was from this complex that Tiffany designed the lavish interiors of the Havemeyer house, once at 66th Street and Fifth Avenue; the stained glass of St. Michael's Church, at 99th Street and Amsterdam Avenue; and parts of the lobby of the Osborne apartment building, at 57th Street and Seventh Avenue. And yet, few people know of the unusual structure.

An 1896 building inspection described the building in the middle of the avenue as a store on the first floor, offices on the second, a workshop and drafting room on the third, "leading glazing workshop" on the fourth, and metal workshop on the fifth.

An account in the *New York Times* of 1894 described a public exhibition of an entire chapel: gold-embroidered vestments for priests, monumental glass windows, interior fountains, enormous lanterns for cathedrals.

In 1897 Cecelia Waern, writing in *International Studio* magazine, reported forty to fifty young women artisans at work in the building and described the mild disarray of the artist's inner sanctum on the fifth floor: "Here choice pieces of blown glass lie around, awaiting attention from Mr. Tiffany."

The writer said that the back stairs were littered with half-completed projects. On view was stained glass, mosaic tile, and other artworks destined for the Chicago Public Library, Princeton University, and unspecified projects in Columbia, Mississippi, and Kansas City, Missouri.

THE TIFFANY COMPLEX *at 25th Street and Park Avenue South, 1895.* COURTESY OFFICE FOR METROPOLITAN HISTORY

Tiffany moved his company to 44th Street and Madison Avenue in 1905 while his business was beginning to peak; by the 1920s his rich colors and dense designs were definitely out of fashion. In 1932 Tiffany Studios went bankrupt, and Tiffany died the next year.

A tour through the inside of the structure, now a cooperative, is a journey of discovery through a maze of interlocking halls and stairways.

The corner building, built in 1875, has a giant central stair and atrium, with the characteristic chunky Victorian Gothic detailing—dating from before Tiffany's occupancy, but an important survivor nonetheless, exceptional for its size, age, and integrity.

Another stairway, circular, winds around a curious 14-inch-wide baluster, strikingly plain, which because of its age and styling must be from the Tiffany occupancy. A third set of stairs on the 25th Street side—in the 1891 building that Tiffany built—is severe enough to be consonant with an industrial building, but so elegant as to have been clearly designed with care.

There are scraps of paneling, fireplaces, and other details throughout the building—like an entire window of leaded glass, battered and patched with tape, facing the rear courtyard.

Louis Comfort Tiffany built a strong artistic reputation, and perhaps his studio building is the last of his works to remain undiscovered.

THE EMMET BUILDING
95 MADISON AVENUE

DR. THOMAS ADDIS EMMET, A NEW YORK GYNECOLOGIST in the 1860s, was also a collector of books and manuscripts and an impassioned critic of English rule in Ireland. His grand uncle, Robert Emmet, had been executed in Dublin in 1803 for starting an uprising.

Dr. Emmet occupied a succession of houses and offices on the east side of Madison Avenue just south of 29th Street and gradually acquired the row of houses at 89, 91, 93, and 95, at the corner. Later, business invaded what had been a residential area, especially after the Metropolitan Life tower went up at 24th Street in 1909.

In 1912, at the age of eighty-four, Dr. Emmet moved out of 89 Madison Avenue, erected a sixteen-story loft building on the site of the four houses he demolished, and returned to occupy an apartment on the top floor of the new building. Designed by Barney & Colt, the Emmet Building has continuous vertical tiers of terra-cotta, superficially neo-Gothic, like the Woolworth Building, but actually early French Renaissance in style.

Spiky dormer windows project above what was originally a red tile roof, and the surface is marked by extensive terra-cotta sculpture of grotesque, medieval figures and

FIG 49.1

THOMAS ADDIS EMMET, M.D.
GYNÆCOLOGIST. PRIV. HOSP. FOR WOMEN. BIBLIOPHILE
PRESIDENT IRISH NATIONAL FEDERATION OF AMERICA

DR. THOMAS ADDIS EMMET. COURTESY OFFICE FOR METROPOLITAN HISTORY

THE EMMET BUILDING, *at right, 95 Madison Avenue in 1912.* COURTESY LIBRARY OF CONGRESS

EMMET BUILDING C-9132
Madison Av. & 29th St.
Copyright 1913 By
IRVING UNDERHILL, N.Y.

other elements. A writer in the magazine *Brickbuilder* praised the building's "exquisite propriety," obviously commercial but also with "the distinction which everyone wants in his own private house."

Dr. Emmet's apartment had a solarium, pergola, and roof garden fountain toward the rear. It was common for superintendents to occupy an apartment on the top floor of office buildings, so Emmet's occupancy was rare—there was tremendous concern in this period about the convention of living in residential sections untainted by commerce.

The 1915 census lists Dr. Emmet, eighty-seven, a widower; his son Thomas, fifty-one; Margaret O'Reily, nurse; and Koricki Myamiata, cook.

An aficionado of American political history, a manuscript connoisseur, an Irish patriot, Dr. Emmet had multiple interests that could have served as the basis for an unusual scheme of ornament.

Early sketches for the building show shields with three bulls' heads, an adaptation of the Emmet family crest, but these were not executed. Although there are some bulls' heads at the top floor, most of the decoration is apparently simply generic work.

In 1919, Dr. Emmet died in his apartment, and his body was taken to Dublin for burial in the family plot. In 1920, the top-floor apartment was converted to commercial occupancy.

THE GORHAM BUILDING

36TH STREET AND FIFTH AVENUE

THE GORHAM COMPANY WAS FOUNDED IN 1831 in Providence, Rhode Island, and by the end of the 1850s it was a leading American silver concern. In the 1870s Edward Holbrook joined the company as its New York agent, and in 1884 it built the unusual Queen Anne–style building that still stands at the northwest corner of 19th Street and Broadway, with showrooms below and bachelor apartments above.

In 1894 Holbrook became Gorham's president. He tried to keep up with the more prominent Tiffany & Company by buying up other silver concerns. Charles H. Carpenter Jr., author of *Gorham Silver* called Holbrook the John D. Rockefeller of the silver industry.

In 1903 both Gorham and Tiffany—which had been on Union Square—began work on new buildings on Fifth Avenue, Tiffany at the southeast corner of 37th Street, and Gorham at the southwest corner of 36th. In September 1905 the two companies opened their new buildings within days of each other. Both were designed by Stanford White, but in very different modes. Tiffany's (which still stands) was rich

INTERIOR OF THE GORHAM BUILDING IN 1905. COURTESY OFFICE FOR METROPOLITAN HISTORY

and heavily modeled, patterned after the sixteenth-century Palazzo Grimani in Venice. The new Gorham Building was more restrained but just as elegant, following general sources of the Florentine Renaissance. "Compared to the Gorham Building, the Tiffany Building is by way of being frivolous," *Architectural Record* said in 1907.

Gorham's eight-story facade is of white limestone and granite, originally heavily trimmed with Gorham-made bronze at the ground and upper floors. *The New York Tribune* said the bronze was one-tenth the cost of the $1.25 million building. Its deep copper cornice apparently had painted details, with additional gold leafing, but what made people stop and stare were the relief sculptures of allegorical silver-making scenes by the sculptor Andrew O'Connor, above the arches on both faces of the structure. The

EXTERIOR OF THE GORHAM BUILDING IN 1955, *before Herbert Tannenbaum's changes of 1960.* COURTESY OFFICE FOR METROPOLITAN HISTORY

main selling floor was a high vaulted space dominated by massive banded columns of granite flecked with gold.

During Holbrook's presidency, Gorham continued to prosper. Evelyn Nesbit Thaw, whose husband, Harry, shot and killed Stanford White, Nesbit's former lover, in 1906 in a jealous rage, purchased more than $2,000 in silver on credit in the same year and gave it away as presents. When Gorham sued her for payment in 1913, she said she had less than $250 to her name.

Gorham moved out of its building in the early 1920s, to 576 Fifth Avenue, and was succeeded by Russek's, a women's clothing store. Russek's made few changes, but in 1960 a new owner, Spear Securities, converted the structure to showroom space and wanted a new look at the street floor. Its architect, Herbert Tannenbaum, tried to persuade the owner to retain the original design. But, Mr. Tannenbaum said, "They told me, 'Do it or we'll get someone else.' " He developed a crisp modern grid of glass and metal, but he said that he had felt terrible, that he hated to see the original details stripped off. "Those arches were lovely," he recalled sadly.

MORGAN LIBRARY BOOKSTORE

37TH STREET AND MADISON AVENUE

WHAT MOST PASSERS-BY KNOW AS THE MORGAN LIBRARY'S BOOKSTORE at 37th Street and Madison was built in 1853. At that time, three related households built three large brownstone houses on the east side of Madison Avenue from 36th to 37th Streets: at the southeast corner of 37th, Isaac N. Phelps.

Isaac Phelps, a distant relative to Anson Stokes, spent his life as a hardware merchant, real estate investor, and banker and amassed an estate estimated at $5 million. He retired in the 1850s to his 37th Street house; in 1888, Isaac Phelps died and left the big brownstone to his daughter, Helen L. Phelps Stokes, wife of Anson Stokes. One of their children was Isaac Newton Phelps Stokes, author of the six-volume *Iconography of Manhattan Island*.

In the same year, Mrs. Stokes retained the architect R. H. Robertson to add a fourth floor. Perhaps it was then that the Stokeses also installed the fantastical ironwork at the ground-floor window balconies, a wild basketwork of leaves and vines. According to Bonnie Yochelson, editor of *Berenice Abbott: Changing New York*, notes made for Berenice Abbott's photographic survey in the 1930s indicate that the metalwork was the design of Oscar Luetke, who was active in bronze and ironwork in the late nineteenth century.

In 1892 there was some unpleasantness in the Stokes household: a maid, Mabel Youngson, fled to England after stealing $2,000 worth of rugs, china, medallions, and other items like a violet silk petticoat. She had smuggled them out of the house over several months, with the help of her lover, Arthur Morley, a servant at 214 Madison Avenue. The police recovered much of the loot, but it appears that Miss Youngson successfully evaded capture.

The banker J. Pierpont Morgan had moved into the house at the 36th Street corner in 1882, and in 1904 he bought the old Stokes house on the 37th Street corner, as a resi-

FIG 51.1

DETAIL OF THE MORGAN BROWNSTONE *stoop and ironwork in 1900.* COURTESY OFFICE FOR METROPOLITAN HISTORY

FIG 51.2

THE MORGAN BROWNSTONE ABOUT 1905, *showing the other houses in the original group.* COURTESY THE MORGAN LIBRARY dence for his son, J. P. Morgan Jr. In 1905 Morgan Jr. retained the firm of Joseph Duveen, better known as art dealers, to redecorate the interior of his new house. The rooms of the 1905 alteration are striking and opulent, with rich woodwork, painting, mantelpieces, and other elements, especially on the main floor.

In January 1912, a burglar got into the house while Morgan was sleeping and stole cash and valuables. The police were baffled, and the case was not solved until September, when officers stopped John Bernauer in the Bronx near a pawn shop—he was carrying a matchbox with the initials "J. P. M. Jr." and had other items at his house. He argued that he was not responsible because he had been hypnotized by someone he met in Battery Park. However he wound up pleading guilty.

The next year J. Pierpont Morgan died with an estate of $68 million, and J. P. Morgan Jr. soon oversaw the dedication of his art collection as a public museum—which also meant the demolition of the father's house, in 1928. The 1915 census lists Morgan Jr., his family of five, and eighteen servants, including three footmen and four laundresses.

THE OLD TIFFANY BUILDING

409 FIFTH AVENUE

CHARLES LOUIS TIFFANY FOUNDED TIFFANY & COMPANY, specializing in stationery and notions, in 1837 at 259 Broadway, at Warren Street. The company moved up Broadway, settling in 1868 at the southwest corner of 15th Street on what had become New York's prime shopping boulevard. But above 23rd Street, elite stores began to favor Fifth Avenue over Broadway, and in 1906 Tiffany moved again, to 37th and Fifth.

The building was designed by the firm of McKim, Mead & White, which modeled it after the sixteenth-century Palazzo Grimani in Venice. According to Leland M. Roth, an expert on the firm's work, Stanford White was the actual designer. He masked seven floors behind three great horizontal divisions, framed by Corinthian columns and piers and topped by a marble cornice.

The main selling floor was surely the most magnificent retail space in New York City—a high, exquisite coffered ceiling, a richly carved marble stair, purplish-gray marble columns, teak floors, silver chandeliers, and open-cage elevators called by *Architects and Builders* magazine "the finest piece of artistic steelwork in this country."

Other floors held the bronze, safe deposit, silver, pottery, glass, clock, leather, and other departments. Some production of gold and jewelry pieces also took place here. The seventh floor was a large, open exhibit hall, with a great elliptical skylight, 20 feet wide by 60 feet long. Although difficult to see from the street, this floor has a great sloping roof of red terra-cotta tile.

THE TIFFANY BUILDING *at 37th Street and Fifth Avenue in 1905.* COURTESY OFFICE FOR METROPOLITAN HISTORY

Tiffany's prospered at the location, adding an adjacent building at 389 Fifth Avenue, also designed by McKim, Mead & White, in 1910. Gradually, other companies passed Tiffany's Murray Hill location, among them Cartier, which moved to its present site at 52nd Street and Fifth in 1917. Saks, Bonwits, Bergdorf's, DePinna, and others followed, and Tiffany's moved to its present location, the southeast corner of 57th Street, in 1940.

The old building remained more or less intact in the 1940s. For a while it was used as a Red Cross training center. But in 1951, the building's character began to change when Charles and Selig Whinston filed plans for Henry Goelet, the owner, to create two floors out of the original main floor and insert shops along Fifth Avenue and offices above.

The main entrance was moved to the side street and given an over-door marble panel engraved with the address in gilt letters. It was elegant for its period, but a jarring change for those who knew the old store.

At the time of the proposed change, Lewis Mumford wrote in his "Skyline" column in the *New Yorker*: "There should be a Society for the Prevention of Cruelty to Buildings."

FLINT TOWN HOUSE

109 EAST 39TH STREET

IN 1886, THIRTY-SIX-YEAR-OLD HELENA FLINT OF LARCHMONT, New York, had an architect, Henry F. Kilburn, file plans for a 25-foot-wide, five-story, $30,000 house at 109 East 39th Street east of Park Avenue.

In later court records, Miss Flint said she had advertised in 1885 for a tutor for some young cousins, and hired Eleanor Ruthrauff for the position. Miss Ruthrauff, a much younger woman, moved in with Miss Flint in 1885, and soon they became "very warm friends," according to an account in the *New York Times* on August 7, 1897.

In 1887, Miss Flint and Miss Ruthrauff moved into 109 East 39th Street just after its completion. A Queen Anne house in New York City is a rarity, this one all the more so because a single woman built it.

FIG 53.1

RENDERING OF THE TOWN HOUSE *at 109 East 39th Street built for Helena Flint in 1887.* COURTESY THE NEW-YORK HISTORICAL SOCIETY, NEW YORK CITY

In the mid-1890s, Miss Flint sued her companion to recover $25,000 in bonds. Miss Flint—who made six wills between 1885 and 1891 favoring Miss Ruthrauff—contended that she had given Miss Ruthrauff the bonds to use their income while Miss Flint was abroad on a trip. But Miss Ruthrauff contended that Miss Flint had wanted to make her secure for life and that the bonds were an outright gift. Miss Flint testified at the trial that "we went everywhere together" and that "I was cut off from my former friends and relatives . . . who disliked Miss Ruthrauff." She also said "my property is in real estate—I manage it," apparently referring to land in Larchmont.

The verdict gave Miss Ruthrauff income on $10,000 of the bonds for life. Miss Flint moved back to

Larchmont and sold the town house to Don H. Bacon, an iron company executive in 1902. In 1921, it was purchased by Princess Vilma Lwoff-Parlaghy, a Hungarian painter with a stormy career.

In Europe, Princess Lwoff-Parlaghy had done portraits of heads of state and other prominent people—including the Kaiser Wilhelm II and Otto von Bismarck. She arrived in the United States in 1907 with a large retinue of servants and a private menagerie including an ibis, an alligator, a bear, and two falcons. She went on to do portraits of Thomas A. Edison, Admiral George Dewey, Andrew Carnegie, and others. She was ultimately evicted from the Plaza Hotel after a $12,000 dispute, and a diamond merchant lent her $218,000 to buy the Flint house.

FIG 53.2

109 EAST 39TH STREEET, AT EXTREME LEFT, IN 1941. COURTESY OFFICE FOR METROPOLITAN HISTORY

On August 27, 1923, a deputy sheriff stood watch outside her front door to take possession of the house because she had not repaid the loan. The *Times* noted at the time "her house resembles an art museum" with works by Van Dyck, Rembrandt, and Rubens, and the sheriff was put off only by pleas from the princess's doctor, who said she was near death. She died at 3 A.M. on August 29—with the deputy sheriff in the hall outside her room.

That was the last gasp for private-house occupancy. In 1926, Emily Hepburn bought the house and renovated it for apartments, removing the stoop. Mrs. Hepburn, who had been influential in the restoration of the Theodore Roosevelt birthplace at 28 East 20th Street, was active in renovating properties in midtown. Three years later she built the Beekman Tower Hotel, an Art Deco structure at the northeast corner of 49th Street and First Avenue.

THE NOTCH IN MACY'S

34TH STREET AND BROADWAY

WHO PUT THE STRANGE LITTLE NOTCH in the "World's Largest Department Store"? Chances are no one asks that question as the store's annual Thanksgiving Day Parade makes its final turn, past the northwest corner of 34th and Broadway. Most people will look no farther than the big Macy's sign on the corner, which stands 70 feet high.

But Macy's has never owned the little corner building underneath its sign. The building survives as a dramatic symbol of the holdout phenomenon in New York City development history.

In the late 1890s Macy's decided to leapfrog the department-store area between 14th and 23rd Streets and build at 34th and Broadway. Secretly, it began to acquire the entire west side of Broadway from 34th to 35th Street, and it had an oral agreement to pay $250,000 to Alfred Duane Pell for the 34th Street corner.

But Macy's plans became known in April of 1901, before the store and Pell went to contract. According to the book *Holdouts!* by Andrew Alpern and Seymour Durst, an agent of Henry Siegel, a Siegel-Cooper partner, offered Pell $375,000 for the 1,154-square-foot plot. Pell accepted.

Siegel could have been interested in the site to embarrass his competitor, perhaps with a big sign on the corner urging people to shop at his store. But he did not do this, and there are two recorded explanations of the motive behind the purchase.

One is that Siegel's agent, Robert Smith, who already had a dry-goods store near Macy's, wanted a site for a new store. Indeed, Smith announced that he would put up a twelve-story building on the corner site to sell women's clothing. However, this was probably just posturing, because the small size of the irregular plot—it is 31 by 46 by 16 by 51 feet—made such a building unlikely.

FIG 54.2

THE HOLDOUT BUILDING IN 1945. COURTESY OFFICE FOR METROPOLITAN HISTORY

The competing, and more credible, account is that Siegel himself wanted to establish a new store on the old Macy's site at 14th and Sixth, to capture its customers. To do this, he offered Macy's the little corner plot in return for its willingness to give up its lease on the 14th Street store, which ran to 1903. But Macy's didn't bite and in July announced its plans for a huge new store, nine stories high with about 1.6 million square feet—and a little notch in the corner.

Macy's architects, DeLemos & Cordes, built around the holdout, creating a ground-floor arcade directly behind it and providing a shortcut connecting Broadway and 34th Street. The store opened in 1902. The next year Siegel demolished the corner building and built a new five-story structure designed by William H. Hume, which was leased to the United Cigar Store Company for $40,000 a year. It is this structure that remains under the big Macy's signs.

Macy's paid to keep its old store vacant until the expiration of its lease, when Siegel took over the property and built the ten-story high "14th Street Store." Robert Smith bought Siegel's interest in the 34th Street corner in 1907 and in 1911 sold the structure for $1 million. This was generally reported as a record price for Manhattan property—$866.55 a square foot. Even then Macy's was rumored as a potential buyer, but it has never acquired it.

FIG 54.1

MACY'S WRAPPED AROUND THE HOLDOUT BUILDING *at 34th Street and Broadway in 1909.* COLLECTION ANDREW ALPERN

WHAT DID YOU DO
FOR YOUR COUNTRY
TODAY
?
Imagine!
Ready-to-Serve Cocktails
Right out of your
Refrigerator
Add No Ice
Just Serve
Pete Hagen's
COCKTAILS
MANHATTAN
DRY MARTINI
SIDE CAR
DAIQUIRI
OLD FASHIONED
Only
1.79
Pete Hagen's
MANHATTAN
Cocktails
AT YOUR NEIGHBORHOOD LIQUOR STORE
BUY
U.S. WAR
BONDS
& STAMPS
Product of POPPER-MORSON CO.
Quality Liquors Since 1889
ROCKEFELLER CENTER
Canadian Club
General Outdoor Adv Co
R. H. MAC
Tastee
FRESH FRUIT
DRINKS
all beef
FRANKFURTERS
NUTS
GREELEY SQ

THE AMERICAN RADIATOR BUILDING

40 WEST 40TH STREET

RAYMOND HOOD, WHO DESIGNED THE STRIKING BLACK-AND-GOLD, American Radiator Building at 40 West 40th Street, rocketed to prominence in 1922 when he won the international competition for the new Chicago Tribune office tower. The young architect had been scraping by on small things, like radiator covers for the American Radiator Company. But after the competition, he got many offers, including one from American Radiator for an office building facing Bryant Park on a block that until then was characterized by brownstones and turn-of-the-century clubs.

Hood embraced both the aesthetic and business sides of architecture and was proud that the Radiator building's steelwork was completed only seven months after the design. The building opened in 1924 and embodied several departures from existing practice.

Although freestanding towers have restricted floor areas because they are not built to the lot line, they can be treated architecturally all the way around and provide good natural light.

Hood also disliked the typical office building facade, where the regular dark glass reflections of the windows contrasted with the light masonry skin, making most buildings look like a "waffle stood on end," as he put it.

So he called for the American Radiator Building to be built of black brick (a product that proved very difficult to obtain) and topped it with gold-colored masonry units, which supposedly recalled the black iron and glowing embers of furnaces of the day.

Special floodlighting made the building "one of the sights of the city" at night, said the magazine *American Architect,* adding that "it has attracted and held the attention of thousands who ordinarily give little heed to street architecture."

In the basement, with its cryptlike low arched ceilings, were boiler and furnace showrooms. Upstairs were offices, including one for Hood, who went on to design the Daily News,

FIG 55.1

RAYMOND HOOD, *designer of the American Radiator Building.* COURTESY OFFICE FOR METROPOLITAN HISTORY

DETAIL OF THE UPPER STORIES OF THE AMERICAN RADIATOR BUILDING IN 1924. COURTESY OFFICE FOR METROPOLITAN HISTORY

McGraw-Hill, and Rockefeller Center buildings, all landmarks of Art Deco modernism.

At the American Radiator Building, the fact that 90 percent of the space was within 25 feet of a window cut both ways. While it provided excellent light, it also meant that elevators ate up much of the interior space, something that Hood sought to mitigate with automatic leveling and push-button car gates to increase their operating efficiency.

In the tower, the far side of the building is never far away, and gives the sense of a flood of light. From it there are close views of other mid-block towers of the same period, and the idea of a city of medium-sized, independent office spires seems very reasonable, even if a bit quaint.

But the efficiency of building to fill the zoning envelope offered a greater logic, and the freestanding tower later appeared only on a huge scale, like the Empire State and Chrysler Buildings.

Hood combined a practical bent with a free spirit and was not loath to admit a style of life that included an appreciation of liquor at a time of Prohibition. He also testified as a witness for the defense in the 1927 obscenity case of the play *Sex,* which was written by and starred Mae West (who was fined $500 and sentenced to ten days in jail).

BRYANT PARK STUDIO
BUILDING.
APARTMENTS
AND STUDIOS
FOR RENT
ASHFORTH & DURYEE
4 WEST 33 ST.
BRYANT PARK STUDIO
BUILDING
APARTMENTS
AND STUDIOS
FOR RENT

BRYANT PARK STUDIOS

80 WEST 40TH STREET

THE MOVEMENT FOR COMMON ARTISTS' STUDIOS is usually considered to date to 1856, when the Tenth Street studios went up at 51 West 10th Street. But buildings put up for studios stayed low until 1879, when the seven-story Sherwood Studios went up at the southeast corner of 57th Street and Sixth Avenue. It was the first tall building for such a tenancy.

The Reverend Jared Flagg built his Rembrandt, a cooperative apartment/studio building at 154 West 57th Street, in 1881, but tall buildings with double-height studios did not reappear until the turn of the century. The well-known colony of such buildings on West 67th Street began in 1901, over a year after Abraham A. Anderson began his Bryant Park Studios, which remains the oldest high-rise artists' studio structure to survive in New York.

Anderson had studied art in Paris after the Civil War and founded the American Art Association there to help struggling Americans. His wife, the former Elizabeth Milbank, was the daughter of Jeremiah Milbank, a banker and a founder of the Borden Milk Company.

At Sixth Avenue and 40th Street Anderson found the ingredients that would become the formula for most later studio operations. The site was near the established elite area along Fifth Avenue. But it was devalued by an adjacent feature others considered a disadvantage, the Sixth Avenue Elevated. It also had a critical asset for turn-of-the-century artists—across Bryant Park flowed uninterrupted north light.

To take advantage of this, Anderson built a twelve-story building with twenty-four north-facing double-height studios, just right for painters of big portraits and giant landscapes. The Beaux-Arts-style building mixed elements of factory and hotel design; indeed the typical artist's studio was both a workshop and a place of residence.

The designer, Charles A. Rich, had worked on various Milbank charitable commissions, among them Barnard College's first building, Milbank Hall of 1896.

Anderson took the top floor as his own studio, and period accounts describe the quintessential Victorian artist's lair. It was littered with such exotica as Spanish tapestries, Louis XV paneling, a suit of armor, a rock crystal fireplace, a Venetian doorway, and a bathroom tiled with abalone shells.

Among the artists who took space were J.C. Leyendecker, Florine Stettheimer, Edward Steichen, and Jo Davidson.

BRYANT PARK STUDIOS *at Sixth Avenue and 40th Street in 1901.* COURTESY OFFICE FOR METROPOLITAN HISTORY

By the 1910s the structure was known as the Beaux-Arts Building, apparently after the cafe of the same name on the ground floor operated by the Bustanoby family.

In 1920, Anderson net-leased the building to a real estate operator but retained his own studio under a complicated leaseback agreement. In 1928, the seventy-eight-year-old artist fought eviction in court with the subsequent owner, a battle he ultimately won. He died in 1940 and, at least in the 1990s, his original studio—with the abalone shell bathroom—was intact.

GRAND CENTRAL TERMINAL TOWER

42ND STREET AT PARK AVENUE

THE CITY IS STILL CELEBRATING THE RESTORATION of Grand Central Terminal, but one large element of the original design is still missing—a twenty-three-story Beaux-Arts-style office tower directly above the concourse.

The idea for a tower in connection with the terminal originates at the turn of the century, when William J. Wilgus—chief engineer and soon to be vice president of the New York Central and Hudson River Railroad—conceived a plan for rebuilding the huge rail yard north of Grand Central to permit the construction of steel-framed buildings overhead. "Thus from the air would be taken wealth," he wrote in a memoir published in *Transactions,* the journal of the American Society of Civil Engineers, in 1940.

In 1903, several architects submitted proposals for a new terminal, and most of them used a monumental tower over the terminal itself as their centerpiece. The winning design, by Charles Reed & Allen Stem, proposed a single twenty-four-story Renaissance-style building that would include the terminal. It looked something like the Plaza Hotel.

The architects Warren & Wetmore were brought in to work with Reed & Stem, and it appears that Warren & Wetmore's influence shifted the terminal's design to its final Beaux-Arts state.

When the nearly complete plans were published in early 1910, the terminal looked much like what was eventually built, with three significant differences. First, there was a giant curved skylight over the concourse. Second, Park Avenue from 45th to 48th Streets was projected as a grand court of honor, with matching colonnaded buildings housing the National Academy of Design and the Metropolitan Opera. The third difference was a twenty-three-story Beaux-Arts-style office tower above the concourse, set back about 100 feet from 42nd Street.

This 219-by-294-foot tower was shaped like a rectangular doughnut, only 49 feet deep on each side, with elevator access from the existing lobbies at the four corners of the terminal; the concourse's east stairway, not constructed until the current restoration, was part of the plan for the office tower—but it was never built.

Wilgus's 1940 memoir said only that it "fell by the wayside" and might still be built. Perhaps the railroad was preoccupied with the continued stream of new hotels, apartment houses, and office buildings that went up in the 1910s and 1920s north of the terminal on Park Avenue.

After World War II the railroad began looking for ways to increase its income, and in 1954 the architects Fellheimer & Wagner announced a fifty-story tower that would completely replace Grand Central Terminal. It was slick and angular and included a 2,400-car garage.

Almost simultaneously, the developer William Zeckendorf said that the architect I. M. Pei had developed a competing eighty-story design with an observation tower so tall it would be higher than the Empire State Building. No plans for this tower were published, and Mr. Pei said that he had no recollection of the design.

Public protest followed, led by the magazine *Architectural Forum*, and in 1955 Emery Roth & Sons published a design for a tower that did not encroach on the station. The result, the Pan Am Building (now the MetLife Building) went up in 1962.

FIG 57.1

DRAWING OF GRAND CENTRAL TERMINAL, *in 1912, and the twenty-three-story tower that was to have soared above it.* COURTESY OFFICE FOR METROPOLITAN HISTORY

THE OLD NEW YORK CENTRAL BUILDING

230 PARK AVENUE

THE THIRTY-FOUR-STORY NEW YORK CENTRAL BUILDING, straddling Park between 45th and 46th Streets, was the last skyscraping gasp of Terminal City, the New York Central Railroad's air-rights development of about three dozen buildings—made possible when it covered over its giant rail yard stretching from 42nd to 50th Streets.

When Grand Central Terminal opened in 1913, published sketches promised a line of matching commercial and public buildings reaching north to make a formal court of honor. Although the stretch was actually developed piecemeal, Warren & Wetmore, the railroad's architects, did design the various office and apartment buildings in a harmonious Renaissance style. Finally only the Park Avenue blockfronts from 45th to 46th Street remained unimproved.

Since 1919 the railroad and the city had been dickering over traffic connections for Park Avenue around Grand Central itself—the rise of the automobile had made the terminal a bottleneck as north-south traffic struggled with local streets around the terminal. At first only the westerly roadway around Grand Central was in public use.

In 1924 the railroad and the city agreed on a complicated network of leases and easements, and in 1926 work began on the New York Central Building, which engulfed 200 feet of what had been a public street. In exchange, the railroad opened up the easterly roadway around Grand Central and threaded both east and west roads through its new building, creating a virtual express highway from 40th to 46th. At the same time the city widened the roadway from 46th to 57th Streets by shaving down the malls from 56 to 20 feet.

In return for the roadway, the railroad got to build a thirty-four-story tower, 560 feet high. Warren & Wetmore designed the lower section to correspond to the Grand Central facade, complete with ornamental clock and flanking sculpture, designed by Edward McCarten.

The middle section is handsome, but the top explodes like a Caribbean coral formation—a field of lacy round dormer windows on the roof, leading up to the delicate, arched lantern with its spire. The ornament on the building is spread out but otherwise every bit as sumptuous as that on Warren & Wetmore's 1899 New York Yacht Club on West 44th Street. The New York Central moved its offices to 230 Park in 1929.

Although 230 Park Avenue is almost universally admired today, observers of the 1920s saw it differently.

George S. Chappell, writing in the *New Yorker* in 1928, was ambivalent, admiring it as "a dramatic stop sign at the end of the thoroughfare, although we cannot help sighing

FIG 58.1

THE NEW YORK CENTRAL BUILDING IN 1928. COURTESY MUSEUM OF THE CITY OF NEW YORK for the bright open sky which we used to glimpse." In 1929 he noted complaints that the lavish lobby had every style "from Pullman to Paramount."

Harry F. Cunningham, writing in the *American Yearbook* in 1928, bemoaned Warren & Wetmore's unreconstructed traditionalism and called the New York Central Building "one of the greatest steps in the present backward tendency shown in *American Architecture*."

And Kenneth Murchison, in his column in the *Architect* magazine in 1928, presciently claimed that better roads would simply increase the number of cars: "Conditions will grow worse and worse, despite anything we can do." And it is Murchison's judgment that has most firmly stood the test of time.

HECKSCHER BUILDING

50 EAST 42ND STREET

IN 1915, THE DEVELOPER AUGUST HECKSCHER announced plans for a new kind of building. This was before the 1916 zoning resolution—which required a series of setbacks on tall buildings to allow light and air to reach the street. The only height restriction on office construction before 1916 was the economic limit of how high a building could go before elevators and other systems ate up the floor area.

Heckscher's new building, designed by Jardine, Hill & Murdock, was quite different—above a five-story base, the twenty-seven-story tower is set back from each side, 23 feet from the 42nd Street side. Heckscher told the *Real Estate Record and Guide* that "it will be a boon to New York if owners of high buildings will build in such a manner that each high building shall be wholly self-contained, light obtained from the outside on each facade."The twenty-third floor was built with a squash court for tenants, who could also use terraces along the top; and the peak of the tower was illuminated.

In 1915 the *New York Times* praised Mr. Heckscher for his early adoption of the ideas for setback towers, which were circulating informally, and would only be made law the next year. If built to the density of the conventional building across the street, the Heckscher Building could have had perhaps double the floor area. "The average structure put up on this site would no doubt have shot up flush with the building line," said the *Edison Monthly* in 1917.

But there is something peculiar about the praise he received for 50 East 42nd: at the same time he was building there, he was also putting up another commercial building at 244 Madison, at 38th Street. But the 244 Madison building was completely conventional in form, filling over 90 percent of the lot and rising straight from the building line—why would setback philanthropy work on 42nd Street, but not four blocks south?

An analysis of Heckscher's title to the property does yield some strong clues. The building at 50 East 42nd Street replaced five old row houses facing Madison Avenue, numbered 307–315 Madison. But Heckscher could only secure ownership of the central three, 309, 311, and 313—he had to lease the northernmost and the southernmost. The lease details of the southerly plot are not clear, but his 1914 lease for the 42nd Street corner required that any new building be erected so that the portion above 315 Madison Avenue—23 feet on Madison and 118 feet down 42nd Street—be built "such that it can be made self contained."

With such a condition, Heckscher would be required to make any tower rising above the joined sites have two sets of fire stairs, two sets of elevators, two sets of plumbing risers and bathrooms, and two lobbies. He also faced the possible loss of any tower above the leasehold site at the end of the lease term. Such costs rose far above philanthropy, and Heckscher and his architects chose to build only five-story sections over the leasehold sites, with the tower portion rising only above the portion for which he owned the land. Mae West might have surmised that philanthropy had nothing to do with it.

59.1 FIG

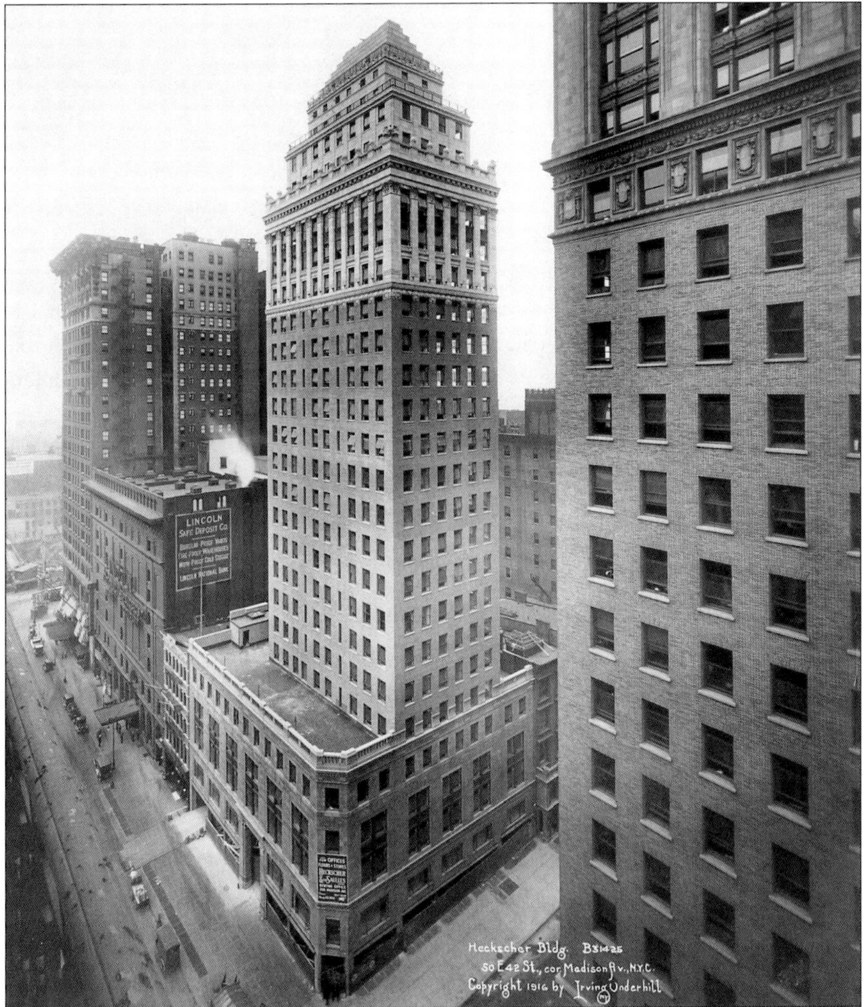

HECKSCHER BUILDING IN 1916. COURTESY LIBRARY OF CONGRESS

THE CHRYSLER BUILDING

405 LEXINGTON AVENUE

IN 1928, WHEN THE AUTOMOBILE MAGNATE Walter P. Chrysler took over an existing development project at the northeast corner of 42nd Street and Lexington Avenue, he got a design for a streamlined skyscraper with a stubby, nearly Moorish top of copper, glass, and terra-cotta. He kept the architect, William Van Alen, but called for a redesign with a more straightforward, pointed top.

Then Chrysler and Van Alen again revised the design, this time in order to win a height competition with the 921-foot tower then rising at 40 Wall Street. This was done in secret, using as a staging area the huge square fire-tower shaft, intended to vent smoke from the stairways. Inside the shaft, Van Alen had teams of workers assemble the framework for a 185-foot-high spire that, when lifted into place in the fall of 1929, made the Chrysler building, at 1,046 feet, 4.75 inches high, the tallest in the world.

The full story of the secret tower has yet to be told, but the new Chrysler Building attracted more popular comment than any other building since the Woolworth in 1913.

Architectural critics were generally offended by the last-minute tower, considering it a gimmicky stunt, trivial and unworthy of Architecture with a capital A. But Kenneth Murchison, an architect and critic, liked the frank, commercial quality of a building erected with advertising clearly in mind. In the September 1930 issue of *American Architect* he observed that Van Alen, who had, like Murchison, studied at the École des Beaux-Arts, was "the only student who returned from Paris without a box full of books."

Murchison also admired the steel crown and "the astonishing plays of light which nature alone can furnish." While other buildings had been put up with distinctive spires, they were all in traditional materials: copper, terra-cotta, iron, stone, brick. But on the Chrysler Building the entire upper section above the sixty-first floor—and much of the ornament below—is gleaming chrome-nickel steel, which reflects sunlight with dazzling brilliance.

The seventy-first-floor observation deck closed long ago, and it is now difficult to look at the metalwork close-up. But anyone who wangles his or her way into an office will find surprise in more than the brilliance of the cleaned metal.

From a distance the Chrysler Building seems like near kin to the Empire State Building, which took away its height record in 1931. But unlike the Empire State, which was proudly hailed by one of its architects as a building where "hand work was done away with," the Chrysler Building is like a giant craft project.

The metal is generally soldered or crimped—all by hand—and the thick, wavy solder lines and the irregular bends all betray individual craftsmanship. The broad surfaces of metal, almost all stamped to form on the site, are wavy and bumpy, like giant pieces of hand-finished silver jewelry.

Just as surprising is the section just below the spire. So solid looking from the outside, this part has no occupants and only intermittent flooring; only a few of the triangular openings have glazing.

Inside, the wind rushes through what seems like a high, thin gazebo-shell of steel, at striking variance with the otherwise modernistic solidity of this continually fascinating building.

FIG 60.1

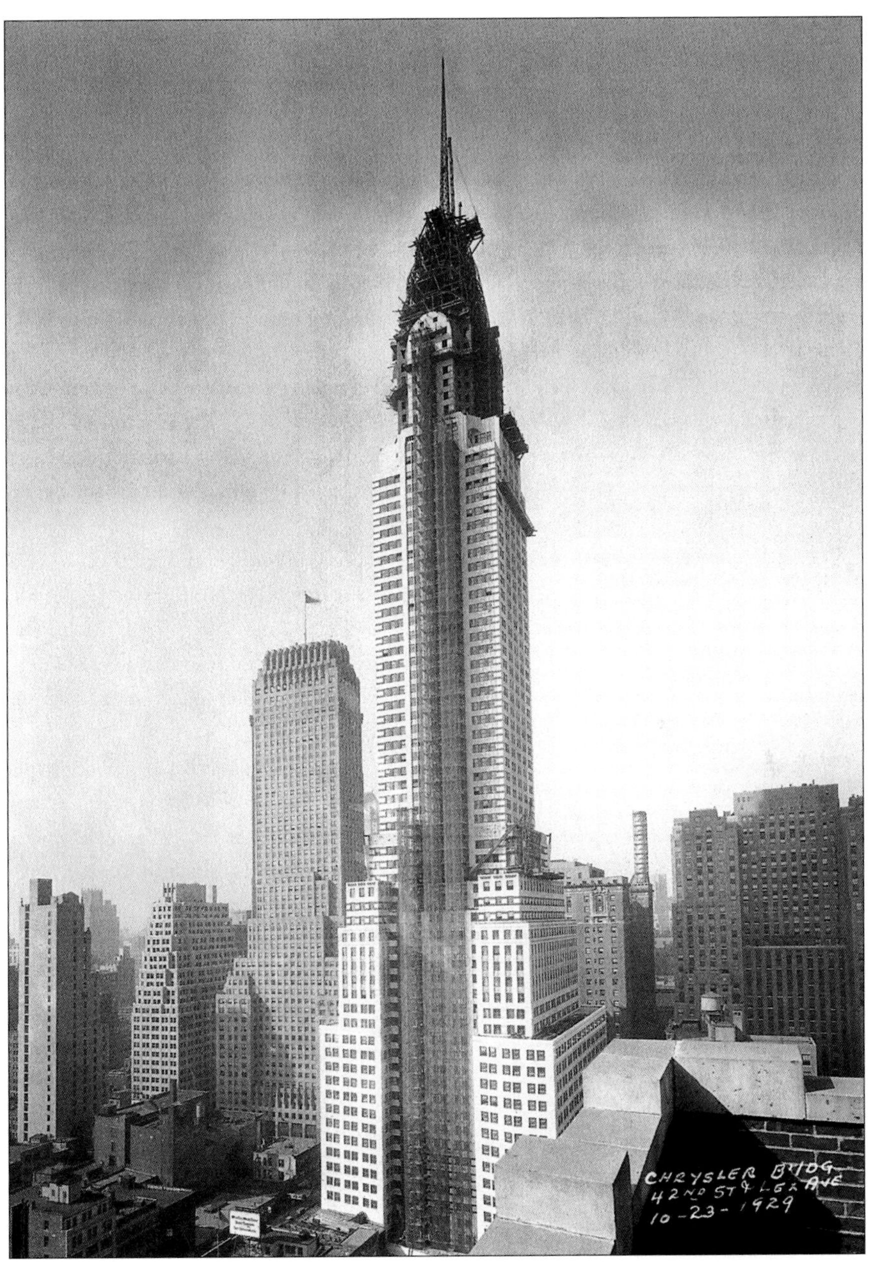

THE CHRYSLER BUILDING *with spire emerging on October 23, 1929.* COURTESY DAVID STRAVITZ

THE CLOUD CLUB

AT THE CHRYSLER BUILDING

ACCORDING TO LINDA ZAGARIA, an officer of the Art Deco Society of New York, the original Cloud Club prospectus said that "the view will be without parallel" and that during the hot summer months it will be "the coolest place in New York." The prospectus called for membership dues of $300 a year. Among the original directors were E. F. Hutton, the financier, and Condé Nast, whose publishing empire had recently moved to the nearby Graybar Building at 420 Lexington.

The rest of the Chrysler Building was uncompromisingly contemporary, from hubcap ornaments on the facade to zigzag Art Deco elevators, but the Cloud Club was a curious mix of historic and modern. The sixty-sixth-floor entry level freely mixed Art Deco elevator surrounds and bathrooms having tiled, abstract cloud motifs with pegged plank floors and neoclassical pilasters and friezes.

One room was for a stock ticker, another a Tudor-style lounge, and another an "Old English" bar and grill. The tower begins to angle in at this level, and service spaces are crammed into odd corners with slanting, triangular windows.

A broad, Renaissance-style stairway of bronze and marble leads up to the sixty-seventh floor, where Walter Chrysler, the owner, kept a private dining room paneled in black etched glass panels, looking north to Central Park.

On the south side is the main dining room with a view of the Battery and a high, curving cathedral ceiling as the tower narrows further. The room is fairly plain, dominated by square polished granite piers and handsome Art Deco woodwork and sconces. On one wall is a huge painting of Manhattan from the top of the Chrysler Building, with the Bank of Manhattan Building carefully depicted as a tiny structure.

In the fire stair off the main hallway is the square shaft where the steel needle was secretly assembled. The sixty-eighth floor consists of service spaces.

The Cloud Club opened in July 1930, seating only eighty in its main dining room. If Van Alen was a member, it must have presented seating difficulties for the maitre d', since he sued Walter Chrysler for most of his fee and even put a mechanic's lien on the building to recover it.

The Cloud Club changed very little over the years, but change went on around it. The Pinnacle Club opened in the new Socony-Mobil Building at 150 East 42nd Street in 1956. Juan Trippe, a charter member of the Cloud Club and head of Pan Am, deserted it for the Sky Club he established in the Pan Am Building in 1964.

A 1971 article in the *New York Times* reported the Cloud Club healthy amid the competition. But in 1975, foreclosure proceedings began against the Chrysler Building, and

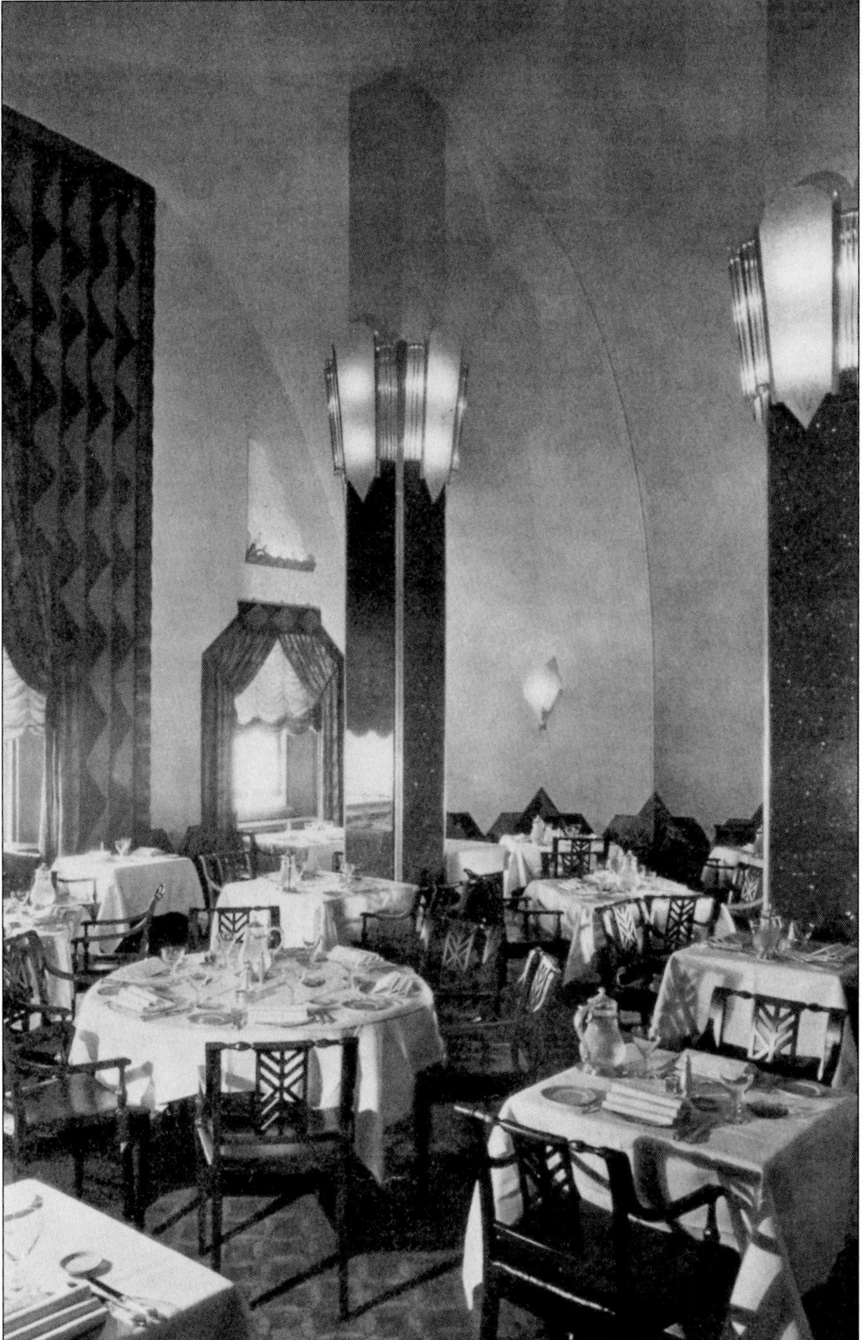

THE CLOUD CLUB DINING ROOM *atop the Chrysler Building in 1938.*
COURTESY LIBRARY OF CONGRESS

the foreclosed building went to the Massachusetts Mutual Life Insurance Company. In 1977, Texaco, whose executives were a mainstay of the club, moved out of the Chrysler Building to Harrison, New York. In 1979, the club closed. Although the club was intact in the 1990s, according to a 2002 article by Claudia Roth Pierpont in the *New Yorker,* all the interiors have been demolished.

THE NEW YORK YACHT CLUB

37 WEST 44TH STREET

FOUNDED IN 1844, THE NEW YORK YACHT CLUB had several modest headquarters for its first half century. But the activity of yachting became so luxurious that by the 1890s—with giant steam yachts of 200 feet or more—a new clubhouse seemed in order.

According to John Parkinson Jr.'s history of the club, members were surprised and pleased at an offer in 1898 by Commodore J. Pierpont Morgan (whose 241-foot-long *Corsair II* was the club's flagship) to pay for three lots "in the new clubhouse district" west of Grand Central Terminal.

A competition attracted entries ranging from the boring—R. H. Robertson's plain design could have been a small-town businessman's lunch club—to the opulent such as Howard, Cauldwell & Morgan's giant, modern French design with three windows shaped like the prows of oared galleys.

FIG 62.1

THE NEW YORK YACHT CLUB *at 37 West 44th Street in 1901.*
COURTESY OFFICE FOR METROPOLITAN HISTORY

THE NEW YORK YACHT CLUB'S MODEL ROOM. COURTESY OFFICE FOR METROPOLITAN HISTORY

The winning design was the first major work of the new partnership of Whitney Warren and Charles Wetmore. They produced a rich, five-story limestone front with three windows patterned after the sterns of early Dutch ships and a large terrace at the fourth floor topped by flagstaffs and a giant wood pergola and trellis.

Warren's original entry called for elaborate torchères atop the windows, but these were never executed. It also envisioned rich plantings covering the wooden elements of the terrace.

The club's $350,000 building opened in 1901, and the 1,561 members found the nautical theme carried out on the inside, especially with a grillroom styled like the interior of a wooden sailing ship, with bowed ceiling beams and curved walls.

It is the model room, though, that will astound the uninitiated visitor. Behind the facade's three great windows, the model room stretches back almost 100 feet under a giant floral stained-glass ceiling. Ringed by a balcony with a galleon railing, the room contains hundreds of full- and half-hull ship models, including one of every defender of the America's Cup.

Scientific American called it "the pride of the clubhouse," but architectural critics did not view it in exactly the same way. *Architectural Review* said that although there was "some semblance of reserve in the exterior," the elaborate stone chimneypiece in the model room was "a riot of swags and spinach, icicles and exotic vegetation. . . . Surely this is not legitimate architectural design. It is very pleasant fooling, but scarcely anything more."

At some point, the pergola and the flagstaffs were removed and the facade was painted gray, giving the club a dull, flat opacity.

But since a restoration project in the early 1990s, the limestone has been stripped of paint, revealing its subtle veining, fossil survivals, color shifts—the material looks almost as alive as wood. And the restored pergola is the whipped cream on this rich architectural dessert.

THE BEAUX-ARTS APARTMENTS

307 AND 310 EAST 44TH STREET

IN 1928 THE BEAUX-ARTS INSTITUTE OF DESIGN—then the club of the elite educated architects in New York—put up a new building at 304 East 44th Street, on a down-at-the-heels block close to the new midtown district of skyscrapers and apartment houses. Several members saw opportunity in the block and formed a consortium to rebuild it, not under orders from developers but using their own ideas—and pocketing the profits themselves.

Raymond Hood, an uncompromising modernist, and Kenneth Murchison, the urbane former president of the institute, assembled a blue-chip group of architect investors, including William Delano, Benjamin Wistar Morris, John W. Cross, and Whitney Warren. Backed by the United States Realty and Improvement Company, a giant real estate investment group, the architects raised money not through a mortgage from a single lender but through the sales of stock, an emerging technique that also helped build Tudor City nearby, London Terrace in Chelsea, and similar projects.

In the spring of 1929 Hood and Murchison designed two facing sixteen-story buildings, the Beaux-Arts Apartments, at 307 and 310 East 44th Street, each set back eight feet from the building line to establish a sense of enclave. Hood perhaps took a more active hand in the design—the buildings combined the sleek Art Deco and factory-functional look common to many of his designs, including the former Daily News building on East 42nd Street.

As in the usual apartment house of the day, the ground floor was all limestone, but with horizontal chrome strips. Above this rose a plain facade of buff brick with wide steel casement windows. Hood thought glass windows read as dark voids, and he linked them in horizontal bands by connecting them with patches of salmon and black brick.

To judge from old photographs, the lobbies were stunning: brown glass, aluminum and brass trim, chrome strips, stepped-down ceilings with silver leaf finishes. The elevator cabs were in lacquered aluminum with ceilings of glass rods. From a distance, the Beaux-Arts Apartments read as clean, modern factories; up close, they were nightclub modern.

On the upper floors some apartments were duplexes with double-height rooms, but the bulk of the building was made up of single studios, 22 by 13 feet. They had cork

THE BEAUX-ARTS APARTMENTS *at 307 East 44th Street in 1930.* COURTESY MUSEUM OF THE CITY OF NEW YORK

floors, tiny kitchens, and twin beds that folded up into the walls. Many tenants took their meals in a central restaurant, the Cafe Bonaparte, also in ultramodern style. The doormen wore gendarme-style uniforms.

The $5.2 million Beaux-Arts Apartments opened in early 1930, and Murchison and his family lived there, but most occupants were singles or couples. In the 1930s prominent tenants included the sculptor Jo Davidson, the architect and writer Talbot Hamlin, and the yachtsman and naval architect Boyd Donaldson.

Murchison, Hood, and their colleagues never began another project together. But the Beaux-Arts Apartments never went into foreclosure in the depression, in part because most of the debt was in the form of stock rather than a mortgage, and in part because a building of new one-room apartments was well-positioned in a time of reduced circumstances.

Neither Trentje Hood Reed, Raymond Hood's daughter, nor Ashbel Green, Kenneth Murchison's grandson, recall family stories of hardship or wealth about the architects' investment—but Murchison "sure didn't die rich," said Mr. Green, an editor with Alfred A. Knopf.

THE OLD PAN AM BUILDING

PARK AVENUE NORTH OF 46TH STREET

THE 1963 PAN AM BUILDING was designed by Emery Roth and Sons and two high-profile modern architects, Walter Gropius, a founder of the Bauhaus in Germany, and Pietro Belluschi. The resulting octagonal structure was faced with nine thousand panels of pre-cast concrete with quartz chips—after partial curing, some of the cement was scrubbed out, to better expose the chips, yielding a slight sparkle to the eggshell-color finish.

Although they were reaching for architectural dignity, critics and citizens were beginning to compare the city's modern architecture with what had come before—the controversy over the demolition of Pennsylvania Station was already under way. In 1962 the writer Wolf Von Eckhardt in the *New Republic* called the new Park Avenue structure—it had been named the Pan Am Building because it housed the headquarters of Pan American World Airways—"conspicuous for its ugliness and arrogant disregard for its surroundings." The next year Ada Louise Huxtable, architecture critic of

FIG 64.1

THE PAN AM BUILDING, *nearing its completion in 1963.* COURTESY AVERY ARCHITECTURAL LIBRARY

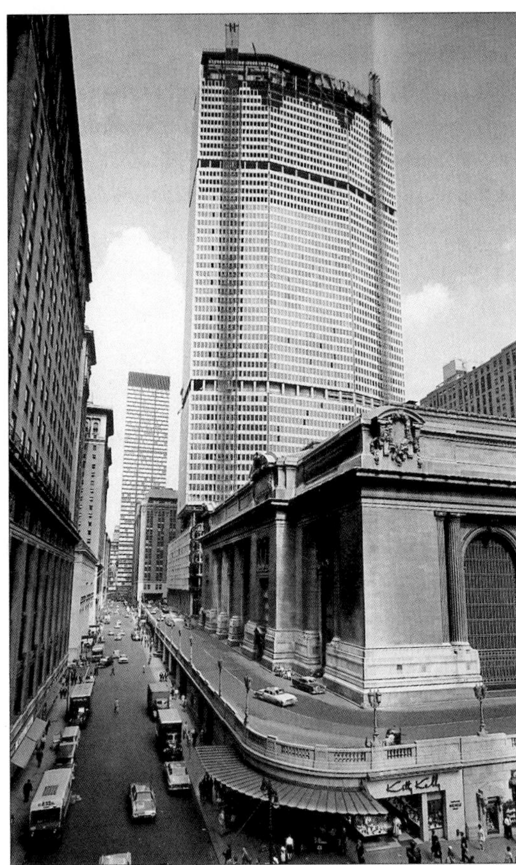

THE PAN AM BUILDING UNDER CONSTRUCTION IN 1962. COURTESY OFFICE FOR METROPOLITAN HISTORY

the *New York Times*, called it "gigantically second rate." She wrote, "A $100 million building cannot really be called cheap. But Pan Am is a colossal collection of minimums."

There was also concern that concentrating twenty-four thousand more workers at a pressure point for midtown transportation would choke the area. The Pan Am Building had some defenders. The editor of *Architectural Record,* Emerson Goble, said that adding office populations near transit points was wise and that the escalators along the north side of Grand Central leading to the Pan Am Building would open the terminal up to the new office buildings erected on Park Avenue north of 46th Street. "The Pan Am Building is planned for pedestrians," he wrote in 1962.

The new Pan Am Building seemed to embody the cosmopolitan age of world travel. MetLife acquired the building in 1981, and in 1992 MetLife announced the replacement of the Pan Am logo with its own. Robert A. M. Stern, the architect, known as a defender of modern buildings, asked the *Times*, "Couldn't they just leave the sign and take the building down?"

But now Mr. Stern, in his early sixties, says he is "ambivalent" about the MetLife Building. A younger viewpoint is that of John Jurayj, a thirty-something painter living in Brooklyn, who has been involved in several preservation efforts and is a member of a preservation organization, the Modern Architecture Working Group of New York City. Jurayj, who was not born when the building went up, said he sees it as "very forward thinking and not antiurban in terms of bringing people back to the city—it's a very high quality building."

Jurayj said he also sees the MetLife Building in a different light since the September 11 attack on the World Trade Center. "The old post office at the south end of City Hall Park was thought of as garish, and it obstructed a view, and so it was demolished in 1939, but now we'd fight to protect it," he said. "It seems that New Yorkers are emotionally connected to what were originally brutal interventions of our skyline. The loss of the World Trade Center shows that buildings that we may not think of as great architecture are important to our sense of ourselves and our city. Aesthetics are dependent upon the passage of time."

THE OLD MCGRAW-HILL BUILDING

330 WEST 42ND STREET

JAMES MCGRAW, WHO BEGAN PUBLISHING IN 1885, joined in 1917 with a competitor—James A. Hill, who began in 1901—to form the McGraw-Hill Publishing Company. The new company's offices and presses occupied the spare, white terra-cotta Hill Publishing Building, built in 1916, at 475 Tenth Avenue at 36th Street. The company grew, and by 1929, it published more than thirty trade journals, among them *Coal Age, Radio Retailing, Engineering News-Record,* and *Electric Railway Journa*l.

For the company's 1931 building at 330 West 42nd Street, McGraw chose one of the most flamboyant and provocative architects possible: Raymond Hood. Hood had struggled in obscurity until 1922, when he won a competition for the Chicago Tribune Tower with a streamlined Gothic shaft. Hood was prone to embrace provocative ideas; he was one of the few to defend, even advocate, urban congestion as a strength, not a weakness.

He also had anti-traditional ideas about design: "If you owned a mountain, would you embroider it?" he told the *New York Sun* in early 1931, criticizing the designs of traditional New York skyscrapers with historical decoration.

Hood designed the inside of the thirty-five-story McGraw-Hill Building with loft-like finishes—plain concrete ceilings and walls—in many areas, even in the office portions. McGraw-Hill rented out the ninth through fifteenth floors. The lower floors held the printing operations: composing room on the seventh floor, pressroom on the sixth, the bindery on the fifth.

The exterior was a startling statement, even to those familiar with Hood's advanced ideas: horizontal bands of factory-style windows framed by fields of green-blue terra-cotta, becoming bluer with height to almost merge with the sky.

Hood took the colors seriously: he had also considered red, yellow, orange, and gray for the terra-cotta, and he fine-tuned the design with a gray-green for the window bands, with a stripe of vermilion at the top of each. Hood also called for buff-colored

MCGRAW-HILL BUILDING IN 1931. COURTESY FAY S. LINCOLN ARCHIVE, PENN STATE UNIVERSITY

window shades, with a green stripe running down the center; the building staff wore green uniforms trimmed with silver.

Traditionalists had fits: a modernistic building was bad enough, but a modernistic blue building was like serving a bacon burger to a vegetarian. The critic Arthur North, writing in *American Architect* in early 1932, called it "a storm center" that showed "disregard for every accepted principle of architectural designing in the most flagrant manner." But he thought the building was worth studying. Lewis Mumford defended most modern architecture but wrote in his *New Yorker* column that the building was just "a stunt," in part because it did not have cantilever construction to allow corner windows. He thought the colors were "heavy and unbeautiful."

McGraw-Hill kept boosting its far-west location, but the striking green tower remained isolated. The company even sold off an adjacent plot to the west, which it had held for possible future expansion. As West 42nd Street declined from honky-tonk to unmentionable, its building became a liability; in 1972 the company moved to its present skyscraper at Sixth Avenue and 48th Street, and its old headquarters has passed through several owners.

THE KNICKERBOCKER HOTEL

42ND STREET AND BROADWAY

THE KNICKERBOCKER HOTEL, AT THE SOUTHEAST CORNER of 42nd and Broadway, was designed in 1901, just as the theater district was turning the corner from Broadway onto 42nd Street. John Jacob Astor IV, who had built the Astoria half of the Waldorf-Astoria Hotel at 34th Street and Fifth Avenue in 1897, owned the southeast corner of the 42nd Street intersection and leased it to a Philadelphia group organized by J. E. and A. L. Pennock.

The Pennocks retained Bruce Price and his former employees, Marvin & Davis, to design a new hotel for the site, and they developed a French Renaissance facade in red brick, limestone, and terra-cotta with a mansard roof.

Something went wrong among the original investors, and work stopped in February 1904 with the exterior complete but the interior just a shell. In May 1905, Astor, who had just finished his own St. Regis Hotel at 55th Street and Fifth Avenue, stepped in to complete the hotel, with redesigned interiors by Trowbridge & Livingston, who had done the St. Regis.

The new hotel had 556 rooms but was organized around the dining and entertaining rooms on the lower three floors—with two thousand restaurant seats to feed the theater district traffic. In 1906, the *New York Times* reported that the operator, James B. Regan,

THE OLD KING COLE MURAL, *in its original location at the Knickerbocker Hotel's bar in 1906.* COURTESY MUSEUM OF THE CITY OF NEW YORK

had spent seven months in Europe studying top hotels and had returned with "radical ideas" like eliminating carpets in the restaurants.

The $3.3 million hotel had its own subway entrance (the door is still visible at the east end of the platform for Track 1 of the shuttle), pneumatic tubes to each sleeping floor for messages and, instead of the usual palm room, a flower room with live and cut flowers. With a gold dinner service for forty-eight and five hundred Paris-made clocks (and an employee dedicated to winding them), the Knickerbocker was advertised by Mr. Regan as "a Fifth Avenue hotel at Broadway prices."

What architectural writers most noted were the decorations of the restaurants, grill, and bar. In other hotels these were typically reproductions of artworks by old masters, but Mr. Regan wanted more contemporary art. These included works by Frederic Remington, Frederick MacMonnies, James Wall Finn, and, in the first-floor bar, Maxfield Parrish's *Old King Cole*, 8 feet wide by 30 feet long, which is now at the St. Regis.

The *Real Estate Record and Guide* predicted that the mural "will do what very few works of art have ever done—it will pay its own way."

Opening in October 1906, on its second night the Knickerbocker turned away five hundred people from the dining room. *Architectural Record* called the hotel "a huge popular success" in large part because of the art program.

In a 1913 interview, Enrico Caruso, the Knickerbocker's most illustrious tenant complained that he could not walk the streets outside in privacy and that audiences wanted only "high notes and loud ones."

Caruso was not listed in the 1915 census but he was definitely living there. Newspapers reported that he had given his overcoat and shoes to Emile Shubert, one of 2,300 unemployed waiting in a bread line at the back entrance to the hotel, on 41st Street.

John Jacob Astor went down on the *Titanic* in 1912, and his son Vincent became head of the firm. In 1920, Mr. Regan surrendered his lease, saying he was ready to retire.

THE KNICKERBOCKER HOTEL IN 1907. COURTESY THE NEW-YORK HISTORICAL SOCIETY, NEW YORK CITY

But Prohibition, enacted the year before, must have affected the Knickerbocker's business: Vincent Astor announced plans to turn the hotel into an office building.

The architect Charles Platt supervised a million-dollar renovation that removed almost all traces of the hotel layout, and rents of $4 to $5 per square foot were projected, along with $400,000 a year for the stores. Vincent Astor crated up *Old King Cole* for storage. In 1935, after being loaned to the Racquet Club on Park Avenue, it was reinstalled in the St. Regis.

THE ELTINGE/EMPIRE THEATER

236 WEST 42ND STREET

THE EMPIRE THEATER WAS BUILT BY THE PRODUCER Al Woods as the Eltinge Theater, named after Woods's moneymaking star Julian Eltinge. By Eltinge's own account, he played a woman in a Harvard production and soon left school for a career as a female impersonator. He was successful enough to perform at Windsor Castle for King Edward VII, who gave him a white bulldog.

FIG 67.1

THE ELTINGE *(later the Empire) Theater at 236 West 42nd Street in 1912.*

COURTESY THEATER COLLECTION, MUSEUM OF THE CITY OF NEW YORK

In 1911 Woods staged *The Fascinating Widow*, written specifically for Eltinge, at the Liberty Theater. It ran four years and made them both rich. The next year he built a theater just west of the Liberty.

It is not clear if Eltinge ever actually played there, but his name lent it luster: in 1912 he was earning $1,625 a week, more than President William Howard Taft's $1,442. He also developed his own magazine (with articles on how he applied makeup and why women should take up "the gentle art of boxing") and his own line of cold cream, whose buyers got a free photograph of him.

The building, designed by the theater specialist Thomas Lamb, has a giant square terra-cotta facade with a great central bay, all covered with the customary garlands, cartouches, and other details, some in polychrome. Compared to other theaters at the time, it marked a new level of composed, urban grandeur.

According to *Lost Broadway Theaters*, by Nicholas Van Hoogstraten, later stage productions at the Eltinge starred such actors as Laurence Olivier and Clark Gable. They were superseded in 1931 by burlesque and then movies.

Eltinge died in 1941, and in 1954 the theater was renamed the Empire. By then the theaters on 42nd Street between Seventh and Eighth Avenues had been in decline for several decades, and there was wishful thinking of somehow returning them to their original cultured vitality.

In the 1960s a series of proposals called for widespread demolition on 42nd Street. Nothing came of them, but in 1998, to make way for new development in the area, the entire 7.4 million pound structure was lifted, placed on rails, and rolled to its new site, 168 feet to the west, over three days.

THE LAMBS CLUB

130 WEST 44TH STREET

THE LAMBS CLUB WAS FOUNDED IN 1874 by a group of theater people who met for dinner and conversation. They took their name from a similar group in London, which had met earlier in the nineteenth century at the house of Charles Lamb, the drama critic and essayist.

In New York, the Lambs occupied a series of rented quarters and in 1888 began what they called their "gambols," special performances by members to which outsiders were invited. In the late 1890s, under the actor DeWolf Hopper, the "Shepherd"—or president—of the club, the gambols were used as fund-raising efforts for a new building. In 1898, the gambols went on a one-week, eight-city tour, raising $67,000.

In 1903 the Lambs bought a site at 128 and 130 West 44th Street, near the emerging theater district, and retained Stanford White, a club member, to design a clubhouse.

THE LAMBS CLUB IN 1905. COURTESY OFFICE FOR METROPOLITAN HISTORY

HARMS

The architect developed a rich neo-Georgian design in brick, marble, and terra-cotta, with six rams' heads and two rams' profiles worked into the facade.

On the first floor were a grillroom and a billiard room, with a bank of telephones in the lobby, on the second floor a banquet hall, and on the third floor a small theater. The top stories were given over to offices and sleeping rooms for members.

In 1914 the *New York Times* wrote "while many of the clubhouses of the Big Town display constantly the dignity and spirit of Greenwood Cemetery on a rainy Saturday afternoon, the Lambs is as full of snap and ginger as an outlaw bronco, a bunch of freshly lighted firecrackers." The club had about 1,400 members (past and present members at the time included Mark Twain, Edwin Booth, the prolific playwright and actor Dion Boucicault, and David Belasco). In 1915 the clubhouse was doubled in size, in an alteration designed by George Freeman.

The 1920 census recorded actors, composers, and movie producers among the residents of the Lambs, of whom the most prominent was Frank Mandel, who cowrote the book for *No, No Nanette*. In 1949 the Lambs began a new television show on NBC, *The Lambs Gambols*, which included bits like Raymond Massey doing a song and dance routine.

A year later the *Saturday Evening Post* was able to point to such high points in the club's history as George M. Cohan's first performance of *Over There* at a gambol, and an early version of *Brigadoon* played by the composer Frederick Loewe on a piano in the grill. But much of the article was retrospective, for it was clear that the Lambs had been hurt by the eclipse of the New York stage by Hollywood.

In 1974 the club was designated a landmark, and a few years later it sold its building to the Church of the Nazarene; the club is now in shared space at 3 West 51st Street.

THE OLD AMERICAN HORSE EXCHANGE

NOW THE WINTER GARDEN THEATER, 50TH STREET AND BROADWAY

LIGHT INDUSTRY SETTLED ALONG THE SLICE OF BROADWAY north of 42nd Street in the 1860s, and by the 1870s wagon factories, harness shops, and horse dealers concentrated in the area, named Longacre after the carriage district in London.

In 1881 William K. Vanderbilt and a group of investors built the area's biggest building, the American Horse Exchange, on the blockfront of 50th Street from Broadway to Seventh Avenue, stretching most of the way up to 51st Street. Vanderbilt's associates included leading millionaire-horsemen like William Jay, George Wetmore, and Frederic Bronson—"gentlemen of vast means," as they were called by the *New York Times* in 1894, to whom profits were "of no consequence."

THE AMERICAN HORSE EXCHANGE, *on Broadway between 50th and 51st Streets, circa 1910.* COURTESY THE NEW-YORK HISTORICAL SOCIETY, NEW YORK CITY

They wanted only that the exchange be self-sustaining, that it provide a scrupulously reliable center for thoroughbred horse trading. Period accounts made it clear that there were plenty of lemons in the equestrian market.

The *Times* quoted auction fees ranging from $5 a head on horses costing under $300 to 5 percent on those over $1,000, and said that the two-story brick building was "the safest in the city."

But in 1896, fire swept though the American Horse Exchange, almost leveling it and killing about 60 of the 265 horses stabled there, the property of owners and dealers from as far away as Chicago, Michigan, and Kentucky. Six thousand people crowded around the blazing building, sometimes blocking horses from escaping. The *New York Times* said that, through the windows, "crazed animals could be seen dashing blindly about in their terror." Loose horses were recovered from all over midtown.

Vanderbilt reconstructed the American Horse Exchange in 1897. His architect, A. V. Porter, reused a portion of the surviving walls to create a two-, three-, and four-story structure with a high covered ring 160 by 80 feet, bridged by open trusswork and with perimeter walls of brick with round-arched windows. In the opening exhibit following the reconstruction, Chester, a brown gelding owned by Adelaide Doremus, won in the category of best saddle horse.

Automobiles became familiar on city streets just after 1900, but in 1906 the *New York Tribune* derided the "totally erroneous impression that the horse is going out of fashion," pointing out that Americans owned $1.2 billion worth of horses—seventeen million animals as opposed to the fourteen million of 1890. The *Tribune* confidently predicted a very long wait for "the funeral rites of genus equus."

But automobiles became increasingly popular, especially to the elite served by the American Horse Exchange. In 1910 the Vanderbilt group leased the entire site to Lee and J. J. Shubert for another theater in the Shuberts' growing chain. The *Times* remarked that this would "remove the last notable landmark of the old horse and carriage trade" and that, even then, the recently arrived automobile dealers were being pushed farther north by theater and hotel construction. Longacre Square had been renamed Times Square in 1904.

The Shuberts were economical, reusing much of the original perimeter walls of the American Horse Exchange and apparently using the riding-ring trusswork for the theater auditorium. They put a new temple-style front on Broadway and, at the 50th Street corner, a three-story nightclub space that extended back behind the old walls to 50th and Seventh. Their architect was W. Albert Swasey. Research by the Landmarks Preservation Commission indicates that Al Jolson made his Broadway debut in the opening theater production in 1911, *La Belle Paree*.

Latterly the building was known for another animal: for two decades the Winter Garden was the home of *Cats*.

ROSELAND

239 WEST 52ND STREET

IN 1916 A NEW COMPANY, ICELAND, LEASED AN OLD ROLLER RINK on the east side of Broadway at 53rd Street and converted it for ice-skating. The original incorporators were three lawyers, including Joseph Force Crater, a powerful Tammany lawyer who later became a State Supreme Court judge and disappeared in 1930 in a famous case that has never been solved. At the time of his disappearance, Judge Crater was under investigation in connection with corruption during the administration of Mayor James J. Walker.

In 1921 the company reorganized with additional partners, among them Irving Brokaw, a patrician skater and clubman who was national figure-skating champion in 1908. In 1922 Iceland built a new $800,000 rink running from 52nd to 53rd Street, west of Broadway—what is now the Roseland Ballroom—as upper Times Square began to fill up with theaters.

The new Iceland was designed by Corry B. Comstock, an architect and refrigeration engineer who had designed the alterations on the Broadway rink in 1916. A thousand skaters showed up for opening of the 80-by-200-foot rink on November 29, 1922.

On 52nd Street, the main facade is a typical white glazed terra-cotta design; the back of the building, on 53rd Street, had a certain industrial drama because of the reinforced concrete piers and the angled roof over the elliptical ceiling. On the interior, a

EXTERIOR OF THE ICELAND ROLLER RINK IN 1923. COURTESY CORNELL UNIVERSITY LIBRARIES

INTERIOR OF THE ICELAND ROLLER RINK IN 1923. COURTESY CORNELL UNIVERSITY LIBRARIES

large oval ice floor was surrounded by a Louis XIV–style gallery in gray and red. At the top, elliptical windows admitted natural light, but at night the smooth, curved ceiling was washed with colored lights.

There is no record that Judge Crater ever skated at Iceland, although a 1964 memoir by his wife, Stella Crater, *The Empty Robe*, does say they often went to the theater. On August 6, 1930, Judge Crater left Billy Haas's chophouse at 332 West 45th Street and was never seen again; his wife believed he had been murdered.

In the summer of 1932 the Central Savings Bank foreclosed on Iceland, although it resumed operation as the Gay Blades Ice Rink. In October of that year Comstock, who was also a major investor in Iceland, shot himself in his office in the Chanin Building, apparently because of financial problems.

By the 1950s Iceland was operated as a roller-skating rink by Louis J. Brecker, an entrepreneur. Three decades before, Mr. Brecker had founded Roseland Dance City in the old Iceland space on Broadway. The 1939 *WPA Guide to New York City* described Roseland as "the downtown headquarters for hot music and such urban dance steps as the Cake, the Collegiate, the Lindy, and the Shag." Tommy Dorsey, Count Basie, and other big-band names played Roseland in the 1920s and 1930s.

In 1956 Mr. Brecker moved Roseland to the Iceland building on 52nd Street. In a 1974 interview in the *New York Times* Mr. Brecker proudly noted that he had never allowed newer dances like the twist; "cheek-to-cheek dancing, that's what this place is all about," he said.

THE WYOMING

55TH STREET AND SEVENTH AVENUE

ALTHOUGH IT IS NOW A DIN OF THEATER TRAFFIC AND STORES, in the 1880s Seventh Avenue above 50th Street was emerging as an elite residential address for the first generation of apartment dwellers. In 1878 Edward Clark had the architect Henry Hardenbergh design his $300,000 Van Corlear apartment house, the full blockfront of Seventh from 55th to 56th Streets, on the west side.

In 1880, the year they also began the Dakota, the same team began the five-story Wyoming, at the southeast corner of 55th and Seventh, and two years later the Ontiora, at the southwest corner of the same intersection. In the mid-1880s the Osborne went up at 57th and Seventh, and also the vast, eight-building Spanish flats, on the east side of Seventh from 58th to 59th.

FIG 71.1

THE WYOMING'S ENTRY HALL IN 1906. COURTESY MUSEUM OF THE CITY OF NEW YORK

THE WYOMING IN 1906. COURTESY MUSEUM OF THE CITY OF NEW YORK

In 1906 the *Real Estate Record and Guide* opined "Seventh Avenue in its middle and upper parts cannot be viewed in any other light than one of the finest avenues of the future." That was the same year that the developer Eugene C. Potter completed a replacement of Clark's old Wyoming—a $900,000, thirteen-story namesake, designed by Rouse & Sloan in a delicate French Renaissance style, with seven- to thirteen-room apartments renting from $2,000 to $5,000 a year.

The earliest tenants of the Wyoming were people like Kenneth D. Chisholm, a Lancia dealer; William H. Truesdale, president of the Delaware, Lackawanna & Western railroad; and Eugene Potter himself.

But the advent of the theater district just to the south brought a new kind of tenant to Seventh Avenue. The 1925 census for the Wyoming lists residents like Clarence Whitehill, a baritone at the Metropolitan, and Mark Brunswick, a composer later prominent in modern music. Most of these households were small, but another family was an exception.

William and Etta Morris were both career actors who began work in the nineteenth century, and they lived at the Wyoming with their children Gordon, a playwright, and Chester, Wilhemina, and Adrian, all actors. Adrian, at seventeen in 1925, the youngest, later appeared in the film *The Grapes of Wrath,* and Chester, twenty-four, had debuted in silent films at the age of nine and was famous for his Boston Blackie detective series in the 1940s. He last appeared as Pop Morrison, the boxing commissioner, in the 1970 film *The Great White Hope*.

Another tenant was Alice Chittenden, fifty-three, who in the 1910s had lectured widely in the unsuccessful fight to oppose extending the vote to women, which was granted in 1913. She told the *New York Times* that letting women vote would not change the outcomes of elections. "Why must two persons do the work one can do?" she told the *Times*; she lived at the Wyoming with three maids.

In the 1940s the porte cochere was filled in with stores, and the roof has recently been mutilated in an aesthetically disastrous renovation campaign.

In 1979 a survey by the Landmarks Preservation Commission categorized the Wyoming as "highest priority" along with buildings like the Osborne, and in 1986 another survey described it as having "outstanding significance." But the commission has never acted.

CATHOLIC APOSTOLIC CHURCH

417 WEST 57TH STREET

A GROUP OF WELL-TO-DO ENGLISH PROTESTANTS established the Catholic Apostolic Church in 1832. They chose twelve new apostles who alone could ordain ministers, but did not provide for any succession—the return of Jesus was originally prophesied for 1835. The word "Catholic" signified a return to the original principles of the church, not because they adhered to Roman Catholicism.

In 1848 a group of Catholic Apostolics began worshiping in New York, and in 1885 the congregation, numbering about four hundred, bought two lots at 417 West 57th Street, in a middling area of tenements and flats, and hired as its architect Francis H. Kimball, who had studied in England.

The critic Montgomery Schuyler, writing about Kimball's church design in 1897, said there was "no more scholarly Gothic work in New York." But the deep red brick and especially the abundant terra-cotta give the church an overriding Victorian cast not really evident in black-and-white photographs. Surrounded by a black iron fence of flame-shaped posts, the blocky verticality of the tower and the hot red color face the street with the strength of a football lineman, ready to knock you over.

Molded terra-cotta leaves—which run along the rims of the doorway arches—seem to jump off the building. And the blocks of terra-cotta that surround them were scraped, before firing, with a tiny, comblike tool, leaving a vibrant electric surface. Each stroke varies, leaving the evidence of human hands on every inch. Above, the apple-sized heads of angels show each wave of hair, as if they were life casts.

In 1893, *King's Handbook of New York City* said that there were two daily services, but the peculiar solitude of the Catholic Apostolics has left few other details. Religious writers call the sect secretive, with no interest in proselytizing or cooperating with outside inquiry.

A Manhattan clergyman who would speak only on condition of anonymity because he has friends in the faith said that the Catholic Apostolics were popular because their apocalyptic vision "provided an explanation for everything" and because "their liturgy was breathtakingly transcendent"—with chanted psalms, incense, and speaking in tongues.

But in 1901 the last of the twelve apostles from the 1830s died and, with him, the power to ordain priests or bishops (called "Angels") and perform other duties. No order of succession had ever been established, and outside accounts say that the Catholic Apostolics considered this "the time of silence," of simply waiting for God's instructions.

Henry O. DuBois was ordained as an Episcopal priest in 1880, but in 1890 became Angel of the Catholic Apostolic Church on 57th Street. He retained his standing as an

FIG 72.1

THE CATHOLIC APOSTOLIC CHURCH *on West 57th Street in 1895.* COURTESY OFFICE FOR METROPOLITAN HISTORY

Episcopal priest. But he was the last Angel to survive in the New York church, dying in 1949 at age ninety-four.

In 1995 the Catholic Apostolic congregation was down to just a handful of members. Seeing the end of their occupancy of the space at hand, they wanted to make sure the building would not be reused as a disco or a rug showroom, and they donated it to a Lutheran congregation. The surviving members are dispersed, have no central place of worship, and are not willing to speak with a reporter.

THE OLD KNOEDLER BUILDING

556 FIFTH AVENUE

MICHEL KNOEDLER CAME TO THE UNITED STATES from France in 1846 and opened an art gallery. By the 1880s M. Knoedler & Company was one of the leading art dealers in America, counting among its customers William K. Vanderbilt and Jay Gould. In 1910, when Knoedler was at 34th Street and Fifth Avenue, Roland Knoedler, Michel's son, was head of the company and broke ground for a five-story mansionlike gallery at 556 Fifth Avenue at 46th Street.

His architects, Carrère & Hastings, were the designers of Henry Frick's mansion at 70th Street and Fifth Avenue and the New York Public Library at 42nd and Fifth. The new gallery was severe in style on the upper floors. But its luxurious, giant bronze show windows were framed in blocks of minutely vermiculated stone, with irregular channels like those made by worms in old wood. Rene Gimpel, in his *Diary of an Art Dealer* (1966), described the ground floor as "an immense stone hall with ten employees to take charge of you and direct you." "This place is a bazaar," he wrote. "You're looking for an engraving for $5 that you'd find on the quays for five sous? You'll get it here. It's a Rembrandt etching you fancy, or a very rare eighteenth-century engraving? Five thousand dollars—it's yours! Name it; they'll show you it."

Knoedler's first exhibition in the new building opened in January 1912, with works by such artists as Romney, Gainsborough and Van Dyck. In 1915, Knoedler held a show of a different kind, one of both old masters and contemporary painters—among them Rembrandt, Rubens, Bronzino, Degas, and Cassatt—to benefit the cause of women's suffrage. It raised more than $2,000. According to Rebecca A. Rabinow, the assistant curator in the Department of European Paintings at the Metropolitan Museum of Art, the collector Louisine Havemeyer was a key promoter. Ms. Rabinow said that Roland Knoedler had agreed to play host to the exhibition in part to lure back Mrs. Havemeyer as a client; she had gone to a competitor, Durand-Ruel.

In a 1918 diary entry, Gimpel did not esteem highly the Knoedler Gallery of those years. "An old name, a long reputation for honesty, but no real intelligence," he wrote.

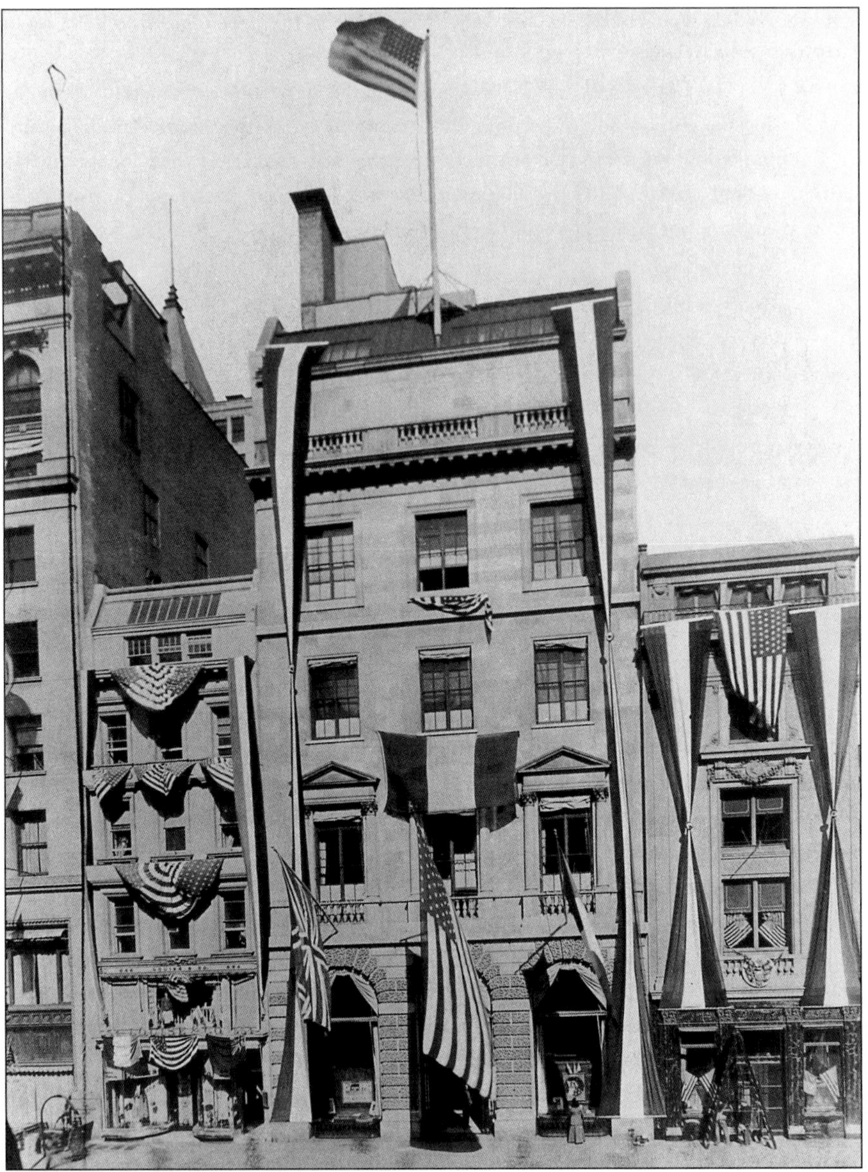

THE KNOEDLER GALLERY *decorated with bunting for a parade about 1918.*
COURTESY PETER H. DAVIDSON

Knoedler was at 556 Fifth Avenue for little more than a decade; Roland Knoedler called back Carrère & Hastings in 1923 to design a new building at 14 East 57th Street, where the company moved in 1925 (now demolished).

When Knoedler moved out of its Fifth Avenue home, Schrafft's took over the building for one of its growing chain of restaurants. Its architect, Charles E. Birge, left the upper facade intact but added an elegant bronze storefront over the lower section of the first floor. In a 1926 column in the *New Yorker*, the critic George Chappell both admired and mourned the addition. "Very good bronze work, too," he wrote, "but as nothing compared with the integrity and suitableness of the original material."

In 1975 the Philippine Government altered the new building for the present Philippine Center, which houses a tourist office, a trade board, the mission to the

United Nations, and the consulate, giving it a completely new facade of pebbled stucco. That has recently been torn away, leaving the partly damaged, partly intact 1912 limestone exposed, a curious palimpsest.

THE GOELET BUILDING

608 FIFTH AVENUE

BY THE EARLY NINETEENTH CENTURY, the Goelet family had become prominent merchants and soon emerged as second only to the Astors as landowners, according to an article on the family by Brooks Peters in *Quest* magazine of March 1989.

In 1882, Ogden Goelet built a mansion at 608 Fifth Avenue at the southwest corner of 49th Street. He died in 1897 but the house remained standing until the death of his widow in 1929. The Goelets rarely sold land, and in 1930 the family chose to erect a new structure on the site adaptable for use as offices, a single department store, or small shops, largely because the pending development of Rockefeller Center made it difficult to forecast the most desirable use.

The columns on the first floor were set in to allow uninterrupted show-window space, and the second floor was hung from the third to increase head room in the first-floor area. But it is the styling of 608 Fifth Avenue that sets it apart—way apart.

Perhaps the term "geometric moderne" is fairly close, but it still doesn't do justice to what the marble trade magazine *Through the Ages* called "a modernist's dream" in 1932.

The building is one giant Art Moderne cigarette case of marble—Dover white at the floor levels; deeply veined verde antique green at the store levels; vertical stripes at the crown; and Yule Colorado golden at the door—all accented by aluminum trim. The bronze doorway was designed after the Goelet family coat of arms and was said to have cost $14,000.

Inside, the lobby is an explosion of zigzag modernism and different marbles—aurora rossa, samosa golden, American pavonazzo, bleu belge, numidian red, and Belgian black, under an aluminum ceiling. It's a key stop on the walking tours given by the geologist Sidney Horenstein, architecturally both exhilarating and exhausting.

The design of the building is subject to competing claims. Roy Clinton Morris, an architect who did other Art Moderne work, actually filed the building application for the Goelet family. But he did so as an agent for Edward H. Faile, an engineer who subsequently did other work for the family. Mr. Faile is also known for his 270 Broadway office building of 1930, unusually austere on the outside but with a highly decorative lobby.

FIG 74.1

THE GOELET BUILDING *on Fifth Avenue at 49th Street in 1931.* COURTESY LIBRARY OF CONGRESS

But the article in *Through the Ages* credits only the architect Victor L. S. Hafner, making no mention of Mr. Faile or Mr. Morris. Charles Savage, an architectural historian at the Landmarks Preservation Commission, has determined that Mr. Faile, a Cornell graduate, began his practice in 1925 and employed Mr. Hafner for a year and a half.

Just how "modern" was the Goelet building in its own time?

Lewis Mumford considered it absurd, sarcastically calling it "an excellent period reproduction—Modernique, 1925" in his *New Yorker* column in 1931. He considered it a *retardataire* holdover of the Art Deco of the 1920s. Indeed, there is an awkward, ungainly quality to the massing and in the restless conflict between the vertical and horizontal elements of the design; the rich facade does not complement the structure itself.

ROCKEFELLER CENTER'S PROMETHEUS

THE PLAZA AT ROCKEFELLER CENTER

ROCKEFELLER CENTER WAS AN ACCIDENT. John D. Rockefeller Jr. had leased the land for a new Metropolitan Opera complex, but when the stock market crash of 1929 forced the opera to bow out, Rockefeller sought a commercial development for the site. Some original elements of the earlier Metropolitan Opera design survived in the new project, including a new mid-block north-south street and a central plaza.

At first circular and later rectangular, the sunken plaza was conceived as an entry point to a shopping concourse underneath 30 Rockefeller Plaza. A central circular fountain was meant to draw pedestrians down a broad stairway and lead them to the retailers.

By early 1933 this design had evolved to a fountain with a sculpture against the west wall, and Paul Manship was hired as the sculptor. Born in Minnesota in 1885, Manship left high school at age seventeen, convinced that his future lay in art.

Manship's muscular, active figures brought him instant fame at his inaugural exhibition in 1912. He quickly developed a reputation as a reliable artist who could work on schedule without histrionics. A 1918 portrait bust of John D. Rockefeller Sr. in the collection of the Rockefeller Archive Center in Sleepy Hollow, New York, was rendered in his typical cool, unemotional style. By the 1920s Manship was the designer of choice for public sculpture projects—he designed the 1933 inaugural medal for Franklin D. Roosevelt.

For the plaza, Manship decided on the theme of *Prometheus*. The finished figure had the stylized hair and blank expression of ancient Greek sculpture that was Manship's trademark. But it also had Manship's typical emphasis on lithe movement.

Installed in early 1934, the eight-ton bronze sculpture had *Prometheus* flying almost horizontally, with a clump of fire in his right hand, through streams of water over a zodiacal ring. Edward Alden Jewel, writing in the *New York Times*, called *Prometheus* "a genuine masterpiece, beautiful in its rhythm." But he acknowledged that another critic, the actor and writer Frank Craven, considered it "a boudoir knickknack." Manship's unhindered success inspired detractors who saw in him an upper-class toady irrelevant to the dead-serious modernism of the 1930s.

Prometheus was originally gilt to a bright finish, but in mid-1934 Jewell wrote in the *Times* that the gilding had been radically toned down, a change he considered a mistake. "For a few weeks," he wrote, "the *Prometheus* was the blithest note in the town's vast architectural scale."

Indeed, Manship had many reservations about the completed work. He thought he had been hurried by the twelve-month schedule, and the horizontal figure of *Prometheus*

FIG 75.1

ROCKEFELLER CENTER'S PLAZA IN 1934. COURTESY MUSEUM OF THE CITY OF NEW YORK

FIG 75.2

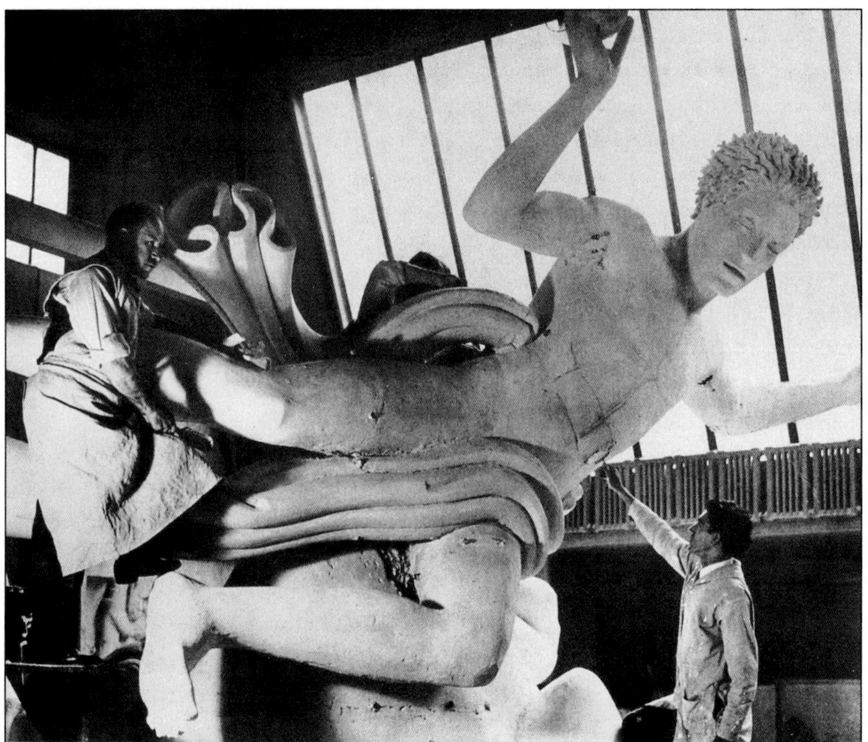

PAUL MANSHIP, LEFT, WORKING ON PROMETHEUS IN 1933. COURTESY ROCKEFELLER CENTER ARCHIVES

was not consonant with the verticality of 30 Rockefeller Plaza. "I'd naturally welcome the opportunity of doing the whole fountain group over again," he told *Rockefeller Center Weekly* in 1935. On reflection, he thought that two huge columns, or two 50-foot-high standing figures, would have been better.

Prometheus, although striking, failed to draw enough shoppers down to the plaza, and in 1936 a skating rink was installed, and the surrounding shops were converted into restaurants, a much more successful arrangement.

THE MARBLE TWINS

645–647 FIFTH AVENUE

THE THREE GIANT VANDERBILT MANSIONS, all completed on Fifth Avenue from 51st to 52nd Streets in 1882, immediately dominated an entire street that until then had been almost uniformly wallpapered with comfortable but boring brownstones. Including lesser houses and stables on the side streets, the Vanderbilts ultimately built fifteen structures on or near Fifth Avenue above 50th Street, and they became naturally identified with its health as a residential boulevard.

But in early 1901 the southeast corner of Fifth and 52nd went to a syndicate of developers, Stewart H. Chisolm, George R. Sheldon, and Charles T. Barney. This group filed plans for an eighteen-story hotel designed by William C. Hazlett on the 12,500-square-foot corner, directly across from the William H. and William K. Vanderbilt houses.

In 1902 the Vanderbilt family, acting as the New York Realty Corporation, paid $1 million for the 52nd Street site to squelch the hotel project—which may have been the developer's point all along.

This left the problem of what to do with the property. The Vanderbilts were able to sell off the actual corner parcel to Morton F. Plant for his town house, now occupied by the jeweler Cartier, but there were no other takers for the mid-block parcels. Taxes had become too high, and there was a growing sense that a major urban thoroughfare was not where millionaires wanted to spend their money.

So the Vanderbilts hired the architects Hunt & Hunt to design a pair of houses directly across from William H. Vanderbilt's famous multiple house at 51st and Fifth Avenue, long known as the "Brownstone Twins." Hunt & Hunt's original elevation drawing dubbed the new buildings the Marble Twins, even though Sidney Horenstein, a geologist at the American Museum of Natural History, says the original facade material appears to be limestone.

A 1905 photograph shows 647 Fifth Avenue with a for-sale sign, but there were no takers. The Vanderbilts later leased it to the real-estate investor Robert Goelet, who

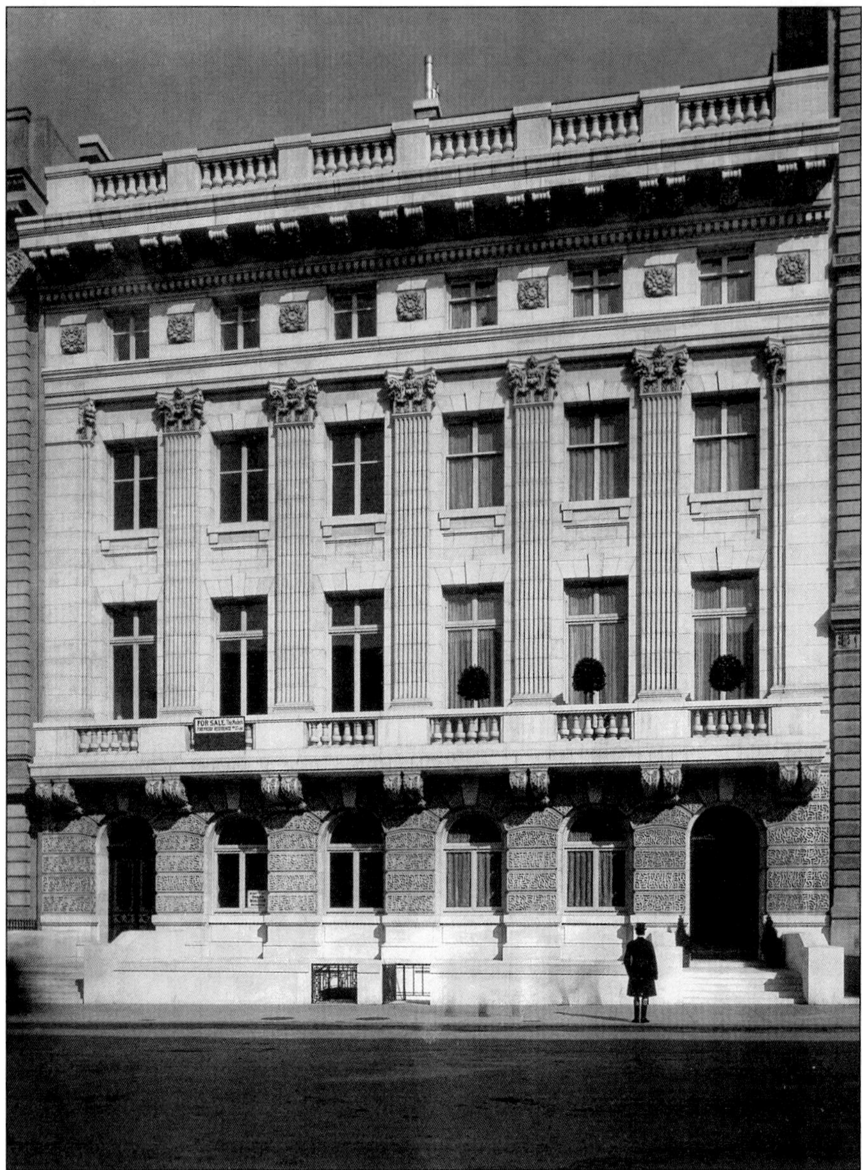

THE VANDERBILT FAMILY'S MARBLE TWINS IN 1904. COURTESY BURR MCINTOSH, THE NEW-YORK HISTORICAL SOCIETY, NEW YORK CITY

lived there with his wife, Elsie; son, Ogden; and fourteen servants. The house at 645 was owned and occupied by William B. Osgood Field and his wife, Lila, granddaughter of William H. Vanderbilt.

The Marble Twins were simply a holding action, a large investment aimed at locking up the use of the land. Despite the obvious change in the Fifth Avenue environment, the *Real Estate Record and Guide* predicted in 1904 that the Marble Twins and the rest of the Vanderbilt holdings "will long act as an absolute barrier" to further business invasion.

But in 1911 the Board of Estimate ordered the removal of all the stoops, gardens, and bay windows that added elegance to the town houses but encroached on the sidewalk. It was at about that time that most householders on Fifth gave up, and William K.

Vanderbilt altered 647 to allow store occupancy and leased it to the art dealers Rene Gimpel and Nathan Wildenstein. Ownership passed from the Vanderbilt family in 1922.

In 1945, 645 Fifth Avenue was demolished for the Best & Company store, which in turn was taken down in 1970 for the present Olympic Tower. The later development uses the air rights of 647 Fifth Avenue, which is the only one of the Vanderbilts' Fifth Avenue buildings to survive.

CARTIER

52ND STREET AND FIFTH AVENUE

BY THE TURN OF THE CENTURY, the Vanderbilts were heavily invested, financially and emotionally, in the future of Fifth Avenue just at the time other mansion builders were moving uptown. In early 1901, Vanderbilt sold the corner parcel at Fifth and 52nd Street to the railroad investor Morton Plant. Plant hired an architect, Robert W. Gibson, to build a richly finished limestone house. When finished in 1905, it was surrounded by an iron fence protecting a deep areaway, with a side-street entrance—Plant used the address 2 East 52nd Street.

But just as William K. Vanderbilt was able to pin down one corner, another came into play. He had bought the northeast corner to prevent another commercial project, reselling to the banker James Henry Smith. But Smith changed his mind about the future of this strip of Fifth Avenue and declined to build. Vanderbilt then thought his problems were solved in 1905 when Frederick G. Bourne, head of the Singer Sewing Machine Company, bought the lot, but Bourne, too, got cold feet—by that time the St. Regis and the Gotham Hotels were beginning to tower over 55th and Fifth.

Morton Plant, gazing out his 52nd Street windows, must have begun wondering about the wisdom of putting his cards in with the Vanderbilts. The first actual business building went up in 1907, at 712 Fifth Avenue, near 56th Street, where the Paris jewelry firm Cartier opened its first New York shop, in 1909. "The advent of the first shops into this sacred precinct brought amazement and indignation to those who dwelt therein," the *New York Times* editorialized, but soon "they experienced that comfortable sensation that invariably accompanies successful investments."

The Vanderbilts' former allies began to desert, and by 1910 even the Vanderbilts conceded, selling the northeast corner of 52nd Street to a developer who built something unthinkable five years before, a garment factory. Still Plant remained, even past

FIG 77.1

MORTON PLANT'S HOUSE *before storefront alterations by Cartier.* COURTESY CARTIER ARCHIVES

FIG 77.2

MORTON PLANT'S HOUSE *after alterations by Cartier.* COURTESY CARTIER ARCHIVES

1911, when the city ordered him to cut back his fence and areaway facing Fifth Avenue; now anyone could sidle up to his Fifth Avenue drawing room windows and look in.

How the Cartier jewelry firm came to acquire the Plant house is a famous story, usually told along the lines of those given in Hans Nadelhoffer's opulent 1984 book, *Cartier—Jewelers Extraordinary*. "Cartier proposed a deal in 1917 to buy the building in exchange for his most valuable two-strand pearl necklace," valued at $1 million, which Plant's wife, Mae, admired, Mr. Nadelhoffer says. Plant agreed, and Cartier moved in.

The "string of pearls" story is now a favorite anecdote for a long-lost chapter in Fifth Avenue history, even though there is something a little off about it. Plant leased the house to Cartier in 1916, a whole year before the supposed trade; and he bought a house site on 86th and Fifth a year before that. But there must be some truth to it, for after the death of Mae Plant (by then Mae Rovensky) in 1956, Parke-Bernet sold a two-strand string of pearls identified at that time as the one traded for the house. They brought only $151,000, far below their $1 million value when she got them—pearls fell in value after the cultured variety came on the market. The jewelry firm says that no one at Cartier knows where the pearls are now.

BEEKMAN TERRACE

455 EAST 51ST STREET

IN THE EARLY 1920S, SOME GENTRIFIERS began fixing up the old brownstones on Beekman Place. But the biggest change took place in 1924 when Joseph B. Thomas bought the plot at the foot of East 51st Street on the north side, then a collection of wooden industrial buildings. Thomas, born in Boston, had admired Fenway Court, the Venetian-style building in his hometown that is now the Isabella Stewart Gardner Museum. In 1910, he had redeveloped East 19th Street between Irving Place and Third Avenue as the "Block Beautiful," transforming the declining brownstones with bright stucco and romantic ironwork.

On the 51st Street plot Thomas had the architects Treanor & Fatio design a six-story apartment house of Venetian design overlooking the water. The earliest design, published in 1924, showed the building with a light court facing the river and a covered arcade with a few steps down to the water.

This was soon revised to a south-facing light court, which gave fewer river views but better light, and a more developed treatment at the riverside—an open lawn

EARLY RENDERING FOR BEEKMAN TERRACE, 1924. COURTESY OFFICE FOR METROPOLITAN HISTORY

bounded by an urn-topped balustrade leading to a Venetian-style dock. There was also an upper garden area, leading to 51st Street.

The principal river traffic at the time was coal barges and tugboats, but in 1924 the *Real Estate Record and Guide* praised the anticipated Beekman Terrace, noting that "the absence of gondolas alone prevents a full conception of the Italian atmosphere," adding that "a profusion of trees and other planting will make the river bank at this

EARLY RENDERING FOR BEEKMAN TERRACE, 1924. COURTESY OFFICE FOR METROPOLITAN HISTORY

point a garden spot." The irregular brick facade is decorated with terra-cotta plaques showing the lion, the symbol of Venice's patron, St. Mark, and maritime symbols recalling Venice's days as a trading empire.

Continuing the Venetian conceit, Thomas's wife, the muralist Clara Fargo Thomas, wrote that New Yorkers were "only just beginning to realize what our waterfronts might mean to us," adding that they provided "an opportunity for the wealth of our present merchant and banker princes to beautify their city."

The $600,000 co-op, with about forty-five apartments, was completed in 1925, and the earliest shareholders included Harold Pulsifer, the poet and editor of *Outlook* magazine, and Charles Poore, book reviewer for the *New York Times*. The territory must have seemed remote, for advertisements for the apartments promised private jitney service.

Original drawings for the building do not call out any unusual uses for the two floors below the grade of 51st Street, but an illustration published in *Arts & Decoration* in 1924 shows a large Gothic-style, leaded-glass window at the level of the river, as if leading to some sort of club room.

The East River Drive wiped out all the interesting wrinkles of the waterfront in the 1940s, and photographs at the time show the lower garden area as a simple grassy area surrounded by a perimeter of hedges. But the constantly increasing traffic on the drive has left the lower garden about as peaceful as the median on the Grand Central Parkway. As in many other cases, one of the biggest threats to our architectural heritage is our own automobile culture.

THE 1 BEEKMAN PLACE GARAGE

THE BEEKMAN FAMILY, COLONIAL-ERA MERCHANTS, built a riverfront mansion near the foot of East 50th Street in 1764. Many sources say that the patriot-spy Nathan Hale was first arraigned there after his capture by the British in 1776. By the mid–nineteenth century the East River waterfront had fallen far from its resort status, and coal

FIG 79.1

PART ONE OF A TWO-PART PANORAMA OF 1 BEEKMAN PLACE IN 1934, *with the garage at right.* COURTESY MUNICIPAL ARCHIVES

yards, lumber mills, and other industries dotted the shoreline, at least where there was good river access. Perhaps because the Beekman mansion's grounds were on a high, rocky bluff without good water access, the house remained standing until the 1870s.

But in 1865 the family sold off much of its land around the newly established Beekman Place, including most of the river-facing lots between 49th and 51st Streets. To protect the light and air of the brownstone row houses that soon went up at 13–39 Beekman Place, the Beekmans promised to restrict the height of future buildings on their remaining waterfront strip of land, directly below the houses, to no higher than that of Beekman Place itself.

By the turn of the century bigger and bigger factories were crowding the shoreline—among them the huge Cremo cigar factory on the current site of River House at 52nd Street—and the once-genteel private houses were filled with boarders. Still, a clipping from the *New York Sun* at the Museum of the City of New York, undated but probably from the 1910s, painted a bucolic picture of the clifftop houses looking down on the rocky shore below: "Mothers in the neighborhood take their knitting and embroidery every afternoon and bask in the shade. . . . Even Coney Island and Rockaway have nothing on the beach at Beekman Place."

By this time the Beekman family estate was trying to void the 1865 height restriction on the waterfront strip—with a free hand, it said, it could have wiped out the beach

FIG 79.2

PART TWO OF A TWO-PART PANORAMA OF 1 BEEKMAN PLACE IN 1934.
COURTESY MUNICIPAL ARCHIVES

and replaced it with a giant steam plant. In 1920 the *New York Times* reported on what had been a six-year fight to remove the restrictions, which the row house owners on Beekman Place had fought strenuously to keep. The Beekmans' lawyer, Herbert L. Fordham, said that radical changes in the area should void the restriction because it was ridiculous to hang on to the "half-forgotten vision of terraces and gardens . . . in the midst of towering steam plants, electric light plants, and coal pockets. New York needs its waterfront for business."

By 1922 the Beekmans gave up the fight and leased the waterfront strip—460 feet long, stretching from 49th up to 51st, and including the empty plot on Beekman Place now occupied by 1 Beekman Place. The lease was acquired by a development group that announced plans for a studio apartment on the Beekman Place frontage, and a one-story garage on the waterfront strip. The studio apartment was not built, but the garage, designed by John J. Dunnigan, later a state senator from the Bronx, did go up. It had simple rubble-stone walls and a curved, wood-truss roof. The garage entrance was at 49th Street.

Perhaps the Beekmans should have held out, because just as they surrendered, fashion came to Beekman Place, and house after house was turned into elite occupancy. The natural outcome, for the empty plot at the south end of Beekman Place, was the luxurious sixteen-story co-op at 1 Beekman, built in 1930 by a syndicate headed by David M. Milton, the son-in-law of John D. Rockefeller Jr. Milton's wife, Abby, was called by the *New York Times* "the wealthiest young woman in America." The Times reported that the couple was taking an eighteen-room triplex with a 33-by-25-foot living room. The building had 335 rooms divided among twenty-four apartments, most of which were duplexes.

Milton's syndicate reached an accommodation with the garage operator and reduced the southerly section of the garage to a narrow driveway encased in the building and running through 1 Beekman's waterside complex of tea room, gym, swimming pool, squash courts, and additional duplex apartments. Early tenants at 1 Beekman included the diplomat David K. E. Bruce, William J. Donovan—who founded the Office of Strategic Services, the forerunner of the CIA—the Miltons, and John D. Rockefeller III.

The architects were Sloan & Robertson, with Corbett, Harrison & MacMurray. The latter firm was also designing Rockefeller Center, for John D. Rockefeller Jr. Rockefeller lent his son-in-law $1 million to build 1 Beekman, and the contractor was Webster B. Todd, whose father, John R. Todd, was working with Rockefeller on the plans for Rockefeller Center. The younger Todd also took an apartment in the building; his daughter, Christine Todd Whitman, is the former governor of New Jersey.

Photographs of the garage in the 1930s show that people still sat along the water's edge, and it was not the Beekmans but the East River Drive, completed in 1939 in this section, that finally wiped out the quiet river view even though a small park, reaching from 49th to 51st Streets, was inserted between the garage and the highway. Although now the traffic noise is almost overwhelming, over time the park has grown in, and the garage structure was surrounded by weeds, trees, and vines, many growing out of the clifflike retaining wall rising above the garage up to Beekman Place. From the park the garage was mysterious—the southern third in the polite Georgian style of 1 Beekman Place incongruously joined to the northern two-thirds, a primitive, anonymous structure.

Recently, the 1 Beekman Place co-op rebuilt the garage—but they were very careful to retain their views.

THE MUSEUM OF MODERN ART

11 WEST 53RD STREET

THE MUSEUM OF MODERN ART OPENED IN 1929 in rented rooms in what is now called the Crown Building, at 57th and Fifth Avenue. Struggling against the orthodoxy of the Metropolitan Museum of Art, the Modern championed, sometimes sanctimoniously, the cubists, surrealists, and others whose art was still controversial and, to some, a joke.

In 1932 the Modern moved to a limestone town house at 11 West 53rd, backing up on the West 54th Street family compound of the Rockefellers, who were important supporters of the museum. In the 1930s there was occasional talk of extending Rockefeller Plaza two blocks north to 53rd Street, and in mid-1936 the museum trustees, hoping to be the terminus of the unusual street, acquired the row houses flanking their little headquarters, a full 129 feet of frontage for a new building.

FIG 80.1

THE MUSEUM OF MODERN ART *under construction in 1938.* COURTESY ALBERT ROTHSCHILD, THE MUSEUM OF MODERN ART ARCHIVES

The Museum of Modern Art set itself apart from traditional museums by including not only painting and sculpture but photography, movies, industrial art, and architecture. Alfred Barr, the museum's first director, was adamant that a first-class modern architect be retained. To him that meant Walter Gropius, J. J. P. Oud, or Mies van der Rohe; they were all Europeans, but no Americans had comparable experience with the International Style.

However, a museum trustee, Philip Goodwin, had been asked to make designs for a much smaller museum project. Because he was handy and agreeable, he was becoming the architect for the new building. Goodwin, a traditionalist, had accepted the need to have a designer of modern training work with him on the project. Perhaps because of the influence of one trustee, Nelson Rockefeller, this turned out to be the young Edward Durell Stone, who had worked on Rockefeller Center.

Because the museum's building plans kept shifting, Barr had let the matter slide. But the point of no return was the summer of 1936—when Barr was in Europe to research an exhibit on Surrealism to open in December. In a 1983 article in the *Journal of the Archives of American Art*, Rona Roob, archivist of the Museum of Modern Art, published the frantic tangle of cables, letters, and messages from the desperate Barr, who accused Nelson Rockefeller of reneging on a promise to wait for Barr's return from Europe and hire a European.

But Goodwin and Stone remained the architects of the most important modernist architectural commission in New York to that date. Goodwin and Stone executed so many studies of their designs, it is hard to guess whether the architects were having a lot of fun or going crazy trying to satisfy their clients.

FIG 80.2

A GROUP EXAMINES A MODEL OF THE MUSEUM, *including Philip Goodwin (extreme left, pointing), Alfred H. Barr (fourth from left), Stephen Clark (fifth from left), and Nelson Rockefeller (third from right).* COURTESY ROBERT M. DAMORA, THE MUSEUM OF MODERN ART ARCHIVES

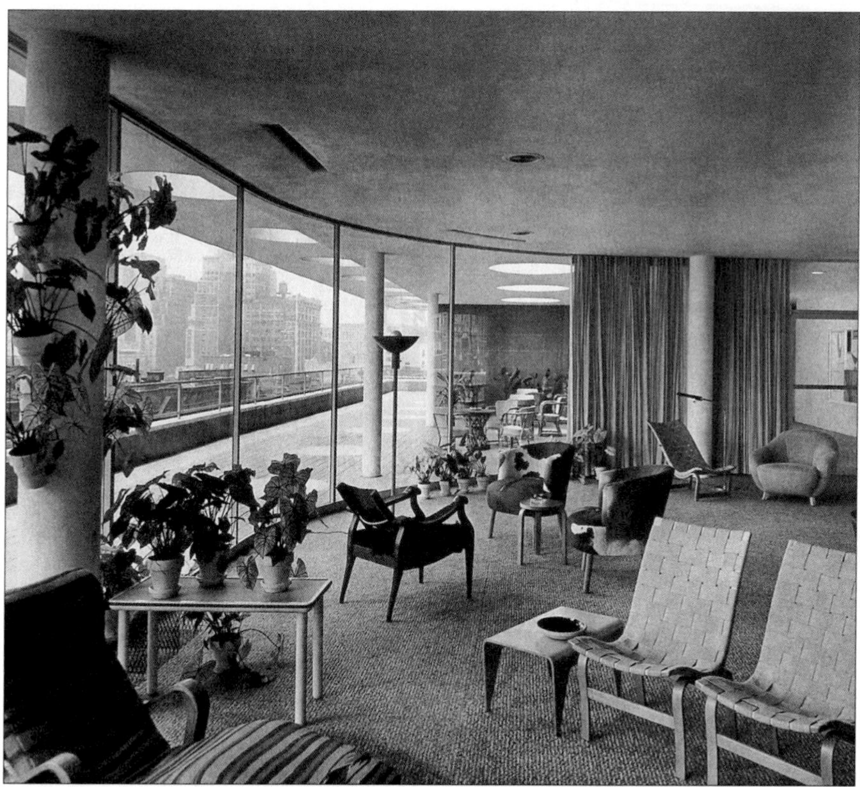

THE MUSEUM OF MODERN ART'S MEMBERS' PENTHOUSE, 1944 COURTESY ROBERT M. DAMORA, THE MUSEUM OF MODERN ART ARCHIVES

Plans kept changing radically even after they filed plans at the Department of Buildings in 1937, but the finished structure was opened in May 1939 with an exhibit pointedly titled *Art in Our Time*. The facade was of deeply veined white marble, with a setback roof story topped by a brise-soleil with round cutouts. The marble did not go below the second floor—the ground floor was just glass. On the second and third floors were square panels of a milky glazing, Thermolux, that filtered light into the galleries. (Within a decade these were covered over by exhibit designers hungry for wall space.)

The opening ceremonies were full of forward-thinking, properly modern sentiments, like those of Edsel Ford, a trustee, who predicted that in the near future everyone's house would be filled with "museum quality" furnishings. Only Walt Disney speaking from Hollywood sounded an ominous off-note. He said, "We'll seem as funny to posterity as an old silent picture looks to us."

Critics were bowled over by the sculpture garden and the simple, modern interiors and were generally pleased with the facade. Henry McBride, writing in the *New York Sun*, was the most doubtful, writing that although it had "been disturbing New Yorkers" for some time "the extreme cleanliness of the affair mitigates somewhat the nudity." But he added that "the Matisses and Picassos and Miros burn with new fire."

Although the museum is now mostly straight lines and gray and white, the 1939 structure was full of angles, curves and color. The gallery partitions were set at a cant, and a curved marquee was reflected by the curved reception desk inside. Blue tile ran up the sides and all over the top; red marble sprang out at you on the ground floor, and the Thermolux was a rich, milky white.

FIG 80.4 THE MUSEUM OF MODERN ART'S MEMBERS' ROOF TERRACE. COURTESY UNIVERSITY OF ARKANSAS LIBRARIES, SPECIAL COLLECTIONS.

Three days after the attack on Pearl Harbor the Modern protected its windows with big, temporary X's of linen framing tape, but that was the only change to the facade until 1958, when firemen chopped out a third of the Thermolux panels to fight a blaze that killed one person. After that the curved canopy was replaced and the panels were either all replaced or altered to eliminate their variegated, milky quality. Age has diminished the veining in the marble, and the facade has acquired a monotone character.

At various times flanking and rear additions replaced the old private houses, lessening the Modern's original shock. Then in 1984 the new Museum Tower, a fifty-two-story condominium apartment building on the museum's roof, opened; Cesar Pelli's design was meant to echo the original building but instead further deadened its effect. And a massive new construction project to the west is under way now.

But what will be impossible to recapture will be the fresh optimism that the Museum of Modern Art brought to West 53rd Street in 1939, as it elbowed its way between the old brownstones and town houses. By making them seem instantly old-fashioned, the 1939 Modern seemed instantly up to date; without their context, and shorn of its original details, it appears to be the back end of a back office, something that no one cared about, let alone fought over.

4 EAST 54TH STREET

THIS RESERVED LIMESTONE TOWN HOUSE was built in 1898–1900 by William Earl Dodge Stokes for himself, his son, and his wife, Rita Hernandez de Alba de Costa. The forty-two-year-old Stokes married her in 1895 when she was nineteen, after falling in love with her picture in a Fifth Avenue photographer's window.

Stokes, a member of the Phelps-Dodge family, with a huge mining fortune, is better known in New York for his real estate development. Lori Zabar has studied his career and has documented the seventy-four row houses he built on the Upper West Side beginning in 1885, as well as his most famous project, the 1902 Ansonia Hotel. Stokes began the Ansonia in 1897 while living in one of his West Side row houses and in 1898 retained McKim, Mead & White to design a new house for his family.

It is a grand, Italian Renaissance design, but without the life or inspiration of the best works of the firm. In 1902, the *Real Estate Record and Guide* called it "tranquil, simple and not ineffective," but observed that the low ground floor seemed cramped.

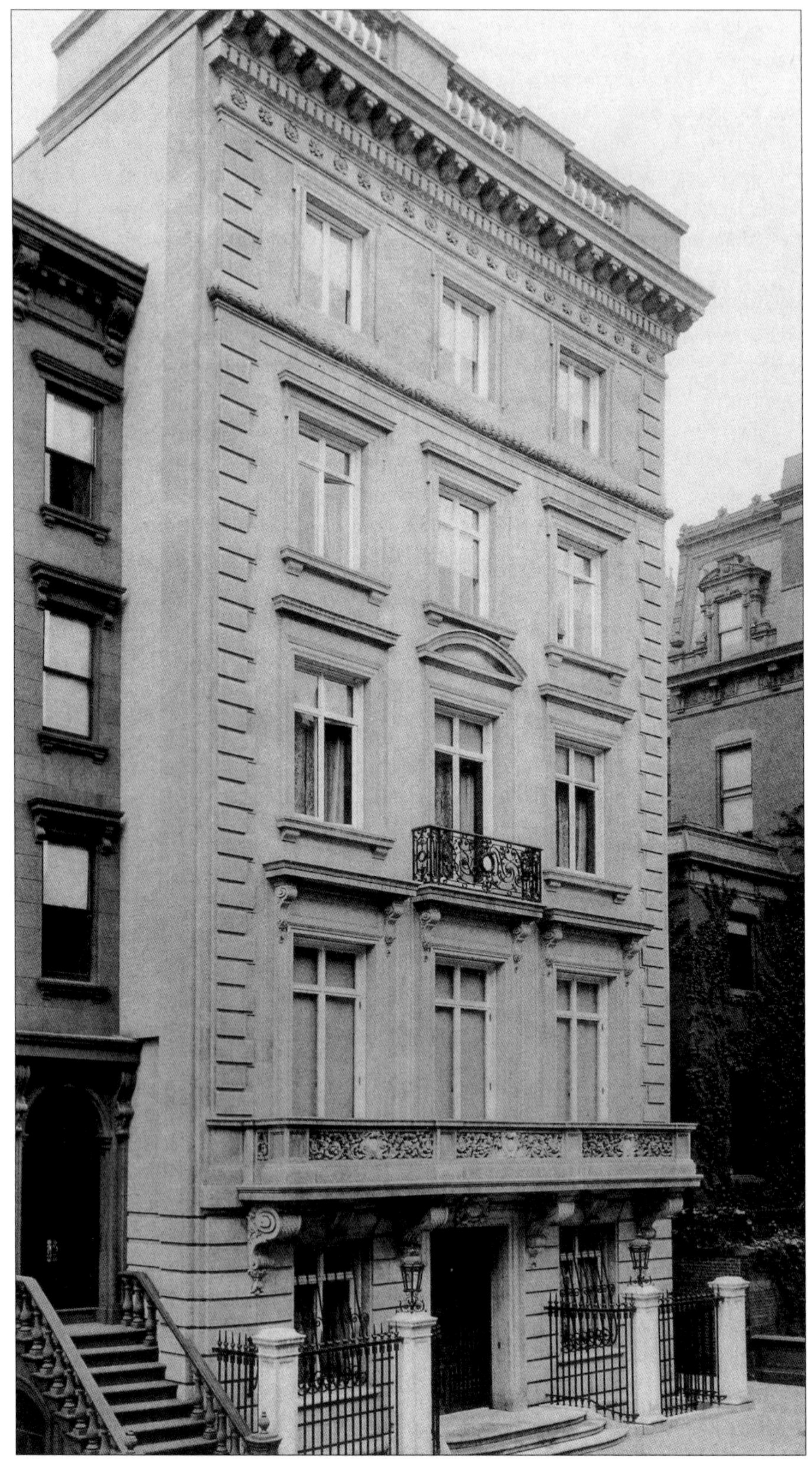

4 EAST 54TH STREET IN 1900. COURTESY OFFICE FOR METROPOLITAN HISTORY

Newspapers regularly reported on suits between Stokes and other family members, and on his sexual escapades. Phyllis Dodge's *Tales of the Phelps-Dodge Family* says that, on their wedding night at the Waldorf-Astoria, "the brutality of the groom and the outraged innocence of the bride" caused the hotel staff to intervene. In April 1900, Mrs. Stokes filed for divorce.

In January 1900 Stokes sold the house to William H. and Ada Moore. Moore, a corporation lawyer, had almost gone bankrupt in 1896, during speculation on Diamond Match Company stock but was soon back on his feet. In 1910, the *New York Times* profiled him with seven other financial titans, including Henry Frick and J. Pierpont Morgan.

The 1910 census provides a good picture of the typical population of an upper-class residence. There were Mr. and Mrs. Moore, ages sixty-two and forty-nine, both native-born Americans. They shared the house with nine servants. Edward Makely, the forty-year-old butler, was the only native-born American.

The others had all arrived in America between 1899 and 1908: the Scottish private secretary Mary Clark, forty; the Scottish second butler, James Finnie, twenty-nine; the Swedish cook, Sigurd Swansson, thirty-one; three Finnish maids—Helmi Mikkaner, nineteen, Betty Knusmein, thirty-one, and Anna Okkonen, twenty-five—and two Irish maids, Margaret Murphy, twenty-eight, and Alice Larcey, twenty-four.

The Moores died in the house—he in 1923 and his wife in 1955. Since then the house has gone through several commercial and nonprofit owners, and was designated a landmark in 1967. Even though it long ago went into commercial use, the exterior is almost untouched, and preserves the illusion of 4 East 54th Street as a real house.

FIG 81.2

WILLIAM EARLE DODGE STOKES
REAL ESTATE OPERATOR AND BUILDER
CAPITALIST. TRUSTEE KENSICO CEMETERY

WILLIAM E. D. STOKES.
COURTESY OFFICE FOR METROPOLITAN HISTORY

CENTRAL SYNAGOGUE

55TH STREET AND LEXINGTON AVENUE

CENTRAL SYNAGOGUE, ORIGINALLY KNOWN AS AHAWATH CHESED, was founded in 1846 by immigrants from Prague and the nearby regions of what was then Bohemia. In 1864 the congregation took over an old church building at Avenue C and Fourth Street, and by 1869 it had decided to move uptown.

Of the group that raised money for the new temple, most lived on the Lower East Side. But many lived in the developing area north of the new Grand Central Terminal, and the congregation bought the southwest corner of 55th Street and Lexington Avenue.

Nineteenth-century Jewish congregations were much concerned about the appropriate style for their synagogues; centuries of religious oppression had left very few historic patterns to emulate. In 1866 a congregation headed by Rabbi Isaac Mayer Wise built a synagogue in Cincinnati in the Moorish style, which in part recalled the medieval flowering of Jewish culture in Spain before the Inquisition.

Like the Cincinnati congregation, Ahawath Chesed was Reform. The members hired the architect Henry Fernbach, and he developed a design in the same spirit, in New Jersey brownstone and a contrasting lighter Ohio stone. Anne Mininberg, the synagogue's archivist, said that Rabbi Wise, considered one of the founders of Reform Judaism in the United States, laid the cornerstone in 1870.

In a city where Christian churches predominated, the resulting building was a spectacular work of horseshoe-shaped Moorish arches in two colors, with twin towers topped by globes with gilded banding. The congregation also installed specially designed streetlamps on the sidewalk.

The building's exterior contrasts the two different stones like chocolate and vanilla, but the interior is eye-popping in its geometric polychromy. Maroon, gold, green, and azure jump out from a dizzying array of stenciled painting.

The synagogue has never fully researched the original finishes, but from early photographs it appears that the basic interior paint scheme is largely unchanged, although it is now lighter—a remarkable survival. Not everything, though, has been saved. In 1872, the *New York Times* reported that the brilliantly colored interior was set off by ebonized woodwork.

John Strauss, the father of a congregation member, has translated the nineteenth-century German-language minutes of the board of trustees. He has run across evidence of the competing issues in synagogue design. Some board members resisted an ornate design, saying: "Excess promotes envy, grudges and hate on the part of our enemies. . . .

We need neither towers nor architectural scrolls on the outside, nor interior ornaments that are overloaded with gold and multicolored splendor."

In 1920, as the midtown area was gradually razed and rebuilt, the temple changed its name to Central Synagogue. Other congregations replaced their Victorian buildings, and the Moorish style became an embarrassment to Reform Jews who generally emphasized assimilation. The old Temple Emanuel-El, at 43rd Street and Fifth Avenue, and the former home of Congregation Rodeph Sholom, at 63rd Street and Lexington Avenue, two Victorian temples, were demolished after 1910.

FIG 82.1

CENTRAL SYNAGOGUE IN 1872. COURTESY CENTRAL SYNAGOGUE ARCHIVE

In an article in *American Architect and Building News* in 1908, the synagogue architect Arnold Brunner offered a typical criticism of the Moorish style, saying it strengthened "the impression that the Jew was necessarily an alien, and did not wish to be regarded as an American." But, after the synagogue recently suffered a disastrous fire, the congregation chose to rebuild in the original 1872 style.

THE BERGDORF GOODMAN BUILDING

57TH STREET AND FIFTH AVENUE

THE LUXURY-GOODS STORE THAT CAME TO OCCUPY the west side of the block from 57th to 58th Streets was founded when Edwin Goodman, a tailor, teamed up with Herman Bergdorf in 1901 and then took over their women's clothing business in 1903. In 1927, Mr. Goodman had plans to lease space at the northeast corner of 52nd and Fifth, but a better site became available: the old Cornelius Vanderbilt mansion, on Fifth from 57th to 58th.

Alice G. Vanderbilt, widow of Cornelius Vanderbilt II, was tired of paying $130,000 a year in taxes on the forty-five-year-old palace, and a plan to redevelop the site with a fifty-two-story apartment hotel had fallen through in 1926.

Frederick Brown, a real estate agent, made a deal with Mrs. Vanderbilt, and in 1928 erected not a skyscraper but a set of seven- and nine-story shops—a mansion-style commercial building.

Mr. Brown's architects, Buchman & Kahn, faced the buildings with white marble, echoing the Metropolitan Club, the lower floors of the Plaza Hotel, and especially Marble Row, a group of sixty-year-old houses then directly across Fifth Avenue. The facades were decorated with slightly different elements of low-relief sculpture, but it is the low mass of the complex, with its green-tiled mansard roofs, that is its distinguishing characteristic.

The shops had separate staircases, storefronts, and elevators. Early tenants included Van Cleef & Arpels, the linen store Grande Maison de Blanc, and, at the 57th Street corner, Dobbs the hatter.

Mr. Goodman had chosen the 58th Street corner during the early stages of construction and had arranged with Mr. Brown to convert the entire ninth floor of the

THE BERGDORF GOODMAN BUILDING *on Fifth Avenue in 1953.* COURTESY OFFICE FOR METROPOLITAN HISTORY

Bergdorf Goodman corner into an apartment. When the store opened in 1928, he sold his brownstone at 320 West 71st Street and moved in. Mr. Goodman bought his own section in 1935 and the rest of the structure gradually, owning it all by 1948.

A 1928 ad in the magazine *Country Life in America* laid out Mr. Goodman's ideals for his store: "Here women of critical taste may observe clothes of the highest fashion. . . . One may judge, before purchasing, how such clothes will look when worn in one's own drawing room."

The French Renaissance interiors were almost bare of display cases and racks. Instead, customers were met by saleswomen who brought out individual pieces for inspection, like high-end art dealers.

In 1952, *Time* magazine called Bergdorf Goodman "Fifth Avenue's finest" store and noted that customers did not pick through racks but were accompanied by a "vendeuse."

The vendeuses included Kay Summersby, Dwight D. Eisenhower's wartime aide, and the Grand Duchess Marie of Russia. *Time* recounted a story about the industrialist Henry Kaiser, who, protesting a three-week wait for his wife's mink coat, exclaimed, "I can build an oceangoing ship in a week." "Mr. Kaiser," Mr. Goodman replied, "you are a great man. I am only a furrier." *Time* said Bergdorf Goodman grossed $11 million a year.

Mr. Goodman died in his penthouse in 1953, and the apartment is now retail space.

THE OSBORNE

205 WEST 57TH STREET

IN 1883 THE STONE DEALER THOMAS OSBORNE conceived a grand project, a giant apartment house rivaling the Dakota, then rising above Central Park West. In 1885 he completed the Osborne, with an unusual staggered arrangement—eleven floors of high-ceilinged rooms in the front and fourteen floors of lower-ceilinged bedroom floors in the back.

Perhaps because of the scale of the project, Osborne hired the architect James E. Ware, who had won a competition for model tenements in 1879. For the period, there is little wasted space in the apartments, which are studded with Queen Anne–style iron and woodwork, decorative glass, and unusual fireplaces. Many original apartments survive intact.

The exterior of the Osborne aggressively captures the eye, perhaps 30,000 square feet of craggy brownstone. This huge clunky mass neatly defeats stylistic description, and it is really the vernacular of the practical builder, quite innocent of aesthetic pretension. The *Real Estate Record and Guide*, unappreciative of the comic transparency of Osborne's effort, called the facade "crude and unskillful."

Early proposals called for a florist, doctor, and pharmacist in the building, and an all-weather croquet lawn on the roof, although there is no indication that any of these were carried out. But the Osborne does boast an astonishing lobby, the most sumptuous in New York, a sparkling treasure chest of marble, mosaic, metal, and glass, which the co-op has also recently restored.

A reverse directory of 1885 lists twenty-nine families in the building's forty-eight apartments. Of these, prior addresses can be determined for twenty-three: Seven came from row houses in Manhattan, nine from the suburbs, and seven from other apartments or hotels. One of those who came from a hotel—the old Hotel Vendome at 41st and Broadway—was J. Walter Thompson, the advertising agency founder.

Osborne intended to sell the building on completion, but he extended himself too far. He lost it at a foreclosure sale that brought $1,009,000 for a building that had cost him $1,209,250. He continued in his stone business, but his next project was a modest set of three tenements at 428–432 East 92nd Street, across from his stoneyard.

A later owner extended the Osborne at the top and on the 57th Street side, and in 1919 created retail space, which took up the entire ground floor except for the entrance and lobby. In 1961 the architect Robert Bien filed plans for a seventeen-story replacement building, a project forestalled by a co-op conversion the next year.

THE OSBORNE *on 57th Street and Seventh Avenue, circa 1885.* COURTESY THE NEW-YORK HISTORICAL SOCIETY, NEW YORK CITY

Early accounts refer to stones of different colors used in the facade. This is unusual for a period in which brownstone was used for its rocky effect rather than for color. However, this variety has been lost by overpainting in a monotonous, flat brown, which defeats a considered judgment of the Osborne.

In recent years a cleaning of the Osborne, supervised by the architect Walter Melvin, has brought back some of the subtle polychromy of the Osborne, returning what's left of the lower balconies to their tan, gray, and taupe stonework.

130 AND 140 WEST 57TH STREET

THE TWO STUDIO BUILDINGS AT 130 AND 140 WEST 57TH STREET went up in 1908 to designs by Pollard & Steinam. They were put up as cooperatives and the original syndicates were apparently arranged by the artist Robert Vonnoh, who was involved with earlier cooperative studio construction on West 67th Street. In 1907, he built 39 West 67th Street, designed by the same architects.

The original configuration of 130 and 140 was five apartments to a floor, with two simplex apartments at the rear, two duplex apartments (with double height studios), and one nonhousekeeping studio at the front. In the 1910s many artists and writers lived in the buildings: like the writer William Dean Howells and the painter Childe Hassam, who was a longtime resident of 130; the unusual trapezoidal window appears in some of his paintings of interiors.

FIG 85.1

130 AND 140 WEST 57TH STREET ABOUT 1908.
COURTESY LIBRARY OF CONGRESS

Hassam's studio was on the thirteenth floor west. That means the society figure Marion Wilson lived just below him, because in 1921 Hassam testified in court that he frequently had to jump up and down on the floor to complain about ragtime concerts at Mrs. Wilson's apartment. "Discords, yelling, catcalling," the painter described them to the *New York Times*. "It's an absolute riot." The filmmaker D. W. Griffith lived at 130 in 1925.

The co-op at 130 failed in the 1930s, and in 1947 it was bought by the Jedwabnik/Van Doren family, which continued an artist-friendly policy. Later tenants included Joseph Heller and Jose Ferrer, who often came to the Jedwabniks' New Year's Eve parties. Lydia Jedwabnik painted the dancers on her windows in honor of a visit by the Moiseyev Ballet Company.

The Jedwabnick/Van Doren family has good lease records back to 1947, so they can document exactly which space Ray Charles rented, where the Rolling Stones practiced, and where Woody Allen's production company rented from the 1960s to the 1990s. They have filled the lobby with memorabilia of the history of the building, including a lease to the writer Joseph Heller; a letter to Mark Twain from William Dean Howells (on 130 West 57th Street letterhead); reproductions of Childe Hassam's paintings showing the windows; and photographs of the painting studio of Irving Wiles—and, on one wall, a giant mural salvaged from the old Russian Tea Room.

This sense of tradition makes 130 West 57th Street all the more unusual, in a city that sometimes seems determined to forget its own history.

THE OLD AMERICAN SOCETY OF CIVIL ENGINEERS' CLUBHOUSE

220 WEST 57TH STREET

THE LIGHT, SOPHISTICATED FRONT of the American Society of Civil Engineers' Building fit right in with the artistic ambience of West 57th, with Carnegie Hall, which was completed in 1891 at Seventh Avenue, and with the 1892 Art Students League building across the street. In 1903, only six years later, the engineers received an offer that few would refuse: a gift of $1 million from Andrew Carnegie to join with the American Society of Mining Engineers, the American Institute of Electrical Engineers, and the American Society of Mechanical Engineers in a combined high-rise professional building. But refuse it they did, because of concerns about a loss of autonomy, even though there were already complaints about the small size of the auditorium.

In 1905 the society brought the original architect, Cyrus Eidlitz, back to expand the building to the west. Still, the members must have marveled in 1907 when the new

THE CLUBHOUSE OF THE AMERICAN SOCIETY OF CIVIL ENGINEERS IN 1898.
COURTESY OFFICE FOR METROPOLITAN HISTORY

thirteen-story Engineering Societies' Building, built by Carnegie for the other organizations, was completed at 29 West 39th Street, with a communal library, one thousand-seat auditorium and other shared facilities.

That was about the time that Nora Stanton Blatch, a Cornell University engineering graduate, was admitted to junior membership in the ASCE, a category for professionals just starting their careers. Late in 1915, age made her ineligible for junior membership, and she applied for associate membership. But the society turned her down, and in 1916 she sued in New York State Supreme Court to force the society to accept her. By that time she was Nora De Forest—she had married the inventor Lee De Forest in 1908, but they were divorced in 1911—and she had worked for various steel companies, as well as on the extension of the subway system along Lexington Avenue and lower Seventh Avenue.

The society defended itself by saying that she did not meet the test for associate membership because of inexperience, but she said the refusal was pure sexual discrimination. Her grandmother was the women's rights advocate Elizabeth Cady Stanton, and she was president of the Women's Political Union, a suffrage organization. The court ruled for the engineering society, citing the society's status as a private organization. A few years later, she moved to Greenwich, Connecticut, where she fought for women's rights while working as a real estate developer. She died in 1971.

The year the lawsuit was filed, the society made plans to join the other engineering groups on West 39th Street, and the 57th Street building was leased to several parties, and then, in 1928, to Schrafft's, whose famous lunchrooms were beginning to blossom all over the city. The Schrafft's architect, Charles E. Birge, put the company's trademark white marble with green trim on the building, where Schrafft's remained until the early 1970s.

THE ALWYN COURT

180 WEST 58TH STREET

BY 1900 SEVENTH AVENUE AROUND CARNEGIE HALL had New York's most important collection of apartment houses: the block-long Van Corlear, from 55th to 56th Street; the Rembrandt (New York's first co-op) at 152 West 57th; the massive Osborne at 201 West 57th; and the eight-building Navarro Flats, stretching east from Seventh Avenue at Central Park South.

In 1907 a group including Alwyn Ball Jr., bought a Seventh Avenue plot at the southeast corner of 58th Street; in September of the same year the *Real Estate Record and Guide* reported the building project would be a "studio palace," designed by Harde & Short. The Alwyn Court had two apartments per floor, each with fourteen rooms and five baths, renting for up to $10,000 a year; one thirty-two-room duplex was offered at $22,000 per year. Harde & Short created a plan with a square, twelve-story central light court and groups of entertaining spaces—music room, living room, library, dining room, gallery, and conservatory—which could be thrown together to create 2,000 square feet. In the typical apartment, the largest room was 18 by 30 feet.

The magazine *Architecture* praised the "consummate skill" of the terra-cotta work and the "considerable charm" of the entrance. But it added that while the design of the facade "if made by a pastry cook, would be of the highest excellence . . . it can hardly be considered at all in the light of architecture." The overall result, it said, "defies description."

ALWYN COURT IN 1910. COURTESY LIBRARY OF CONGRESS

In late 1909, the Alwyn Court opened to tenants. Most of them moved from private houses, like Jacob Wertheim, president of United Cigar Stores, who left a 50-foot-wide house at 5 West 76th Street to occupy the duplex. Another was Frederick Steinway; in 1925, as president of his family's piano company, Steinway moved the firm from East 14th Street to its new headquarters at 119 West 57th Street.

Only five apartments had been taken by the night of March 4, 1910, when Patrick Quinn, a doorman, saw the reflection of flames in the windows of the Navarro Flats across 58th Street. He raced to alert the occupants, and Edward King and Robert Casson ran the elevator through the smoke until the motor shorted out.

No one was seriously hurt, although three housemaids, thinking the entire building was in flames, almost jumped from the roof to Seventh Avenue.

"Great Blaze Lights the City," said the *New York Tribune* on page one, and ten thousand people watched; the *Times* described the Alwyn Court as "a huge torch." The fire had started in an unoccupied apartment on the ninth floor and broken through the windows; tongues of fire leapfrogged the blaze to the top.

By 1937 the building was empty as Seventh Avenue fell out of fashion, and the interior was gutted in 1938, creating seventy-five apartments where there had been two dozen.

HAMPSHIRE HOUSE

150 CENTRAL PARK SOUTH

IN 1884 JOSE DE NAVARRO COMPLETED HIS VAST, eight-building cooperative, the Navarro Flats, at 150 to 180 Central Park South running back to West 58th Street. The Navarro Flats failed, and when its eight buildings were put up for sale in the '20s the first replacement building begun was what is now known as Hampshire House, designed in 1926 by A. Rollin Caughey and William F. Evans Jr. Its site fronts 117 feet on Central Park South and 127 feet on 58th Street. The project started as a two-part venture, and a thirteen-story building at 145 West 58th Street was built first, completed in late 1929.

The stock market crash that October did not bring real estate development to a halt. Indeed, some real estate analysts welcomed it, believing investors would now favor real estate over stocks, and some major projects were actually begun in 1930—the Carlyle Hotel, parts of London Terrace, the old McGraw-Hill Building at 330 West 42nd Street, and the Majestic at 115 Central Park West. But uncertain conditions delayed the start of the Central Park South sections of Hampshire House until January 1931.

According to Rollin Caughey, son of A. Rollin Caughey, the 1926 design for what was to be called the Medici Tower envisioned a combination medical building and apartment hotel rising in a slender shaft to a streamlined dome. The cornerstone included examples of "the modern spirit in art, literature and science" including photographs of Thomas Hart Benton murals and a copy of Ernest Hemingway's *A Farewell to Arms*. But by 1931 the $6 million project had been redesigned into a thirty-six-story mix of Regency and Art Deco, rising in a series of white-brick setbacks to a giant pyramidal copper roof.

In June 1931, with the building complete except for interior finishes and closing in the roof, the owners, Eugene E. Lignante and the H. K. Ferguson Company of Cleveland, stopped work, apparently out of funds.

ESSEX
HOUSE

HAMPSHIRE HOUSE, *second building from left, in 1959.* COURTESY OFFICE FOR METROPOLITAN HISTORY

The New York Title and Mortgage Company, which had advanced $2.2 million for construction, began foreclosing. But as other projects failed, the mortgagee soon went into receivership. And, as the depression deepened, Hampshire House loomed over the elegant skyline, a dark mass by night, an empty hulk by day.

It was a nagging reminder that the building boom of the'20s had imploded as foreclosures multiplied and co-op shareholders abandoned apartments for the sake of a few months' overdue maintenance, even in established buildings on Park and Fifth Avenues.

The receivers for New York Title and Mortgage felt that the almost completed property was worth at least $3 million, but the only serious offer was for $800,000. So they finally decided to complete the project themselves, spending $1.5 million.

Working with A. Rollin Caughey, the decorator Dorothy Draper redesigned the public rooms into some of the most significant interiors of the '30s or '40s, with daring contrasts of black, white, and turquoise, overscale plaster carving, mirrors and glass block and extraordinary door moldings of cast clear glass.

Hampshire House finally opened in the fall of 1937 as a rental building and the *Real Estate Record and Guide* wrote: "When the history of real estate financing is written, at least a footnote will be devoted to the strange story of Hampshire House," which it called "Manhattan's Monument to Frenzied Finance." For six years an almost completed building on one of the choicest streets in Manhattan had gone begging.

240 CENTRAL PARK SOUTH

IN 1939 THE MAYER FAMILY, which had developed apartment houses on Park Avenue in the 1910s and 1920s, bought the entire east blockfront on Broadway between 58th Street and Central Park South. Albert Mayer, a member of the family firm, was also an architect in partnership with Julian Whittlesey. They worked out a solution for a twenty-eight-story, H-shaped structure on Central Park South and a smaller, fifteen-story section on 58th Street to accommodate a total of 325 apartments.

The $4.5 million building carried out several new ideas. It covered only 48 percent of its plot—far less than the typical Manhattan apartment house of its day—and the remaining space was landscaped. Above the seventh floor the corner rooms were made into balconies with large picture windows behind them, giving an outdoors character to the interior. The lobby had a conservatory that faced onto a central garden. High above the

240 CENTRAL PARK SOUTH.
COLLECTION ELLIOTT GLASS

park was a public sunroof with an indoor recreation area. On 58th Street, an off-street truck dock was designed to ease deliveries and reduce street congestion.

The kitchens all had windows, even though recent changes in building law permitted mechanical ventilation. Shops on Broadway and a restaurant on Central Park South had lobby access, so tenants did not have to go outside.

In 1940 the magazine *Buildings and Building Management* complimented the variety of the plans and views, saying, "Each apartment becomes a sort of penthouse."

Over the front door is a brilliantly colored mosaic panel, *The Quiet City*, by the artist Amédée Ozenfant, who worked with Le Corbusier. Otherwise the exterior is undecorated in the traditional sense, but the patterns of the delicately framed casement windows still make an elegant statement.

The earliest tenants included Antoine de Saint-Exupéry. The French aviator-author was already famous as a combat hero and for his best-selling *Wind, Sand and Stars*, but was dejected by the fall of France in 1940. He came to New York on December 31, 1940, to resume writing and puzzle out a course of action. He moved to a high-floor apartment at 240 Central Park South—one account says the twenty-third floor, another the twenty-seventh.

Stacy Schiff's 1994 biography *Saint-Exupéry* recounts that the author made his bathtub into a wave laboratory to investigate invasion techniques, and littered Central Park South with paper helicopters—he hoped a fleet of motorless autogiros could surprise the German occupiers. Saint-Exupéry moved from 240 before he wrote *The Little Prince* (published in 1943) and disappeared in action on a mission out of Sardinia in 1944.

Few buildings in New York, even those on much larger budgets, can equal the original grace and sophistication of 240 Central Park South.

UPPER EAST SIDE

HOTEL PIERRE

61ST STREET AND FIFTH AVENUE

CHARLES PIERRE WAS SICILIAN, born Pierre Casalasco about 1880 to a father who operated a hotel. At age eighteen he ran away to Monte Carlo and then went on to work at the Ritz in Paris. From there he went to London and became headwaiter at the Savoy, where he met Louis Sherry, the New York restaurateur.

Around 1915 Sherry took Pierre back to his legendary restaurant, Sherry's, on Fifth Avenue, and by 1920 Pierre had established his own restaurant at 290 Park Avenue. It became synonymous with chic dining.

In February 1929, Pierre, backed by a group of investors that included Otto Kahn, E. F. Hutton, and Herbert Pratt, filed plans for the $15 million, forty-two-story hotel at the southeast corner of 61st Street and Fifth Avenue that would bear his name. The promoters promised that their Georgian-style skyscraper would have "simplicity and refinement" with the "atmosphere of a private club or residence."

Designed by Schultze & Weaver, the 714-room hotel offered very large suites—up to nine rooms—and mixed permanent with transient guests. The plan of public rooms was complicated, multilevel, and elegant. The oval foyer (the room with the strange murals of recent vintage) connected an Edwardian-style dining room (since destroyed), facing Fifth Avenue, with a double stairway leading to the Louis XV–style main ballroom, at the Madison Avenue end.

The hotel's three main entrances faced 61st Street, as did Pierre's private office. Zoning regulations prohibited shops, and on Fifth Avenue the architects kept the facade elegantly simple, although later doorways and canopies have diminished this character.

Higher up, the urns and neoclassical ornament keep to the Georgian theme, but the huge scale makes the style more "New York" than anything else. The top is crowned by a modest setback story and then a giant copper mansard roof, which covered a double-height supper club.

The roof has always been a distinctive feature of the hotel, which the *New York Times* said in 1930 produced a "picturesque effect of real charm and individuality."

A year after the stock market crash of October 1929, the hotel opened with a dinner at which the eighty-five-year-old Auguste Escoffier upbraided his American audience for the "feverish" pace of modern life that did not allow sufficient time for meals.

THE PIERRE SEEN FROM CENTRAL PARK IN 1930. COURTESY OFFICE FOR METROPOLITAN HISTORY

The Hotel Pierre capped the evolution of Grand Army Plaza itself, ringed by Bergdorf Goodman, the Squibb Building, the old Savoy-Plaza Hotel, and the thirty-eight-story Sherry-Netherland. Together they defined what had become the city's most elite public square in a grouping that survived intact until the Savoy-Plaza was demolished for the General Motors Building in the '60s.

In April 1931 Pierre stated that New York had "passed the low ebb of the depression," but the following September a foreclosure action began: The hotel had begun missing interest payments on its $6.5 million mortgage around the time Pierre made his comment. The hotel corporation declared bankruptcy in March 1932 but continued under Pierre's management.

Pierre died from an infection following appendicitis in September 1934. His obituary described the hotel as the realization of "dreams of his youth," and in 1935 the employees installed a bronze memorial plaque in the lobby with the maxim by which he worked: "Be courteous. This is the most important rule of all."

421 EAST 61ST STREET

WHAT BEGAN AS A BARN, BECAME A HOTEL, and only later a country house is so old it's off-angle from the city street plan. It was planned in 1795 as the barn for Mount Vernon, the country estate of Colonel William S. Smith and his wife, Abigail. Smith was an aide to George Washington; his wife was the daughter of John Adams, the second president of the United States. They planned a main house near what is now 61st Street and First Avenue but lost the entire property before completion in 1796; they probably never spent a night there.

In 1806 the estate was advertised for sale in the *New York Evening Post* as a twenty-three-acre "country seat . . . near the five mile stone." The ad described the barn as "a very ornamental building, and well arranged for convenience and use," with stables for six horses, a coach room, shelter for cattle, pigeon houses, and a loft for thirty tons of hay.

But perhaps the private estate idea was too ambitious, because by 1808 the main house was operating as the "Mount Vernon Hotel" with a one-mile racetrack. But the main house burned in 1826, and Joseph Hart purchased the surviving barn and renovated it as an inn, the new Mount Vernon Hotel.

In 1829 James Stuart, duke of Lennox, visited the hotel, a trip he described in *Three Years in North America*, published in 1833. He praised "the view of the river and of the gay sailing craft constantly passing, and tossed about by the eddies in every direction."

FIG 91.1

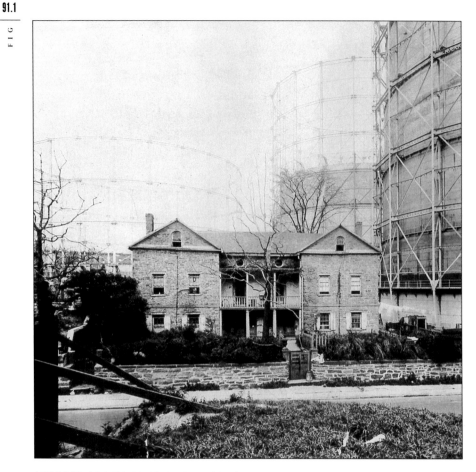

ABIGAIL ADAMS SMITH ROBINSON'S HOUSE IN 1919. COURTESY COLONIAL DAMES OF AMERICA

FIG 91.2

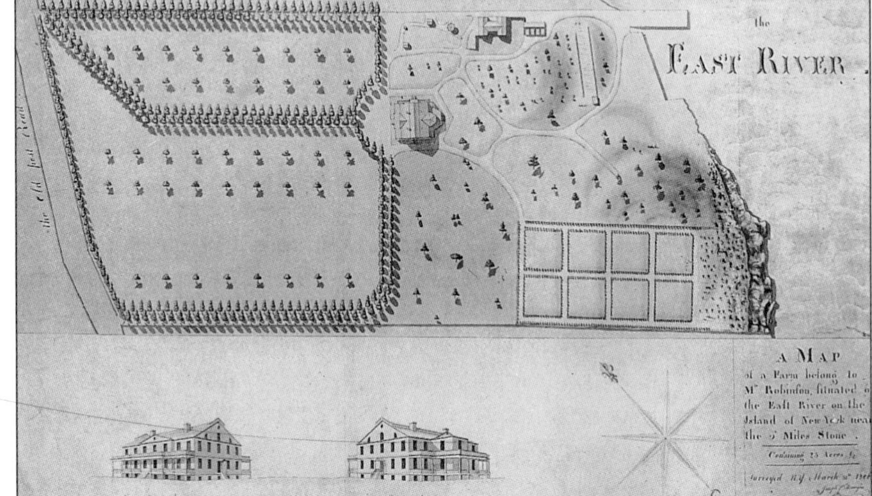

MAP OF THE SMITH ESTATE *in 1806, when it was up for sale.* COURTESY THE NEW-YORK HISTORICAL SOCIETY, NEW YORK CITY

"Near as we are to New York," he wrote in surprise, "and within three hundred yards of the high road, there is neither a shutter nor a bar to a window in the house. Clothes are laid out to bleach all night without the slightest fear of their being carried off."

In 1833 Jeremiah Towle bought the hotel and made it into a country house. It must have been Towle who put in the high-style trim on the interior—the fluted columns and rosettes, and some astoundingly rich Greek Revival mantles, which are no longer in the building. Towle's two daughters, Isabella and Mary, continued to live in the house past 1900, by which time the area had been taken over by industry and tenements.

In 1919 Jane Teller Robinson took over the house, apparently on a lease. She renovated the place as "Jane Teller's Mansion" and began a program of spinning and weaving to enable poor people to manufacture their own clothing.

In 1921 Robinson, who organized the Society for the Revival of Household Industries and Domestic Arts, relayed something of her missionary zeal to the *New York Times*. She wanted to recapture an earlier time of self-sufficiency, noting that "up to 1830 nearly every house had its own flax wheel and wool wheel, and 90 percent of all goods was made at home." Brochures from her organization said that they were selling regularly to Abercrombie & Fitch, and that they custom-made clothes from the sheep's wool of their clients.

In 1924 the house was purchased by the Colonial Dames of America, for use as its headquarters; today they operate it as a house museum, the Mount Vernon Hotel Museum and Garden.

THE WEYHE BOOK STORE AND GALLERY

794 LEXINGTON AVENUE

ERHARD WEYHE EMIGRATED FROM ENGLAND on the eve of World War I and soon specialized in the sale of art books. Business was good, and in 1923 he bought a four-story, 1870s brownstone at 794 Lexington and altered the front.

His architect, Henry S. Churchill, shaved off most of the brownstone decoration and added what makes the building arresting. The upper three floors were reduced to an abstract blocky design of brown and red tinted stucco, and show windows were opened up on the first and second floors, with deep blue tile surrounds above and a yellow and blue tile checkerboard below. Above the door and first-floor windows are three floral tile medallions in red, tan, blue, and yellow.

Either Churchill or Weyhe got Henry Varnum Poor, a painter-ceramicist-sculptor-architect, to design a four-part floral tile plaque rich in blue, green, orange, and purple. Poor's signature is still visible under the cracked glaze. Rockwell Kent, the writer and artist, designed ironwork and a sign over the door with a wrought-iron "W" monogram.

THE WEYHE BOOK STORE AND GALLERY, *794 Lexington Avenue in 1924.*
COURTESY THE NEW YORK SOCIETY LIBRARY

The Weyhe shop became a center of modernist artistic activity. Carl Zigrosser, its manager for many years, recalled that patrons like Lewis Mumford, Frank Crowninshield, Alfred Lunt, and Jo Mielziner bought books and prints by the gallery's circle of artists, among them Kent, Louis Lozowick, Aristide Maillol, Gaston Lachaise, John Sloan, Reginald Marsh, and Diego Rivera.

The gallery published their prints singly and in portfolios and indeed was organized around the idea of presenting less expensive works by emerging artists.

David Kiehl, associate curator of prints and photographs at the Metropolitan Museum of Art, calls the building "a shrine for modern art."

"They had early exhibits of the German Expressionists, of Matisse, of Picasso, of Mexican and African art," he said, adding that Weyhe published an art magazine, the *Checkerboard,* named after the tile work on the building. Alexander Calder had his first wire sculpture display at the gallery.

From 1923 until the early 1990s, the bookshop and gallery upstairs remained unchanged—wooden floors and shelves, dusty out-of-print books, inexpensive artwork informally presented. Those who can remember it are among New York's most fortunate. In 1972, Mr. Weyhe died and his daughter, Gertrude Dennis, continued the business.

In the summer of 1991 the gallery and bookstore moved out, and the results would make for a Shakespearean tragedy. The family leased the space to the Glendale bakery, a franchise. Phil Rudnick, a spokesman for Glendale, said at the time that he wanted a "very modern, really upscale" bakery/deli.

Mrs. Dennis says that the family did not require or even suggest the facade be saved. "I don't think it would be appropriate for anyone except Weyhe" she said. And the Kent ironwork, the tile work the subtle modeling of the storefront, were all smashed and discarded—essentially at the direction of the family which should have been proud to preserve it. Oh, and Glendale? They got their new shop—a cheap, tinny, disposable thing—but they moved out a few years later. Only the soft pastel stucco of the upper floors survives, a reproach to those who ought to have known better.

ROCKEFELLER UNIVERSITY

62ND TO 68TH STREETS ALONG THE EAST RIVER

ALTHOUGH FACTORIES OVERRAN MUCH OF THE EAST RIVER shoreline in the late nineteenth century, the cliff-top stretch from 64th to 67th Streets offered poor water access and was not developed. Period photographs show open, uneven ground, used by an athletic club, with a few frame houses and an old chapel.

In the 1890s John D. Rockefeller left his position as active head of the Standard Oil empire to devote his life to philanthropy. His adviser, Frederick T. Gates, had been urging him to create something in the medical field and, after the death of his three-year old grandson John Rockefeller McCormick of scarlet fever in 1901, Rockefeller pledged $200,000 for what was initially known as the Rockefeller Institute of Medical Research. His son, John D. Rockefeller Jr., guided much of the planning.

At the time, American medical research was a sometime thing. One institute trustee was Dr. Christian Herter, a leading medical researcher; Herter worked out of a laboratory he had built in his home at 819 Madison Avenue, near 68th Street. (His nephew, also Christian Herter, was appointed secretary of state by President Dwight D. Eisenhower in 1959.) At first the institute gave away grants and conducted research in makeshift quarters at 50th Street and Lexington Avenue. An outbreak of meningitis in the winter of 1904–5 led the institute's first director, Dr. Simon Flexner, to develop a serum to fight the disease.

FIG 93.1

LOOKING EAST ALONG 66TH STREET *toward Rockefeller Institute in 1916, showing the original building (center) and the hospital (right).* COURTESY ROCKEFELLER UNIVERSITY ARCHIVES

FIG 93.2

THE ROCKEFELLER INSTITUTE *from the East River in 1937.* COURTESY ROCKEFELLER UNIVERSITY ARCHIVES

The trustees, headed by Gates, soon began looking at building sites. After considering the small block from 57th to 58th Streets fronting on the East River, Rockefeller gave money to buy the riverfront parcel from 64th to 67th Streets. The first building opened in 1906, at the head of a long drive at the foot of 66th Street, followed in 1910 by a hospital and other buildings, variously designed by York & Sawyer, and Shepley, Rutan & Coolidge.

Early photographs show the hospital with open balconies so patients could be wheeled out—even in beds—for fresh air. The first buildings were set well back from the city proper, behind a tall fence and large planted grounds from what is now York Avenue. Perched high above the East River, the buildings had panoramic views over the water and to Queens, and the massive, craggy retaining wall is still a familiar feature on the Franklin D. Roosevelt Drive.

Flexner's staff included Hideyo Noguchi, a Japanese-born bacteriologist, and the Frenchman Alexis Carrel, who became the institute's first Nobel Prize winner, for transplant research, in 1912. Flexner also hired the bacteriological researcher Paul de Kruif in 1920, but Flexner dismissed him in 1922—de Kruif's 1922 spoof, *Our Medicine Men*, satirized Rockefeller Institute personnel too closely. De Kruif later assisted Sinclair Lewis on Lewis's 1925 novel, *Arrowsmith*, itself based loosely on the institute.

The Rockefeller University is a sweet, blessed place, cool and serene, normally closed to the public. But watch for its once-a-year Spring Neighborhood Day, when anyone can stroll around the campus.

FRANKLIN, ELEANOR, AND MOTHER'S HOUSE

47–49 EAST 65TH STREET

IN 1905, WHEN ELEANOR AND FRANKLIN MARRIED, the future president was living with his widowed mother in their old row house at 200 Madison Avenue, at 35th Street. The couple moved into a brownstone at 125 East 36th Street, but at the end of 1905 they got a Christmas present—Sara Roosevelt promised them a new home. But there was a little extra surprise: the architect Charles A. Platt designed two houses hidden behind one facade, 47 East 65th for her and 49 for her son and daughter-in-law. The twin-house aspect had not been mentioned in the letter that originally described the gift. Platt provided for connections between 47 and 49, especially at the rear of the first and second floors, where the dining and drawing rooms could be linked for entertaining.

The houses were finished in 1908, and, according to Geoffrey Ward's 1989 book about FDR, *A First Class Temperament*, Eleanor complained that she wanted a house

FRANKLIN D. ROOSEVELT *(center) with Mayor Fiorello H. LaGuardia (right) and Grover Whalen standing in front of FDR's home, next to the removable railings that gave the president extra support on the stairway.* COURTESY FRANKLIN DELANO ROOSEVELT LIBRARY

completely her own, but Franklin brushed her off gently and convinced her that she was "quite mad."

In 1921, while vacationing in Maine, Franklin Roosevelt was stricken with polio; after six weeks in the hospital, he came back to the 65th Street house to recuperate. Mr. Ward's book quotes Roosevelt as writing to a friend that "by the spring I will be walking without any limp."

But he never again walked unaided, and it was in the 65th Street house that Roosevelt planned his political future and also developed the strategies that kept the public from concentrating on his disability. A special removable stairway was built for the front stoop, with railings set close together; he could stand and wave from it and even descend, with the help of assistants and his massive upper body strength.

According to the 1925 census, Franklin, Eleanor, and their five children shared their home with seven servants: E. H. Gibson, thirty-two, and Will Pickett, thirty, butlers; "Captain" Taylor, thirty, cook; Noah Gibson, forty-seven, second cook; Leroy Jones, thirty, valet; and Mary Connor, nineteen, and Cora Robinson, forty-one, maids.

FIG 94.2

SARA ROOSEVELT'S HOME *at 47 East 65th Street, in the distance, in 1908.* COURTESY OFFICE FOR METROPOLITAN HISTORY

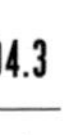

FIG 94.3

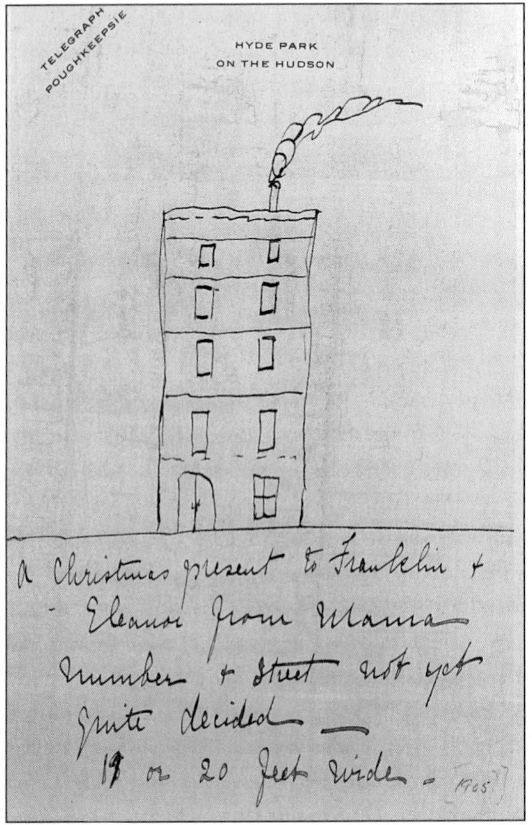

SKETCH BY SARA ROOSEVELT *of her Christmas present to her son and daughter-in-law, 1905.* COURTESY FRANKLIN DELANO ROOSEVELT LIBRARY

Joseph Lash wrote in his 1971 book *Eleanor and Franklin* that Eleanor had repeated difficulties with her all-white household servants in the 1910s and in March 1919 replaced them with a staff that was largely black (of the servants listed above, six were black and one was white). Census records for twentieth-century New York City indicate that there was a distinct prejudice against hiring nonwhites (except, occasionally, Japanese) for household work, and so Eleanor Roosevelt's decision has some of the character of a move for racial equality.

In 1928 Franklin Roosevelt was elected governor of New York, and in 1932 he won the presidency. Although the Roosevelts kept the 65th Street house, it was often vacant.

Sara Roosevelt died in 1941, and in 1942 the president sold the twin house to a group of private citizens to operate as an interfaith meeting place for Hunter College students.

THE CHARLES SCRIBNER HOUSE

9 EAST 66TH STREET

FIG 95.1

IN 1879 CHARLES SCRIBNER TOOK OVER the family publishing company, founded in 1846. For the next half century he groomed its list until it stood for the most cultured taste, "a kind of blue ribbon" for authors, according to the *Dictionary of American Biography*.

CHARLES SCRIBNER. COURTESY OFFICE FOR METROPOLITAN HISTORY

Scribner was married to the former Louisa Flagg, and in 1893 he gave her brother Ernest one of his first major architectural commissions, a new store and office building at 155 Fifth Avenue, near 22nd Street.

In 1909 Charles and Louisa Scribner asked Flagg to design their new town house at 9 East 66th Street. Completed in 1912, it has many of the earmarks of the Flagg style: a gridlike order to the facade, intelligent ironwork designs, contrasting red brick and light-colored stone, the use of marble instead of the more common limestone, and large windows.

The *AIA Guide to New York City*, by Norval White and Elliot Willensky, calls it "an airy and masterful facade with so much glass that it presages . . . curtain walls by half a century."

THE CHARLES SCRIBNER HOUSE *at 9 East 66th Street in 1945.* COURTESY OFFICE FOR METROPOLITAN HISTORY

This was another instance in which Flagg persuaded a client to adopt an interior garage instead of keeping the family automobile at a public garage or converted private stable. At the Scribner house, what appears to be simply a grand entryway is a double door at grade leading into an interior driveway and a vehicle elevator to the basement.

The tiled vaulted driveway also leads to a side-facing door into the main hall. The hall interiors are finished in plain plaster, with black and green marble trim of refined but vigorous beauty. The paneled main salon at the front of the second floor is conventional in style, but the dining room at the rear is covered with painted panels in ivory and brown with scenes of cherubs, urns, and foliage. A concealed door from this room leads to a small, square, skylit library.

Soon after the 66th Street house was completed, Scribner called on Flagg to design a new headquarters for his company, the tall limestone building with an elegant selling floor at 597 Fifth Avenue, near 48th Street. Many New Yorkers still remember buying books in that sophisticated, vaulted room, the equivalent of Grand Central Terminal for book retailing.

At the time that Charles Scribner built his 66th Street house, his company had reached the pinnacle of impeccable taste, with authors like Edith Wharton, Henry James, George Santayana, John Galsworthy, Robert Louis Stevenson, and Rudyard Kipling. But the company is better known today for the younger generation of writers it brought along: It published F. Scott Fitzgerald's first novel, *This Side of Paradise*, a sensation in 1920.

Fitzgerald also enthusiastically recommended a promising writer he referred to as "Ernest Hemmingway," and in 1926 Scribner's brought out *The Sun Also Rises* to critical acclaim. Charles Scribner admired the two authors' vigor and inspiration but was shocked by their use of vulgar words, and only the influence of his editor, Maxwell Perkins, got them published intact.

Scribner died in 1930 and Mrs. Scribner in 1937, and 9 East 66th Street passed out of the family in 1943.

2 EAST 67TH STREET

EVERYBODY KNOWS THE BEST ADDRESSES: Park Avenue and foremost, Fifth Avenue. So who would ever consider the side street address more prestigious? Consider the case of 2 East 67th Street for one answer.

In the early nineteenth century, householders almost always took Fifth Avenue or Broadway addresses. But as Fifth Avenue developed north of the Grand Army Plaza beginning in the late nineteenth century, new standards of judgment came into play. For one thing New York "society" was now rapidly changing as outsiders attempted to take their place alongside more established families. To winnow out the newcomers from the established society, the Social Register was created in 1887 followed a year later by Ward McAllister's list of the "Four Hundred."

Henry Havemeyer, the sugar refiner, took 1 East 66th Street for his Romanesque-style mansion at the northeast corner of Fifth in the 1880s, and Andrew Carnegie chose 2 East 91st Street for his mansion, now the Cooper-Hewitt Museum, at the turn of the twentieth century.

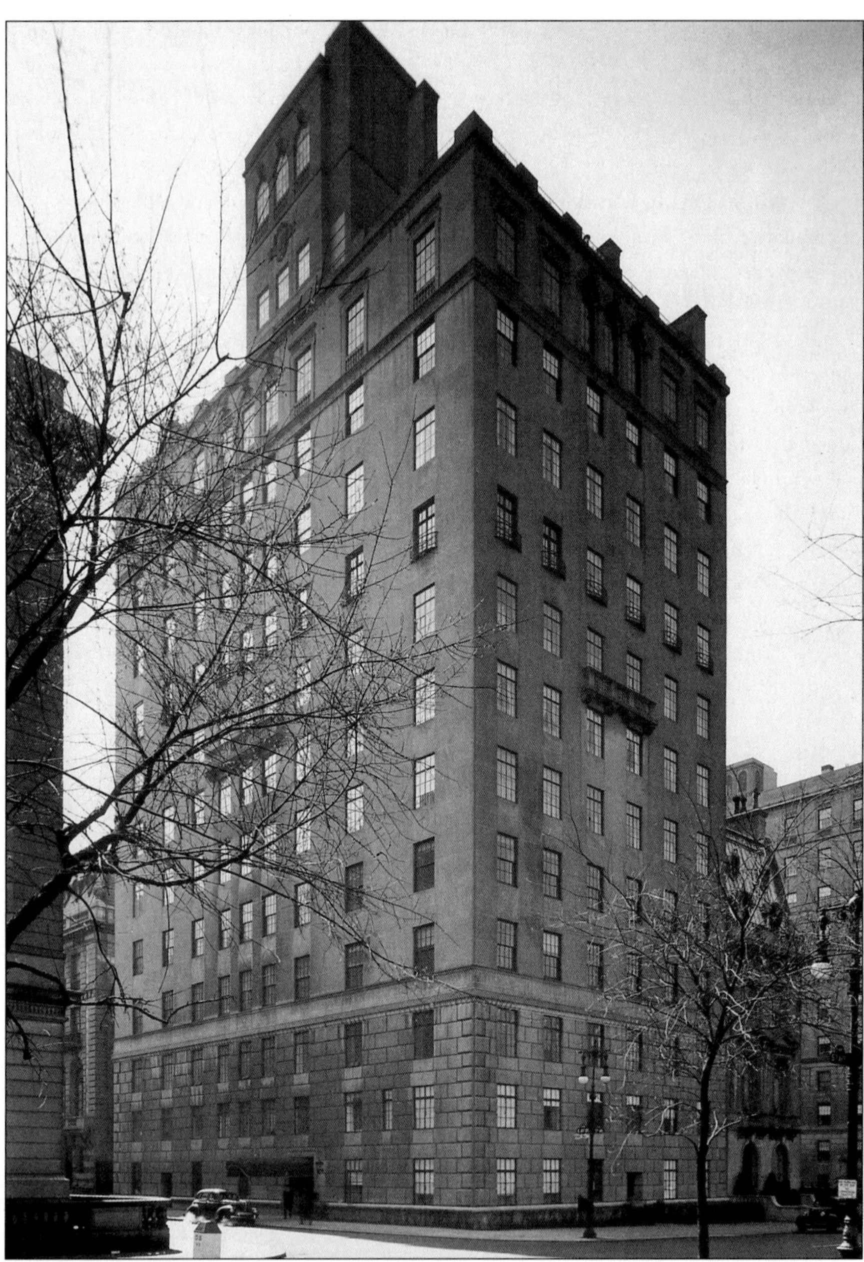

2 EAST 67TH STREET IN THE LATE 1940S. COURTESY OFFICE FOR METROPOLITAN HISTORY

Stuart Duncan, an importer, felt safe numbering his double-width, limestone mansion 1 East 75th in 1903; it was 100 feet off Fifth Avenue. But Edward Harkness, a Standard Oil heir, building on the corner lot in 1907, demanded the No. 1 number, bumping Duncan to No. 3. At least half of the other corner mansions took the side street address.

Although there is little writing on the subject, the presumption is that the code of "1 East" or "2 East" separated the knowledgeable from the newcomer.

In 1926, Michael Paterno, a developer, acquired a mansion at the southeast corner of 67th Street and Fifth Avenue known as 856 Fifth Avenue. He took title in the name of the "855–856 Fifth Avenue Corporation," and early news accounts and ads uniformly referred to the proposed fourteen-story co-op as 856 Fifth Avenue.

But in September 1927, as construction was under way, Paterno applied to the borough president for the address 2 East 67th Street, already used by former New York Governor Nathan L. Miller, who owned a town house on the next inside lot.

Relations between Miller and Paterno had been friendly, with Miller permitting construction fences to partly block his property. But in early 1928 Miller complained that Paterno's blasting had damaged a grandfather clock and that construction waste had been dumped on his building; he claimed damages of over $1,000. Paterno sent $23.60.

In September 1928, Borough President Julius Miller (no relation to the former governor) denied Paterno's request. Paterno and then Miller vowed to sue for the "2 East" designation. The *New York Herald Tribune* noted "that most persons now considered side street numbers just off Fifth Avenue more valuable than Fifth Avenue addresses."

Only in 1930, with Paterno's apartment completed and occupied, did Miller offer 2 East to Paterno solely through "kindness and courtesy," according to the *New York Times*. Crisscross telephone directories show that the initial shareholders gradually shifted to the 2 East 67th Street designation; by 1950, "856 Fifth Avenue" no longer existed as an address.

THE CHRISTIAN HERTER HOUSE

817–819 MADISON AVENUE

IN THE 1880S, SOME FAMILIES WHO COULD HAVE AFFORDED MANSIONS on Fifth Avenue opposite Central Park chose instead to build more expansive houses on lower-priced land along Madison Avenue, then a street of polite but unassuming brownstone row houses. Henry Marquand, financier and art collector, put up a three-house complex at the northwest corner of 68th in 1884, and the Tiffany family built a sprawling, castle-like house at the northwest corner of 72nd in 1885. By the early 1890s, half a dozen other grand houses had followed, all in the subdued palette of red brick and brownstone typical of the period.

But in 1893, a new kind of house appeared in the middle of a high-stoop brownstone row on the east side of Madison between 68th and 69th Streets. It was the latest thing from Paris, "modern French" in the terminology of the time, a bright, light limestone building with a rusticated stone base, colossal Corinthian pilasters and a street-level entry. The first Manhattan residence designed by the firm of Carrère & Hastings, it was built for Dr. Christian Herter, whose father, also Christian Herter, was a partner in the Herter Brothers decorating firm.

Dr. Herter had a ground-floor office in the house and did research on the top floor, which was fitted out as a laboratory. He was later associated with the

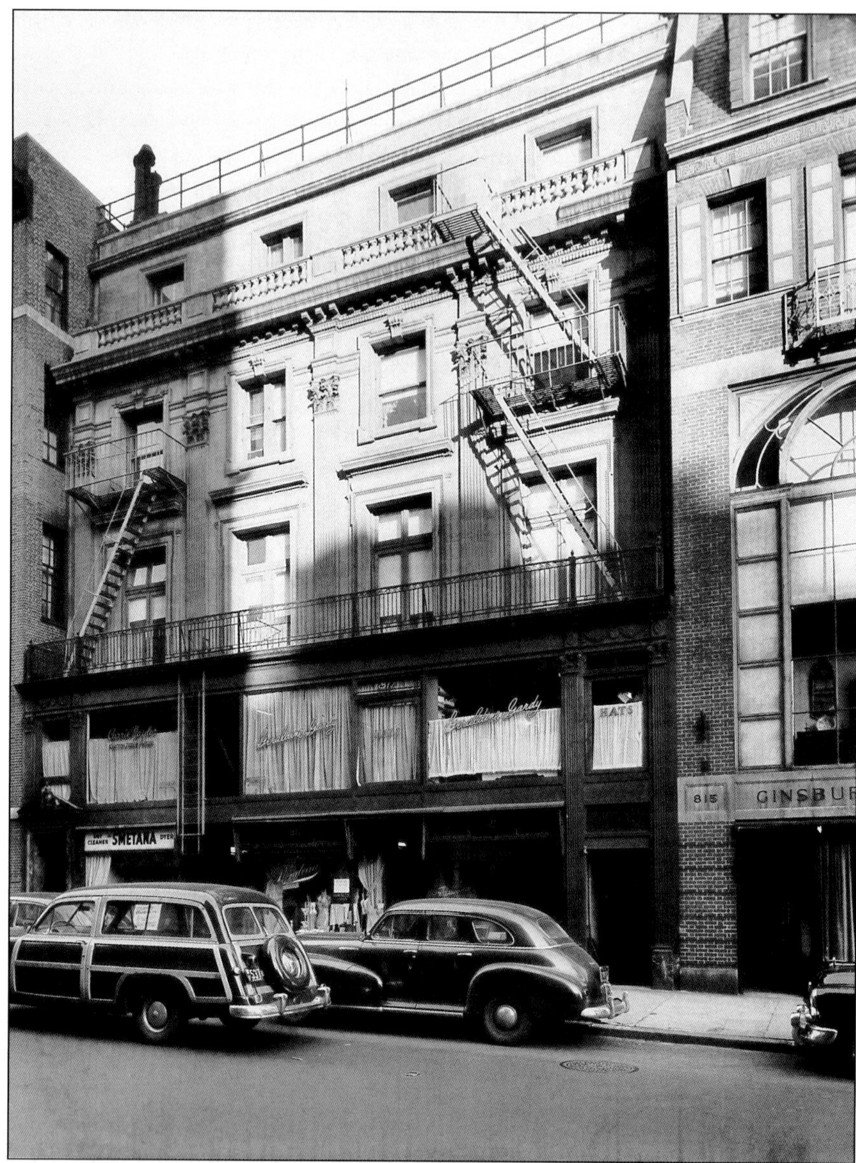

THE CHRISTIAN HERTER HOUSE *at 817–819 Madison Avenue, near 68th Street, in 1951.* COURTESY OFFICE FOR METROPOLITAN HISTORY

Rockefeller Institute hospital and studied the chemical aspects of disease, metabolism, and food preservatives.

At his death in 1910, he was described by the *New York Times* as "a pioneer in medical science." After 1900, Madison Avenue began to develop as a commercial thoroughfare, linking mansions on Fifth Avenue with the new apartment houses on Park Avenue. One by one, storefronts popped out of the lower floors of formerly residential brownstones, and even mansions fell to the wrecker's ball. Marquand died in 1902, and his house at 68th Street was replaced in 1908 by the apartment house now on the site, which bears the "M" monogram on its facade.

The Herter family remained in its house for a few years but sold it around 1920 to the decorating firm of White, Allom & Company. Sir Charles Allom had worked on the interiors of the Frick residence and retained Carrère & Hastings to alter the Herter interior into offices. In 1929, an article in the *New York Times* noted that "in less than ten years' time, this section has built up an unbroken line of smart, small shops."

The White, Allom firm moved out in 1933, and the subsequent owner again altered the Herter house. This time, the architect Phelps Barnum changed the upper three floors into apartments, but inserted two levels of stores on the original street level, behind an attractive iron storefront with paired, two-story-high pilasters at each end. Since that time the building has had a charming if dual presence on the street: a refined residential fragment of limestone above an elegant storefront at street level.

655 PARK AVENUE

IN THE LATE NINETEENTH CENTURY, Park Avenue had medium-grade apartment houses, brownstones, and a dozen or so major institutions, like the Seventh Regiment Armory from 66th to 67th Streets, Normal (now Hunter) College between 68th and 69th Streets, and the German (now Lenox Hill) Hospital between 76th and 77th Streets. Hahneman Hospital, a homeopathic institution, got the east blockfront between 67th and 68th Streets from the city for a hospital it opened in 1878.

After the turn of the century, luxury development swept up Park, especially on the elevated ground between 67th and 72nd Streets. In 1919, Harold I. Pratt, son of a founder of Standard Oil, began a limestone town house at the southwest corner of 68th Street. His neighbors up to 69th Street, including the families of Percy Pyne, William Sloane, and Arthur Curtiss James, occupied a string of mansions.

The entire row benefited from light and air let in by the low-rise institutional buildings across the avenue from 66th to 69th—the armory, the hospital, and the college.

But apartment development began to succeed mansion construction, especially in large sites available in one purchase. In 1919 Hahneman planned a new hospital on Fifth Avenue between 105th and 106th Streets. It offered its Park Avenue property for sale. The Pratts, Pynes, Sloanes, and Jameses bought the blockfront for $1.25 million, intending to keep out tall apartment development.

They resold the blockfront and placed unusual permanent restrictions on the land, permitting either private houses built to a maximum height of 80 feet (measured at 68th Street) or "a first-class, high-grade apartment house" limited to 75 feet—half the height permitted by the zoning then in effect.

655 PARK AVENUE IN 1924. COURTESY THE NEW-YORK HISTORICAL SOCIETY, NEW YORK CITY

The restrictions permitted somewhat greater heights farther back from the Park Avenue building line and also required that the facade be executed in brick with limestone and or marble trim. One story in circulation is that the restriction was meant to protect the sunlight in the Pratts' breakfast room, but their sole surviving in-law, who spoke on condition of anonymity, said, "My mother-in-law wanted to allow sun for her bedroom on the third floor."

That is indeed what Harriet Pratt got, because Mott Schmidt and James E. R. Carpenter, the architects for 655 Park Avenue, produced a building that rose only seven stories at the 68th Street corner. With its large, street-opening garden court, refined Georgian detailing, and low height, 655 Park is an anomaly among luxury apartments, which are almost uniformly built to their highest allowable height.

With the armory to the south and the college to the north, 655 Park forms the centerpiece of a group that is almost Bostonian in its relatively even balance with the street. In Manhattan south of 110th Street even the broadest boulevards are typically overpowered by tall buildings.

No. 655 was built as a "100 percent cooperative," a shift from the previous "group ownership" schemes where the shareholders occupied about half the building and rented out the other half for income. None of its fifty-one apartments of seven to fourteen rooms had access to the wide, green, T-shaped courtyard, which had only a gate from Park Avenue. This is a garden for looking at, not sitting in.

THE EXPLORERS CLUB

46 EAST 70TH STREET

IN 1912 STEPHEN C. CLARK, GRANDSON OF THE BUILDER OF THE DAKOTA, built his Jacobean-style townhouse at 46 East 70th Street. Clark was born in 1882, the year his grandfather, Edward Clark, died. The elder Clark had become rich as the head of the Singer Sewing Machine Company, the business partner of Isaac Merritt Singer, and began investing in real estate in the 1870s. In 1882 his Dakota apartment house at 72nd Street and Central Park West, finished in 1884, was still being roofed in.

By the 1910s the Dakota—and other Clark real estate operations—were controlled by Stephen Clark, and in 1911, Clark began a 50-foot-wide town house at 46 East 70th Street, in a center of mansion-building activity.

His architect, Frederick Sterner, had begun to make a name giving old brownstones new Mediterranean-style fronts, and for Clark's house he was equally picturesque. With a soaring brick front, the house has double-height window bays of leaded glass that make its five floors seem like only three. The roofline terminates in twin Flemish-style gables. Sterner gave the Clarks an interior rich with paneling, softly lit by the giant sheets of leaded glass.

FIG 99.1

STEPHEN C. CLARK. COURTESY NATIONAL BASEBALL HALL OF FAME

Clark was active in publishing, politics, and art but he is better known for a major effort in popular culture—in 1939 he founded the National Baseball Hall of Fame in Cooperstown, New York.

According to Stephen Birmingham's 1979 book, *Life at the Dakota*, by the late 1950s the Dakota's tenants were concerned about the building's future and tried to stay on Clark's good side with gifts and dinner invitations. When he died in 1960, they were chagrined that he left the Dakota to a family trust that offered the building for sale. There were fears it would be demolished, but after a last-minute scramble, they were able to buy the building as a co-op.

STEPHEN C. CLARK'S HOUSE *at 46 East 70th Street in 1913.* COURTESY LIBRARY OF CONGRESS

In 1964, the Clarks sold the house to the Explorers Club, which was established in 1904 and was in small quarters in the Majestic, across from the Dakota at 72nd and Central Park West. Since then the explorers have filled up the former Clark house with a wide collection of souvenirs of members' expeditions. On the ground floor is the globe on which Thor Heyerdahl planned his Kon-Tiki ocean trip in the 1950s. On a wall in the stair hall—where the Clarks had hung an El Greco—the club has a sledge that was used to supply a trans-Arctic expedition.

These are mixed with a stuffed, standing polar bear; the ship's bell used by Admiral Richard F. Byrd for his second Antarctic expedition; a sledge used by Admiral Robert F. Peary to reach the North Pole; lion-skin shields from the Samburu tribe in Africa; and many elephant, mastodon, and narwhal tusks.

THE REAR GARDEN ON 70TH AND 71ST STREETS

BETWEEN MADISON AND PARK AVENUES

BUILT AS A GROUP IN 1929, SEVEN CONTIGUOUS HOUSES facing 70th or 71st Street between Madison and Park Avenues were put up by the developer Alfred Rheinstein with restrictions to preserve their rear gardens as a unit. For him, the whole was greater than the sum of its parts. As the first owners left, fences went up, but the great, green interior of the block still remains an enclave of peace and beauty.

When Presbyterian Hospital decided to move to 168th Street and Broadway and leave its Upper East Side complex in the mid-1920s, the whole block from Madison to Park, between 70th and 71st Streets, came on the market at once. In 1927, the developer Louis Abrons told the *New York Times* that a group he headed would build "the finest apartment house in the world" on the 200-by-400-foot property. But the block was soon divided into four development parcels, with apartment buildings at 720 Park Avenue, 730 Park Avenue and 33 East 70th Street (which stretches along Madison Avenue to 71st Street), and, for the mid-block area, private houses protecting the apartments' light.

The Abrons group transferred the mid-block parcel to Rheinstein, who had built commercial buildings, among them 21 West Street. Rheinstein and his family took for themselves the site at 42 East 71st Street, and in 1928 sold the other lots, persuading five of the other six buyers to use his architect, Aymar Embury. On East 70th Street, No. 41 was built by Walter and Carola Rothschild; he was the chairman of Abraham & Straus and Federated Stores. The house at No. 43 was built by Walter and Florence Hope; he was a lawyer and Republican Party leader. No. 45 was built by Arthur and Adele Lehman; he was a partner at the Lehman Brothers banking firm and son of one of its founders.

On 71st Street, No. 40 was built by Charles and Alice McVeigh; he was a banker and lawyer. The house at No. 44 was built by Richard and Katherine Hoyt; he was a banker, pilot, and yachtsman. The house at No. 46 was built by Richard and Dorothy Bernhard; he was a banker, and she was the daughter of Arthur and Adele Lehman, directly across their rear yard. Completed in 1929, the houses are complementary, even the Hope house, designed by Mott Schmidt.

The owners generally stayed out of the newspapers, although in 1925 Richard Hoyt set the speed record to Albany in his boat *Teaser*; he also backed Charles Lindbergh's transatlantic flight. They all shared a giant backyard, kept open and free from rear extensions by deed restriction.

THE COMMON GARDEN *of 41, 43, and 45 East 70th Street and 40, 42, 44, and 46 East 71st Street, 1966.* COURTESY OFFICE FOR METROPOLITAN HISTORY

Charles McVeigh Jr. says that "we didn't talk over the fence." But Walter Rothschild Jr. recalls throwing a football back and forth with the McVeighs, and said that "there was a good deal of conversation about dogs who barked too early in the morning." Mr. Rothschild also remembers one of the Hoyt daughters sneaking cigarettes. "We could see her hanging out the window," he said. The Bernhard and Lehman houses were unusual in that a path connected their two yards. Rheinstein's concept gave the place a civility rare in New York. Instead of the usual warren of little slots surrounded by high board fences, the backyards formed a sort of common forest. Instead of utilitarian rear facades of absolutely plain brick, each house had a fully developed garden facade.

If you can sneak a look through the service courtyard of an adjacent apartment building, it is still a special place.

43–45 EAST 70TH STREET IN 1943. COURTESY OFFICE FOR METROPOLITAN HISTORY

THE FRICK MANSION
1 EAST 70TH STREET

HENRY FRICK WAS BORN IN PENNSYLVANIA in 1849, and by the age of thirty he had made his first million by supplying coke to the growing steel industry. In the 1880s he began an association with Andrew Carnegie, and by 1889 he was the head of Carnegie's steel company. Carnegie profited by Frick's tough attitude toward labor: in the Homestead steel strike in 1892, several strikers were killed, and the plant's labor movement was crushed.

Even during their alliance, Carnegie had several bitter disputes with Frick, and after Frick became locked in a battle for control over Carnegie's holdings, they were permanently estranged. Frick was living in Pittsburgh in the late 1890s, when Carnegie planned his huge house at 91st Street and Fifth Avenue; it is now the Cooper-Hewitt National Design Museum. In 1901, the *New York Tribune* reported Carnegie's boast that he had bought his block-long site with the profits of a deal in which he had bested Frick. It's estimated that Carnegie spent at least $2.5 million on his house, but a firm total is hard to pin down.

Frick moved from Pittsburgh to New York around 1905 and rented the old Vanderbilt mansion at 640 Fifth Avenue, at 51st Street, where he hung his growing art collection. In 1906, he bought the most impressive house site available on Fifth Avenue, the blockfront between 70th and 71st Streets.

Frick must have gauged his own project at least in part against Carnegie's. Frick's architects, Carrère & Hastings, drew upon eighteenth-century French sources when they designed his three-story limestone palace, which cost $5 million.

The late Wynne Fooshee lived on 70th Street as a child, and in a 1982 interview said she recalled passing the house right after it opened: "I had a piece of chalk and wrote on the wall, 'Robbers rob this rich man'—too much reading of Robin Hood, I guess. At that instant, the gates opened, and Mrs. Frick drove out in her little electric car, saw what I had done, and said: 'Wipe that off immediately! I have a little girl, and she would never do anything like that.' Of course, I felt awfully ashamed."

Like most big houses, Frick's required a huge staff. The 1915 census return lists Frick; his wife, Adelaide; daughter Helen; and twenty-seven servants. These included first and second butlers; first, second, and third footmen; first, second, third, and fourth chambermaids; a chef; a second cook; two vegetable cooks; three laundresses; and a "servants' hall girl." But even with Frick's millions, there was a revolving door

FIG 101.1

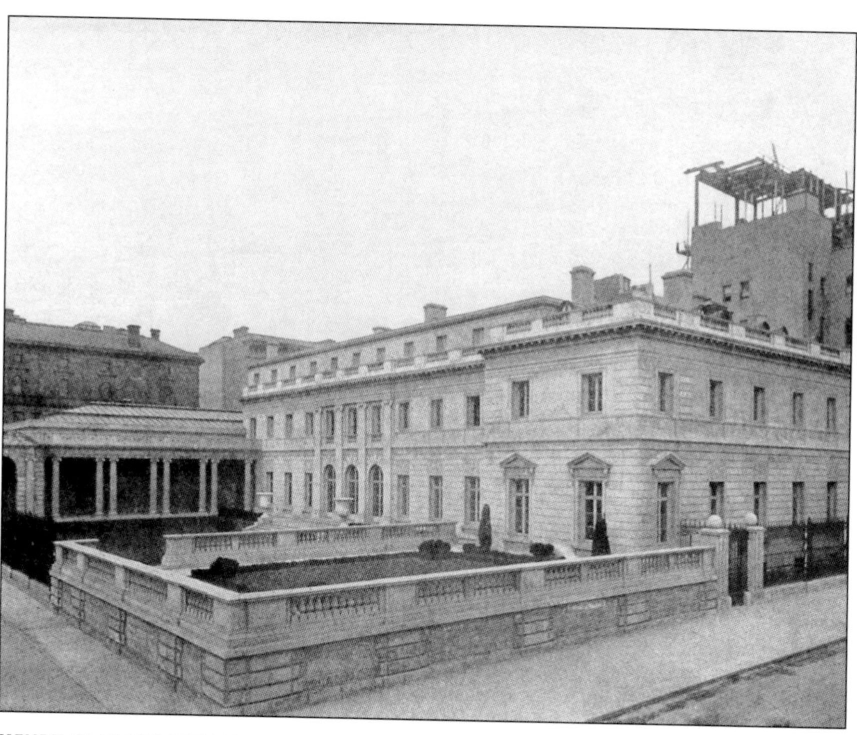

HENRY CLAY FRICK'S MANSION IN 1914. COURTESY OFFICE FOR METROPOLITAN HISTORY

FIG 101.2

HELEN CLAY FRICK, *founder of the Frick Art Reference Library, in the 1950s.* COURTESY THE FRICK COLLECTION

downstairs: of the twenty-seven household staff members listed in 1915, only one also appears on the 1910 census in the Frick household: Percy Martin, then forty, who was listed as a "choreman." Frick did not enjoy his house long. He died in December 1919, just four months after his former ally Andrew Carnegie.

THE FRICK ART REFERENCE LIBRARY

10 EAST 71ST STREET

HENRY FRICK'S DAUGHTER HELEN NEVER MARRIED and developed a close bond with her father, especially over his growing art collection. According to *Henry Clay Frick: an Intimate Portrait*, by his great-granddaughter Martha Frick Symington Sanger; Helen was hobbled by guilt that she may have given her father an improper sedative the night he died in 1919.

In the 1930s she bought two adjacent town houses on 71st Street, demolished them, and hired John Russell Pope to design what remains a stunning work of side-street architecture, with a facade suggesting a war memorial or mausoleum, but with thirteen levels of shelving and offices inside.

The large windows light a high, sunny reading room with tile floors and, in the painted frieze, images of the heads of Helen Frick's two dogs, Bobby and Pat. On the top floor, she installed the paneling from an eighteenth-century Massachusetts house in the staff lounge, but also built a tiled lunchroom with southwestern and Art Deco overtones. The Frick Art Reference Library opened in 1935.

A 1939 profile of Helen Frick by John McCarten in the *New Yorker* described her as "a frail little woman, weighing less than one hundred pounds . . . who looks not at all like the forceful character that she really is." Mr. McCarten noted that Helen Frick had barred researchers with Teutonic names because of her disgust with Germany's actions in World War I and that she was "quick to resent an actual or imagined affront."

She was in frequent conflict with John D. Rockefeller Jr., whom her father had also appointed a trustee of the Frick Collection. Helen Frick wanted to keep the house as it had been lived in, but Rockefeller thought it should be a real museum; to him the furniture and personal effects that Helen Frick wanted kept in place were extra baggage. In 1948, Rockefeller offered to give paintings by Botticelli, Goya, and Fragonard to the Frick Collection but was so vehemently opposed by Helen Frick, who wanted to keep non-Frick acquisitions out of the collection, that the matter went to court, where she lost.

FIG 102.1

THE EXTERIOR OF THE FRICK ART REFERENCE LIBRARY IN THE 1950s. COURTESY THE FRICK COLLECTION

In 1961, during a similar battle over accepting artworks from the Rockefellers, she resigned from the board of the Frick Collection in a fury. Helen Frick was director of the Frick Art Reference Library until 1983, when she was persuaded to resign. Martha Sanger's book quotes a witness who said that, after Helen Frick resigned, she "turned her face to the wall and said she wanted to die." Helen Frick died in Pittsburgh the next year at age ninety-six. Today the Frick library reading room is one of the most civilized places to read in New York. Everyone passes the reserved plaque she installed, which names not the founder but her inspiration: "This library was founded in loving memory of Henry Clay Frick by his daughter."

THE BLACK AND WHITES

527–541 EAST 72ND STREET

IN THE LATE NINETEENTH CENTURY NEW YORK'S RIVERS, full of industry and sewage, were leftover areas, unattractive to the elite New Yorkers who built their town houses at the center of the island. In 1894 several different owners built a row of eight walk-up apartment houses at 527 to 541 East 72nd Street, in the midst of an area of malt houses and cigar factories.

As the depression settled over New York, real estate owners began walking away from their tenement properties, in the face of increasingly restrictive housing regulations and declining rents. At the same time, a new housing market was emerging: formerly prosperous New Yorkers who had fallen on hard times or just wanted to spend their money more conservatively.

On Sutton Place between 55th and 56th Streets, the Phipps Estate hired the decorator Dorothy Draper to redo some old tenements, and Draper had the idea to paint the outside black with white trim, an instant mark of chic.

Into these and other buildings flowed a wave of veterans of town houses and Park Avenue apartment buildings, and in 1933 *Vogue* praised "The Rise of the Walk-Up." In the same year *House & Garden* remarked that these new tenants were "living gallantly in simplicity and liking it."

Up on far-east 72nd Street there were still only factories and tenements, but in 1938 George Palen Snow, real estate investor and husband of Carmel Snow, the trend-setting editor of *Harper's Bazaar*, bought the eight tenements at 527 to 541.

The Snows' circle included the art and literary worlds and old New York money. The guests at their 1926 wedding included Rockwell Kent, Winthrop Aldrich, and Condé Nast. Among them they had memberships in the Piping Rock, Brook, Colony, and Racquet & Tennis Clubs.

The architects Sacchetti & Siegel designed an alteration that gutted and combined the eight tenements into four buildings with two-, three-, and four-bedroom apartments of simple finish, many with wood-burning fireplaces, but painted a stylish black and white on the outside. There is no evidence of a separate designer or stylist in the project—perhaps Mrs. Snow simply adopted the black-and-white treatment herself.

The Snows themselves left their apartment in the Ritz Tower at 57th Street and Park Avenue and moved to the easternmost building, facing the river. Five of the nine

FIG 103.1

THE BLACK AND WHITES IN 1940. COURTESY EDWIN PARKER

recorded tenants in 1939 were in the Social Register; this was a new building type, the Social Register tenement.

By 1940 tenants included Lathrop Brown, Franklin D. Roosevelt's roommate at Harvard, who left River House for Big Sur in California and kept a pied-à-terre in the 72nd Street complex; A. Thornton Baker, an investment banker just back from a round-the-world cruise on his 50-foot yacht; and W. S. Baring-Gould, an authority on Sherlock Holmes.

T. Woodfin Keesee Jr., who had just graduated from Harvard Law School in 1938 when he moved into the 72nd Street buildings, remembers that his neighbors were "always going to El Morocco and the Stork Club—they were all sort of Social Registerites." Edwin Parker, the superintendent in the buildings from 1952 to 1976, said, "They just wanted to be left alone at the end of the world."

19 EAST 72ND STREET

IN 1936 JOHN THOMAS SMITH WAS LIVING in comfortable circumstances at 1115 Fifth Avenue, at 93rd Street. After getting his Yale law degree in 1901, he went on to become vice president and general counsel to the General Motors Corporation, and also pursued outside investments in gold, copper, real estate, oil, and banking. According to his grandchildren, he was concerned about the continuing depression and its effect on New Yorkers of lesser means, and he wanted to provide jobs.

So in 1936 he bought the northwest corner of 72nd Street and Madison Avenue and began work on New York's first luxury apartment house since the 1920s, paying $2.25 million for the land and construction out of his own pocket.

For his architects Mr. Smith teamed up Rosario Candela and Mott Schmidt. One Smith grandchild, who spoke on condition of not being named, says that John Thomas Smith "brought in Mott Schmidt to ride herd on Candela, who was thought too extreme, too Art Deco-y."

Their design for 19 East 72nd Street was fifteen stories of limestone, sumptuously carved along discreet Art Moderne lines at the lower three floors. In 1936 an article in the *New York Times* told of fifty-nine apartments in the new building, but this was revised to only thirty-four units—twenty duplexes of from seven to thirteen rooms each, one duplex of twenty-one rooms, and thirteen simplexes of eleven rooms each—for which the monthly rentals ranged from $330 to $1,000. At the time, a large eight-room apartment on Park Avenue rented for less than $200 a month.

In an interview in 1984, the since-deceased Gregory Smith, John Smith's son, said that his father had adamantly opposed allowing stores in the building along Madison Avenue, even though doing so would have generated the most revenue, but that steel was put in at the second-floor level to permit such a conversion in the future. Another relative says the senior Mr. Smith thought the presence of stores "would cheapen the building."

The basement had separate laundry rooms for each tenant and seven vaults for valuables. According to the *Real Estate Record and Guide* the elevators were operated by attendants, but had push buttons "in case of a labor strike." But air-conditioning was not offered because, the *Record and Guide* noted, "it is expected most of the tenants will live in their country or shore places in hot weather."

Only one of the new tenants moved from a private house; the others came from top apartment houses like River House (435 East 52nd Street); 79 East 79th Street; and 740, 770, and 775 Park Avenue. Charles E. Merrill, founder of Merrill Lynch, moved from

19 EAST 72ND STREET IN 1937. COURTESY OFFICE FOR METROPOLITAN HISTORY

925 Park. John Smith and his family moved to the twenty-one-room duplex on the fourteenth and fifteenth floors, which has since been broken up into two apartments.

What passersby now notice are the carved marble panels surrounding the main doorway. Designed by Carl Paul Jennewein, they present a puzzling group of classical figures with no clear theme—putti around a sundial, exotic animals, figures with musical instruments. Perhaps Jennewein also did the frog and the snail in the doorway woodwork, and the sensuous marine and bird carvings in the elevators, among the finest such work in New York.

THE HENRY SLOANE HOUSE

9 EAST 72ND STREET

IN THE EARLY 1890s, HENRY AND JESSIE SLOANE were living on 54th Street, but midtown was almost fully developed and the streets next to Central Park were being built up as the new luxury quarter. Sloane was an executive at W. & J. Sloane, the family firm established in 1843, and the company was running at full tilt carpeting and furnishing the new mansions, hotels, and clubs of New York. In 1894, Sloane hired the architects Carrère & Hastings to design one of the most sumptuous town houses to survive in New York.

Sloane bought a 54-foot site at 9 East 72nd Street, just off Central Park, a block that already had the mansions of the Tiffanys, Cuttings, and other families. Carrère &

FIG 105.1

HENRY SLOANE'S HOUSE ABOUT 1900. COURTESY OFFICE FOR METROPOLITAN HISTORY

Hastings pioneered the French style of New York, and they pumped the new Sloane House up to colossal Francophilian proportions, all in limestone. Above a ground story of rusticated stone rises a double-height screen of columns bracketing giant French windows with garlands, cartouches, scrolls, and other details applied in profusion. This midsection supports the fourth floor, a mansard roof with dormers screened by a balustrade.

The streets in this section filled up with such mansions, many of them in the exuberantly French style of the Sloane House, like the Jennings House next door at 7 East 72nd Street, built in 1898. In 1900, *Architectural Annual* published a picture of the two houses with an ironic commentary using the French expression for an urban town house, "Enigmas: Hotels particuliers a New York—BUT not the French Quarter."

The Sloane House was completed in 1896, and Jessie Sloane gave a dinner dance for two hundred in January 1897, which included the cream of New York society—but not, according to newspaper reports, her husband. Indeed, Henry Sloane soon moved out to a hotel and divorced his wife in 1899. Within five hours she remarried, taking as her husband Perry Belmont, a diplomat and prominent figure in the Democratic Party. Mr. Sloane considered himself the injured party and extracted an unusual concession—Jessie Sloane could have no contact with their two daughters, Jessie, fifteen, and Emily, ten, until they were twenty-one. She could not write to them or even speak to them on the street, although the *New York Tribune* noted that the order might be rescinded if she could show, after several years, that she "had led a moral life."

After this, neither of the Sloanes wanted their palatial house. The Belmonts moved to Washington and Henry Sloane, who never remarried, built a much more modest house for himself and his daughters at 18 East 68th Street. He rented 9 East 72nd Street for a year or two and then sold it in 1901.

CHARLES DANA GIBSON HOUSE

127 EAST 73RD STREET

CHARLES DANA GIBSON WAS BORN IN MASSACHUSETTS in 1867 and as a child became adept at cutting silhouettes of animals. He launched his career in the early 1880s and sold his first drawing to the old *Life* magazine for $4 in 1886.

More commissions followed, and by the early 1890s Gibson was well established as an illustrator-cartoonist. He soon published the first of what became his series of "Gibson Girls," pen-and-ink portraits of aristocratic young women. Attractive, intelligent looking, Anglo-Saxon, and apparently single, they were typically at summer places,

CHARLES DANA GIBSON'S *house about 1905.* COURTESY MUSEUM OF THE CITY OF NEW YORK

horse shows, or fancy dress balls—often attended by young men, who were very handsome and very interested.

Gibson made some political sketches, but his fame rested on gently poking knowledgeable fun at American aristocracy: young lovers eyeing each other during a society concert, a matriarch's "house warming" in her palatial but empty ballroom, young American women marrying enfeebled European royalty.

The demand for Gibson's clear, distinctive sketches grew frantic, and he was soon living very well. In 1902, he bought a lot on East 73rd Street between Park and Lexington Avenues. The block included such householders as the lawyer Newbold Morris, president of the Metropolitan Club, and the novelist Arthur C. Train, president of the National Institute of Arts and Letters. Gibson hired Stanford White to design a new town house, not in showy Beaux-Arts style but in old-shoe neo-Federal. It was completed in 1904.

In April 1905 the *New York Times* called it "the House the 'Gibson Girls' built." In an interview Gibson acknowledged that, artistically, he was struggling to get out of a Gibson Girl rut: "She has had an adhesive quality that has at times been slightly annoying," he said.

But if the Gibson Girl and her variations kept the artist in bondage, it was with a golden cord: Just as he completed his 73rd Street residence, Gibson was able to build a summer house on a seven-hundred-acre island near Isleboro, Maine.

Gibson was so well off—and so restless—that in December 1905 he left New York to travel through Europe for several years to study painting. News accounts stated that he made $20,000 a year from the old *Life* magazine, $25,000 a year from *Colliers*, and $20,000 a year in royalties from books like *The Social Ladder* and *The Weaker Sex*.

The depression, financial woes, and the Gibsons closed the 73rd Street house and moved to Maine. In 1942, the same year that *Life* magazine called them "America's most romantic couple," they put the house on the market. In September 1944 President Roosevelt sent an amphibious plane to bring a seriously ill Gibson from his island home back to New York. That December, the artist died in "the House the Gibson Girls built."

FIG 106.1

CHARLES DANA GIBSON. COURTESY OFFICE FOR METROPOLITAN HISTORY.

FOR SALE
570 FIFTH AVE
THE NINETY AND NINE
NEW STAR
15
EVENT OF THE SEASON
O.J. ASHMAN
THE NINETY AND NINE

820 PARK AVENUE

ALBERT J. KOBLER, WHO PUT UP 820 PARK AVENUE, started out in business around 1910 by selling newspaper ads. He proved so able that in 1917 William Randolph Hearst appointed him head of Hearst's *American Weekly* syndicated Sunday magazine supplement. In 1923, Kobler bought a severe stone mansion at the northwest corner of 75th and Park for his own use, filling it with art treasures and antiques. In 1925 the magazine *Arts & Decoration* said that Kobler's "priceless art collection" made the house reminiscent "of the baronial castles of England."

But in 1926 Kobler demolished the house for a dramatically new kind of dwelling. He retained the architect Harry Allan Jacobs to design a fourteen-story building with duplexes above the ground floor for five tenants—and with the top three floors as Kobler's triplex. Jacobs predicted in a 1925 article in the *New York Times* that soon "the private house will be forgotten and a thing of the past," because of taxes, problems with servants, and the construction of other tall apartment buildings in elite neighborhoods, most of which "are rather barrack-like and unattractive."

Jacobs's design remains unusual: above a two-story stone base rises a facade of mottled amber brick with windows arranged in vertical bays. These terminate at the Kobler apartment, marked by bands of plum-colored terra-cotta and, on the north end, a three-story slate-shingled roof arranged as a mock-mansard roof. The base is delicious orange and yellow Ohio sandstone from the Mississippian era, three million years old, according to Sidney Horenstein, a geologist at the American Museum of Natural History.

The ironwork at the entryway is some of the most unusual on Park Avenue: dark, hammered shapes worked in medieval designs, including the shapes of blades and a knight. William J. Whitaker, collections manager at the architectural archives of the University of Pennsylvania, said that records in their collection indicate that the work was done by Samuel Yellin, one of America's most prominent metalworkers.

Kobler owned the building and leased the duplexes for $25,000 to $40,000 a year. The typical twenty-room duplex had a 22-by-38-foot living room, a 19-by-23-foot dining room, a library, and five master bedrooms, with six servants' rooms. Kobler's triplex, decorated by French & Company, had a 37-by-39-foot living room with a 20-foot ceiling and a great stone arch. *Arts & Decoration* visited the apartment in 1928 and noted that "bewildered New York sunlight filters through the splendor and ancient stained glass."

THE APARTMENT OF ALBERT J. KOBLER, *with its great stone arch, in 1928.*
COURTESY NEW YORK SOCIETY LIBRARY

Kobler's new neighbors included Herbert Lehman, governor of New York from 1932 to 1942 and United States senator from 1949 to 1957. Another tenant was Herbert S. Martin, a vice president at the investment bank of S. W. Straus & Company. Martin, his wife, and their three young sons lived in the eighth- and ninth-floor duplex, from which Martin fell or jumped in January 1930, not long after the stock market crash of 1929. He had previously had a nervous breakdown and was getting ready to go on a three-month vacation in Egypt and Europe.

Sometime before Kobler's death in 1937 at age sixty, he leased his custom-built apartment to the automobile manufacturer Walter Chrysler. The Kobler/Chrysler triplex was subdivided into six apartments in 1941, and the other duplexes in the building were gradually split up, although it is hard to tell from the outside.

820 PARK AVENUE IN 1944. COURTESY OFFICE FOR METROPOLITAN HISTORY

THE CARLYLE HOTEL

76TH STREET AND MADISON AVENUE

THE CARLYLE WAS THE SIGNATURE PROJECT OF MOSES GINSBERG, who was born in Poland in 1885 and came to the United States via London in 1896. Ginsberg started out in banking, but in the mid-1920s he was putting up small apartment buildings in Brooklyn. By 1929 he was in full swing, buying sites on the West and East Sides of Manhattan for large-scale apartment development. After the stock market crash of 1929 many of his plans foundered, but the buildings he did complete were suave and sophisticated. They include the thirteen-story co-op at 133 East 80th Street, at Lexington Avenue, with its Gothic-style detailing and flying buttress rising over the penthouse terraces. Ginsberg finished 133 East 80th in mid-1930.

But for what he planned as his largest project to that point, he hesitated. He had bought the east blockfront of Madison Avenue from 76th to 77th Streets, and in early 1929 he filed plans to build a hotel and an apartment tower. It was not until a year later, however, in February 1930, with the effects of the stock market crash still uncertain, that Ginsberg began the steelwork for a project that the *Real Estate Record and Guide* said was "influenced by the campanile of Westminster Cathedral in London." He built a forty-story hotel and apartment tower on the south end of the site and a complementary fourteen-story apartment house at the north end. Designed by Bien & Prince, both buildings are seamlessly joined and Art Deco in style.

When the Carlyle opened in the fall of 1930, George Chappell, the architecture critic of the *New Yorker*, praised the "sturdy" tower, although he said the top looked like "a gigantic screw-plug for an electric light." The hotel gained its name from Ginsberg's daughter, Diana. Her daughter, the novelist Rona Jaffe, said that her mother, while studying at Cornell, had read and admired the English critic Thomas Carlyle. Ms. Jaffe said that her mother had taught English to foreigners but had not been particularly literary. She recalled that her grandfather was "very smart, but not necessarily book smart." He was 4 feet, 11 inches tall, "spoke with an accent, and despite the fact that he was short, had a very forceful presence," she said. "I admired him tremendously."

In November 1930, Marcia Zimbalist, writing in the *New Yorker* under the name "Penthouse," said that the hotel had apartments ranging from one to nine rooms renting for up to $20,000 a year. They were, she said, "intended for those who live in hotels from choice, and not because they ran away from their families and are doing penance in cubicles."

The earliest hotel tenants included Chester Dale, an investment banker and art collector who was later president of the National Gallery of Art. His collection of French

THE CARLYLE IN THE 1940S. COURTESY OFFICE FOR METROPOLITAN HISTORY

nineteenth- and twentieth-century paintings was one of the finest of the mid-twentieth century. Another tenant was Truman H. Talley, a director for Fox Movietone News, who sometimes appeared in and narrated the newsreels. Ginsberg's triumph, however, was short-lived. The Carlyle and the apartment house on 77th Street were sold at a 1932 foreclosure auction for $7 million.

823 PARK AVENUE

THE INITIAL REACTION TO THE OCTOBER 1929 CRASH by real estate professionals was relief. They felt the stock market was a sort of indecent crap game, siphoning off dollars that should have gone into stone, steel, and bricks, whether from investors or potential homeowners.

Indeed, on Park Avenue between 59th and 96th Streets there were no foreclosures in 1930 and no wave of panic selling. But the next year four buildings were foreclosed—mostly new, partly occupied structures like 778 and 895 Park Avenue. Despite continuing rosy predictions, this kept up throughout the '30s and into the mid-'40s. By 1945, 52 of the 105 big apartment houses on this stretch of Park Avenue had gone through foreclosure or been bought back by the mortgage holder in lieu of foreclosure. This even happened twice to 791, 1085, and 1192 Park, and three times to 891 Park.

Metropolitan Life Insurance took back the most, seventeen, but there were no tax foreclosures. In rental buildings the mechanism was simple: Rents came down. But in the co-ops, ownership complicated the issue. The falling market slowed sales, and even when temporary subleasing was permitted, the lower rents often did not cover maintenance charges. Shareholders began walking away from apartments, exacerbating the problems for the remaining tenants.

The building at 823 Park Avenue was erected in 1912, a near duplicate of 829 Park Avenue, put up the year before. Designed by Pickering and Walker, it had twelve duplexes, each with a library, living room, and dining room across the front, a kitchen and three servants' rooms in the middle, and four master bedrooms at the rear, in the upper part of the duplex. Interior photographs show a 55-foot sweep from the dining room through to the library, and kitchens with dinosaur-sized appliances.

Twelve apartments is not a very broad base, especially with such large apartments in times of shrinking expectations, and in 1940 the shareholders gave the building back to the principal lender, the Dry Dock Savings Bank, and the building was emptied. Dry Dock rebuilt it with thirty-eight two- to four-room apartments in place of the original twelve. They introduced push-button elevators, kitchenettes, glass-block partitions, and an outside servants' bathroom on each public hallway.

The work at 823 Park Avenue reflected a wave of similar alterations. Most buildings had just a few apartments cut up, but in 1940 Metropolitan Life emptied 969 Park Avenue, between 82nd and 83rd Streets, and reconstructed it, and City Bank Farmer's Trust did the same with most of 970 Park Avenue.

823 PARK AVENUE *under reconstruction in 1942.* COURTESY MUSEUM OF THE CITY OF NEW YORK

The facades of the buildings changed little, but inside it was as if completely new buildings had gone up, with corresponding social changes. Park Avenue was an elite thoroughfare: In 1930, 70 percent of the tenants at 823 were in the Social Register.

Most other buildings on Park Avenue, except those that were predominantly Jewish, had similar percentages. But in 1950, after reconstruction, only 10 percent of 823 Park Avenue's tenants were in the Social Register. At 830 Park Avenue, which had been through foreclosure but not wholesale reconstruction, the drop was only to 30 percent.

The foreclosures and alterations stopped only a year or two after World War II. The turmoil of the depression years is invisible; Park Avenue looks much as it did in the peak years of the 1920s.

THE PAUL FORD HOUSE

53 EAST 77TH STREET

IN 1900 THE THIRTY-FIVE-YEAR-OLD PAUL FORD, disabled from birth with a spinal injury, was on a roll. He had been transformed from a respected but obscure historical writer into a best-selling novelist, had married into a socially prominent Brooklyn family, and had almost finished a luxurious new house at 53 East 77th Street.

His father, the Brooklyn lawyer Gordon Ford, had expected all his children to pursue literary and scholarly careers, and Paul, while still a youth, founded a historical publishing house with his brother, Worthington, who was later chief of manuscripts at the Library of Congress.

Hunchbacked and a dwarf, Paul Ford was privately educated. In 1876, at age eleven, he published a genealogy of his grandfather Noah Webster; in 1892, he put out the first in a ten-volume set of Thomas Jefferson's writings.

In the early 1890s he began to publish historical fiction, and *The Honorable Peter Stirling* (1898) and *Janice Meredith* (1899) were both best-sellers. Although he had said he was a confirmed bachelor, in 1900 he married Grace Kidder, daughter of a prominent Brooklyn family, and began their newlywed house on 77th Street. Worthington Ford was the best man, but another brother, Malcolm, did not attend.

Designed by Ford with the architect Henry Rutgers Marshall, the new house was completed in 1901 in a rich Georgian style on a 34-foot-wide lot. Ford installed much of his father's library in a 30-foot-square office at the rear of the second floor. He was there around 11 A.M. on May 8, 1902, when his brother Malcolm came by.

Malcolm Ford had disappointed his father by pursuing a career as an amateur athlete. When Malcolm was fifteen, his father took him out of school to punish him for his interest in sports, but the boy followed his own abilities to national success in track and other events—amid strident protests by his father and the rest of the family. In 1891, Malcolm was the only one of seven children left out of his father's will, and in 1894 he unsuccessfully sued his siblings, saying they had promised privately to pool money for a seventh share.

They replied that they had made the offer on condition he give up athletic contests, which they felt brought the family name into the public eye in the wrong way. Feelings in the family had gone from open disagreement to grim bitterness, in part because Malcolm was a spendthrift.

After a hushed conversation between the brothers, Malcolm shot Paul and then himself in the chest. According to newspaper reports, Malcolm died instantly, but Paul

110.1 FIG

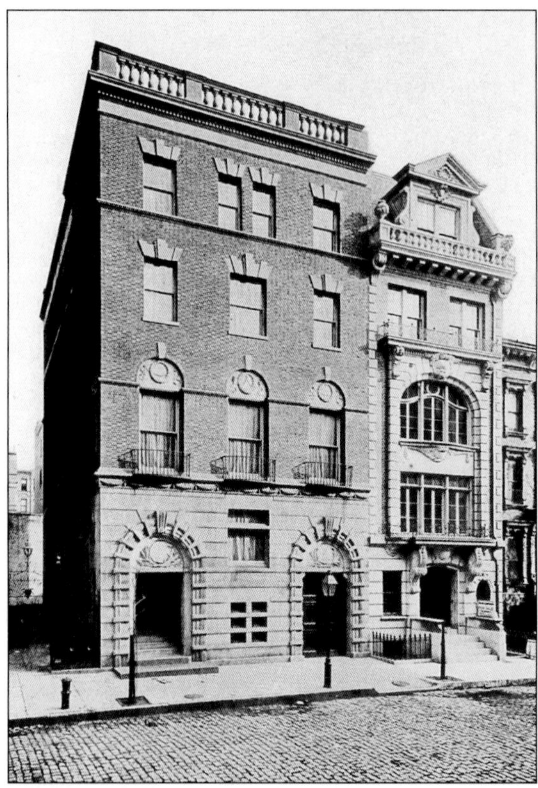

EXTERIOR OF PAUL FORD'S TOWN HOUSE IN 1910. COURTESY OFFICE FOR METROPOLITAN HISTORY

110.2 FIG

PAUL FORD'S STUDY IN 1901. COURTESY OFFICE FOR METROPOLITAN HISTORY

lived for half an hour, saying to his secretary, "Miss Hall, I must die like a brave man." Grace Ford, pregnant, was upstairs and heard the gunshots.

On May 10, coffins for Paul and Malcolm Ford sat side by side in the house's library. On June 3, Grace gave birth to a daughter, Lesta.

Mrs. Ford remarried in 1908, and the house went through several hands until 1926, when it was bought by Joseph Kerrigan, who gave the building its present medieval style brick front. But the traces of the Ford house—including the windows lighting the stairway that Malcolm Ford ascended in 1902— are still visible on the side wall.

THE PAYNE WHITNEY HOUSE

972 FIFTH AVENUE

AT THEIR MARRIAGE IN 1902 PAYNE WHITNEY AND HELEN HAY received as a present a Fifth Avenue plot with a house to be designed by Stanford White. This gift was not from Whitney's father, William C. Whitney, who had made millions in street railways—the son had quarreled with the father on the latter's remarriage after the death of his first wife, Payne Whitney's mother.

Rather, the new house was the gift of Payne Whitney's uncle, Oliver H. Payne, who ultimately gave Payne Whitney $75 million. Payne Whitney had just graduated from Harvard Law School; his wife, Helen, had written several books of poetry.

For them Stanford White not only designed an imposing granite house with a full southern facade looking over a garden plot but also selected furnishings, sculpture, and paintings that drove the final cost to about $1 million.

According to David Garrard Lowe, author of *Stanford White's New York,* White was careful enough to consult with Helen Hay's father about the color of marble in the house where she grew up. But ultimately, he had to write Oliver Payne, who was paying the bills, that "I have dreaded to speak to you about" the increasing bills.

At the time, White was in financial trouble even though he was collecting a 10 percent commission on interiors.

Visible in one historic photograph of the foyer are antique plaques, ironwork, furniture, statuary, and, at the center, an odd marble fountain ringed by greenery and topped by the damaged figure of a nude boy with a quiver.

White bought the statue in Rome. Although there is not yet any evidence that he had any particular idea about the sculptor, he did put it at the center of a circular room right in line with the main entrance.

THE PAYNE WHITNEY MANSION IN 1909. COURTESY OFFICE FOR METROPOLITAN HISTORY

White, slain in 1906 in a notorious murder, did not live to see the house completed in 1909. It was filled with tapestries, furniture, architectural elements, and paintings that White had brokered. Mr. Lowe's book quotes a 1911 account in *Town & Country* calling the Whitney residence "a triumphant blending of decorative art, old and new, a marvelous assembling of . . . voices of that ancient Italy of Leonardo da Vinci, of Benvenuto Cellini, and others of the Cinquecento."

Whitney and his wife divided their time between 972 Fifth Avenue and their Manhasset, Long Island, country house, Greentree, with their two children, Joan (later Mrs. Charles Shipman Payson) and John Hay, called Jock.

After Whitney's death in 1927, his wife continued in the house and also maintained her husband's interest in racehorses. In 1931 her horse, Twenty Grand, won the Kentucky Derby. In the late 1930s Jock Whitney bought the film rights to *Gone with the Wind,* and one scene of the movie was shot on the staircase of 972 Fifth Avenue.

In the 1990s the little marble Cupid, which had been purchased by White for the Whitneys and somehow survived in place, was attributed by Professor Kathleen

Weil-Garris Brandt to Michelangelo. The building is now occupied by the office of the French Cultural Services, a division of the French Embassy, and you can ask admission to examine the curious statue and the magnificent room that surrounds it.

890 PARK AVENUE

THE HOUSE AT 890 PARK AVENUE was part of a row of five at 882–890, built in two stages from 1884 to 1886. The houses at 888 and 890 were built first, designed by James E. Ware with gabled roofs and red brick, a picturesque contrast to the dour brownstones typical until then.

The houses at 882–886 were built slightly later and shared the Queen Anne–style multipane windows and the arched parlor floor windows with stained glass, but they were built with full top floors and a more traditional roofline.

The first resident of 890 Park Avenue—at that time 1390 Fourth Avenue—was Harry A. Groesbeck, a stockbroker who occupied it with his family in 1886. Five years later, the New York Stock Exchange censured Groesbeck for following another broker's courier to determine the other broker's client. Groesbeck's neighbors included Edward and Edith Wharton, who had married in 1885 and moved into 884 Park Avenue, three houses down.

Edith Wharton began writing in earnest after her marriage, perhaps in response to her husband's emerging mental illness. She drew on her own patrician upbringing to write fiction, and in 1897 her first important book was published, *The Decoration of Houses*, an influential treatise on design she wrote with the architect Ogden Codman.

Just as her book came out, 890 Park Avenue was altered to include a store in the basement (the present entry floor) and an office with a large show window on the parlor floor with two apartments above.

By 1899, when Wharton published her first important work of fiction, *The Greater Inclination*, she was spending little time in the New York house, which was boarded up in a 1907 photograph. In 1900 the census taker recorded an English-born "furnace man" at 884, noting, "House closed—Paris France."

Park Avenue's fortunes began looking up when the railroad replaced its steam engines with electric ones in 1907. The switch reinvigorated the house market. David Keppel, a prominent dealer in old master prints, took over 890 Park Avenue and retained the store but converted the upper floors back to single-family use in an alteration designed by Hewitt & Bottomley. The architects installed a sophisticated Italian Renaissance–style mantel on the second floor, but otherwise little of their work is discernible.

888 AND 890 PARK AVENUE, CIRCA 1890. COURTESY OFFICE FOR METROPOLITAN HISTORY

The 1920 census recorded Keppel in the house with three servants, and, in a separate household, Isaiah Waters, fifty-nine, born in Virginia, who worked at Lenox Hill Hospital. Waters lived with three family members, all born in southern states. Unlike almost all others on Park Avenue, the Waters household was African American.

In the 1930s the Greenwich Savings Bank took the bank back in foreclosure, and in 1940 the bank's architects, Cross & Cross, renovated what the building application described as a rooming house. The current entry vestibule is probably their work; the rich red marble walls and highly figured black-and-white marble floor recall Cross & Cross's building for Tiffany & Company at 57th Street and Fifth Avenue of the same year. Although the exterior of the house is bedraggled, this little touch is a nice surprise on the art gallery of the New York streets.

THE DUKE CHATEAU

1 EAST 78TH STREET

JAMES DUKE BECAME THE MOST ACTIVE MEMBER OF A FAMILY TOBACCO FIRM in Durham, North Carolina, and in 1890 he joined with other companies to form the American Tobacco Company. He later said, "If John D. Rockefeller can do what he is doing in oil, why should I not do it in tobacco?" And indeed, his company controlled four-fifths of the American tobacco business within twenty years.

Duke moved to New York in the 1880s and in 1909 bought a site at the northeast corner of 78th Street and Fifth Avenue on one of two blocks on the Upper East Side completely restricted to private houses. As architect he retained Horace Trumbauer, who had become prominent for his designs of palatial houses around Philadelphia but who had not yet built at such a scale in New York.

Duke's new house was completed in 1912, with a giant main hall, dining room, drawing room, music room on the first floor, eight bedrooms on the second, and, on a third floor hidden from the street behind a balustrade, twelve servants' rooms.

Dreck S. Wilson of the Maryland Department of Environmental Protection has researched the career of Horace Trumbauer. He says that the Duke house is particularly notable as an early work by one of Trumbauer's designers, Julian Abele, an African American. Mr. Wilson says that Abele was a top student at the University of Pennsylvania School of Architecture and began working for Trumbauer in 1906. "Trumbauer had no formal education as an architect," says Mr. Wilson, and had to rely on staff architects for much of any commission.

According to Mr. Wilson, Abele "considered himself above and beyond racial description" and was light skinned. He did not focus on his racial makeup—others may have thought he was Spanish—and carved out a place as senior designer in Trumbauer's office without controversy or remark. However, Michael Adams, an architectural historian in New York, says that there is evidence that Abele was a member of the National Association for the Advancement of Colored People (NAACP) and that Trumbauer was criticized for hiring Abele, criticism that he ignored.

The 1915 census shows James B. Duke in occupancy with his wife, Nanaline, his two-year-old daughter, Doris, and fourteen servants. The 1920 census showed plenty of turnover downstairs: the only servant remaining was Mathilda Andrews, fifty, the Swedish cook. Duke died of pneumonia, at home, in 1925, and his daughter inherited about $50 million.

Doris Duke went through several troubled marriages and until the late 1950s shared the house off and on with her mother, who died in 1962. Doris Duke gave the house to New York University in 1957, and since then it has served as the Institute of Fine Arts. The well behaved may be able to talk their way past a security guard into the main hallway, which is still as gracious as it was nearly a century ago.

FIG 113.1

THE DUKE MANSION, *the exterior(top) and an interior bedroom(bottom), in a* New York Times *photograph from January 1914.* COURTESY MUSEUM OF THE CITY OF NEW YORK

39 EAST 79TH STREET

EMILY POST WAS BORN IN 1873, the daughter of the architect Bruce Price, who designed the gated Tuxedo Park enclave in the 1880s. Divorced around the turn of the century, she moved to Tuxedo Park. To support herself, she followed Edith Wharton's path and began writing fiction, but with moderate success, and in 1922 published *Etiquette—The Blue Book of Social Usage*.

Although matters involving Emily Post and etiquette are widely lampooned, anyone who reads her book finds an eminently pragmatic guide. Far from foppish concerns over the right knife or the right greeting, her advice on many issues was that "it doesn't matter," and that the most sensible and comfortable thing was almost always the most correct.

Her passages on servants, invitations, and introductions to royalty don't seem to have much relevance now, but other observations still have resonance: "Nothing shows selfish want of consideration more than being habitually late." "Who does not dislike a boneless hand extended as though it were a miniature boiled pudding?" "It is a waste of breath for the father to order his sons to keep their temper, or to behave like gentlemen, or to be good sportsmen, if he does or is himself none of these things."

Mrs. Post's deft writing and disarming practicality made *Etiquette* a best-seller. She was happy living in Tuxedo Park until around 1924, when her son told her that increasing traffic out of New York City would curtail the regular Sunday visits that brought him, his wife, and his son out to see her.

His account says that she announced her plans to build and live in a co-op apartment building at lunch at the Colony Club, the women's club on Park Avenue, and that "by the time coffee was served" she had a list of likely buyers.

Mrs. Post hired the architect Kenneth Murchison. In Mrs. Post's view, this was the right way to build a co-op: keeping it in a small circle of friends and family instead of involving a professional developer tempted to cut corners.

The finished building had large duplexes on the west side, facing Madison Avenue, and smaller simplexes on the east side. The apartments cost from $25,000 to $60,000.

Every tenant was listed in the New York Social Register; the typical figure in a Park Avenue building of the time was 60 to 80 percent. Today, about 20 percent of the building's residents are in the Social Register. Mrs. Post died in her apartment, 9B, in 1960.

39 EAST 79TH STREET IN 1941. COURTESY OFFICE FOR METROPOLITAN HISTORY

ISAAC FLETCHER HOUSE

2 EAST 79TH STREET

IN 1897 ISAAC D. FLETCHER, A BANKER AND BROKER, retained the architect C. P. H. Gilbert for a new house at the southeast corner of 79th and Fifth, and Gilbert delivered a design in limestone of the French Gothic style so characteristic of his work. The Fletcher house is marked by a profusion of crockets, pinnacles, moldings, and other details that make Gilbert's elaborate Warburg house of 1907 (at 92nd Street and Fifth Avenue, now the Jewish Museum) seem relatively chaste.

In an article in the *Real Estate Record and Guide* in 1899, an anonymous critic generally praised the design (especially the rather plain east wall) but noted that much of the ornament was ecclesiastical rather than domestic in origin. The writer closed with the observation that the Fletcher mansion had "too much the air of an archeological reproduction to be accepted as an appropriate New York City house of 1898."

Fletcher died in 1917 and left the house and his art collection to the Metropolitan Museum of Art. The Met sold the house to Harry F. Sinclair, a self-made oil prospector who had founded the Sinclair Oil Company in 1916. Sinclair was occupying the house in the 1920s when the Teapot Dome scandals of the Harding Administration broke over him. Sinclair was accused, with Secretary of the Interior Albert Fall, of conspiring to defraud the government in a lease of oil reserves owned by the navy in Teapot Dome, Wyoming. Fall served time for related offenses; Sinclair was acquitted, although his lease of the reserve was canceled.

In 1930 Sinclair sold the house to Augustus Van Horne Stuyvesant Jr. Stuyvesant and his sister, Anne, descendants of Governor Peter Stuyvesant and rich with inherited real estate, had been driven by commerce from their house at 3 East 57th Street, where they lived together; both were unmarried.

Anne Stuyvesant died in 1938, and the article "Death and Taxes" in *Fortune* magazine of July 1939 remarked that the Fifth Avenue mansions had become "symbols not of power but of decay"—of the seventy-two private houses then left on Fifth Avenue, thirty-three were closed. The article reported that even a moderate-sized house required ten servants at a yearly payroll of $14,000, with $4,000 alone in food for the staff. The bare minimum for keeping a house open was $30,000 a year. The magazine

THE ISAAC D. FLETCHER MANSION IN 1898. COURTESY OFFICE FOR METROPOLITAN HISTORY

reported that Stuyvesant "eats utterly alone at the big dining room table . . . served by Vernon, the butler, and an assisting footman."

Stuyvesant died in 1953 and was buried in the family vault after services at St. Mark's in-the-Bouwerie, at Second Avenue and 10th Street. The *New York Times* reported that in the front left pew, "Ernest Vernon, Mr. Stuyvesant's white-haired, ruddy-faced butler, dressed in formal black, sat alone, weeping into a handkerchief."

In 1955 the Ukrainian Institute of America bought the house, and they are often open for cultural events. A walk through the Fletcher house is a time trip: the house is astonishingly intact, even down to the woodwork in the servants' areas. The occasional modernization so often seen in big old houses is entirely absent, as if the Stuyvesant butler had locked up for the last time just yesterday.

THE GREEK CONSULATE

69 EAST 79TH STREET

IN 1908 GEORGE L. RIVES HIRED CARRÈRE & HASTINGS for the new house he planned to occupy after leaving Murray Hill. Rives, a lawyer and a Democratic politician, had been first assistant secretary of state under President Grover Cleveland and was part of the fusion-reform movement that elected Seth Low, a Republican, to the mayoralty in 1901 over Tammany Hall's opposition.

An unsigned article in a 1909 issue of the *Architectural Record* praised the design of the five-story Rives house, based on Parisian town houses on the Place Vendôme: "Its total effect is characterized by repose, distinction and style, and it is these qualities which make this house front worthy of study and imitation."

Around 1919, the Rives family left the house and leased it to others. It was purchased in 1958 by the government of Greece, which then completely rebuilt the fourth and fifth floors and added a sixth as it altered the house for consular use. The alteration, completed in 1962, was one of many adaptations of obsolete mansions in New York—but with a difference. The Greek architect in charge of the project, Pierre Zannettos, designed the new top three floors with astonishing sensitivity to the original design. On the exterior, his work is seamless—the limestone upper floors are indistinguishable from the original ones below.

Mr. Zannettos carefully reproduced, with slight simplifications, the eared window frames and other details of the original fourth floor. The original fifth-floor balustrade was either reproduced or disassembled and repositioned. Mr. Zannettos also added two bronze flagpoles and bronze lanterns at the front, elegant works of metal, particularly considering the date of execution.

Many of the rooms—like the pine-paneled reception room in the front—were left intact or nearly so. In the sections of the house that were rebuilt, Mr. Zannettos did work in a more contemporary style. On the fifth floor, he created a large, U-shaped reception desk in green and white marble for visa and passport applications, with square marble columns and bronze metalwork. It could be a 1950s airport ticket counter in Crete. Generally, the house lacks the cheap dropped ceilings and similar construction typical of the time. Mr. Zannettos's project on 79th Street does not appear to have received any awards or public notice in architectural journals, perhaps because it was so far out of the mainstream. But today even the classicist and historian Henry Hope Reed admires it, saying: "It's got good manners. He was not trying to express himself like modern architects are always trying to do."

In 2001 Dmitris Platis, the consul-general, oversaw a cleaning project that recaptures much of the 1909/1962 elegance, which is pleasing to Mr. Platis; he appreciates the evident age of the stone and said he wanted to avoid a "like new" appearance.

FIG 116.1

THE RIVES HOUSE AT 69 EAST 79TH STREET IN 1909.
COURTESY LIBRARY OF CONGRESS

FIG 117.1

THE VINCENT ASTOR HOUSE ON EAST 80TH STREET IN 1927.
COURTESY MUSEUM OF THE CITY OF NEW YORK

116-130 EAST 80TH STREET

THE ENTIRE SOUTH SIDE OF 80TH STREET between Park and Lexington Avenues was built up with modest three-story brownstones in 1871, occupied by people of modestly comfortable means. But the social geography of the East Side was changing. The row was fairly intact in 1921 when Lewis Spencer Morris, a lawyer and an eighth-generation descendant of Lewis Morris, a signer of the Declaration of Independence, bought the brownstones at 116 and 118 and put up a double-width town house for himself and his wife, Emily Coster Morris. Designed by Cross & Cross and completed in 1923, this suave neo-Federal design successfully evoked the age and social position of the Morris family, and the 36-foot width of the house announced that a new level of householder had settled on the street.

Two years later Vincent Astor bought the houses at 128 and 130 East 80th. At age twenty, Astor had inherited the $87 million estate of his father, Colonel John Jacob Astor, after his father died on the *Titanic* in 1912.

Vincent Astor hired Mott Schmidt to design a house for a man who could have anything, and the architect developed what remains one of the most stately residences in New York, in a soft yellow limestone reminiscent of London town houses.

Astor and Morris both began buying up properties on the 79th Street block to the south, to preserve the light to their south gardens. Their actions appear to have attracted two more multimillionaires in 1929: George Whitney, who bought the brownstones at 120 and 122, and Clarence Dillon, who bought 124 and 126.

Whitney hired Morris's architects, Cross & Cross, and they designed a lighter, more cosmopolitan Federal-style house. Dillon retained Astor's architect, Mott Schmidt, and got a richer, more modeled neo-Georgian-style design than Astor's house.

Both Dillon, head of Dillon, Read & Company, and George Whitney, partner and later head of J. P. Morgan & Company, had been spectacularly successful in banking. Dillon, an alumnus of Harvard, Class of 1907, must have had something to talk about over the back fence with Whitney, also a Harvard alumnus, Class of 1905.

These four houses, of identical width and similar design, form the type of streetscape that urban designers often dream of emulating—but these quadruplets arrived entirely by accident. Surviving children of the original owners agree that their parents had no concerted plan, and there are no comprehensive property restrictions such as those that were essential to colonies like Sutton Place and Turtle Bay Gardens.

The Morrises were the first to sell, in 1942; Astor sold in 1947 to the New York Junior League, a combination women's social club and charity organization. That group is now the senior owner in the group of four: the Dillon house, at 124, is the residence of the Iraqi ambassador to the United States; the Whitney house, at 120, is now apartments; and the Morris house, at 116, has gone through several hands but is still a private residence. They make an elegant foursome.

1009 FIFTH AVENUE

ALTHOUGH THE SIX-STORY BUILDING AT 1009 FIFTH AVENUE presents itself as a custom-built mansion, it was actually one a group of four houses, 1006–1009 Fifth, built in 1901 for sale by the developers William and Thomas Hall, and designed by Welch, Smith and Provot. In late 1901 the critic Montgomery Schuyler ridiculed this building and others in an article in the magazine *Architectural Record* entitled "The Architecture of the Billionaire District."

Schuyler conceded some competent touches in the house but generally dismissed 1009 Fifth Avenue (and other mansions on Fifth), singling out the sheet-metal cornice painted to imitate stone. "We hold these truths to be self-evident," Schuyler wrote, "that, when a man goes into 'six figures' for his dwelling house, he ought not to make its upperworks of sheet metal. That is a cheap pretence which nothing can distinguish from vulgarity."

By the time of Schuyler's review, the Halls had sold the house to Benjamin N. Duke of Durham, North Carolina. With his brother, James B. Duke, Benjamin had built up the family tobacco business into the American Tobacco Company. The brothers were also associated in the endowment of what became Duke University.

At one time Benjamin Duke's fortune was estimated at $60 million, and it is not clear why he bought 1009 Fifth Avenue instead of building a house of his own design. In addition, census, city directories, and other sources list no occupant of the house until 1907, when Benjamin Duke moved in from the old Hoffman House Hotel.

He moved to the Plaza Hotel in 1909, and his brother replaced him at 1009 Fifth. In 1912 James built his own mansion at 1 East 78th Street, now owned by New York

University, and Benjamin built one at the southeast corner of 89th Street and Fifth Avenue that was demolished years later for the Guggenheim Museum.

Other family members moved into 1009 Fifth; they were followed in 1922 by Anthony J. Drexel Biddle Jr. and his wife, Mary, Benjamin's daughter. It was during their occupancy that the modern designer Karl Bock added to the existing French-style interiors. At various times in the 1930s and 1940s Bock installed a ribbon-striped sycamore dressing room, an oval, black-marble-and-mirror bathroom, and a royal-blue glass-tile bathroom with a modernistic sink that looks like a robot. These are among the most unusual interiors on Fifth Avenue.

Mrs. Biddle died in 1960, and her daughter, Mary Biddle Semans, took over the house. In the 1970s, Mrs. Semans refused offers from a real estate developer for a project that brought about the demolition of 1006–1008 Fifth Avenue and resulted in the apartment house now next door, so this house remains as her testimony that money isn't everything.

FIG 118.1

1009 FIFTH AVENUE, AT LEFT, IN 1910. COURTESY OFFICE FOR METROPOLITAN HISTORY

THE METROPOLITAN MUSEUM OF ART

FIFTH AVENUE FRONT

THE ARCHITECT RICHARD MORRIS HUNT had been among the original organizers of the museum and was frustrated that he had never been asked to design for it. But he got his chance, with the Met's building campaign in the 1890s, when it built what is now its main entrance, facing Fifth Avenue.

The new design broke with the older wings. Instead of red brick, he envisioned white marble encrusted with columns, classical decorations, and plenty of sculpture. Hunt died in July 1895, but not before he produced nearly final designs for the facade more or less as it was built; he included thirty-one separate works of sculpture. Those that were executed include standing caryatid figures on the wings, heads of Athena as keystones for the three arches, and six medallion busts of old masters flanking the arches.

But much of Hunt's sculptural program was not carried out, including long inscriptions in the upper frieze and panels on the wings; reproductions of famous sculpture in the niches behind the columns; and, at the top of the building, four large figural groups, meant to represent ancient, classical, Renaissance, and modern art. Also, limestone was substituted for the originally specified marble.

Hunt died before he could make more than generic designs for the four figural groups, but preliminary drawings suggest that in scale and arrangement they would have looked something like the *Four Continents* series on the Bowling Green front of the old United States Custom House. The new wing was finished in 1902, praised by critics as one of Hunt's finest works. "His success, as we can all now see, has been really brilliant," the *Architectural Record* said.

But the question of the unexecuted sculptures still bothered the trustees. Around 1900 the sculptor John Quincy Adams Ward advised the trustees that "if the term modern art means to include any art later than the Renaissance you would be getting into a sea of difficulties where there would be danger of disaster." Contemporary art, Ward said, was "too chaotic" to find a common representation. And the cost of completing the sculptures was huge. In 1904 Louis di Cesnola, the museum's director, complained that the exterior limestone was already disintegrating. "Anyone can see what condition the exterior is in, however, and the necessity of action of some kind," he told the *New York Tribune*. The large piles of limestone blocks, meant to be carved, remained in place. They are still there, a cohort of perplexing cubist monuments.

FIG 119.1

THE FIFTH AVENUE FRONT OF THE METROPOLITAN MUSEUM OF ART *about 1905.* COURTESY LIBRARY OF CONGRESS

FIG 119.2

DETAIL OF AN 1896 DRAWING *showing the facade sculptures that were never created.* COURTESY THE METROPOLITAN MUSEUM OF ART

THE METROPOLITAN MUSEUM OF ART

WING A

THE FIRST BUILDING OF THE METROPOLITAN MUSEUM OF ART, later termed Wing A, followed the High Victorian Gothic style, red brick with a patterned slate roof and polychromed Venetian-style arches. Although now enveloped by the rest of the museum, it is now familiar as the location of the annual Christmas tree display.

The museum did not open until March 30, 1880. A writer for the *Critic*, an art magazine, thought the new Metropolitan—along with St. Patrick's Cathedral—represented America's "backwardness of architecture." But the interior was generally praised: A writer for the *Art Journal* described the inside as "an honest, good building, with no meretricious gewgaws about it."

The main feature of the interior was a giant central skylit hall, with a roof supported by pierced metal beams. The flooring was of giant geometric slabs of white and black marble and red slate, and the four stairways had iron decoration in the High Victorian style, with clustered columns and capitals of hybrid plant and floral forms.

More than 912,000 visitors came to the Metropolitan in the first year. Within two decades Wing A was boxed in on the south by Wing B, on the north by Wing C, and on the east by Wing D—which remains the main entrance to the building. In 1935 the architect Otto Eggers enlarged the central hall as a medieval gallery and destroyed most of its Victorian elements.

In 1954 the architects Robert O'Connor and Aymar Embury boxed in some of the Victorian ironwork of the remaining eastern staircases with the best of modernist intentions. The magazine *Architectural Forum* softly demurred, calling the new stairs "cleaner but devitalized."

The coup de grace came with the 1970 Master Plan for the museum by Kevin Roche, John Dinkeloo Associates. While proclaiming "restoration," the plan ruthlessly hid the parkfront Victorian facades of Wings A, B and C, recapturing part of the front of Wing A as an airless backdrop for the sleek new Lehman Wing. Bernhard Leitner, writing in *Art Forum* that year, decried the new homogeneity and called it "the Metropolitan Bank of Art."

For decades the little fragments of the original Met have tantalized visitors who know where to look: the medieval tapestry gallery has a large swath of original mar-

INTERIOR OF WING A *of the Metropolitan Museum in the 1930s.* COURTESY THE METROPOLITAN MUSEUM OF ART

ble and slate flooring, with giant fossil snails that six-year-olds spot immediately. Off to each side the two original stairways survive partially intact, although with the dimmest legal lighting and dull gray paint covering surviving ironwork. Despite the preservation revolution of the last thirty years, nothing changed the Met from its course of designed neglect of these unusual elements.

But in 1994 the Met uncovered, during a gallery renovation, a small part of the original eastern facade of the museum. It is now visible in a room to the left of the top of the main staircase. Later the museum squeezed out a tiny budget for a homemade restoration of these stairs, which have received a casual paint job in the original colors—taupe, maroon, buff, and black, according to Amelia Peck, associate curator. Now finding Wing A no longer requires the help of a detective.

THE BREARLEY SCHOOL

610 EAST 83RD STREET

THE TYPICAL NEW YORK PRIVATE SCHOOL BUILDING seems to cross town house with private club—neo-Georgian, genteel, and particularly, only four or five stories high.

For over a century the Brearley School, now at 83rd Street and the East River, has followed a different course, building an unusual series of three high-rise buildings in 1890, 1912, and, in 1930, its present ten-story-high factory-style structure.

Samuel Brearley Jr. announced his new girls school with a large advertisement in the *New York Times* on June 19, 1884, to open on October 8 in an old brownstone at 6 East 45th Street. Tuition was set for $350 a year, and Brearley offered Latin, Greek, botany, and elocution as well as the more usual subjects. His goal was to develop a girls school equal in every way to those for boys.

He died of pneumonia in 1886 and his obituary in the *New York Times* called his efforts "very successful." The parents banded together to continue, and by 1890 enrollment had grown to such a degree that the parents did something that almost no proprietary school had done—they developed their own building.

Their architect, Henry Rutgers Marshall, filed plans in 1890 for a medieval-style school, 82 feet high and 50 feet wide, at 17 West 44th Street, in a growing district of private clubs. The facade gives the impression that the building has only five stories, but sidelong views indicate it was at least six and possibly nine stories high—and this at a time when New York was still largely a city of three- to five-story walk-ups.

The $100,000 building opened in the fall of 1891 and the school remained there until 1912, when the growing number of office buildings (and the increasing migration of families uptown) caused trustees to move again. This time they bought the southwest corner of 61st Street and Park Avenue, building a ten-story-high neo-Georgian building, similar in detailing to many East Side town houses—but it was ten stories tall. In 1928 Brearley sold the 61st Street building and bought its present site at the south corner of 83rd Street and the East River, in the developing East End section.

Brearley's third architect, Benjamin Wistar Morris, designed another ten-story building. This facade mixes factory modernism with trim, elegant detailing, like ornamental pilasters of serrated brick. This was the type of styling that was remaking the face of Europe. It seemed revolutionary at a time when the traditional styles still reigned supreme in the United States.

The same spare modernism was carried out on the interior, where the walls were a sand-finished plaster and the concrete beams and cork and brick walls of the gym carry the same decorative value as the slight Art Deco of the auditorium. Although the school has been indifferent to its building over the last several decades, it is still an architectural treat, inside and out.

FIG 121.1

BREARLEY AT 17 WEST 44TH STREET IN 1892. COURTESY OFFICE FOR METROPOLITAN HISTORY

RENDERING OF BREARLEY'S *present building at 610 East 83rd Street, 1929.*
COURTESY BREARLEY SCHOOL

3 EAST 84TH STREET

JOSEPH MEDILL PATTERSON GREW UP IN CHICAGO, a member of the Medill-McCormick-Patterson publishing family. His grandfather Joseph Medill had built up the *Chicago Tribune,* which Patterson's father, Robert W. Patterson, took over in the 1890s. When Joseph Medill Patterson took it over with his cousin, Robert McCormick, in the 1910s, they doubled its circulation. Patterson then had the idea of starting a tabloid-type newspaper in New York.

FIG 122.1

A DETAIL OF THE DOORWAY AT 3 EAST 84TH STREET ABOUT 1930. COURTESY OFFICE FOR METROPOLITAN HISTORY

First published in 1919, the *Daily News* did well, aiming at mass circulation with sensational stories. In 1926, with a circulation of one million, it became the most popular newspaper in New York, and Patterson came here from Chicago to supervise its continuing success.

In 1928 Patterson built the house at 3 East 84th Street with an apartment for himself, apparently the penthouse. His architect was Raymond Hood, a provocative modernist, who designed a jazz-modern riff of smooth limestone and zigzag ornament, arranged in alternating vertical piers. The limestone frieze above the first floor is hypnotic—is it abstract, or is it a pattern of chubby birds over faces with stylized hair?

Although this type of ornament had become familiar in commercial buildings, it was unusual in residential buildings, especially luxury ones. The arrangement of the facade into vertical bays was antithetical to the palazzo model of horizontals that still dominated the design of such buildings. The interior was also surprising, a wild combination

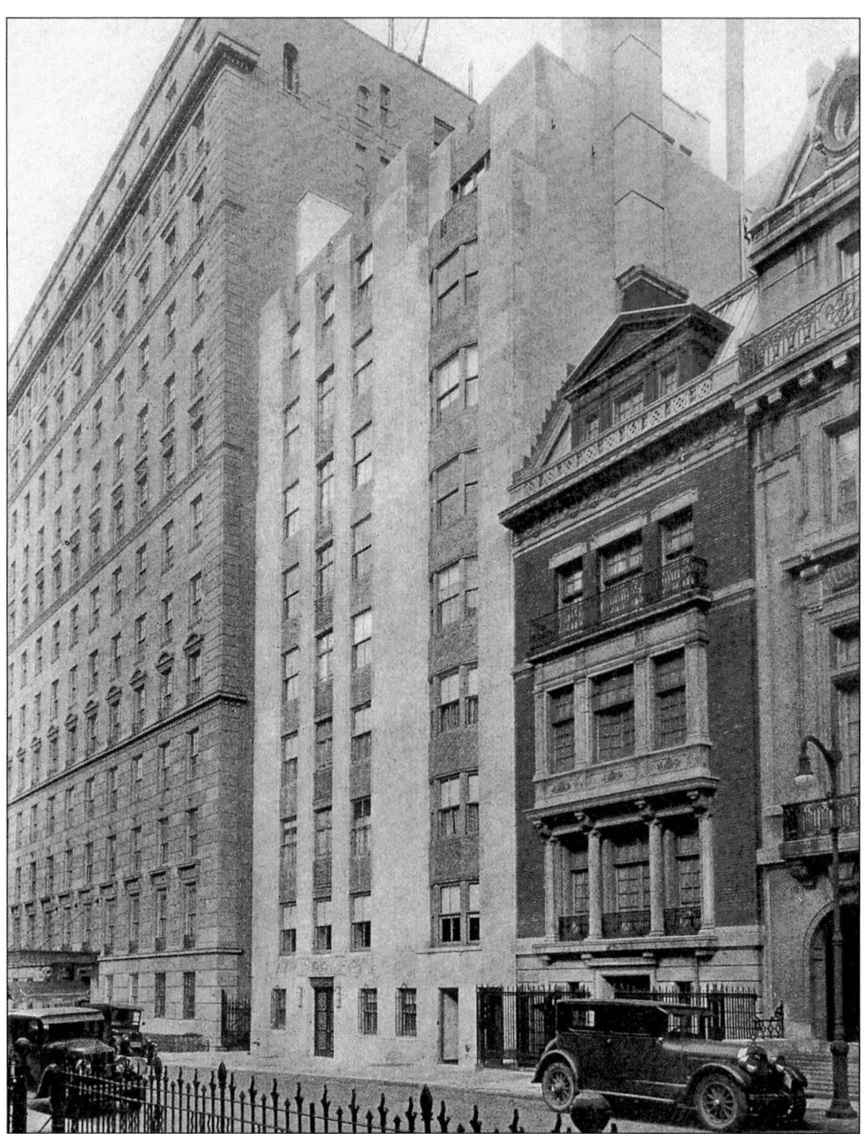

3 EAST 84TH STREET ABOUT 1930. COURTESY OFFICE FOR METROPOLITAN HISTORY

of abstract patterns and ornament—the elevator was nearly Mayan in character.

In 1929, when Hood was designing the Daily News Building at 220 East 42nd Street for Patterson, he reused the vertical banding of 3 East 84th Street for what is considered one of the most important of New York's skyscrapers.

Patterson was outspoken and unconventional, a socialist from a rich family who subscribed to the *Daily Worker* and frequented the Bowery incognito to keep in touch with the masses.

Soon after 3 East 84th Street went up, he also built a country house near Ossining, New York, designed by Hood. A sprawling, cubic mass with no attempt at symmetry, it had a rooftop observatory and was painted with the irregular, blocky forms used for naval camouflage in World War I. According to John Tebbel's *An American Dynasty* (1947), Patterson was also claustrophobic to the extent that he required doors of metal instead of wood. He was afraid that the wood might swell and trap him inside.

Other apartments at 3 East 84th Street were taken by James A. Farley, the Democratic political boss who was postmaster general under Franklin D. Roosevelt, and Patterson's daughter, Alicia, who founded *Newsday* in 1940. She also shared with her father an interest in flying—they got their pilot's licenses on the same day in 1930.

Loiter at the elaborate front doorway to peer inside at the remarkable lobby, a small but delicious legacy of an unusual architectural team.

1040 PARK AVENUE

IN 1923 JOSEPH L. B. MAYER, a developer, began work at the northwest corner of 86th Street, an apartment house that is still a piquant addition to rest of the avenue's rather sober architecture. Although Mayer had used commercial architects on other projects, he retained Delano & Aldrich, better known for upper-class town houses and clubs.

The architects gave it a chaste limestone base of three floors and an amusing third-story frieze of tortoise-and-hare figures. At the top is an inventive attic story with an elegant iron balcony of anthemion pattern. This top story also has rounded windows and a frieze of triglyphs and shells, a mild but imaginative mix. Barely visible at the top is the glassed-in terrace on the 86th Street side of the building's roof. This was the penthouse apartment of Condé Nast.

Nast began his publishing empire in the 1910s and by the mid-1920s was riding high. Creating a triumvirate of *Vogue, Vanity Fair,* and *House & Garden*, Nast emphasized quality printing on flatbed presses and the highest artistic and literary standards. Jean Cocteau, Aldous Huxley, Pablo Picasso, Paul Robeson, Cecil Beaton, and the photographers Edward Steichen and Charles Sheeler were typical of the people who worked for or were portrayed by Condé Nast Publications.

Nast may or may not have been in on the initial planning of 1040 Park Avenue in 1923, but in 1924 Delano & Aldrich revised the top-floor plans to provide for a huge apartment for Nast with a wide surrounding terrace, an unusual although not unprecedented feature in a luxury apartment house.

Nast inaugurated his apartment, decorated by Elsie de Wolfe, with a housewarming dance on January 18, 1925. His wide-ranging guest list included George Gershwin, Edna St. Vincent Millay, Rube Goldberg, Katharine Cornell, Jascha Heifetz, Fannie Hurst, Fred Astaire, Edward Steichen, and John Drew.

FIG 123.1

THE VIEW NORTH ON PARK AVENUE *showing 1040 Park Avenue at 86th Street (at center, left) with its penthouse in 1930.* COURTESY MUNICIPAL ARCHIVES

FIG 123.2

CONDÉ NAST WITH GUESTS IN HIS PENTHOUSE IN THE 1930S. COURTESY LESLIE BONHAM-CARTER

Nast must have been one of the first New Yorkers to recognize that an open terrace is of only seasonal use: In 1926 he hired Delano & Aldrich to design a greenhouse-like glass canopy to cover the terrace and had the ballroom extended to the edge of the building.

The stock market crash of 1929 wiped Nast out and left him with marginal control over his beloved magazines. He was in debt until he died, but he held on to his apartment and still entertained New York society. In 1941 he gave a party for Henry R. Luce, the head of Time Inc., and his wife, the writer Clare Boothe Luce, before they left on a trip to China. The party was attended by the Chinese ambassador to the United States, Dr. Hu Shih, as well as by the French writer André Maurois, Mrs. Cornelius Vanderbilt, John D. Rockefeller Jr., and Joseph Medill Patterson, the publisher of the *Daily News*. Nast died in his penthouse in 1942; his employees filed past his coffin in the drawing room.

CHURCH OF THE HOLY TRINITY

320 EAST 88TH STREET

ALONG WITH THE ASTORS AND GOELETS, the Rhinelanders, who made their money in importing, were one of the great building families in nineteenth-century New York. Beginning in 1879, they put up scores of small houses and flat buildings, mostly on the far Upper East Side, the seventy-two-acre grounds of the family's summer house in the early 1800s.

In 1895 Serena Rhinelander decided to give $500,000 for a church complex in the working-class neighborhood, using a long mid-block site on the south side of 88th Street between Second and First Avenues. She entrusted the details to her nephew, William Rhinelander Stewart, treasurer of Grace Church, and he brought in the architects J. Stewart Barney and Henry Otis Chapman.

They made the most of the expansive site, designing a tawny string of buildings in orange, iron-spot brick, and lacy terra-cotta: a vicarage, the main church (with its 150-foot-high central tower), a chapel, and the parish house. In 1899 the *New York Evening Post* called it "in effect, a park for the surrounding tenements."

The church has a very unusual dark brown terra-cotta interior, designed to set off the lush stained-glass windows by Henry Holiday. Almost perfectly intact, this Victorian interior contrasts nicely with the tiny chapel, modernized in the 1950s and given glass by Robert Sowers. Although heavily worn, most of the parish house interior is unchanged, with banks of oak closets and delicate Renaissance-style interiors.

On the outside, the parish house was expanded in 1959 in an alteration designed by

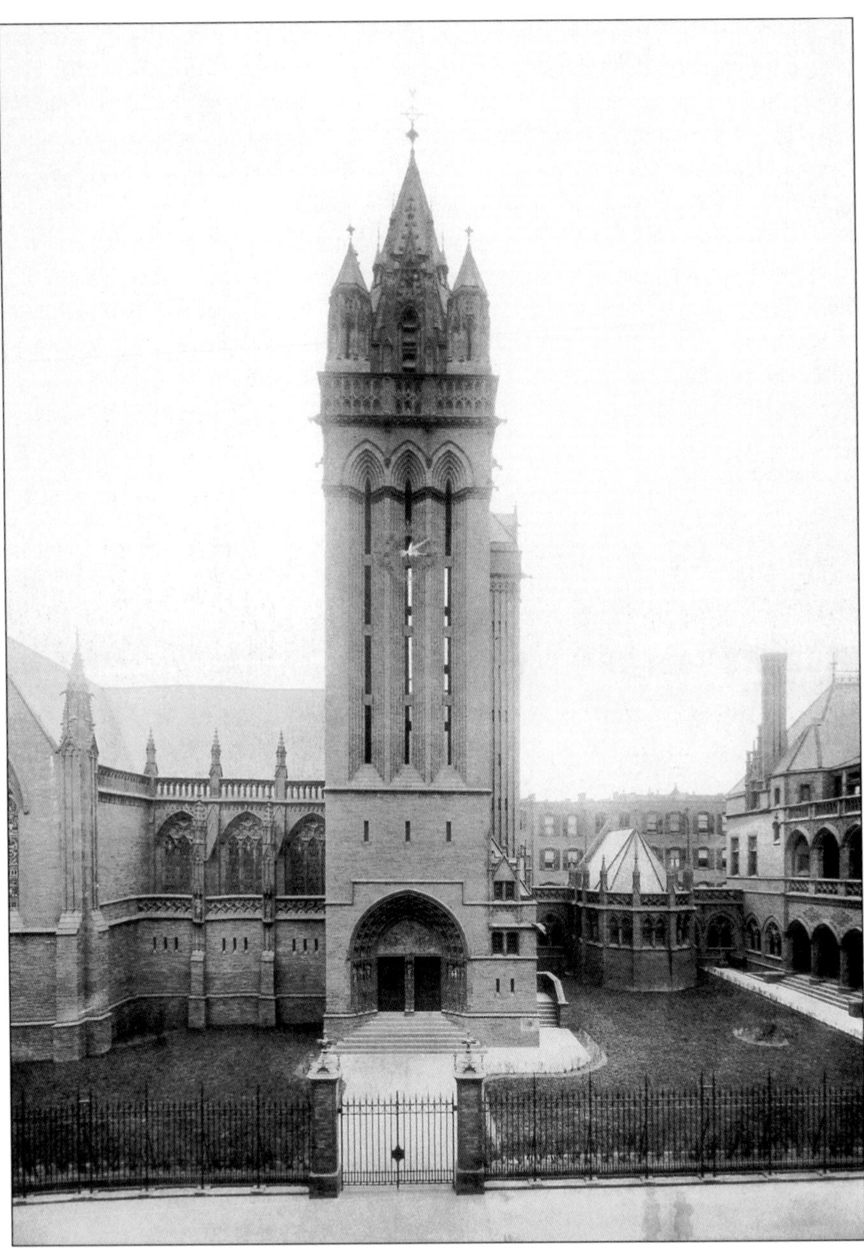

THE CHURCH OF THE HOLY TRINITY *and its French Renaissance–style bell tower in 1899.* COURTESY OFFICE FOR METROPOLITAN HISTORY

Frank and Walter Eberhart. Anyone who thinks the '50s was all white brick should come see this remarkable, contextual work, with carefully chosen brick laid in crisscross patterns, custom-molded terra-cotta, and a soaring chimney stack that bridges the gap between a Loire Valley chateau and the Finnish architect Alvar Aalto.

The entire complex is unified by a long arcaded gallery snaking through the buildings—you can walk from one end to the other without going outside.

According to J. Stewart Barney's daughter, Mary Alice Barney Kean, her father took her mother, Mary Alice Van Nest, up to the top of the bell tower to propose to her sometime before their marriage in 1901, and Mrs. Kean's late husband, John, did the same with her.

THE CHURCH OF THE HOLY TRINITY, CIRCA 1920. COURTESY ARCHIVES, CHURCH OF THE HOLY TRINITY

Holy Trinity remains a particularly tranquil mid-block enclave, far removed from the thundering trucks on First and Second Avenues. At an 8:15 Sunday morning service a few years ago, a visitor walked beneath the shade of tall trees, past the giant, spreading lawn, and into the dark sanctuary, where the only non-ecclesiastical sounds were the melodies of singing birds outside and the clink of dog collars—four canines to twenty-four humans. The church allows dogs at its early service, one of only many reasons to kneel within this unusual building.

THE NATIONAL ACADEMY MUSEUM AND SCHOOL OF FINE ARTS

1083 FIFTH AVENUE

FROM AN EARLY AGE, ARCHER HUNTINGTON WANTED TO CREATE MUSEUMS. For his tenth—and last—he donated his town house at 1083 Fifth Avenue to the National Academy of Design in 1940. Huntington—originally Archer Worsham—was born in 1870 to John and Arabella Worsham. According to James T. Maher, author of the 1975 book *Twilight of Splendor,* which discusses the Huntington family, John Worsham, a gambler, seems to fade from sight. In 1884 Arabella Worsham married Collis P. Huntington, a ship and railroad builder and one of the richest men in New York. Mr. Maher says that Collis Huntington informally adopted Archer Worsham, who took his stepfather's last name.

When Archer was a child, Arabella Huntington took him to European museums, and at an early age he developed an interest in art collections and Spanish art and culture. In the 1890s Collis Huntington wanted Archer to take over his shipbuilding company in Newport News, Virginia, but the young man chose instead a life of connoisseurship.

When Collis Huntington died in 1900, he left a third of his estate to Archer, a legacy estimated by Mr. Maher at no less than $50 million. In 1902 Archer Huntington bought 1082 and 1083 Fifth Avenue, two of a row of three new speculatively built town houses near 89th Street, and moved into 1083.

Over time he financed the construction of buildings at the complex for the Hispanic Society of America, the American Numismatic Society, the American Geographical Society, the Museum of the American Indian, and the American Academy of Arts and Letters. Huntington also founded an art museum in Austin, Texas—the Archer M. Huntington Art Gallery—a forest station in the Adirondacks, the Mariners' Museum in Newport News, and Brookgreen Gardens, an outdoor sculpture museum at Murrells Inlet, South Carolina, near Myrtle Beach.

In 1913 Huntington embarked on a radical change for 1083 Fifth Avenue. The high-style architect/decorator Ogden Codman expanded the house in an L-shape to 3 East 89th Street and reworked the interior and redbrick front into a more sophisticated

ARCHER HUNTINGTON'S TOWN HOUSE *at 1083 Fifth Avenue (far left) in 1904.*
COURTESY OFFICE FOR METROPOLITAN HISTORY

French–town house design. Joining the new building with the old was a circular rear extension with a round stairway, a luxurious feature for a New York house.

In early August 1914, while the alteration was under way, the Huntingtons were motoring through Europe as war tensions mounted. In Nuremburg, German authorities noticed that Huntington was traveling with some of his map collection and arrested him on suspicion of being a Russian spy. The *New York Times* later reported that he was released but that his English valet and French chauffeur were made prisoners of war.

Huntington published several books, many relating to Spanish culture, and seems to be one of the few Fifth Avenue mansion owners to have written poetry. One stanza of *A Wave at Javea*, published in 1936, gives the flavor of his work:

> I woke in the midst of the sea,
> My heart was an opal fire,
> And kisses of foam I flung
> To the sun of my desire.

When Huntington gave the house at 1083 Fifth Avenue to the National Academy of Design in 1940, it was a final parting gesture to the world of art.

CHURCH OF THE HEAVENLY REST

90TH STREET AND FIFTH AVENUE

THE SOUTHEAST CORNER OF 90TH AND FIFTH AVENUE was vacant in 1901 when Andrew Carnegie built his blocklong mansion, now the Cooper-Hewitt National Design Museum, just to the north. Carnegie, who became rich from steel and railroads, also bought the vacant land on the north side of 91st Street to protect his own site. But the property on the south corner of 90th Street remained undeveloped, covered with billboards and a ramshackle lemonade stand.

Carnegie must have given frequent thought to that corner, and in 1917 he paid over $1.7 million for it—just after a sign was posted that read "For sale—without restrictions." He might have been thinking of Henry Phipps, who had a big mansion at 87th and Fifth, declined to buy the empty land to the north—and was then unpleasantly surprised when the apartment house at 1067 Fifth Avenue went up next door in 1915.

In 1926, the Episcopal Church of the Heavenly Rest, then at Fifth Avenue and 45th Street, came shopping for a new site. Carnegie's widow, Louise, sold the church the corner for $1 million, with restrictions through 1975 that the land be used only for a Christian church no higher than 75 feet, exclusive of steeples.

The church hired the architects Mayers, Murray & Phillip, successors to Bertram Goodhue, one of America's most sensitive and influential designers. They developed a design for a giant limestone mass in the neo-Gothic style, with bursts of sculpture by Malvina Hoffman, Lee Lawrie, and other artists. The church opened in 1929 at a final cost of $3.2 million, seating 1,050, with the twin innovations of a sound system and indirect lighting.

On the inside, the architects gave every pew an unobstructed view of the altar. The resulting wide span and the high, nearly plain stone walls produce a vast nave. George Chappell, the architecture critic for the *New Yorker* at the time, admired the gold stars and gold ribbing on the ceiling and praised the clever use of mortar joints to add to the sense of soaring height—the joints are wide on the flagstones on the floor, medium on the walls, and small on the vaulted ceiling, making it appear even farther away than it is.

126.1

FIG

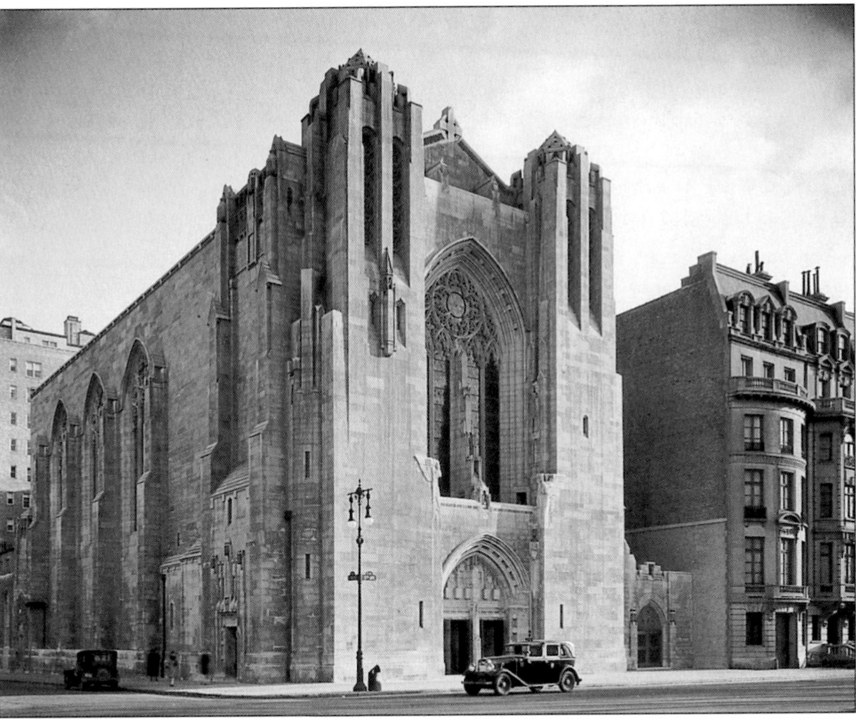

CHURCH OF THE HEAVENLY REST ABOUT 1928. COURTESY MUSEUM OF THE CITY OF NEW YORK

126.2

FIG

BILLBOARDS ON THE CHURCH OF THE HEAVENLY REST SITE *opposite the Andrew Carnegie house, 1913.* COURTESY MUNICIPAL ARCHIVES

The finishes marry modern materials with delicate artistry. The glazed screen behind the entry doors is a dramatic work in Monel metal with gilded steel. The door hardware, of nickeled steel with Chinese red highlights, is astonishing. Every detail in the church came from the designer's hand—nothing was a formula, or left to chance.

Over two-thirds of the ambitious sculpture program was never executed. In 1928 the artist Janet Scudder said she withdrew from a commission for a life-size "Madonna and Child" because the church had reduced it from five feet, four inches to four feet, seven inches. In reply, Dr. Henry Darlington, the rector, said: "Did you ever have anything to do with artists? One day she wanted the statue one size, and the next day she wanted it another."

The stock market crash of October 1929 was probably the chief obstacle to completion, and the streamlined blocky forms that were meant to be carved give the church an abstract, modernistic quality that many have admired. But the smooth, uncompromising masonry of the Church of the Heavenly Rest, especially after a recent cleaning, is as majestic as a 1930s dam.

THE CARNEGIE MANSION

91ST STREET AND FIFTH AVENUE

THE STEEL MAGNATE ANDREW CARNEGIE WROTE widely and developed the "Gospel of Wealth," the idea that the rich had a social responsibility to spend their fortunes for the common good. By the time of his death in 1919 he had established several institutions—among them the Carnegie Endowment for International Peace—underwritten New York's system of branch libraries, and given away about $350 million.

But in the 1890s Andrew Carnegie was living at 5 West 51st Street at a time of controversy about the character of New York City mansions. Real estate writers and architectural critics considered typical rich men's housing—narrow, densely built houses with dark rooms and poor ventilation—ludicrous considering their architectural pretensions.

There was even a prediction that mansion builders would soon relocate to the open blockfronts of Riverside Drive and that the social center of gravity would jump Central Park. The northerly limit of mansion construction on Fifth Avenue, it seemed, would remain in the '70s.

Carnegie made his contribution to this discussion only as he was nearing retirement. He was unconvinced of the future of Riverside Drive and in 1898 began assembling what would ultimately amount to two blockfronts on Fifth Avenue between 90th and 92nd Streets. This, the highest area of the Upper East Side, had been called Prospect

127.1
FIG

THE CARNEGIE MANSION *on 91st Street and Fifth Avenue about 1903.* COURTESY THE NEW-YORK HISTORICAL SOCIETY, NEW YORK CITY

127.2
FIG

THE MAIN HALL OF THE CARNEGIE MANSION, *with its pipe organ and portrait of Andrew Carnegie.* COURTESY OFFICE FOR METROPOLITAN HISTORY

Hill but was soon dubbed "The Highlands" by newspapers agog over Carnegie's grand purchase of two largely vacant lots that few thought would ever see such a buyer.

In 1899, he selected the architects Babb, Cook & Willard. Published plans later in the year show the house generally as it was built, essentially Georgian but with the heavy decorative elements typical of French styling popular in the 1890s. In 1901, the *New York Tribune* remarked that "many people are disappointed by the plainness of the house," but that is exactly what Carnegie had requested: "The most modest, plainest and most roomy house in New York," he said.

More significant was the siting and environs: A big house, yes, but set within an even bigger yard. The 1895 Astor mansion at 65th Street and Fifth Avenue had about 100 square feet of yard—Carnegie got almost 30,000.

Carnegie explained to the *New York Tribune*: "The precious little life that has come to us needs the Park and sunshine. . . . We not only concurred in the advice of our physician but deemed it a duty to move up to the highest ground and where there is plenty of room."

"He set an example to other billionaires," wrote Montgomery Schuyler in *Architectural Record* in late 1901. But only two others followed it: Charles Schwab, who built a huge, freestanding house at 73rd and Riverside, and Henry Frick, whose wide, low house still survives as a museum at 70th and Fifth. Carnegie sold the 91st–92nd Street land to other mansion builders, and in 1903, the first use of the term "Carnegie Hill" appears as the Carnegie Hill Hotel, now the Hotel Wales, at the northeast corner of 92nd Street and Madison Avenue. It is now one of the most sought after residential areas in New York, in part because of Carnegie's 30,000-square-foot yard, which now surrounds the Cooper-Hewitt National Design Museum, which took over the house in 1976.

THE BURDEN HOUSE

7 EAST 91ST STREET

WHEN ANDREW CARNEGIE BOUGHT THE FIFTH AVENUE blockfront between 90th and 91st Streets as the site for his mansion—now the Cooper-Hewitt National Design Museum—he sought to avoid uncongenial neighbors by buying up much of the surrounding land, concentrating on the north side of 91st off Fifth Avenue, opposite his main entrance.

In 1899 he sold off a 136-foot front lot at Nos. 7 and 9 to Florence and James A. Burden Jr., who were married in 1895, and Emily and John H. Hammond, married in 1899. Florence Burden and Emily Hammond were sisters, daughters of William D. Sloane, head of W. & J. Sloane, and descendants of Commodore Cornelius Vanderbilt.

BURDEN AND HAMMOND HOUSES *at 7 and 9 East 91st Street in 1907.*
COURTESY LOUIS AUCHINCLOSS

In 1905, the Hammonds finished the imposing Italian Renaissance–style 9 East 91st Street, designed by Carrère & Hastings. The Burdens built the Beaux-Arts-style 7 East 91st Street, slightly shorter but just as grand.

Designed by Warren & Wetmore, at that time the favored Vanderbilt family architects, the Burden house plays turn-of-the-century French luxury off against the sober High Renaissance of the Hammond house.

The wide and deep rustication on the ground floor of the Burden house is almost frantic; above it the second-floor windows seem squashed by the heavy balcony. Then the ballroom-floor windows yawn open, twice the height of the second floor, and the fourth-floor windows push through the rich, fluted frieze, their heavy, projecting sills emphasizing the interruption.

The individual elements are elegant, like the concave recessed arches around the ballroom windows, but the combination is exuberant, even comic.

The handling calls to mind Warren & Wetmore's first major project, the nearly riotous facade of the 1899 New York Yacht Club on West 44th Street.

In 1906 the Burdens became less congenial neighbors. When Carnegie sold the 91st Street properties to the Burdens and the Hammonds, he promised that he would sell the remaining Fifth Avenue corner as a single parcel. But he found no takers—even then mansion building was beginning to decline—and sought to divide it in two. The Burdens and the Hammonds sued and successfully prevented the sale. A decade later the banker Otto Kahn bought the corner to build his own house, which is still on the site.

The 1910 census-taker found the Burdens at home with their three children and seventeen servants, including four laundresses, three footmen, and a chauffeur. Mr. Burden died in 1932 and Mrs. Burden remarried, leasing the house to John Jacob Astor VI, who had been born in 1912, shortly after his mother, Madeleine Astor, was rescued from the sinking *Titanic*.

THE HAMMOND HOUSE

9 EAST 91ST STREET

IN 1903, AFTER ACQUIRING THE LAND FROM ANDREW CARNEGIE, John H. Hammond, a banker, put up a majestic high Renaissance-style limestone house at 9 East 91st Street. The land, and perhaps the building, was a wedding gift to Hammond and his wife, Emily Vanderbilt Sloane, from her father, William D. Sloane, of W. & J. Sloane.

Designed by Carrère & Hastings, the house is among the grandest mid-block residences in the city, as elegant as any building of its size in Rome. Period photographs show a rich series of Louis XVI–style rooms with elaborate marbles, carving, tapestries, and furnishings.

The house is faced with limestone on its western side, flanking a private courtyard with a fountain, since removed.

Writing in the *New York Herald Tribune* in 1962, Henry Hope Reed called East 91st "the noblest perspective in the city." By that year, however, most of the original families had gone. The Burdens left in the 1930s and the Hammonds and Carnegies in the 1940s.

The Hammonds sold the house in 1946 to Dr. Ramon Castroviejo, who operated the building as an eye hospital with minor changes. But the Landmarks Preservation Commission still thought 91st Street fairly noble, designating the remaining buildings as landmarks in the 1970s—in the case of the Hammond House, over the owners' objections.

The Soviet Union bought 9 East 91st Street from Dr. Castroviejo in 1975 for $1.3 million. William Gleckman, who designed its alteration and modernization—including new electrical service, the installation of a theater, air-conditioning, and a huge metal gate in front of the courtyard—recalls that "Mr. Myshkov, the consul-designate, loved classical things and loved this house" because it reminded him of imperial architecture in Russia.

The Soviets finished their renovation a year after purchase, but its use as a consulate was dependent on a treaty with the United States, and in December 1979, President Carter froze the consulate program, because of the Soviet invasion of Afghanistan.

For many years the house was empty, dark, and moody like some grand, mothballed ocean liner, with heavy metal shutters covering its giant second-floor windows. But in 1990 the cold war went into defrost mode, and both governments reopened discussions, leading to an opening of the building later in the 1990s.

FIG 129.1

THE HAMMOND HOUSE, *9 East 91st Street, in 1904.* COURTESY OFFICE FOR METROPOLITAN HISTORY

OTTO KAHN MANSION

91ST STREET AND FIFTH AVENUE

OTTO KAHN CAME TO THIS COUNTRY FROM GERMANY in 1893, began work with the banking house of Speyer & Company, and became a partner at Kuhn, Loeb & Company in 1897. His skill with railroad issues helped Kuhn, Loeb develop as a leading investment bank, and he became one of the richest men in New York.

In 1913, Kahn bought the mansion's site from Andrew Carnegie, whose mansion on the other side of 91st Street is now the Cooper-Hewitt National Design Museum. He completed his house in 1918 and moved in with his wife, Addie, four children, and twenty-two servants.

The house, which was designed by C. P. H. Gilbert and J. Armstrong Stenhouse, was the last great mansion to rise on Fifth Avenue. Although it looks like a giant box, the rear of the building is cut to open up a deep winding courtyard that penetrates almost to the middle of the building.

This unusual feature brings light deep into the Kahn house and animates what otherwise might have been a succession of airless but magnificent interiors.

The rear yards of most mansions were mere light shafts, but the Kahn house courtyard is fully developed, all in stone, with half-stairways and small arcades of windows.

Kahn, who came from a banking family, had an appreciation of art from an early age. As a teenager he wrote a blank-verse tragedy in five acts. He supported or helped many individual artists and small organizations, and at his death in 1934 the *New York Times* wrote that he had "saved" the Metropolitan Opera.

Beginning in 1903 Kahn pumped money and talent into the Met, then an old-line institution strangling on tradition. He hired Arturo Toscanini as conductor and Giulio Gatti-Casazza as manager and even bought a site for a new opera house, on 57th Street west of Eighth Avenue, although it was never built. He was named chairman of the Met in 1911.

Rene Gimpel, in his *Diary of an Art Dealer*, published in 1966, recorded a different perspective: "With so much money at his disposal, Otto Kahn resolved to storm the gates of the Four Hundred, a tremendous undertaking in this fiercely anti-Semitic society; so he invaded their sanctum, the opera [and] bought up its shares."

FIG 130.1

OTTO KAHN MANSION *at Fifth Avenue and 91st Street, circa 1918.* COURTESY MUSEUM OF THE CITY OF NEW YORK

According to *Our Crowd,* Stephen Birmingham's book on Jewish families in New York, Kahn joined the opera board when Jacob Schiff, another Kuhn, Loeb partner, declined an invitation to join but suggested that the seat go to Kahn. Birmingham also says that Kahn had been planning to convert to Roman Catholicism in the early 1930s, but chose to remain a Jew out of solidarity after Hitler's rise to power.

Perhaps because of his artistic interests, Kahn brought a distinct grace to banking, and often cited ten golden rules of success, which included, "Be a good sport. Remember, you can't lift yourself by drowning others," and, "Meet your fellow-man frankly and fairly. You don't have to go through business armed to the teeth."

When Kahn died in 1934 the Convent of the Sacred Heart acquired the building from the family in exchange for the school's three old brownstones on the corner of 54th Street and Madison Avenue. Few changes have been made to the onetime mansion, and the lower floors are informally open to the public during its annual Christmas tree sale in early December.

CARNEGIE HILL WOODEN HOUSES

120 AND 122 EAST 92ND STREET

THE YORKVILLE AREA DEVELOPED TO VILLAGE PROPORTIONS in the mid-nineteenth century, reinforced by the East 86th Street ferry to Astoria, the Third Avenue railroad, and the industries that sprang up along the upper part of the East River. In 1859 Adam Flanagan, a custom house officer, built the Italianate-style wooden house at 122 East 92nd Street. Twelve years later Catherine Rennert, wife of John C. Rennert, a California wine importer, built the wooden house at No. 120. The Rennerts lived in a wooden house at 114 East 92nd, now demolished.

The Rennerts held No. 120 for rental; the 1880 census lists the head of household as Jonathan Kimmens, a captain with the fire insurance patrol, which was organized by insurance companies to protect property affected by fire. Kimmens lived there with nine family members and was in occupancy in 1882 when the Yorkville photographer Peter Baab climbed atop a house at 94th Street and Park Avenue to make a ten-part panorama of the city.

One frame shows several wooden houses, among them the three at Nos. 114, 120, and 122. Another frame shows 128 East 93rd, which dates from 1866, and was built by Henry Shaw, who made artificial limbs. The fourth wooden house, 160 East 92nd, dates from 1853. But the photographs also show masonry construction taking over. Wooden buildings were prohibited south of 86th Street in 1866 and south of 155th Street in 1888.

In 1890 Anton Hoffmann, a barrel maker who served the beer and liquor industry, purchased 120 East 92nd Street for his own residence. Hoffmann, born in Germany in 1842, may have had a few things to talk about with his neighbor in No. 122, the stone dealer Henry Hanlein, born in Germany in 1850. Both had first immigrated to Pennsylvania in 1870. The Hoffmanns and the Hanleins remained neighbors into the 1930s, well after the town houses and then the big apartment houses had taken over Carnegie Hill. In 1938 Anton Hoffmann Jr. told the *New York Sun* that with high taxes, "an apartment builder cannot come too soon."

Both families sold their buildings within a few years, but the houses survived without incident. The house at 128 East 93rd lost its stoop, and the one at 160 East

PANORAMIC PHOTOGRAPH LOOKING DOWNTOWN *at the south side of East 92nd Street in 1882, including Nos. 120 and 122 East 92nd Street (left).* PHOTOGRAPH BY PETER BAAB. COURTESY MUSEUM OF THE CITY OF NEW YORK

92nd was somewhat modernized, but Nos. 120 and 122 retained almost all of their decorative trim.

The number of frame houses that survive in Manhattan is difficult to estimate. In a format discarded in the early 1980s, the Sanborn land maps rendered masonry buildings in pink and frame buildings in white.

One of the last maps of the old format indicates that there were 308 frame buildings remaining on Manhattan Island at that time: 83 south of 14th Street, 33 between 14th and 59th, 13 between 59th and 110th, and 179 north of 110th. Perhaps a third of the overall group were buildings like diners or sheds, or buildings that have subsequently been faced with brick.

The survival of four frame houses in a built-up area is remarkable.

THE FELIX WARBURG MUSEUM

1107 FIFTH AVENUE

BORN INTO AN ESTABLISHED GERMAN-JEWISH BANKING FAMILY in 1871, Felix Warburg arrived in New York City in 1894. The next year he married Frieda Schiff, daughter of Jacob Schiff, a senior partner at the banking house where he worked, Kuhn, Loeb & Company. Over the next several years the couple occupied a mildly Renaissance-style town house at 18 East 72nd Street.

In 1907, the *Real Estate Record and Guide* reported that Charles Steele, a banker at J. P. Morgan & Company, would build at the northeast corner of 92nd and Fifth Avenue from plans by C. P. H. Gilbert. But in 1907 the Warburgs bought the corner and filed plans for a mansion designed by the same architect. Jacob Ruppert, the Yorkville brewer, had built a mansion at 93rd Street and Fifth Avenue in 1882, but the Warburgs' mansion was the northernmost mansion on the avenue built by a family moving uptown.

FIG 131.1

FELIX WARBURG MANSION *on 92nd Street and Fifth Avenue in the 1940s.* COURTESY OFFICE FOR METROPOLITAN HISTORY

Gilbert was a specialist in mansion design and used his trademark French Renaissance style for Warburg with drip moldings, ogee-arched windows, and crocketed gables standing out from broad planes of Indiana limestone walls and steep slate mansards.

The 1910 census listed thirteen servants—ranging from a nurse to an engineer—along with Mr. and Mrs. Warburg and their five children. Edward M. M. Warburg, then nearly two years old, still remembers the giant stairwell and games of spitting from above into a bowl kept for visiting cards—"which never had a chance to dry up," he says.

An electric train wound its way around the fourth-floor children's rooms, and in a 1984 account, Mr. Warburg recalled the building as "full of children and pranks."

"Father used to say had he had any idea what kind of family he was going to have," Mr. Warburg said, "he never would have built so formal a house."

Indeed, the story is widely repeated that Mr. Schiff was outraged by the opulence of the design, believing that such a building would inspire anti-Semitism. But Edward Warburg says this is a distortion of his view, and that his grandfather, who lived in a Beaux-Arts mansion, voiced only mild disapproval of the François I style.

In 1944, Frieda Warburg, Edward's widowed mother, gave the building to the Jewish Theological Seminary for its Jewish Museum, which opened in 1947 in the Warburg mansion. In 1988, after numerous attempts to build a high building on the site, the Museum retained Kevin Roche to design a matching annex to the building. This was meant to be a gesture to historic preservation—although the museum destroyed many of the nearly intact interiors at the same time—but the result is a kind of exhausted "architecture of compliance," denaturing the original building.

THE WILLARD STRAIGHT RESIDENCE

94TH STREET AND FIFTH AVENUE

AFTER 1902, WHEN ANDREW CARNEGIE BUILT HIS HOUSE at 91st Street (now the Cooper-Hewitt National Design Museum), it was slow going for upper Fifth Avenue as a street of millionaires. The district was hemmed in on its northern border by institutions like Mount Sinai Hospital, the railroad tracks above 96th Street, and the steep slope of the Upper East Side over to the tenements and factories east of Park Avenue.

It looked as if the northernmost mansion on Fifth Avenue might remain Jacob Ruppert's gawky 1880s house at the northeast corner of 93rd Street (demolished in the 1920s).

But a final burst of confidence in the future of upper Fifth Avenue as a street of single-family houses came in 1914, when Willard D. and Dorothy Straight began work on

THE WILLARD STRAIGHT HOUSE IN 1915. COURTESY OFFICE FOR METROPOLITAN HISTORY

their trim brick-and-marble house on the northeast corner of 94th Street. Straight, the son of a missionary and a schoolteacher, worked in commercial and diplomatic affairs in the Far East and so impressed the partners at J. P. Morgan that they hired him as their agent in China.

In 1911, Straight married Dorothy Whitney, the daughter of William Collins Whitney, a financier and streetcar millionaire. Within a few months the couple went to China, and they barely escaped the unrest that soon toppled the Manchu rulers. Back in New York, the Straights hired Delano & Aldrich who designed a reserved trim brick building, almost Bostonian except for its generous scale, with dark shutters and round windows at the attic floor. Instead of a series of baronial rooms, Delano & Aldrich developed Georgian-style spaces comparable to their elegant Knickerbocker Club design of the same period, still at 62nd Street and Fifth Avenue. The ground floor of the Straight house is organized around a circular hallway in the eighteenth-century Adam style topped by a dome, with a hypnotically patterned black-and-white marble floor.

Delano & Aldrich also designed a garage for the Straights, a complementary building at 162 East 92nd Street, which is still standing.

The Straights were particularly interested in liberal politics, and while their house was under construction they founded the *New Republic* magazine for their friend, the writer Herbert Croly, who became its president and one of its editors. Early issues had articles by Walter Lippmann, John Dewey, and Rebecca West. The journal was outspoken in favor of women's rights, the labor movement, and American involvement in international affairs. Straight died in the influenza epidemic of 1918, and the 1920 census records Dorothy Straight in the house with her three children and twenty servants. According to *After Long Silence*, a 1983 memoir by Michael Straight, the Straights' son and a longtime editor of the *New Republic*, after his father's death, his mother frequently held cultural events at the house, including a reading by Joseph Conrad and a performance by the pianist Ignace Paderewski.

Dorothy Straight soon remarried and moved to England. She put the house up for sale, with a restriction against apartment construction for twenty-one years, and it was this peculiar detail that probably allowed the house to ride out the apartment boom of the 1920s.

Later the house was sold to the International Center of Photography, which horribly abused one of the most refined houses in New York. They have since moved, and the house is under renovation as a single-family residence.

THE CATHEDRAL OF ST. NICHOLAS

15 EAST 97TH STREET

THE CHURCH OF ST. NICHOLAS WAS ESTABLISHED IN THE EARLY 1890S in rented rooms on lower Second Avenue to serve an increasing number of Russian immigrants. By 1899 it had three hundred members, and a movement began to build a new church. The congregation chose an inexpensive uptown location at 97th Street off Fifth Avenue, in an area that was beginning to emerge as a neighborhood of modest flats.

Czar Nicholas II made the first donation to the building fund, and in May 1901, when the cornerstone was laid, it bore a silver plaque praising him. "Long live the emperor of Russia and the president of the United States," proclaimed the Reverend Alexander Hotovitsky, the minister. President McKinley died from an assassin's bullet in September.

The 1902 building was designed by John Bergesen according to the characteristic Russian model, with seven domes above a dark red brick facade trimmed with limestone and glazed tile in green, blue, and yellow.

In 1904, a *New York Times* reporter marveled at the exotic, incense-laden atmosphere: "The air was heavy with perfume, and the multitude of sacred candles shedding a dim light throughout the church combined with the solemn chant of choristers and the psalm singers to produce a quaint splendor seldom surpassed in this city." But Montgomery Schuyler, the critic for the *Architectural Record,* was not similarly moved, calling the church building "ugly and freakish."

Soon, amid rising civil strife in Russia, Grand Duke Sergius was assassinated by a bomb in Moscow, rumors of a bombing plot against the cathedral were circulating, and the czar granted some powers to the Duma, a new legislative body. Czar Nicholas abdicated in 1917 and was murdered the next year.

CATHEDRAL OF ST. NICHOLAS IN 1903. COURTESY OFFICE FOR METROPOLITAN HISTORY

After the Communists came to power they began remaking the Russian church to fit the goals of an atheist state. Early in 1920 Bolshevik sympathizers disrupted a communion service at St. Nicholas but were thrown out by the faithful. In 1923 the Reverend John. F. Kedrovsky was sent by Moscow to take over the Cathedral of St. Nicholas—and the $3 million in property controlled by the Russian Orthodox Church.

However, newspaper accounts indicate that the congregation was generally anti-Communist, and Father Kedrovsky was carried out of the building and down the steps onto 97th Street, kicking and screaming. The police helped the Communists enter the rectory in July 1925 and take over St. Nicholas, but it was reoccupied by the anti-Communists in August, and pictures of the late czar were still being sold in the church in December of that year. The police came back in April 1926, when the New York State Appellate Court ruled in favor of the Communists, and Father Kedrovsky was installed again—although he had to send to Hartford for robes, because those in the church had been removed by the losing faction.

At Sunday services, it is not uncommon to find the cathedral crowded with Russian speakers, old and young, some born in the reign of Lenin, others in the reign of Putin. The service, in Russian and Latin, resonates through the incense-laden air, while some worshipers light candles in front of various icons, saying prayers, and kissing the frames. Communion is served in traditional style, bits of bread soaked in wine placed by the priest with a spoon in the mouth of the worshiper. Conspicuously non-Russian visitors are received in a friendly manner, and without fuss.

GLEN SPAN ARCH IN CENTRAL PARK

FREDERICK LAW OLMSTED AND CALVERT VAUX'S ORIGINAL DESIGN for Central Park consisted of two zones. The lower area was one of pastoral landscapes, like the Sheep Meadow, and dramatic vistas, like a view up the mall terminated by Belvedere Castle. But in the upper end, north of the reservoir, the designers accepted the existing rocky landscape as a canvas for a more rugged composition.

Just inside Central Park West near 101st Street, the park's designers created alternating bodies of still and rushing waters that begin with the large, triangular pool—a first-time visitor may still gasp at the romantic vista of flat water brushed by weeping willows.

The pool empties eastward over the cascade, a twelve-foot-high drop of boulder-steps. The boulders were painstakingly assembled by Olmsted and Vaux. But by 1980,

THE CASCADE, *a twelve-foot-high drop of boulders in Central Park, circa 1870.*
COLLECTION HERBERT MITCHELL

when the nonprofit Central Park Conservancy was established, erosion and vandalism had reduced them to a jumbled heap. In 1992, using old photographs from the collection of Herbert Mitchell, the former rare-book librarian at Columbia's Avery Library, the conservancy repositioned the rocks into the original scheme.

The cascade plummets into a still, slow-moving channel at the bottom of a ravine, with rocky, soil-studded slopes on each side. It then flows on under Glen Span Arch, a giant rough stone bridge that carries the west vehicular drive overhead. Then the watercourse meanders forward into a shady oval unnamed in early Central Park maps except by inference—the glen.

An irregular canal about five feet wide and perhaps 150 feet long, the glen empties under another rustic bridge where it proceeds on into the loch, now a swamp of neglect.

This stretch, from the cascade on down, is a masterpiece of landscape manipulation. As visitors follow the streamside path, they see the noisy, sunny brightness of the cascade disappear into the silent, tomb-like darkness inside the massive arch.

On the other side, soft forest light and sounds emerge—birds twitter under the rustling green canopy. Turning back, they get a visual recapitulation of this sensory trail—a sheet of placid water leads back through the dark arch, which frames the sunny cascade. It is typical of the Olmsted and Vaux concept of the park as a series of sophisticated experiences meant to be uplifting for all, but especially for the lower classes.

But it is out of character with later-day concepts of a park as a roofless sportsplex for dirt biking, ball playing, roller blading, and other active recreations.

The natural edges of the stream are fragile and the steep banks on either side of the Cascade are natural climbing spots, magnetically attractive, and therefore threatening to the vegetation that holds the soil on the slopes. Many of the stones that form a picturesque contrast with the surrounding foliage can easily be dislodged.

It is not yet clear whether the great experiment of more intelligent park use that began in the 1980s can remain in force—it requires intense maintenance and is diametrically opposed to American park culture of the past century. But if anything can convince New Yorkers of its value, it is a meandering walk through Glen Span Arch and its surrounding landscape.

CENTRAL PARK BASEBALL FIELDS

CENTRAL PARK WAS CONCEIVED AS A MORALITY PLAY, a place where millionaire and laborer could be physically and morally refreshed by reflecting on the intricately designed landscape. The Central Park Conservancy's 1985 report, "Rebuilding Central Park," calls it "a bold democratic experiment in which all social classes were invited to mingle in scenic surroundings of uplifting poetic beauty."

But "Casey at the Bat" was not one of the poetic selections. The designers, Frederick Law Olmsted and Calvert Vaux, both opposed active sports and, especially, the dedication of areas for specific uses. So their original plan specifically excluded the playgrounds, tennis courts, croquet lawns, baseball diamonds, and other elements that now make up the modern definition of park.

A NEW YORK EVENING JOURNAL CARTOON, *depicting the Great Lawn baseball field controversy in 1933.* COURTESY THE NEW-YORK HISTORICAL SOCIETY, NEW YORK CITY

This distinction began to vanish at the turn of the century when athletics became a moral force for the uplifting of the poor and the working classes. By the 1920s permanent baseball diamonds, tennis courts, and other features had encroached on the park. A great controversy was touched off in 1930 when the Lower Reservoir, on the site of the Great Lawn, behind the Metropolitan Museum of Art, was declared obsolete and drained.

At first, Mayor Jimmy Walker accepted a plan for a huge grassy oval proposed by the American Society of Landscape Architects. But the *Daily News* and other organizations campaigned for facilities for active sports—baseball diamonds, a cinder track, pole-vaulting pits, and the like. The new administration of Mayor John P. O'Brien was more receptive to such an idea, and the battle was fought largely along class lines.

On the one side were elite civic organizations supporting the original park ideal—the City Club, the Fine Arts Federation, the League of Women Voters, the Architectural League, and others—who allied themselves with Fifth Avenue and Central Park West real estate interests opposed to the rough element they thought baseball would bring.

On the other side were churches from working-class areas and organizations like the Public Schools Athletic League and East Side House Settlement who thought that any big open space was appropriate for baseball diamonds. They argued that the original park ideal was insufficient for many in the city.

The battle seesawed, but in May 1933 the first baseball diamond opened, although Parks Commissioner John Sheehy promised it would be temporary. The subsequent chronology is unclear but it appears that by the 1950s dirt baseball diamonds were in place; there are now eight.

In more recent years the Conservancy's 1985 report singled out the diamonds for turning the Great Lawn into "a hardpan desert," and the Conservancy's report said only 9 percent of Central Park visitors came for active sports. But such is the power of the baseball lobby that, after the glorious reconstruction of the Great Lawn in the 1990s, baseball diamonds again dotted the great oval. Since the reconstruction, tight rules have been observed about closing the lawn when it needs to rest—amid complaints by the baseball players. Even with intensive repairs, the perimeter areas of the baseball diamonds are ragged. Perhaps in another five or six years, park users will be able to fairly judge whether or not Olmsted & Vaux's masterpiece can accommodate the great American pastime.

CENTRAL PARK ROCK TUNNEL

A KEY DESIGN ELEMENT OF CENTRAL PARK was a series of four sunken transverse roads separating east-west traffic from the park landscape. The north-south drives in the park pass over the transverses on brick-lined arches. But for the path leading to Belvedere Castle, the designers, Frederick Law Olmsted and Calvert Vaux, wanted to blast through the solid knob of stone for picturesque effect.

The rock tunnel, completed in January 1861, is 141 feet long, 17 feet, 10 inches high, and 40 feet wide. Shortly after the tunnel was completed, the commissioners of Central Park cautiously reported that it appeared "thus far, firm and reliable."

Indeed, the rock tunnel's spectacular malevolence is one of its chief attractions; it is like a particularly nasty roller coaster that blurs the line between thrill and kill. In *The Central Park,* published in 1864, Fred B. Perkins described what he called the chasm: "the great, heavy, beetling mass, bare of earth, that overhangs its front, undoubtedly will not fall, but somehow you think, as you look at it, what if it should fall while I was under it?"

At the same time, the rock tunnel can offer a kind of peace and solitude unique in the wide, uncovered Central Park. In the early 1860s, Julian K. Larke, in *Davega's Handbook of Central Park*, noted that "the difference in the temperature of the atmosphere from that in the walk above, and a few moments thus spent by a thoughtful man will give him a subject for after reflection."

Gas torches were added at each end of the tunnel, and a special stairway leads to the park above. This is the only access of its kind in any of the transverses, and it suggests that the designers of the park intended the rock tunnel to be a destination point.

Research by the Olmsted historian William Alex suggests that the first change to the rock tunnel took place in 1915, when loose rock was pried out, seams were grouted, and iron bars were driven into the rock to prevent slippage.

In the last fifty years grime and exhaust have cloaked the craggy interior, but the stony, turbulent arch still leaps across the roadway like a roiling sea. At various points ground water seeps through crevices, spreading a dark stain and producing a grotto effect. Seven or eight million vehicles drive through the rock tunnel every year, but only the most eccentric "thoughtful man" would now seek reflection amid the deafening traffic, although anyone there when traffic is shut down will have a sublime experience.

In 1993 the Department of Transportation, ignoring requests from the Landmarks Preservation Commission for less visible changes, installed raised bolts in various areas on the rock tunnel; it has thus sprouted two dozen giant carbuncles.

A rusty, modern conduit now supersedes the elegant gas fixtures. No sign of the tunnel exists at Belvedere Castle directly above, a popular tourist destination. It is particularly sad that the last twenty years of park restoration have, mysteriously, ignored the rock tunnel, which is one of the most remarkable interiors in New York.

FIG 136.1

THE ROCK TUNNEL *in the 79th Street Central Park transverse road with its special torchères in 1898.* COURTESY OFFICE FOR METROPOLITAN HISTORY

THE OLD YORKVILLE RESERVOIR IN CENTRAL PARK

IN 1835 NEW YORKERS APPROVED A VISIONARY PROJECT to replace private wells and cisterns with a forty-mile-long masonry aqueduct from a new dam across the Croton River in Westchester. The aqueduct channeled eighty million gallons a day to an Egyptian-style distributing reservoir on the site of the present New York Public Library at 42nd Street and Fifth Avenue.

But few people ever mentioned the Yorkville Reservoir up the line in what would later become Central Park. This reservoir was nestled neatly into the imaginary street plan of the section, between Sixth and Seventh Avenues and 79th and 86th Streets.

FIG 137.1

THE OLD YORKVILLE RESERVOIR *as viewed from Belvedere Castle, looking toward Central Park West in the early 1890s.* COURTESY NEW YORK BOUND BOOKS

More than six times the size of the 42nd Street reservoir, the Yorkville Reservoir held 150 million gallons in a giant rectangular chamber 836 feet wide and 1,826 feet long. According to a report by the reservoir's chief engineer, John B. Jervis, its principal purpose was to let dirt and sediment settle out of the water after its walking-speed journey from Westchester County and before its trip downtown.

At 4:30 P.M. on June 27, 1842, thousands of spectators lining the flag-topped walls of the empty reservoir watched as a thirty-eight-gun salute greeted the first water to pour in, a stream 12 feet wide and 12 inches deep coming from a pipe on the west side of the reservoir at 85th Street. Exit gates on the east side of the reservoir at 82nd Street and 80th Street fed the water down to 42nd Street.

The exterior walls were of rough masonry and were steeply sloped, with no ornamental trim or decoration, and were 18 feet wide at the top and up to 38 feet high.

The 1858 design by Olmsted & Vaux for the new Central Park made a virtue of this giant obstacle, placing Belvedere Castle at the southwestern corner for a sweeping view over the flat sheet of water, which would vary with the weather, sky, and wind.

In 1933, H. I. Brock in the *New York Times,* said that the water lapping at the base of the castle suggested "Tristan's Castle on the coast of Brittany."

In the 1910s the new Ashokan Reservoir allowed a shutdown of the Yorkville Reservoir, and in 1925 the Department of Parks took over the structure. There followed a succession of plans for replacement: playgrounds, an open-air theater, a garage, and a formal mall.

From 1933 to 1936 the reservoir walls were partly taken down and the Great Lawn was built. A *New York Times* editorial lamented the "lost charm and seclusion" of the area. The ball fields that turned it into a dusty wasteland insinuated themselves later.

But a walker in the city can still trace the outlines of this great public work, which left faintly visible ridges on each side of the Great Lawn. There is a 20-foot stretch of wall just peeping out over the ground on the western side, and a full corner, about 4 feet high, that survives just east of the Central Park Precinct, south of the 86th Street transverse. Together, they form a ghostly outline of one of New York's oldest and most important public works.

UPPER WEST SIDE

MEETING HOUSE OF THE SOCIETY FOR ETHICAL CULTURE

1 WEST 64TH STREET

THE FOUNDER OF THE ETHICAL CULTURE MOVEMENT, FELIX ADLER, was born in Germany in 1851, but came to New York as child when his father, Samuel L. Adler, took over as the rabbi of Temple Emanu-El, where he became one of the most influential figures in Reform Judaism. Felix Adler graduated from Columbia College in 1870 and then went to the University of Heidelberg, where he studied the ethical philosophy of Immanuel Kant.

After returning to the United States in 1873, he made what was to be his only address to his father's congregation, "The Judaism of the Future"—which advocated eliminating what he described as superstitious traditions from Judaism to concentrate on the study of ethics. Three years later, he put these ideas into practice and founded the New York Society for Ethical Culture, which mixed the spiritual and the practical.

Throughout the 1880s and 1890s, the charismatic Dr. Adler frequently spoke on social issues; in 1888, he opposed spending money on the new Protestant Episcopal Cathedral of St. John the Divine as "a deviation from the true spirit of religion," according to the *New York Times*. He arranged several open discussions on the future of blacks in American society.

But the Society of Ethical Culture never had its own house, instead renting auditoriums like Carnegie Hall. In 1899, the society bought an entire blockfront on Central Park West, from 63rd to 64th Streets.

FIG 138.1

FELIX ADLER, PH.D.
FOUNDER OF THE SOCIETY FOR ETHICAL CULTURE
LECTURER AND EDUCATOR

FELIX ADLER. COURTESY SOCIETY FOR ETHICAL CULTURE, ARCHIVES

The society first built a five-story school building at the northwest corner of 63rd Street, completed in 1904. Of brick and limestone, it was modest considering its designers: John Carrère and Thomas Hastings, who were generally known for opulent architecture. Felix Adler's remarks at the laying of the school's cornerstone were characteristic of his continued social activism. He criticized the growing trend of the rich to educate their children in private schools: "We believe that a class school is an evil for the rich as well as for the poor." At the Ethical Culture school there were 400 on the rolls, but only 119 were paying tuition.

FIG 138.2

THE SOCIETY FOR ETHICAL CULTURE IN 1910. COURTESY SOCIETY FOR ETHICAL CULTURE, ARCHIVES

In 1909, Ethical Culture began work on a meeting hall on the 64th Street corner. The building was designed by Robert D. Kohn, who had been a member of the society since childhood and who had become a principal practitioner of the Art Nouveau style in New York. Like Christian Science, the Ethical Culture movement was searching for its own form—it had no historic precedents from which to draw.

Kohn's exterior, all Bedford limestone, took its cornice and base course lines from the adjacent school, but nothing else. Instead of the school's broad window facing Central Park, the meeting house had wide, limestone expanses, like a mausoleum, and simple, blocky detailing. When the building opened in 1910, the *Times* wrote: "The severe plain wall is eloquent in its protest against the breathless rush and hustle of the modern city; it beckons to the hastening, sordid throng, Tarry a while; there is in life more than stocks and shekels and vain show."

THE PRASADA

65TH STREET AND CENTRAL PARK WEST

IN 1904 PLANS WERE FILED FOR THREE TALL APARTMENT HOUSES on Central Park West: the St. Urban at 89th Street, the Langham at 73rd Street, and the Prasada at 65th Street. The developer Samuel B. Haines retained the architect Charles Romeyn, who designed the twelve-story Prasada with typical turn-of-the-century ebullience, with Beaux-Arts detailing capped by a two-story-high mansard roof.

The planning showed the typical quirks of apartment planning of the time. None of the bedrooms had private bathrooms, and many rooms had sinks set inside closets, presumably to reduce the load on sanitary facilities. Each apartment had a long hall—visitors generally made a substantial trek past kitchens and bedrooms until they got to the entertaining rooms.

It is often said that the early apartment buildings primarily lured families away from the bother of private houses, but this is not consistent with a random sample of the Prasada's early tenants. Charles Fowles, an art dealer, moved to the Prasada from an 1880s apartment house at 63rd and Park. Henry B. Harris, a prominent theater producer who owned the Hudson Theater on 44th Street near Broadway, moved with his wife, Irene, from a fairly new apartment building at 69th and Central Park West.

In 1912, Harris was returning to the Prasada from Europe, traveling on the *Titanic*. According to his wife's obituary in the *New York Times* in 1969, he died after persuading her to step in the last lifeboat to get off. She took over her husband's responsibilities, becoming, according to the obituary, the first woman theatrical producer in New York.

Only three years after the *Titanic* disaster, Fowles was lost on the *Lusitania*—he had moved to Harperley Hall, next door to the Prasada, in 1914, the year the Prasada was sold in foreclosure.

In 1919 two investors, Walter Russell and Penrhyn Stanlaws, bought the Prasada. They announced that they were going to gut the Prasada—eliminating the long halls and other anachronisms, adding a swimming pool, gym, dining room, and full housekeeping services. They replaced the elaborate two-story mansard with plain brick, but their interior work was much more limited: to judge from a later rental plan, they squeezed in more bathrooms and ripped out the sink-closets but made few other substantial changes.

One new tenant was the writer Edna Ferber. She had been living in the old Majestic

THE PRASADA ABOUT 1910. COURTESY MUSEUM OF THE CITY OF NEW YORK

apartment hotel at 72nd Street and Central Park West and said she was sick of the semitransient atmosphere. Julie Gilbert, Ferber's great-niece, wrote about her great-aunt in the 1978 book Ferber: *Edna Ferber and Her Circle.* Ms. Gilbert quoted one of Ferber's essays about moving to the Prasada: "I'm never going to give up this wonderful place. Never. They'll have to wheel old 'Gamma Ferber' out when they tear the building down. The very nicest thing, though, is to have a mattress that you know no one else has ever slept on."

Despite her prediction about staying until the Prasada was demolished, she moved in 1929 to the Lombardy, at 111 East 56th Street.

55 CENTRAL PARK WEST

IN THE LATE 1920s CONSTRUCTION SURGED UP and down Central Park West, in part because of the anticipated IND subway line, which opened on the street in 1932. A handful of builders adopted the new Art Deco style, and the results were prominent enough to make Central Park West a sort of display case for the movement.

The first of the buildings was 336 Central Park West, at 93rd Street, designed in 1928 by Schwartz & Gross for the developer Edgar Levy. Its streamlined redbrick piers rise from an abstract entryway up to a plum-colored terra-cotta cornice, whose Egyptian character sets the building apart from mainstream Art Deco.

The next year, Schwartz & Gross filed plans for 55 Central Park West, at the southwest corner of 66th Street, the first full-blown Art Deco building on the thoroughfare. They were working for Victor Earle and John C. Calhoun, who had been active on the Upper West Side since the 1910s. Victor Earle and his brother, Guyon, developed a dropped living room design that distinguished the interiors from others of the time. Opened in 1930, the building had apartments of from three to nine rooms—the largest with four bathrooms.

On the exterior Schwartz & Gross also departed from tradition, designing a brick facade that changed in shade from bottom to top, from deep purple to yellow-white on the water-tank enclosure. Color was a tool increasingly used in the 1920s, both with polychrome terra-cotta and also in overall effects, like Raymond Hood's black and gold 1924 American Radiator Building at 40 West 40th Street.

"New modernistic design of exterior with beautiful shaded color scheme," the rental brochure for 55 Central Park West read, and in 1930 *Real Estate* magazine wrote that "on a bright sunny day the effect will not be unlike that of the Jung Frau, that most beloved snowcapped Alpine peak."

George S. Chappell, the *New Yorker*'s architecture critic, praised the use of color, saying that "the total effect is exhilarating" and singling out for particular praise the lobby and hallways, in gray-green marble and green plaster with metal trim.

After 55 Central Park West came five more Art Deco buildings—including 241 Central Park West, at 84th Street, also by Schwartz & Gross for Earle & Calhoun—all completed by 1931.

Not every builder was sold on Art Deco—in mid-1929 Schwartz & Gross filed an Art Deco set of drawings for the developer Abraham Bricken, for the full blockfront

FIG 140.1

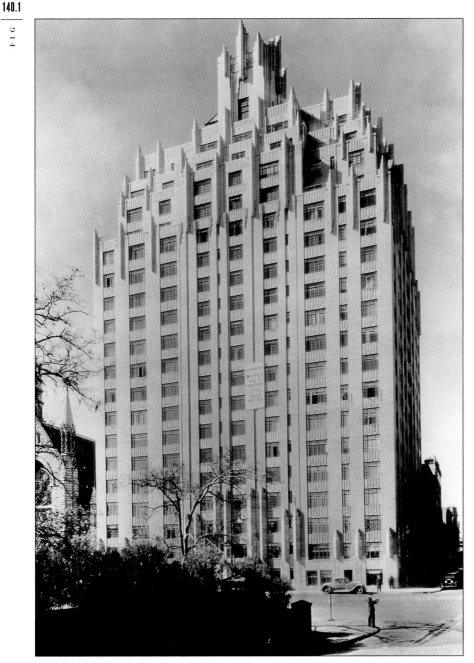

55 CENTRAL PARK WEST IN 1930. COURTESY MUSEUM OF THE CITY OF NEW YORK

apartment house now known as 101 Central Park West, at 70th Street. But in December 1929, Bricken had the architects change the design to the present Renaissance style.

Early tenants of 55 Central Park West included Rudy Vallee, the Yale graduate who had just made it big as a radio singer with tunes like "I'm Just a Vagabond Lover." When Vallee moved into the building he was earning $20,000 a week. Another recent success was Raymond Loewy, the industrial designer, who had redesigned the gawky Gestetner duplicating machine of the era with the streamlining he later used on railroad engines, Studebakers, and even Air Force One.

DURLAND'S RIDING ACADEMY

7 WEST 66TH STREET

IN 1901 GEORGE DURLAND, WHO RAN A RIDING ACADEMY on Columbus Circle, built a new stable complex, designed by Henry Kilburn, on a T-shaped lot on 66th and 67th Streets, off Central Park West. The central building, with 100 feet of frontage on each street and running 200 feet through the block, was a huge riding ring under long trusses, surrounded by balconies for six hundred spectators.

To the west, on 66th Street only, was a plain five-story building for stables and carriage storage; to the east, also only on 66th Street, was a more ornate five-story building for lounging and various club rooms. Although the *New York Tribune* called the complex "severely plain," the easterly portion—with the club rooms—had an elaborate portico, a cornice, projecting window bays, and shields bearing figures of horseshoes.

A gallery held forty musicians for entertaining indoor riders at "music rides" every afternoon. Parks Commissioner George C. Clausen—a regular rider at Durland's—promised to cut a new gate at 66th Street through the stone wall to the bridle paths in Central Park.

The *New York Tribune*'s report on the 1903 Christmas horse show at Durland's told of races, a basketball game on horseback, and a staged "attack on a settlers' camp by Indians."

Durland retired in 1927. He said that even though Central Park and upper Seventh Avenue had been "ruined by automobiles," cars would never displace saddle horses. He sold the complex to the New York Riding Club, an elite private group, and in 1930 the magazine *Country Life* reported that the club fielded several polo teams in the cavernous riding ring, which was fitted for night polo.

The Riding Club closed in 1936, but the old Durland's complex returned to service as a public stable. Six years later, Michael Korda, the book editor and publisher, came to New York. In an account published in *New York* magazine in 1987 he recalled New York as "full of stables and horses." At the stable, grooms would deliver horses to riders' buildings, and many women still rode sidesaddle in the park.

Paul Novograd, the owner of Claremont Riding Academy on West 89th Street, says that Durland's "was our chief competition" and that stables had distinctive colors for the brow bands above the horses' eyes; Claremont's was blue, Durland's was checked.

In 1949 the American Broadcasting Company bought and occupied Durland's, and shows like *Soupy Sales, Wide World of Sports,* and *Good Morning America* were produced

FIG 141.1

DURLAND'S RIDING ACADEMY IN 1903. COURTESY MUSEUM OF THE CITY OF NEW YORK

FIG 141.2

THE STALLS IN DURLAND'S RIDING ACADEMY IN 1903. COURTESY OFFICE FOR METROPOLITAN HISTORY

from that location. Looking up from the sets, a visitor—or a broadcaster—can see the giant trusses of the original Durland's Riding Academy.

In the 1980s the new ABC headquarters expansion involved the demolition of the westerly portion of the Durland complex, but much of the Durland complex is still evident.

HOTEL DES ARTISTES

1 WEST 67TH STREET

BY 1915 WEST 67TH STREET OFF CENTRAL PARK WEST had been transformed into an artists' haven, with four tall co-ops of varying designs. That was the year the painter Penrhyn Stanlaws, living in the second studio building, at 33 West 67th, organized a syndicate to build the biggest co-op building yet, taking the address 1 West 67th Street and the name Hotel des Artistes.

The architect George Mort Pollard, who had done some of the earlier buildings, worked out a broad Gothic-style H-plan building, 150 feet wide, with seventy-two apartments. Unlike the earlier buildings, the Hotel des Artistes not only had studios with northern light, it had southern-light studios facing the street.

Despite its name, it was a building not just about art. Stanlaws said that the ten-floor, $1.2 million structure was the largest studio building in the world. It had a swimming pool, a squash court, a sun parlor, a ballroom, a first-floor grill, and, on the second floor, a much larger restaurant. The apartments did not have kitchens (they were added later); rather, the chef's salary and other dining expenses were figured into the building's budget.

Although many apartments were customized during construction, the typical floor had eight small studios facing 67th Street and six small and two double-size studios facing the rear. The Hotel des Artistes was completed in 1917, and the 1920 census captures the building partly full. In the tally of occupations, there were fourteen artists, musicians, or writers; eleven actors or movie executives; and twenty-two stockbrokers, engineers, and other business people. The most frequent occupation listed was household servant—twenty-six in all.

The artistic contingent included Walter Russell, a Paris-trained artist who had studied with Howard Pyle and painted Theodore Roosevelt's children, and who was one of the originators of the studio idea on West 67th. His neighbors included Howard Chandler Christy, who did the murals in the present Café des Artistes, which is adjacent

THE HOTEL DES ARTISTES IN 1917. COURTESY CORNELL UNIVERSITY LIBRARIES

STUDIO
APARTMENTS
FOR RENT
ASHFORTH

A STUDIO IN THE HOTEL DES ARTISTES. COURTESY OFFICE FOR METROPOLITAN HISTORY

to the building's lobby; and Carolyn Wells Houghton, a popular writer of mysteries and humor books, among them *The Rubaiyat of a Motor Car*.

The motion-picture side of the building included Alan Crosland, who directed Al Jolson's *Jazz Singer* of 1927, and George Fitzmaurice, who directed Greta Garbo in the 1931 *Mata Hari*. In 1925 Fitzmaurice had predicted that, since movies were already being shown on Paris-to-London airplanes, they would soon be available in New York subway cars.

Most of the apartments were small, and there were plenty of one-person households. But Aaron Naumburg, a fur dealer, had an expansive top-floor apartment, filled with art and furnishings. He left his collection to the Fogg Art Museum at Harvard, which still displays it in a reproduction of Naumburg's 67th Street studio, though it is primarily used for staff events and receptions and is not usually open to the public.

2 WEST 67TH STREET

IN 1916 THE SEVENTH ARTISTS STUDIO on West 67th, at 2 West 67th Street, turned a corner, both onto Central Park West and beyond the realm of art. The painter and illustrator Penrhyn Stanlaws had organized the Hotel des Artistes across the street the year before, and for 2 West 67th Street he had the architects Rich & Mathesius design a building with a pronounced arts-and-crafts influence.

They eliminated the usual projecting cornice and finished the top of the building with a simple frieze of panels and delicately worked copper coping. They used roughly textured brick on the facade and rendered it with details that emphasize a handmade character.

Delays with structural steel—possibly related to the need for steel in World War I—put off completion until 1919. Plans in the building varied from floor to floor, but there were about two dozen duplex apartments with double-height studios—19 feet high—and an undetermined number of regular apartments. Written accounts suggest that half the apartments were for sale at prices ranging from $5,000 to $30,000; the co-op rented out the other half at rates that paid the entire cost of operation—the co-op tenants were to pay no maintenance.

The original double-height studios on West 67th were designed for working artists who needed the spaces for large sculptures or canvases, but the 1920 and 1925 censuses record only two artists at 2 West 67th Street. Rather, the tenants were business owners and stockbrokers, people like the Cuban-born Leandro Rionda, head of the Francisco Sugar Company. Instead of artists, there were the "artistic," like the husband and wife authors Charles and Kathleen Norris—his 1930 novel about birth control, *Seed*, sold 70,000 copies.

The most famous was Burton Holmes, who began a travelogue business in 1894 that, according to *Variety*, the entertainment journal, had grossed $5 million by 1947. Holmes developed five new illustrated travel lectures a year, many from his expansive studio at 2 West 67th. Holmes's architect was Iwahiko Tsumanuma, who worked in Japan and in the United States, here under the name of Thomas S. Rockrise. The Holmes studio, which survives with few changes, was modeled after the seventh-century Horyuji Temple on Honshu Island in Japan and held Holmes's collection of Asian antiquities.

After 2 West 67th Street, only regular apartment houses went up on the block, marking the expanding attraction of supposedly artistic neighborhoods. Like Soho

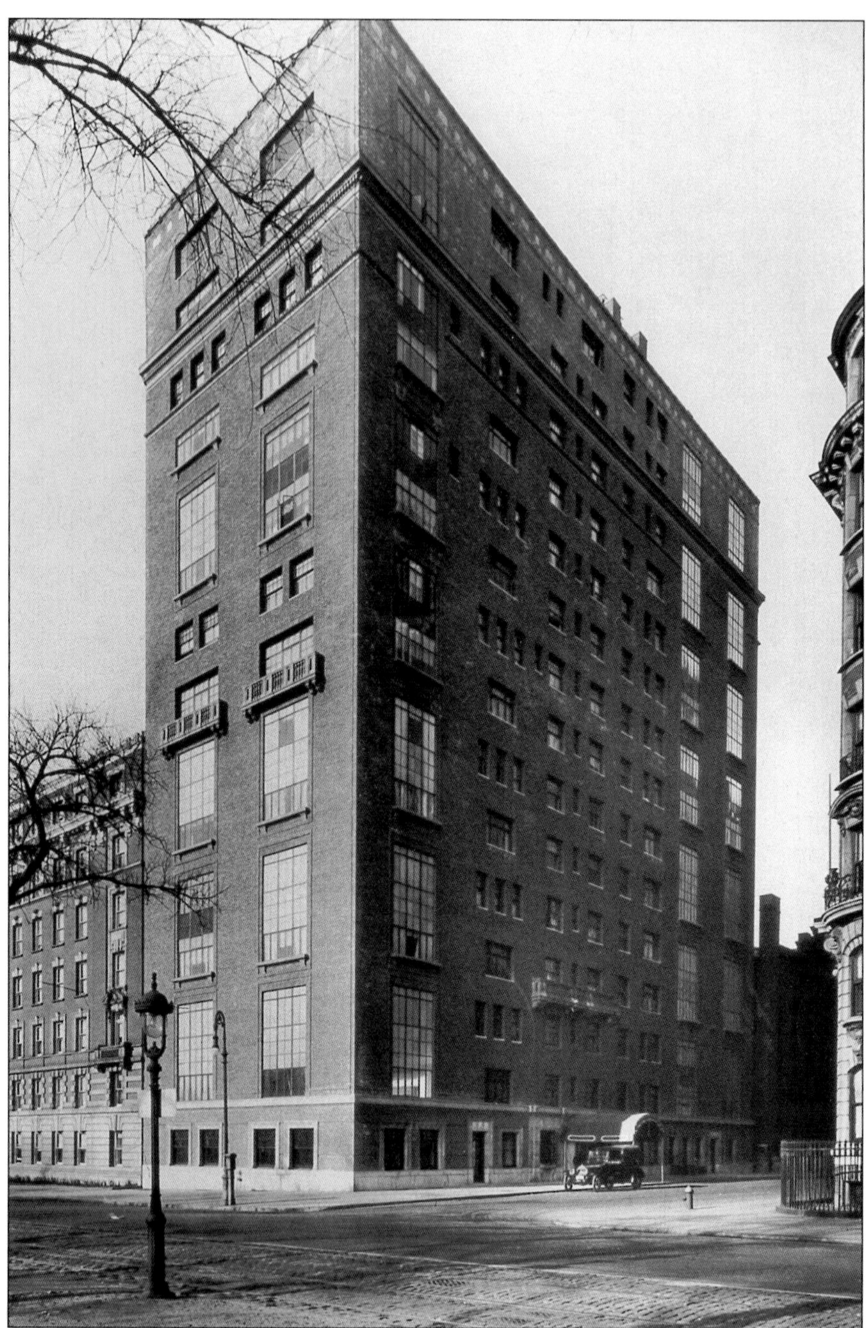

2 WEST 67TH STREET AT ITS COMPLETION IN 1919. COURTESY MUSEUM OF THE CITY OF NEW YORK

decades later, West 67th Street had been discovered.

Penrhyn Stanlaws had grand plans for future construction—even before 2 West 67th Street was finished, he announced a gigantic project for Manhasset Bay on Long Island. The project consisted of a multibuilding co-op complex of eight- to sixteen-story buildings—with towers 375 feet high—served by communal schools, restaurants, a theater, and yacht ferries to and from Manhattan; however, it was never realized.

27 WEST 67TH STREET

IN THE 1890S THE PAINTER, HENRY WARD RANGER, conceived of a plan to build a high-rise studio/co-op for artists but was rebuffed by speculative builders. He finally persuaded nine other artists—including Childe Hassam, Frank Dumond, and Walter Russell—to do it themselves.

In 1901 they chose West 67th Street, off Central Park West, a ragged block of stables, a planing mill, a warehouse, and vacant lots. But it was next to Central Park and it backed up onto the row houses of West 68th Street, where restrictions effectively prohibited tall buildings. Assurance of light and proximity to an established residential district and Central Park made it a smart real-estate move.

The artist syndicate's architect, Sturgis & Simonson, refined the duplex/studio plan that had been used in the 1880s, matching a double-height studio in the rear—facing north—to single-height living and sleeping rooms doubled up in the front. Completed in 1903, the building had fourteen studios, plus smaller rental apartments. Photographs of the studio interiors show them decorated in grand, Romantic style, filled with carpets, artistic knickknacks, and giant artworks.

But the industrial Gothic exterior of red and black brick with green window frames was "not a thing of beauty," said the *New York Times,* which called it "a somewhat ornate factory . . . tall, bulky and sad."

This, too, fit in with the artists' scheme, avoiding the cheap tin cornices and tawdry catalogue ornament that speculative builders used to dress up their buildings. The lobby, with its plain marble wainscot, simple classical mural by Robert Sewell, cramped spaces, and low ceiling, would have puzzled a commercial builder, but the absence of show suited the tenants just fine.

It appears that the original ten artists split the total cost of $350,000, and there is no evidence that they sought anything but a roof over their heads—at first. But later reports indicate that they returned a 23 percent profit on their investment, and of course they had their apartments.

In 1905 a related syndicate, this time with more than shelter on its mind, successfully built 33 West 67th Street, this time with a more decorated front, and everyone saw that the game had changed. Ranger, Dumond, Hassam, Russell, and others spread out and built co-ops at 130 and 140 West 57th Street; 2, 15, and 40 West 67th Street; and 44 West 77th Street.

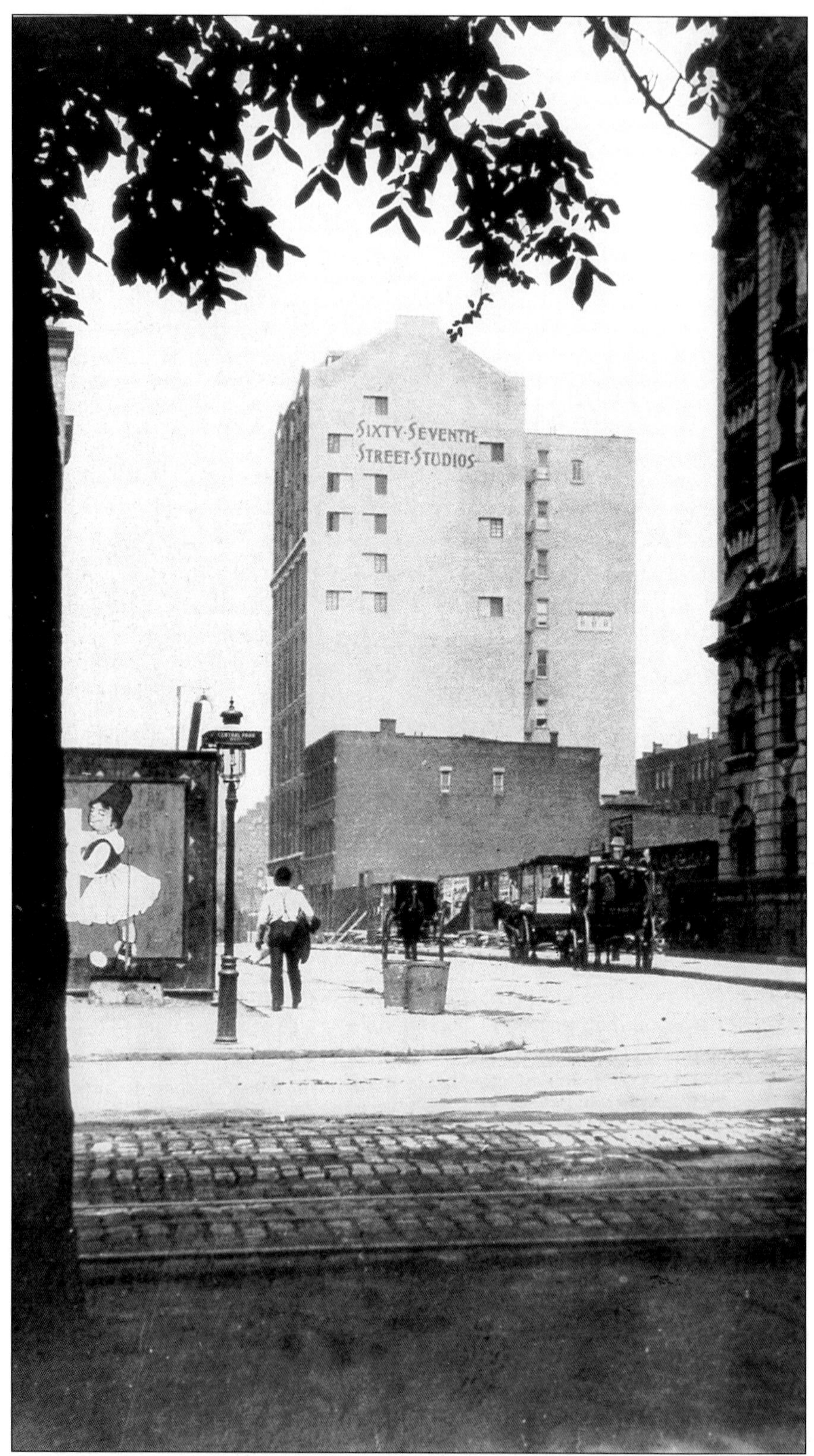

27 WEST 67TH STREET *rising above the low buildings on West 67th Street about 1903.* COURTESY LANDMARK WEST!

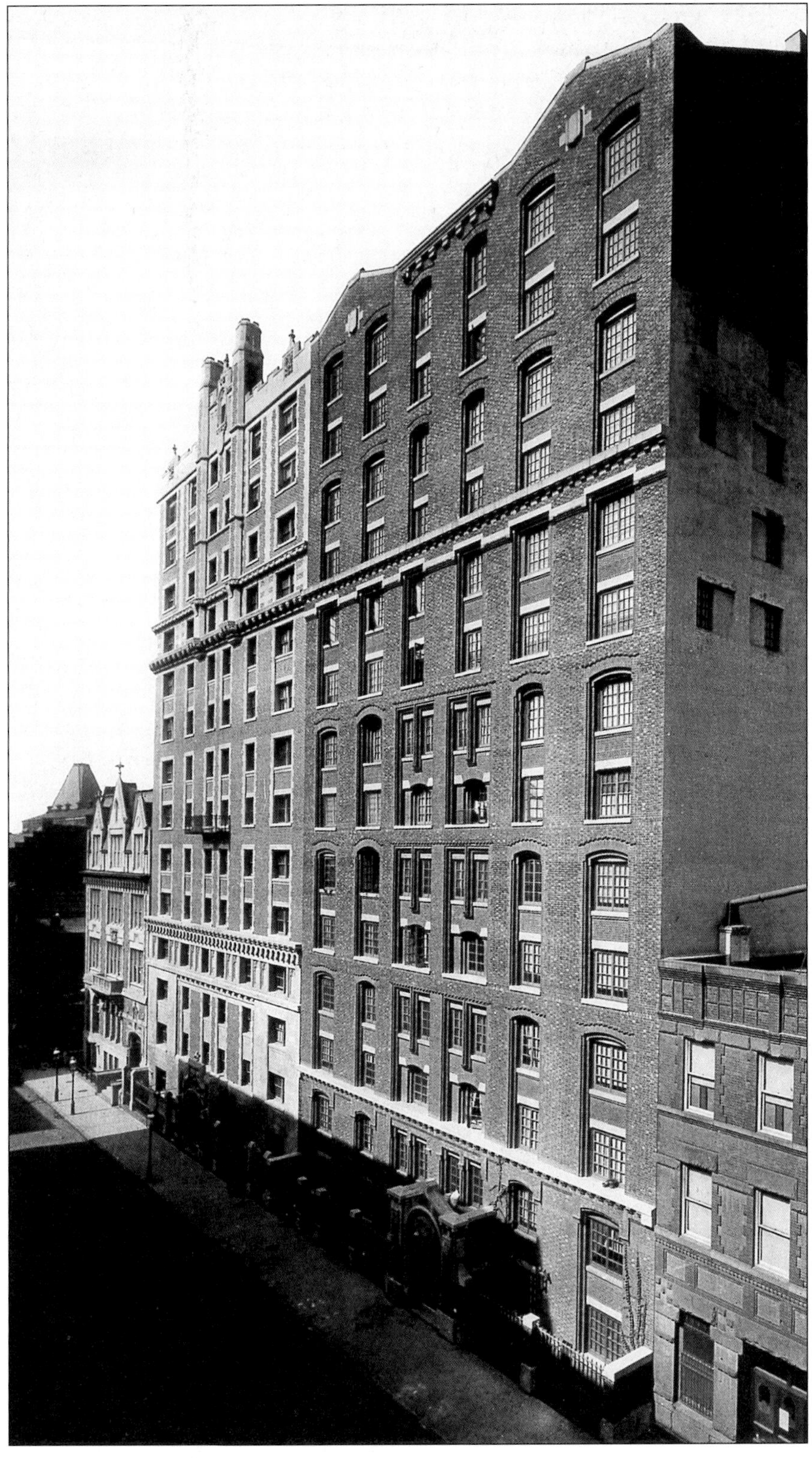

27 WEST 67TH STREET, CIRCA 1906. COURTESY MUSEUM OF THE CITY OF NEW YORK

In 1929 Pease & Elliman advertised the thoroughly conventional building at 40 West 67th Street using the phrase, "You'll find them fascinating—these new cooperative apartments in 'The Artists' Colony.' " The original development of 27 West 67th Street can fairly be said to have opened the way—as to social class and co-op theme—for the development of elite apartment houses all over Manhattan after 1910.

THE SWISS HOME

35 WEST 67TH STREET

IN 1846, UPPER-CLASS NEW YORKERS OF SWISS EXTRACTION founded the Swiss Benevolent Society, which finally bought an old row house at 108 Second Avenue in 1883.

Prominent families like the Iselins, the de Coppets, the de Rhams, and the Couderts supported the society, and in 1904 it began a building from scratch on the Upper West Side. It appears that the Swiss sought a site near both Central Park and an established neighborhood. They economized wisely by buying at 35 West 67th Street: their land backed up on an existing neighborhood of brownstones stretching north, but West 67th itself was then predominantly a street of light industry and stables.

The Swiss-American architect John E. Scharsmith designed the $117,000, five-story building, which "resembles somewhat the city hall of Basel," according to the society's 1905 annual report. The report also praised the location as "in the most salubrious part" of the city.

The interiors had the plainness of sensible charity: a dining hall on the first floor and, above, rooms for up to eighty people in spaces that are, by New York standards, one notch up from a servant's room.

The opening ceremonies in December 1905 were in French, German, and English, and attended by groups like the Helvetia Wheelmen and the Swiss Choral Society. They looked with pride on a building that still had the seals of the United States and Switzerland above the second floor and those of all twenty-two Swiss cantons in the cornice.

Histories of the Swiss Benevolent Society refer to a constant schism in the organization; apparently the French Swiss were generally better off than their German- and Italian-speaking countrymen, dominating the affairs of the society. Census records for 1910 show that almost all those living in the Swiss Home were of German extraction, like Adam Gasser, seventy-four, a widower and retired machinist.

After the opening of the new home, the society adopted English as its official language to reduce tensions.

In 1916 a new president, Robert J. Schwarzenbach, expressed concern that the residents of the home were in danger "because of its proximity to saloons" on Columbus Avenue. He also said that, in part because the society could never more than half-fill the building with deserving poor, it was spending $400 a year per person. This was, he said, an extravagance "of which economically thinking and thrifty Swiss should not be guilty."

Perhaps his judgment was also affected by the later development of West 67th Street, which had become a center for expensive apartment buildings, like the Hotel des Artistes.

Under Schwarzenbach's leadership, the aged occupants were moved to an estate that the society bought in 1923 for that purpose in Mount Kisco. In 1924 the Swiss Home became the Swiss Town House, a dormitory for working women; the stated purpose was to house women of Swiss extraction, but exceptions were numerous. The charge was $9 to $14 a week for room and board.

FIG 145.1

THE SWISS BENEVOLENT SOCIETY *at 35 West 67th Street in 1905.* COURTESY OFFICE FOR METROPOLITAN HISTORY

The 1925 census shows a new crop of residents, including a corset saleswoman, a child's nurse, a lady's maid, and a dental hygienist. Erma Ringh, a stenographer, twenty-three years old and nine months in the United States, lived in one room, and Ida Haas, a seamstress, fifty-two years old and fifteen years in the United States, lived in another. The Swiss Home remained in operation until 1991 but has since been sold.

THE DORILTON

71ST STREET AND BROADWAY

NEW YORK'S FIRST SUBWAYS SPURRED REAL ESTATE DEVELOPMENT, especially along upper Broadway, where land was relatively unimproved. Early in 1899—before the subway route was officially set—Hamilton M. Weed bought the northeast corner of 71st and Broadway for $275,000.

In March 1900—just after the route up Park Avenue, across 42nd Street, and on up Broadway had been fixed—Weed filed plans for the first tall apartment house on Broadway to take advantage of the proposed subway line, which was completed in 1904.

He had just finished the Alimar, a seven-story apartment house at the northwest corner of 105th Street and West End Avenue, in the Beaux-Arts style, and for his new Dorilton he retained the same architects, Janes & Leo.

They, in turn, used the same approach as they did with the smaller Alimar—a stone base, redbrick middle section and curving mansard—but both inflated and multiplied. The limestone lower stories are voluptuous in their deep carving. The middle section is an epidemic of quoining, ironwork, brackets, cartouches, oriels, and other details. At the top, the mansard roof explodes in large intersecting curves, a profusion of elaborate dormers and chimneys and rich copper cresting. It's an architectural fistfight.

FIG 146.1

THE ENTRANCE TO THE DORILTON IN 1902.
COURTESY OFFICE FOR METROPOLITAN HISTORY

THE DORILTON APARTMENT HOUSE *at 71st Street and Broadway in 1902.*
COURTESY OFFICE FOR METROPOLITAN HISTORY

The one- to four-bedroom apartments, four to a floor and renting for $100 to $300 a month, had long halls, unusual paneling, and mirrored bathrooms. But there was marginal closet space and a skimpy bath-to-bedroom ratio, both typical of early apartments.

In 1902, the critic Montgomery Schuyler chose the Dorilton for his "Architectural Aberrations" column in *Architectural Record*. He remarked on "the wild yell with which the fronts exclaim, 'Look at me,' as if somebody were going to miss seeing a building of this area, twelve stories high."

"The incendiary qualities of the edifice may be referred, first to violence of color, then to violence of scale, then to violence of 'thinginess,' to the multiplicity and importunity of the details."

"Motley elements," he said, "set the sensitive spectator's teeth on edge." But this did not hurt the Dorilton in the marketplace; a report in the *Record and Guide* in 1902 said it was fully rented. Over time, stores were installed in the Broadway frontage, and starting in the 1950s, large sections of cornice, whole dormers, lengths of cresting, and other elements crumbled or were removed.

Notwithstanding this, the building was designated a landmark in 1974; the Landmarks Preservation Commission described it at the time simply as "exceptionally handsome."

Over the last fifteen years the dedicated cooperative board has brought the building back from an aesthetic total loss, rebuilding cornices, roofs, cresting, stonework, and other elements. Somehow this has tamed the Dorilton—its near dereliction emphasized the violence of the original design, and gave it a surreal, even menacing look. But now, with the facade tuned up, the contrast is diminished—perhaps this is closer to what the original tenants of the building saw.

THE DAKOTA

72ND STREET AND CENTRAL PARK WEST

THE FAMOUS 1884 DAKOTA IS INVARIABLY WRITTEN up as a wildly improbable venture. Is that really the way it seemed to New Yorkers a century ago?

Many popular guidebooks retell the well-known story that the huge apartment building was ridiculed for being so far out of town that it might as well have been in the Dakotas, and that the name stuck.

This amusing account is repeated in scores of guidebooks and supposedly authoritative histories. That it always appears without a source, without variation or elaboration, and without the flavor of real life apparently never raised the authors' suspicions. Or perhaps they just didn't want to rock the quote.

It is true that when the Dakota was built there was little in its immediate area, but that "little" included the American Museum of Natural History, the fast elevated trains running up what is now Columbus Avenue, and several score of row houses.

However, everyone was agreed on the great prospects for the area: The El made commuting downtown from the West Side faster than by surface transit from much farther south, and Central Park had been a major tourist attraction for a decade.

Beyond the park, the East Side had largely filled up with row houses and apartment buildings, and the price of West Side real estate, especially along what is now Central Park West, had increased dramatically. West Side terra was hardly incognita, or even Dakota.

THE DAKOTA IN 1886. COURTESY OFFICE FOR METROPOLITAN HISTORY

Andrew Alpern, the apartment house historian, has located what seems to be the first appearance of the usual story, not in the nineteenth century, but in the twentieth. It is given in an interview in 1933 in the *New York Herald Tribune* with George P. Douglass, the Dakota's manager since 1897.

Douglass had known members of the family and staff of Edward Clark, the builder, who were alive when the building went up, but this is how he put it: "Probably it was called 'Dakota' because it was so far west and so far north."

But for someone with his tenure at the building to present the story as a casual conjecture does not give it the flavor of authenticity.

Indeed it is significant that, in the several dozen articles covering the construction of the building in the trade and popular press, not one makes anything at all of the supposed remoteness of the area. The first publication of the name "Dakota," in the *Real Estate Record and Guide* of June 3, 1882, is straightforward and without evidence of any gibe.

The occupancy of the fifty-eight apartments also does not reinforce the idea that the Dakota's location was beyond the pale. Prior addresses can be determined for forty-four of its original residents: six came from outside Manhattan, one from below 14th Street, eleven from between 14th and 42nd, ten from between 42nd and 57th, and sixteen from between 57th and 110th. Nine of this last group were already living on the West Side and several had lived on 57th Street or on Central Park South. But there were also others, like Solon Vlasto, a merchant, who had lived at 72 West 92nd Street.

THE GATE TO THE DAKOTA COURTYARD ABOUT 1890.
COURTESY OFFICE FOR METROPOLITAN HISTORY

Nor was the Dakota tenanted by oddball visionaries. The typical head of household was a lawyer, banker, or businessman, often socially established, like Tarrant Putnam, a commodore of the New York Yacht Club, or Charles Knoblauch, a Wall Street broker. The Knoblauchs were one of two Dakota households listed in the first issue of the Social Register in 1887. Indeed in the same issue a "magnificent apartment" at the Dakota was offered for rent, along with a first-tier box at the Metropolitan Opera.

But . . . how did the Dakota get its name?

In February of 1880, more than six months before plans for the Dakota were even filed at the Department of Buildings, Clark spoke out on the topic of names for the principal streets, then known as Eighth through Eleventh Avenues, but now known as Central Park West, Columbus, Amsterdam, and West End Avenues. He derided a proposal to name Eighth Avenue "West Central Park" and suggested a different model.

"The names of the newest states and territories have been chosen with excellent taste," he said, and suggested Montana Place for Eighth Avenue, Wyoming Place for Ninth Avenue, Arizona Place for Tenth Avenue, and Idaho Place for Eleventh Avenue.

Eighth Avenue was renamed Central Park West within a few years, and Clark's other suggestions were also ignored.

Of his ideas on names in "excellent taste," he left only one example, the Dakota—and even that gesture has been turned on its head.

EDWARD "DADDY" BROWNING'S BUILDINGS

42 WEST 72ND STREET, 118 WEST 72ND STREET, AND 126 WEST 73RD STREET

EDWARD BROWNING WAS BORN IN 1874 and from an early age wanted to be a builder; his earliest identified building is the strangely narrow twelve-story structure put up in 1908 at 11 West 17th Street, designed by Otto Strack. Tall mid-block loft buildings were becoming common at the time, but, at 27 feet wide, this one was unusually narrow.

In 1913 Browning built a more imposing office structure, the World Tower Building at 110 West 40th Street, designed by Buchman & Fox, twenty-five stories on a 50-foot front lot. Then in 1914 Browning filed plans for three identical apartment houses designed by Buchman & Fox: 42 West 72nd Street, 118 West 72nd Street, and 126 West 73rd Street.

Each building is 25 feet wide and thirteen stories high, faced in white terra-cotta of Gothic design. Browning's initials, "EWB," are in cartouches at the third-floor levels. The buildings are peculiar in that they are designed with banks of windows flush against the neighboring property line, but a title search shows no easement or restriction—Browning was relying on luck.

These buildings had one- and two-room apartments, a new kind of development for the Upper West Side, where brownstones and big apartments were still the rule. The tenants were singles and married couples, probably deserting boardinghouses and other makeshift accommodations.

In 1915, the year these structures were completed, the forty-one-year-old Browning was married for the first time, to Nellie Adele Lowen. They moved to a rooftop apartment at 35 West 81st Street, where Browning built an expansive garden. After moving, he announced plans to build a hangar atop the World Tower Building, saying he would commute there by airplane. He also promised he would drop leaflets and dummy bombs on Times Square, because he felt New Yorkers were insufficiently concerned about the perils of aerial bombing.

He did not follow through on his plans. Instead, he put up a fourth narrow building, at 31 West 71st Street, similar but not identical to the earlier three.

In 1918 Adele Browning adopted the couple's first child, three-year-old Josephine Herbst, the daughter of a truckman who already had two children and could not provide for a third. They renamed her Margery. Two years later Edward adopted a child, a five-year-old named Dorothy, whom they nicknamed "Sunshine." Browning built the children a sort of playland on his rooftop, with a lake, captive songbirds, Japanese temples, and colored lights.

42 WEST 72ND STREET IN 1940. COURTESY OFFICE FOR METROPOLITAN HISTORY

In 1923, Adele Browning left suddenly for Paris on the liner *Olympic*. Detectives hired by Edward Browning determined that she was traveling with the family dentist, Dr. Charles J. Wilen, but Wilen said they were on the same ship only by coincidence. "My only relations with Mrs. Browning have been to install bridgework," Dr. Wilen said.

The Brownings separated and divorced, and Edward Browning retained custody of Dorothy; Adele kept Margery.

In 1925 Browning sought a third girl for adoption, selecting Mary Spas of Astoria, Queens, who was said to be sixteen. When it turned out she was actually twenty-one, Browning had the adoption annulled.

FIG 148.2

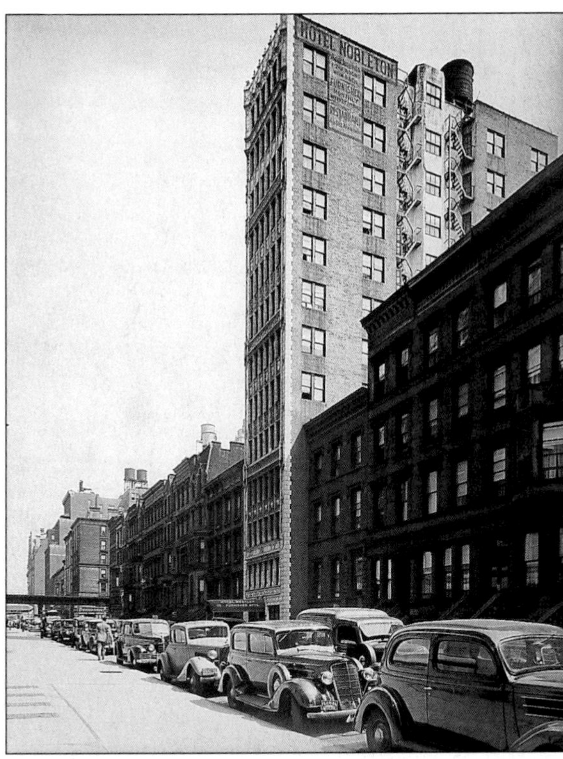

126 WEST 73RD STREET *in 1940.* COURTESY OFFICE FOR METROPOLITAN HISTORY

By this time word had got out that a millionaire real estate investor was looking for someone to share his wealth, and he regularly received mail addressed to "Daddy, New York" and "The Millionaire Daddy, U.S.A."

In 1926 Browning married fifteen-year-old Frances "Peaches" Heenan, with the consent of her parents. They lived together for ten months, but then Peaches left him and tried to make her way on the stage. In 1931 she charged in a divorce suit that a private detective following in a car had spotted him in his limousine between two blonde sisters, Marion and Evelyn James, twenty-one and twenty-four, respectively.

There were charges that one of the sisters was sitting on Daddy's lap, but he said that the rides were entirely proper, that they had discussed things like fresh air, sunshine, and proper diet. Peaches Browning lost her divorce suit.

Edward Browning died in 1934 with his adopted daughter, Dorothy, at his bedside. He left his estate—with several properties, including 42 and 118 West 72nd and 126 West 73rd—in a life trust for his daughter, to go to charity on her death. The three buildings were leased out as a package for $30,000 a year in 1939, while litigation tied up his estate.

"Peaches" Browning died in 1944, and the three buildings were sold on behalf of the estate to different owners. Dorothy, who apparently wound up with most of the estate, died in 1968.

In 1971 the New York Community Trust, using charitable funds from the estate, gave the first Browning Achievement Awards, five $5,000 prizes for things like food, study, and Christian missionary work. Robert Edgar, the trust's manager of donor services, said the award program was reduced in 1981 because of a decline in value of the Browning funds, which are now worth about $110,000. But Browning's four peculiar buildings built within a one-block radius, still memorialize "Daddy's" unusual career.

THE LANGHAM

73RD STREET AND CENTRAL PARK WEST

WHEN THE CLARK FAMILY BUILT THE DAKOTA from 1880 to 1884, they also bought the blockfront of Central Park West from 73rd to 74th Streets but left it vacant. In 1902 the *Real Estate Record and Guide* reported that the Clarks put the 73rd–74th Street blockfront on Central Park West up for sale, with an unusual restriction: that any subsequent building not exceed the Dakota in height.

The restriction was apparently designed to protect the prestige of the Dakota. If the family had been concerned about the views from the Dakota's 73rd Street windows they would more likely have required the construction of four- or five-story houses. Apparently the Clarks could not sell with such a restriction, for the actual sale deed, later in 1902, included only a boilerplate prohibition of stables and billboards.

The new owners, Abraham Boehm and Lewis Coon, did not move ahead until 1904, when their architects, Clinton & Russell, filed plans for a $2 million structure, "the finest apartment house in the city," the *New York Times* said on its front page.

FIG 149.1

A DETAIL OF THE LANGHAM'S ENTRANCE. COURTESY OFFICE FOR METROPOLITAN HISTORY

THE LANGHAM APARTMENT HOUSE IN 1907. COURTESY MUSEUM OF THE CITY OF NEW YORK

The Langham had four apartments on a floor, with a parlor, dining room, library, three to four bedrooms, and servants' rooms in each. The biggest entertaining rooms were generous, 17 by 22 feet, but architects had still not figured out how to divide an apartment efficiently into entertaining, service, and dormitory zones—the bedroom wings stretched out along hallways more than 40 feet long.

The rooms were finished in Adam, Elizabethan, colonial, and other styles, and under the mansard were laundry rooms. The thirteen-floor building is perhaps 25 feet higher than the Dakota and appears even taller because of differences in the mansard roof.

Completed in 1907, the Langham had $500-a-month apartments that attracted moneyed and successful tenants, among them Isadore Saks, who moved from the old Hotel Majestic, just south of the Dakota, with his son, Joseph. Isadore Saks founded Saks & Company in New York in 1902, building his giant store at 34th Street and Broadway, just south of Macy's. Joseph joined him in the business, and together they were instrumental in establishing Saks Fifth Avenue at 50th Street and Fifth Avenue in 1924.

Later tenants included Edward F. Albee, head of the Keith and Keith-Albee-Orpheum theater chains and grandfather of the playwright Edward Albee; Samuel I. Rosenman, the confidant of Franklin D. Roosevelt who coined the term "New Deal," and Lee Strasberg, the actor and teacher.

Recent restoration work on the Langham by the owners resulted from the 1993 "luxury decontrol" law. In that year, state and city rent regulations were changed to permit the deregulation of apartments with rents of $2,000 or more a month whose tenants had incomes in excess of $250,000 a year (later lowered to $175,000).

One of these was the actress Mia Farrow, who had been paying less than $2,300 a month for an eleven-room apartment overlooking Central Park that had been featured in the film *Hannah and Her Sisters*. The owners filed to increase Ms. Farrow's rent under the new provisions, but she left the building, and the increased rents on her apartment have paid for new roofing, copperwork, cleaning, slate, and other elements.

18–52 WEST 74TH STREET

BY 1880, WHEN EDWARD CLARK FILED PLANS FOR THE MAMMOTH DAKOTA, he had also bought other large chunks of land.

He died in 1882, two years before the Dakota was finished, but the Clark family continued to buy; in late 1882 his son Alfred Corning Clark acquired the lots where 18–52 West 74th now stand. These and other purchases by the family on and off Central Park West from 70th to 86th Streets suggest a comprehensive or at least a grand plan.

The Clarks put up several dozen row houses on 73rd and 85th Streets by the end of the 1880s, but there they stopped, still holding large unimproved parcels. By the turn of the century these stood out clearly amid a sea of newly built apartments and houses, and the Clark estate began to search for other options.

It was Frederick Ambrose Clark, son of Alfred Corning, who returned the family to the ranks of the builders, and in 1902 he hired Percy Griffin to design eighteen row houses for the south side of 74th Street off Central Park West. As with most of their other projects, the Clarks were building for investment, not sale, and required a uniformly high level of quality, with concrete floors and fireproof construction.

150.1

FIG

18–52 WEST 74TH STREET IN 1904. COURTESY MUSEUM OF THE CITY OF NEW YORK

150.2

FIG

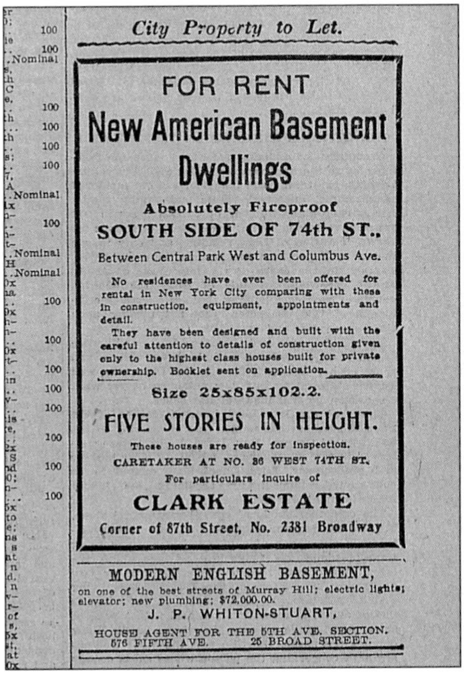

City Property to Let.

FOR RENT

New American Basement Dwellings

Absolutely Fireproof

SOUTH SIDE OF 74th ST.,

Between Central Park West and Columbus Ave.

No residences have ever been offered for rental in New York City comparing with these in construction, equipment, appointments and detail.

They have been designed and built with the careful attention to details of construction given only to the highest class houses built for private ownership. Booklet sent on application.

Size 25x85x102.2.

FIVE STORIES IN HEIGHT.

These houses are ready for inspection.

CARETAKER AT NO. 36 WEST 74TH ST.

For particulars inquire of

CLARK ESTATE

Corner of 87th Street, No. 2381 Broadway

MODERN ENGLISH BASEMENT,

on one of the best streets of Murray Hill; electric lights; elevator; new plumbing; $72,000.00.

J. P. WHITON-STUART,

HOUSE AGENT FOR THE 5TH AVE. SECTION.
576 FIFTH AVE. 25 BROAD STREET.

A RENTAL ADVERTISEMENT FOR *apartments at 18–52 West 74th Street in 1904.* COURTESY OFFICE FOR METROPOLITAN HISTORY

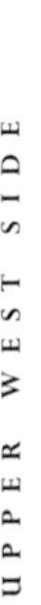

Each five-story house had 17 to 19 rooms and its own dynamo to generate electric current for elevators, a radical (and perhaps unique) innovation in row house construction. Griffin's row emulates London's sophisticated terraces, cohesive rows of houses also often built for investment. In 1906 a writer in the *Architectural Record* noted, "To the passerby, the block presents an orderly and attractive picture," something architects and critics had been seeking for New York since the 1880s. Part of this order was the subtle variation in design from house to house, part was the purposeful planting of street trees—unusual in that period—and part was the solid aspect of the houses themselves, which eschewed the cheap show typical of speculative houses.

By this time private houses were facing stiff competition from apartment houses, and the Clark row had water filters, wine refrigerators, silver safes, and similar details. Plans for the row generally show a butler's room, coal bin, and servant's hall in the basement; kitchen, reception, and billiard room on the first floor; parlor, dining room, and library on the second floor; and bedrooms above—including six or seven servants' bedrooms on the top floor.

It is not clear how the Clarks made out in their investment, but the 74th Street row is apparently the last thing they built on the West Side. They sold the rest of their vacant land, between 85th and 86th Streets west of Central Park West, to speculative townhouse builders. The Clarks held on to 18–52 West 74th until 1920, when they began selling off the houses. Now only two of the houses are private residences, and of the 18 Clark houses, seven are occupied by institutions.

THE SAN REMO

74TH STREET AND CENTRAL PARK WEST

THE DEVELOPER OF THE SAN REMO, at 74th and Central Park West, is shrouded in obscure financial records, but it may have been the Bank of United States that financed the project. The Bank of United States—which collapsed spectacularly in 1931—was established in 1913 and was headed in the 1920s by Bernard Marcus, whose aggressive expansionism increased the bank's branches from five in 1925 to sixty-two in 1930.

Whoever conceived the San Remo benefited from a law passed in the spring of 1929 that permitted high towers on plots greater than 30,000 square feet. The twenty-one-story Beresford, begun at 81st Street before the law passed, sprouted its three short, stubby towers, but they were for mechanical and water-tank use. The San Remo, designed in mid-1929 and finished in 1930, was the first of the four twin-tower buildings

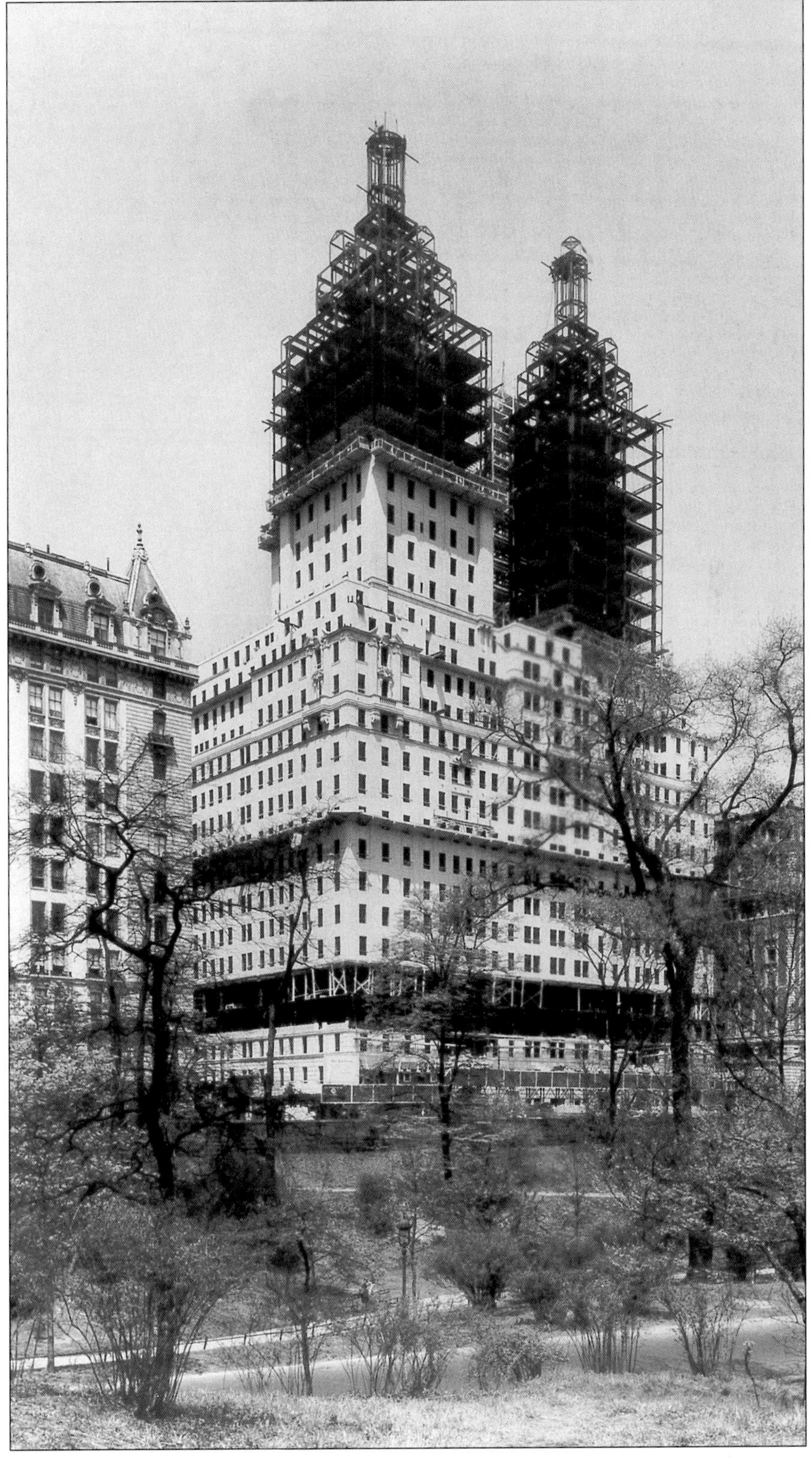

THE SAN REMO UNDER CONSTRUCTION, 1930. COURTESY MUSEUM OF THE CITY OF NEW YORK

THE SAN REMO IN 1942. COURTESY OFFICE FOR METROPOLITAN HISTORY

to go up on Central Park West. It had freestanding square towers rising to twenty-seven floors—ten floors above the seventeen-floor base—measuring 400 feet high to the tops of the temple-topped peaks.

According to the architectural historian and lawyer Andrew Alpern, Emery Roth, the San Remo's architect, gave the south tower the best apartments, five thirteen-room duplexes with 22-by-35-foot living rooms. One was originally offered for rent for $21,000 a year. The north tower had ten six-room simplexes.

An ad for the San Remo in the *Times* in April 1930 called it "as modern as a flying boat, as luxurious as the Ile de France and designed for people who are at home on both. Birds in the sky are your only neighbors."

The writer George Chappell, under his byline of "T-Square" in the *New Yorker*, considered the San Remo a successful design but singled out for particular praise a comparatively minor detail—the typical window has the usual swing-out casement, plus smaller transoms above and below. The top one swings out and the bottom one swings in, providing multiple alternatives for ventilation.

The San Remo was only partly filled in October 1930 when the reserves of the Bank of United States began falling, precipitating a run in December of that year, when the bank closed for good. Public hearings disclosed that bank officers had burned ledgers and other records in the incinerator of the Beresford, where at least one of the bank officers lived, and both the Beresford and the San Remo were foreclosed after the bank collapsed.

The San Remo is now considered a celebrity building, and telephone listings from the 1930s indicate that it housed prominent show business people in its early years as well. They included Albert Warner, one of the Warner Brothers; Joseph Vogel, vice president of Loew's; and Eddie Cantor, the comedian. Cantor, named Isidor Iskowitch when he was born in 1892 into a tough life on Eldridge Street on the Lower East Side, made his way into vaudeville in the 1910s and became a favorite of Florenz Ziegfeld and other producers. He was making a half million dollars a year in the early 1930s as he moved into radio and movies.

44 WEST 77TH STREET

HERBERT S. HARDE AND R. THOMAS SHORT DESIGNED fairly conventional tenement houses until 1903, when they created the five-story, overtly Gothic-style Red House at 350 West 85th Street. Then, in 1906 and 1907, they designed three tall apartment houses that established their enduring fame—the neo–French Renaissance Alwyn Court, at 58th Street and Seventh Avenue; the neo-Gothic Park View, at 66th Street and Madison Avenue; and 44 West 77th Street.

The West 77th Street building was a project organized by Walter Russell, who had been instrumental in the development of the high-rise artists' cooperatives on 67th Street off Central Park West. In 1907, as the cooperative movement spread to nonartists, he filed plans for 44 West 77th Street with great double-height studio spaces.

Completed in 1909, the fourteen-story building was occupied by some artists,

44 WEST 77TH STREET *scaffolded for facade repairs in 1911.* COURTESY LIBRARY OF CONGRESS

44 WEST 77TH STREET IN 1909. COURTESY MUSEUM OF THE CITY OF NEW YORK

among them the sculptor Karl Bitter, but also by lawyers, brokers, doctors, and others with more conventional occupations.

What they thought of the exterior is unrecorded. But it was not just eye-catching; it made people "stare and gasp," according to a review in 1909 by Montgomery Schuyler in *Architectural Record*.

A "Brobdingnagian cathedral," said *Architects & Builders* magazine the same year. And Andrew Alpern, the architecture historian, said that the elaborate terra-cotta decoration "appears to have been squeezed out of a pastry tube."

Indeed, the *Real Estate Record and Guide* noted in 1909 that the recent advent of terra-cotta had opened up "a mine of possibilities for architects." Shaped in soft clay and then fired, terra-cotta was lighter and much less expensive than carved stone.

This development was not without its critics, however, and chief among them was the stone industry. When the entire front of 44 West 77th Street was scaffolded in 1911, the trade journal *Stone* gloated that the work involved a replacement of "much" of the terra-cotta after pieces had fallen to the street.

Stone predicted the "craze" for terra-cotta had peaked and "we are ready to return to safe and sane methods of construction."

But modeled terra-cotta continued in use with structures like the Woolworth Building of 1913 and went out of fashion only with the advent of Modernism in the 1930s.

In 1940, the Metropolitan Life Insurance Company took over the 77th Street building with a deed in lieu of foreclosure. In 1944, the company's architect, Samuel R. Bishop, removed the bulk of the terra-cotta, calling it "a hazard and likely to fall." The banks of cathedral windows still create an impressive effect, but all the projecting work has been cut away.

The other similar Harde & Short buildings with similar facades have kept most of their terra-cotta, and David Pearce, a building resident interested in its history, hypothesizes that Metropolitan Life took an extra-cautious approach. In 1992 Raymond Pepi, president of Building Conservation Associates, invited to speculate on what it would take to replace the missing facade elements, said that such work could easily cost $5 million. "And the more I look, the more detail I see."

WEST END COLLEGIATE CHURCH

77TH STREET AND WEST END AVENUE

THE DUTCH FOUNDED THE NEW AMSTERDAM COLONY in New York in 1625 and built a Dutch Reformed church three years later. Dutch rule ended in 1664, when the English seized the island, but Dutch culture and customs continued generally unimpeded.

The Dutch Reformed churches became more and more Anglicized—the 1854 Marble Collegiate Church, at 29th Street and Fifth Avenue, is generically Gothic. The churches adopted the term "collegiate" from their practice of sharing multiple ministers as colleagues, not competitors.

As the West Side developed in the 1880s, some developers and architects saw in the Dutch and Flemish styles a way to shake off the traditional brownstone corset of the urban row house. McKim, Mead & White's 1885 group of brick houses with stepped

FIG 153.1

THE WEST END COLLEGIATE CHURCH COMPLEX IN 1893. COURTESY OFFICE FOR METROPOLITAN HISTORY

gables at the southwest corner of 83rd and West End Avenue, which is now mostly demolished, is considered the first of a half-dozen such groups.

In the 1880s the Reformed Dutch Church noticed this emerging quarter—the associated Collegiate School moved from 29th Street and Seventh Avenue to 74th Street off West End Avenue in 1887. In 1891, the architect Robert W. Gibson designed a new church and school complex for the northeast corner of 77th Street and West End Avenue. Working in orange brick, tan terra-cotta and red tile, he modeled it after a seventeenth-century butcher's guildhall in the Netherlands, although he omitted the heads of livestock that decorated the original. According to a history of the church, parishioners paid an extra $5,000 to have the roof done in tile instead of plain slate.

By comparison, the Middle Collegiate Church built in 1892 on Second Avenue at Seventh Street, designed by S. B. Reed, is a more conventional Gothic-style building.

West End Collegiate Church, seating 750, and the school, with 110 students, opened in 1892. The *New York Times* approved of the new building, saying that "people are beginning to pay more attention than ever before to the history of the city." The *New York Post* called the building "a constant surprise and delight."

Both church and school emphasized a Dutch heritage, although surnames of parishioners and students do not show a large number of obviously Dutch names. In 1894, the church's men's group, De Vereeniging (The Association), heard lectures on prison reform and "The Saloon in Politics." The school's sports cheer was "Endracht maakt macht; Endracht maakt macht; Yea; Collegiate, Collegiate, Collegiate!" The first phrase means "in unity there is strength."

THE BELLECLAIRE

77TH STREET AND BROADWAY

IN 1900 ALBERT SAXE HIRED THE YOUNG ARCHITECT EMERY ROTH to design an apartment hotel on newly fashionable Broadway. Completed in 1903, the ten-story Hotel Belleclaire had nonhousekeeping apartments of one to four bedrooms. Tenants took their meals in a Moorish dining room or a Louis XVI ladies' dining room or a Flemish cafe.

The Belleclaire made a solid addition to the growing list of impressive, generally French-inspired apartment houses on Broadway, like the Dorilton and the Ansonia. What set it apart was the outside: the fullest example yet of the Art Nouveau and Secession styles, related movements sweeping Europe.

FIG 154.1

WEDDING DINNER AT THE BELLECLAIRE IN 1908. COURTESY MUSEUM OF THE CITY OF NEW YORK

FIG 154.2

THE BELLECLAIRE AT 77TH STREET AND BROADWAY IN 1910. COURTESY THE NEW-YORK HISTORICAL SOCIETY, NEW YORK CITY

Characteristic elements of that style as seen in the Belleclaire's exterior include the pendant panel decorations on the tall limestone pilasters, the stone spandrel and lintel ornament on the fourth floor, and the asymmetrical windowpanes, twelve in the top sash, three in the bottom. As originally built, the Belleclaire also had elaborate sidewalk railings that could have come from Hector Guimard's Metro stations in Paris. There was also similar ironwork at the roof and the ninth-floor balcony and a long bay of sinuous, Art Nouveau windows lighting a dining room on 77th Street.

In 1915, Roth designed an apartment house for Saxe at 601 West End Avenue where the Art Nouveau influence is barely discernible, but it was a stale reference, for by that time architects shook their heads at the silly "Art Nouveau craze."

The 1905 census listed sixty-three families at the Belleclaire, most of them headed by brokers, merchants, and businessmen. It was into this upper-middle-class environment that Maxim Gorky, the Russian socialist author, arrived in 1906 on a lecture tour, taking rooms at the Belleclaire. He and his companion, who was listed as his wife, were there but a few days when it was discovered that his supposed spouse was actually the Russian actress Madame Andreieva and that his legal wife, from whom he was separated, was in Russia.

Milton Roblee, manager of the Belleclaire, ejected the Gorky party, saying, "My hotel is a family hotel." Indignant, Gorky replied to newspaper controversy, "for us still remains the human right to overlook the gossip of others." After being ejected from two other hotels, Gorky found peace at the house of the John Martin family on Staten Island, whom the *New York Times* described as "less scrupulous than their neighbors."

In the '20s the ground-floor public rooms of the Belleclaire were replaced with storefronts, and by the 1930s the hotel had lost any claim to distinction. At some point after 1950 its unusual corner dome was removed, but several years of recent renovations offer promise for this unusual jewel.

THE THEODORE ROOSEVELT MEMORIAL HALL
OF THE AMERICAN MUSEUM OF NATURAL HISTORY

IN THE 1880s AND 1890s CADY, BERG & SEE COMPLETED THE GRAND, Romanesque-style south front of the museum facing West 77th Street, departing from the earlier style but keeping the same concept of a giant, square complex of museum buildings that now extends to 81st Street.

Construction slowed after 1900, but the death of Theodore Roosevelt in 1919 brought other opportunities. Roosevelt had been an active explorer and adventurer, and his many expeditions were often associated with the museum's research.

New York State established a commission to create a suitable memorial to him, and the museum's empty Central Park West blockfront was designated to receive a state-sponsored memorial building. In 1925, John Russell Pope won an architectural competition for its design.

Built from 1929 to 1935, the hall was also part of a larger, failed proposal for an "Intermuseum Promenade" between the American Museum of Natural History and the Metropolitan Museum at Fifth Avenue and 80th Street.

The broad landscaped and terraced swath "will be hailed by the art-loving people of the West Side and the science-loving people of the East Side," Henry Fairfield Osborn told the *New York Times* in 1927. He also called the new building "the most inspiring me-

FIG 155.1

THEODORE ROOSEVELT MEMORIAL HALL *at the Museum of Natural History in 1932.* COURTESY AMERICAN MUSEUM OF NATURAL HISTORY

morial ever designed, excepting perhaps only the Taj Mahal." Mr. Osborn, a paleontologist and the president of the Museum of Natural History since 1908, lived at 998 Fifth Avenue, at 81st Street—at the other end of the projected promenade.

Pope planned the Roosevelt Memorial to be seen from a distance as the terminal feature of this long promenade, a giant triumphal arch of granite projecting from plain, undecorated flanking wings. The interior is dominated by a giant, barrel-vaulted main hall, 67 feet by 120 feet and 100 feet high, in marble and limestone, with murals of Roosevelt's African trips and his role in the Panama Canal and in settling the Russo-Japanese war.

Because the promenade was never completed, the Roosevelt Hall is usually seen obliquely from Central Park West; published studies by Pope show that it was meant to be viewed from well inside the park. Because of the lack of an appropriate setting, it has something of the character of a beached whale—grand but out of place.

Mumford—writing in his *New Yorker* column in 1932 when the facade was half completed—was horrified, in part because he admired the existing Romanesque-style museum buildings.

"This classic monument, so painfully, so grotesquely inappropriate, will never look better than it does now," he wrote. "Today one can swallow it as a sheer ghastly fantasy, [but] in a year it will be finished and then it will not even be funny."

President Franklin D. Roosevelt dedicated the building in 1936. Over the years, the memorial has seen only modest changes, among them the installation of visitor gates and an information desk. For all intents and purposes it is in original condition, the better to invite critical judgment in its setting on the art gallery of the New York streets.

AMERICAN MUSEUM OF NATURAL HISTORY

WING A

IN 1994 THE AMERICAN MUSEUM OF NATURAL HISTORY TOUTED what it called a "sympathetic restoration" of one floor of its original building, a polychromed extravaganza designed by Calvert Vaux, but it was a work of opportunism rather than respect. Vaux came to the United States from England in 1850 as a partner of the landscape architect Andrew Jackson Downing. Downing died in 1852, but Vaux continued on his own, teaming with Olmsted to win the Central Park competition in 1858. That victory led to Prospect Park and other municipal commissions, including the American Museum of Natural History, built 1872–77, and the Metropolitan Museum of Art, 1874–80.

Both museums were designed by Vaux with the assistance of Jacob Wrey Mould, and were part of much larger schemes. Vaux's plans for the Museum of Natural History would have covered its entire present site—from Central Park West to Columbus Avenue and from 77th to 81st Streets—with the largest museum in the world. The current 1.2 million-square-foot museum covers about half the site.

The American Museum of Natural History opened in 1877, a bright sparkle of polychrome: deep red brick, a patterned slate roof, and Venetian Gothic arches of two shades of granite.

The interior was arranged in large single galleries. On the ground floor, mammals (later Northwest Coast Indians); on the first floor, birds (later African People); on the mezzanine, anthropology (later North American Birds); and on the top, fossils (later the library). The exhibit cases were designed by the engineer George K. Radford, and the original contents of the museum were not so different from those of today.

The decorations of the halls mixed aesthetics and engineering. Vaux used iron frankly and expressively, with intricately worked column capitals in floral forms unlike any seen in ancient history and a delicate openwork railing at the mezzanine. For the ceilings, he simply plastered over the low brick arches supported by iron beams. The floors were laid in geometric patterns of richly colored Minton tiles.

The detail sheets reproduced in William Alex's 1994 *Calvert Vaux Architect & Planner* show how carefully he worked out both the structure and the decoration of the two museums, conceiving as a continuous element what other architects treated separately. A detail of the staircases at the Metropolitan shows both the iron framing and bolt holes but also the intricate column capitals and the patterned tread plans.

FIG 156.1

THE INTERIOR OF THE NATURAL HISTORY MUSEUM'S WING A, CIRCA 1890. COURTESY AMERICAN MUSEUM OF NATURAL HISTORY

FIG 156.2

THE EXTERIOR OF WING A OF THE MUSEUM OF NATURAL HISTORY, CIRCA 1890. COURTESY AMERICAN MUSEUM OF NATURAL HISTORY

Both museums grew, but not in accordance with Vaux's master plan or his designs; later administrations have consistently neglected the original sections of their buildings. At the Museum of Natural History the magnificent Minton tiles on the ground floor have been often abused and always ignored, and the ironwork of the mezzanine was long ago boxed in. Knock on the modern plasterboard and imagine what treasure is buried inside.

The top-floor exhibition hall—the original fossil gallery—was converted to a library in the 1950s with dropped ceilings and the other usual insults. A 1994 reconstruction of much of the fourth floor, by the museum's architect, Kevin Roche, John Dinkeloo & Associates, and its designer, Ralph Appelbaum Associates, did remove the dropped ceilings, exposing the Vaux ironwork, calling it a "sympathetic restoration." Sadly, that is just lip-service preservation. There was no sense of the original character of the museum as a series of distinct buildings; they have been homogenized for the sake of convenience.

For the Vaux building the museum did no historic paint analysis in 1994; testing of the surviving ironwork at the Metropolitan Museum of Art shows a polychrome scheme of coral, ochre, red, and white. Instead, the Vaux interior was to be simply painted white to match the other interiors.

Saddest of all was to see the Minton tile floors. The linoleum that covered them in the library years was removed, but during this "restoration," iron-wheeled Dumpsters ran back and forth, breaking the tiles into shards. These floors were covered up, so they, too, could "match" the rest of the building.

THE BROCKHOLST

85TH STREET AND COLUMBUS AVENUE

THE SIX-STORY GINGERBREAD-COLORED BROCKHOLST at 85th Street and Columbus Avenue was designed in 1889 by John G. Prague, a prolific West Side row house architect who owned the building with a partner, Thomas E. D. Power. Along with other investors, Prague and Power built 232 row houses in the area from 85th to 87th Streets and from Columbus to Amsterdam Avenues, creating an entire community where, in the mid-1880s, there had been only open land.

An 1890 issue of the *Real Estate Record and Guide*, called the $250,000 Brockholst "truly noble," with an interior "such as one would expect to see in one of the old English castles." The lobby ceiling was decorated with aluminum leaf by Tiffany & Company, and two dining rooms, a cafe, and a barbershop served tenants and passersby. Most of the thirty-two apartments had three bedrooms and rented for $125 a month. They had gas

THE EXTERIOR OF THE BROCKHOLST IN 1890. COURTESY OFFICE FOR METROPOLITAN HISTORY

and electric lighting, and Wilton carpets in the hallways. The earliest tenants were prosperous leaders in the mining, brokerage, printing, and fancy-goods businesses.

But a 1917 article in the trade magazine *Building Management* noted that rents had declined to $75 a month; at that time, dinner in the restaurant could be had for 75 cents, and full board was $10 a week. By the 1920s, when the Brockholst had been eclipsed by more advanced buildings, a more varied group of tenants had moved in. They included Margaret Beecher White, a Christian Science practitioner who lived there with her mother, Harriet Beecher, daughter of the controversial Brooklyn preacher Henry Ward Beecher.

Hilda Englund, the Swedish-born actress, well known for performing in the plays of Henrik Ibsen, also lived there, and the census returns for the 1920s show occupations like "manager-musical," "artist-painter," and "writer–literary critic" among the lodgers in the informally subdivided apartments.

By the 1950s, the dining rooms had been replaced by stores on the Columbus Avenue side, cornice and trim details had been removed, and "the West Side was very much on a downward movement—people wanted to move to Westchester, Long Island, and New Jersey," said Marcus Retter, who was the head of the group that bought the building in 1956.

In March 1939, as a teenager, Mr. Retter fled Vienna for England. He had hoped that his parents would follow, "but they were with the unlucky ones—they were deported to Riga and gassed," he said from his office at 88th Street and Riverside Drive. His desk is awash in papers, and his own office has a 1960s IBM electric typewriter and an old adding machine—he is one of the last of the old-line West Side landlords who was there long before the fancy co-ops and restaurants.

THE INTERIOR OF THE BROCKHOLST IN 1890. COURTESY OFFICE FOR METROPOLITAN HISTORY

Mr. Retter said that when he bought the Brockholst he had planned to divide the large apartments into smaller units, but that plan was too expensive, and so most of the large apartments remain intact. The rent on these apartments was about $300 a month in the 1950s; now, he estimates that the market rent is $2,500 a month. In retrospect Mr. Retter and his contemporaries may be viewed as early participants in the historic preservation movement, for it was they who kept older buildings like the Brockholst functioning during hard times, banking them for a more prosperous future.

THE CLARENDON

137 RIVERSIDE DRIVE

IN THE 1890S THE YOUNG WILLIAM RANDOLPH HEARST came to New York, buying the *Morning Journal* in 1896 and battling Joseph Pulitzer's *World* for circulation. He later launched the *Evening Journal* and by 1908 had major newspapers in five cities. Hearst also served as a representative in Congress and stoked his appetite for politics with campaigns for mayor of New York City, senator, governor, and even president—none of them successful.

In April 1907, when he was living in a brownstone at the corner of 28th Street and Lexington Avenue, the *Real Estate Record and Guide* reported that he would build a mansion at the southeast corner of 105th Street and Riverside Drive. But Hearst, perhaps

FIG 158.1

WILLIAM RANDOLPH HEARST'S ARMOR HALL *in his Clarendon apartment in 1924.* COURTESY LIBRARY OF CONGRESS

THE CLARENDON ABOUT 1915. COURTESY OFFICE FOR METROPOLITAN HISTORY

seeing that Riverside Drive's days as a street of private houses had ended, soon arranged for Ranald Macdonald—a developer building a conventional twelve-story apartment house at the southeast corner of 86th Street and Riverside Drive—to take over the top and possibly other floors in the building.

The building, the Clarendon, opened in 1908. In 1913 Hearst bought the entire structure from Macdonald. He had Macdonald's architect, Charles E. Birge, draw plans for further work on the apartment, which already took in the tenth, eleventh, and twelfth floors, plus the addition of a metal and glass marquee at the main entrance.

In 1913 or 1922 Hearst took over the eighth and ninth floors and also added the giant rectangular mansard along the 100-foot-long Riverside Drive front. This was really the upper section of what plans identify as a two-story-high "Tapestry Gallery" running the length of the building and furnished with suits of armor, stained glass, tapestries, and other artworks. Other rooms were identified as the North Museum and the South Museum, the Greek Room, the English Room, a two-story-high Spanish Gallery, the Gothic Room, and the Julius Caesar Room.

The apartment was the nerve center of Hearst's three-part empire of publishing, real estate, and especially politics, in which his candidates were backed vociferously by his ever-expanding media chain. Hearst was an isolationist. In 1918, after America entered World War I, the New York State attorney general was conducting an investigation into cooperation with Germans before and during the war. Building employees at the Clarendon testified that in 1916, Bolo Pacha, who was later executed by France as a German spy, was a frequent visitor to the Hearst apartment.

By 1920 Hearst was having an affair with the actress Marion Davies and his day-to-day domicile seems to have varied widely. In 1925 he and his wife had separate listings in the New York City directory. In 1927 he moved to California, in part to oversee the motion picture business he built around Davies; Mrs. Hearst stayed at the Clarendon.

Then in 1935 Hearst angrily announced his departure from California for New York because of high California taxes, even predicting that other movie studios would leave. Then in 1939 the Mutual Life Insurance Company took the Clarendon back from the Hearst company in foreclosure and, in 1940 gutted it, including the fabulous Hearst apartment.

THE ST. URBAN

89TH STREET AND CENTRAL PARK WEST

THE ST. URBAN WAS PART OF THE EARLY GENERATION of tall New York apartments, big-blowzy buildings like the Dorilton at 71st and Broadway of 1902 and the Ansonia at 73rd and Broadway of 1904.

In 1904, Peter Banner, a wool and animal hides dealer then living at the Majestic at the southwest corner of 72nd and Central Park West, filed plans for a twelve-story apartment house at the southwest corner of 89th, also facing Central Park.

Designed by Robert T. Lyons and completed in 1906, the St. Urban is made distinctive by its high mansard roof and round corner tower, culminating in a dome and lantern of copper. The elaborate copper dormers, trimmed by equally elaborate copper cresting, are framed by the sloping, dark slate mansard roof.

The completed building was flanked by lower structures and the high mansard and corner tower have always given it a prominence beyond its height. It is hard to believe that the narrow turnaround of the Central Park West porte cochere was functional, but a

FIG 159.1

A DETAIL OF THE ST. URBAN'S EXTERIOR IN 1907. COURTESY OFFICE FOR METROPOLITAN HISTORY

FIG 159.2

ST. URBAN APARTMENT HOUSE *on Central Park West at 89th Street in 1907.* COURTESY OFFICE FOR METROPOLITAN HISTORY

1907 photograph does show a carriage partway inside, and the pavement was scored in the manner common to stables.

Apartments in the St. Urban all had twelve rooms, full-length mirrors, solid porcelain tubs and other fixtures, large wall safes, and oak-paneled dining rooms. The water was filtered and ice was delivered from a basement ice plant. They rented for $250 to

$375 a month. Most unusual, to later eyes, is the great variety of original windows: in-swing, out-swing, double-hung, French, transom, and other types.

Peter Banner lost the building in bankruptcy in the year it was completed.

By the 1910s and 1920s, apartment designs settled into less flamboyant patterns, and buildings like the St. Urban, with its separate carriage driveway on Central Park West, became obviously dated. A 1928 article in *Building Management* reported that the building was popular, and that new tenants were received mostly by referral, even though leases were drawn for five-year terms. "Children who grew up in the building have now married and established new homes there."

But the interior still was altered, merging the older, smaller bedrooms, and removing some of the older-style decorations. Older features—like a centrally placed library, with sliding doors on each side—were derided as wasted space, used simply as a corridor, and many of these were completely demolished to simply enlarge the adjacent living rooms. Mechanical refrigerators superseded iceboxes, high-tank toilets were taken out, and freestanding bathtubs were replaced with built-in models.

The older generation of elaborate buildings also proved to be more difficult to maintain, and finials, cresting, roofwork, the slate roof, and balconies gradually disappeared. In 1989 the roof was redone after Landmarks Commission review, but they assumed the original roof was copper—and that's the way it was restored.

THE ISAAC RICE MANSION

89TH STREET AND RIVERSIDE DRIVE

AS EARLY AS THE 1870S THERE WERE PREDICTIONS THAT FIFTH AVENUE would be eclipsed by Riverside Drive, where millionaires could build the freestanding mansions typical of other cities. A few mansion builders did come to Riverside, among them Elizabeth Clark, owner of the Dakota and other West Side properties. She started her house at the northeast corner of 89th and Riverside Drive in 1898.

The next year Isaac L. Rice bought the southeast corner of 89th Street and Riverside for his own house. Rice was an academic turned corporate lawyer and had become rich through railroad and other investments. In 1900 he had the new architectural firm of Herts & Tallant design a large freestanding house with a reflecting pool and colonnaded garden along the south side of the lot. The landscape elements were reduced in revisions of 1901, and the house was completed in 1903. Isaac Rice called it Villa Julia, after his wife.

FIG 160.1

A VIEW NORTH ON RIVERSIDE DRIVE *toward the Isaac L. Rice mansion, circa 1904.* COURTESY OFFICE FOR METROPOLITAN HISTORY

FIG 160.2

ISAAC L. RICE. COURTESY OFFICE FOR METROPOLITAN HISTORY

Herts & Tallant produced a typically individualistic design, mixing Beaux-Arts, Georgian, and Renaissance elements. Particularly distinctive are the deep overhanging eaves and the repetition of curves—the porte cochere on the north side, the bay above it, and the large marble arch above the main entrance.

In 1903 the *Real Estate Record and Guide* praised "the rare combination of white marble and dark redbrick" on a site that commanded "the finest view up the Hudson that is obtainable on Manhattan island."

In 1905 Julia Rice began a campaign against noisy river traffic, especially against tugboat pilots who would use whistles and sirens for personal messages at all hours. She focused on hospital areas and hired Columbia University students as monitors. One recorded 2,500 "unnecessary" whistles in a twenty-four-hour period.

The issue was not only a pet peeve of Mrs. Rice's. She got endorsements from hospital and medical authorities, and she got results, although one tugboat captain who was taken to court, Patrick McGurl, said that the whole thing was "foolery" and that he wouldn't change his ways.

In early 1906 Mrs. Rice told the *New York Tribune* that she was happy with what was, operationally, a one-woman crusade. "There is no haggling about expenses, because I pay them all myself," she said. But later that year she did found the Society for the Suppression of Unnecessary Noises, of which she was elected president.

The society expanded its mission to lobby for rubber tires on milk wagons and oppose factory whistles, firecrackers, and boys clacking sticks along iron fences.

Mr. Rice was a chess expert and invented the strategy called the Rice Gambit. In his basement chess room he organized matches via overseas cable between United States and British competitors.

Perhaps because of the panic of 1907, the Rices moved to the Ansonia apartment building at 73rd Street and Broadway. Mrs. Rice continued her antinoise activities and, after her husband's death in 1915, donated to the city the Betsy Head Memorial Playground in the Brownsville section of Brooklyn and the Rice Memorial Stadium in Pelham Bay Park in the Bronx.

THE ASTOR COURT

89TH STREET AND BROADWAY

JOHN JACOB ASTOR'S GREAT-GREAT-GRANDSON, Vincent, was a first-year student at Harvard in 1912 when he heard that his father John Jacob Astor IV had sailed, and perished, on the *Titanic.* Vincent Astor left Harvard that year, the heir to $87 million, of which $65 million was in real estate, and set to work in the family office at 23 West 26th Street. Guided by his father's manager, Nicholas Biddle, he began building modestly, favoring educated but not ostentatiously stylish projects. In 1914, Astor began work on the $1 million Astor Court apartments, on the east side of Broadway from 89th to 90th Streets.

For this project he retained the artist-turned-architect Charles Platt, who had already designed an unusual set of duplex co-ops on Lexington Avenue from 66th to 67th Streets. These were luxurious on the inside, but their rear courtyards were barren concrete spaces. Perhaps it was Astor who had the idea to design more modest apartment in-

FIG 161.1

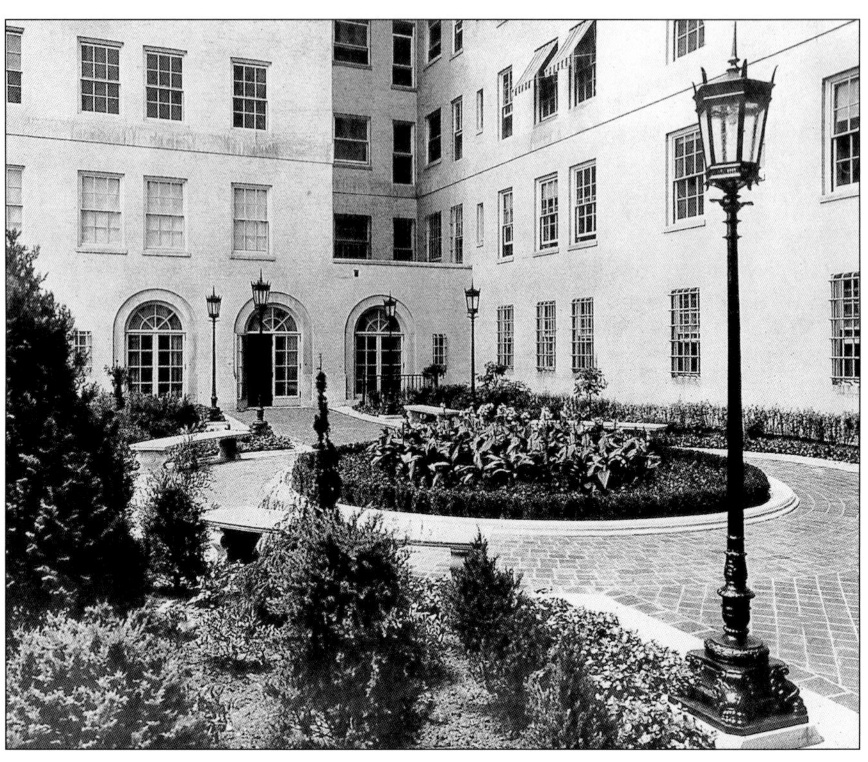

THE ASTOR COURT'S GARDEN IN 1916. COURTESY LIBRARY OF CONGRESS

FIG 161.2

teriors but develop a real garden for the court. Rising thirteen stories above Broadway, the Astor Court has a reserved facade, except for its spectacular projecting copper cornice, originally stenciled with colored designs.

The building's two lobbies have coffered ceilings set into low, curved vaults. What sets Astor Court apart from its competition is something a passerby can only glance at from a distance through the lobbies' doors—in place of the customary prisonlike rear yard, there is a great garden court. If a resident wished, she could enter an apartment as if it were a country house, down a brick walkway, past plantings of ivy, evergreens, hedges, and flowers. A few of Platt's drawings for the building bear the initials

EXTERIOR VIEW OF THE ASTOR COURT IN 1916. COURTESY LIBRARY OF CONGRESS

"E. S."—perhaps the garden was designed by Ellen Shipman, who attended Radcliffe, studied under Platt, and was related by marriage to Biddle, the manager.

Shipman often collaborated with Platt in this period, and by the 1920s she was one of the leading American landscape architects. In 1938 she said in an interview that "until women took up landscaping, gardening in this country was at its lowest ebb." She died in 1950.

Although the front of the building is in red brick, Platt designed the rear facades in buff brick, lighting up what might at some points be gloomy. And he raised the garden level a few feet above the lobbies, avoiding the sunken feeling present in some rear areas. In 1916 the magazine *American Architect* reviewed the Astor Court and said, "We hope that it marks the beginning of a new era in apartment house design." Anyone who has ever decried the abysmal state of most New York backyards will revel in the Astor Court's garden. The early tenants were prosperous families with several servants. The residents included Frank Vincent, a theatrical manager, and Jacob de Jong, fifty-two, who had been born in Holland and ran an artificial-flower business. Astor sold the building in 1922, and by 1935 it was owned by Henri Bendel, of women's clothing-store fame, who divided some of the apartments.

Over the last ten years the Astor Court cooperative has brought back the garden court from an impenetrable mass of weeds, making the building one of the most popular on the West Side.

THE ELDORADO

90TH STREET AND CENTRAL PARK WEST

IN THE LATE 1920S, REAL ESTATE BOOMED on Central Park West and spawned the four twin-towered apartment buildings that loom over the park on the New York skyline: the San Remo, between 74th and 75th Streets; the Majestic, between 71st and 72nd Streets; the Century, between 62nd and 63rd Streets; and the Eldorado. In July 1929, the investor Frederick Brown bought the first El Dorado, a 1902 apartment house of modest character, and resold the site to Louis Klosk, a Bronx-based developer.

At first Klosk had his architects, Margon & Holder, file plans for a sixteen-story building, but in early fall they revised the designs to a twenty-nine-story building, with twin towers; the Multiple Dwelling Law of 1929 allowed such towers where lot sizes were large. Margon & Holder and their associate architect, Emery Roth, developed multiple designs for the new Eldorado. The earliest published version showed fairly simple streamlining on the base and towers but squared-off tops. On his own, Roth developed a nearly Romanesque design with red tiles on the roof areas, similar to his Oliver Cromwell apartment house at 12 West 72nd. The drawings that Margon & Holder filed at the Department of Buildings in 1929 show a twin-towered design very similar to what was executed, but it delineated the tower finials as angled, faceted spires. The drawings bear the note "gold leaf" for the finials. The completed building has spires with a distinctive stepped design, like a ziggurat.

The stock market crash of 1929 did not instantly hurt construction projects. In January 1930, *Real Estate* magazine said that the Eldorado had been "designed with impressive simplicity" and would open in the fall. In June 1930 Edgar Stix, a real estate agent, sent out a promotional letter for the building saying that the apartments "do not attempt to appeal to the popular demand; the idea has been, rather, to create the exceptional and offer them at fair rentals."

By November 1930 the *New York Times* said that mechanics' liens for several hundred thousand dollars had been filed against the building, but that an agreement had been reached and the building would be completed. In 1931, however, the building was in foreclosure, and Klosk lost it; it was reorganized with a new owner, the Central Park

FIG 162.1

THE ELDORADO ABOUT 1947.
COURTESY OFFICE FOR METROPOLITAN HISTORY

Plaza Corporation, and then opened. Among the earliest tenants were Rex Cole, who made millions marketing General Electric refrigerators, sold from his trademark stores built to resemble giant refrigerators. Another was Royal Copeland, who served as mayor of Ann Arbor, Michigan, from 1901–1903, then senator from New York from 1924-1938. Copeland unsuccessfully ran for mayor of New York City in 1937. According to his obituary in the *Times* in 1938, Senator Copeland's failed opposition to the confirmation of Hugo Black as a United States Supreme Court justice in 1937 led to the disclosure that Black had once been a member of the Ku Klux Klan. Another tenant was Barney Pressman, who founded the Barneys clothing store in 1923.

THE NIPPON CLUB

161 WEST 93RD STREET

AFTER THE ATTACK ON PEARL HARBOR on December 7, 1941, Japanese restaurants were closed down, Japan's embassy was shut, and Japanese Americans who had been in the country for decades were sent to internment camps. A few traces of the aftermath of Pearl Harbor survive in New York, especially in an elegant 1912 building at 161 West 93rd Street that was seized by the federal government during World War II.

The building, between Columbus and Amsterdam Avenues, is now a Seventh-Day Adventist Church. Few New Yorkers know that it was originally the Nippon Club, built by Jokichi Takamine, who brought about the gift of the cherry trees that blossom in Washington, D.C. Takamine, born in 1854 in Takaoka, Japan, learned English in school and moved to New York in the 1890s, where he did research in applied chemistry. In 1901 he isolated the hormone adrenaline in his laboratory.

In 1905 he organized the Nippon Club, and in 1912 the club put up its own building. The Nippon Club's architect, John Vredenburgh Van Pelt, was a careful designer who wrote books on the history of ornament. He annotated the facade drawing for the building, "brick colors to be selected to give the effect desired by the architect." The building is now painted, but the magazine *Edison Monthly* wrote in 1915 that "something in the architecture, alien but not at all bizarre, attracts one to this substantial building in light gold brown brick." It continued that "the broadly projecting ledge of the cornice is the only discoverable hint of Asia" on the exterior, and that the interior also was subdued as to Japanese influence, with "a charm of finish, a certain subtlety of ornament, that transforms the conventional, rendering the place exotic and curious."

There was also, in the kitchen, "a queer-looking fish table, marble topped and knife girdled, a device indispensable to the requirements of the Nippon appetite." Carved sycamore chairs, upholstered in gold leather and laced with delicate flower

FIG 163.1

NOTICE OF SALE

Notice inviting citizens of the United States of America to make purchase proposals to Leo T. Crowley, United States Alien Property Custodian, for the real property and improvements thereon located at 161-5 West 93d St. in the City and County of New York, New York, and all furniture, fixtures, office equipment and miscellaneous personal property owned by Leo T. Crowley, United States Alien Property Custodian, at the premises at 161-5 West 93d Street, New York. Bids are invited for (1) Real property only, (2) Real and Personal property together, (3) Personal property only. Contents will be on display in the premises on Tuesday, September 7, Wednesday, September 8 and Saturday, September 11, next, between the hours of 1:00 o'clock P. M. and 5:00 o'clock P. M.

The aforesaid parcels of real property are more particularly described as follows:

PARCEL ONE

All those three certain lots, pieces or parcels of land with the buildings and improvements thereon erected, situate, lying and being in the Borough of Manhattan of the City of New York in the County and State of New York, bounded and described as follows:

Beginning at a point on the northerly side of 93rd Street, distant 168 feet easterly from the corner formed by the intersection of the northerly side of 93rd Street with the easterly side of Amsterdam Avenue; running thence easterly along the northerly side of 93rd Street 51 feet; thence northerly parallel with Amsterdam Avenue and part of the distance through a party wall of 104 feet 8½ inches more or less to the center line of an old road or lane formerly called Apthrop's Lane; thence northwesterly along the center line of said lane 51 feet and 9/16th of an inch more or less to a point distant 168 feet easterly from the easterly side of Amsterdam Avenue measured along a line drawn at right angles thereto, and thence southerly parallel with the easterly side of Amsterdam Avenue 106 feet 10¼ inches to the point or place of beginning.

PARCEL TWO

All that certain lot, piece or parcel of land with the buildings and improvements thereon erected, situate, lying and being in the Borough of Manhattan, City of New York, in the County and State of New York, bounded, and described as follows:

Beginning at a point on the northerly side of 93rd Street distant 219 feet easterly from the corner formed by the intersection of the easterly side of Amsterdam (10th) Avenue with the northerly side of 93rd Street; running thence easterly along the northerly side of 93rd Street 15 feet; thence northerly parallel with Amsterdam Avenue part of the way through a party wall 104 feet, 1 inch to the center line of an old road called Apthrop's Lane; thence northwesterly along said center line of Apthrop's Lane 15 feet and ⅛th of an inch to a point distant 219 feet easterly from the easterly side of Amsterdam Avenue measured on a line drawn at right angles thereto; thence southerly parallel with Amsterdam Avenue part of the way through a party wall 104 feet 8½ inches to the point or place of beginning.

Sealed bids addressed to Alien Property Custodian, 120 Broadway, New York, will be received until 10:00 o'clock A. M. on the 17th day of September, 1943, at which time and place bids will be publicly opened, and declared. Each bid must be submitted in duplicate and on forms prescribed by the Alien Property Custodian. Forms will be made available on request. Bids involving the payment of a brokerage commission must state the gross bid, the amount of the commission and the net amount to be received by the seller. The net amount of said bid will be considered in determining the successful bidder. A bank draft or certified check in the amount of 5% of the gross bid must accompany the same. The Alien Property Custodian reserves the right to accept or reject all bids. Real property is to be conveyed by quit-claim deed without covenants or warranties.

Further particulars with regard to the said real and personal property can be obtained by communicating with Guy T. Reid, at the Office of the Alien Property Custodian, 120 Broadway, New York, New York.

EO T. CROWLEY
Alien Property C dian of the United State erica

Bids for Personal Property will be received for the whole or by lot numbers as follows:

Lot (1) Bedroom Furnishings
Beds, cots, springs, mattresses, chairs, pillows, quilts, bed spreads, pillow slips, sheets, dressers, mirrors, carpets, curtains.

Lot (2) Dining Room Furnishings
Tables, buffet tables, chairs, table cloths, sideboards, china cabinets, rugs, carpets, plated silver, glassware, napkins, china.

Lof (3) Living Room Furnishings
Lamps and shades, rugs, carpets, hanging mirrors, chairs, Grand Piano, oil paintings, pictures, wood-cuts, lithographs, curtains, sofas, tobacco stand.

Lot (4) Large Selection of Kitchen Utensils and Frigidaire

Lot (5)
Bar, chromium steel stools, ping-pong table, billiard table, furnishings, fixtures, furniture, bric-a-brac, golf clubs, fishing rods, safe, etc.

AN ADVERTISEMENT RUN BY THE FEDERAL GOVERNMENT DURING WORLD WAR II, *placing the old Nippon Club up for sale.* COURTESY OFFICE FOR METROPOLITAN HISTORY

patterns, were brought from Japan, along with deep gold screens, deeply carved marble-topped tables, and lanterns of sycamore slats, and rice paper. The club frequently entertained Americans.

A dinner in February 1940 was exclusively Japanese, as 250 gathered at the club to celebrate the 2,600th anniversary of the founding of the empire. The anniversary was celebrated with folk songs and sake, and the evening was presided over by the Japanese consul general, Kaname Wakasugi, who led a low bow to the flag of the rising sun. The *New York Times* quoted him as saying that Japan was going to "do our best in a humble way to make this world a better place."

After the attack on Pearl Harbor, about 200 of the 2,500 Japanese nationals in New York and its suburbs were taken into custody. At the Nippon Club, twelve Japanese members were escorted by police to their homes, and the club was closed. It was confiscated by the Office of the Alien Property Custodian, and in 1943 the office put the building up for sale. In early 1944 it was bought by the Elks for a clubhouse, complete with its furniture; the club said that the interior would be remodeled and that the Japanese artifacts would be sold to art collectors.

There is nothing left inside now except for a heavy, timber-style stair baluster topped with large brass finials.

115 WEST 95TH STREET

MOST OF 95TH STREET BETWEEN COLUMBUS AND AMSTERDAM AVENUES went up in the late 1880s, a furious mixture of Queen Anne, Victorian picturesque, and just plain builder-vernacular. For the row at Nos. 111–121, the architect Charles T. Mott designed modest, straightforward facades of brownstone-trimmed red brick with peaked roofs. But he also gave the houses some intricate touches: two stringcourses of scallop and tendril shapes, and curiously irregular quoining around the window openings.

The first occupant of No. 115 appears to have been Dennis Moloney, a Ninth Avenue meat dealer who moved up from West 44th Street. In 1896, Dr. Philip F. O'Hanlon moved in with his wife, Laura, and their daughter. The O'Hanlons had been living on East 20th Street.

In the summer of 1897, the daughter of Dr. O'Hanlon, who was a police surgeon and deputy coroner, asked her father a difficult question. He suggested that the *New York Sun* would be a final authority, and the paper printed her letter on September 21:

> Dear Editor:
> I am eight years old. Some of my little friends say there is no Santa Claus.
> Papa says,"If you see it in the *Sun* it's so." Please tell me the truth; is there a Santa Claus?
> Virginia O'Hanlon 115 West Ninety-Fifth Street.

The editorial reply was long on reassurance but short on specifics. It runs in part:

> Virginia, your little friends are wrong. They have been affected by the skepticism of a skeptical age.
> They do not believe except they see. . . .
> Yes, Virginia, there is a Santa Claus. He exists as certainly as love and generosity and devotion exist. . . . You might get your Papa to hire men to watch in all the chimneys on Christmas Eve to catch Santa Claus, but if they did not see Santa Claus coming down, what would that prove? Nobody sees Santa Claus, but that is no sign that there is no Santa Claus. The most real things in the world are those that neither children nor men can see.

115 WEST 95TH STREET IN 1940. COURTESY MUNICIPAL ARCHIVES

The editorial was unsigned, but the author is generally accepted as Francis P. Church, age fifty-eight (and childless) in 1897. By 1918 the *New York Times* noted that the editorial had become famous. The *Sun* reprinted it yearly, until it merged with the *World-Telegram* in January 1950.

The O'Hanlons had rented 115 West 95th Street, but in 1900 they bought and moved into 121 West 95th Street. In the '20s Virginia, now married, lived at 121 with her parents and her daughter, but without her husband. By that time No. 115 had become a rooming house, with eleven occupants.

Mrs. Virginia Douglas taught in the public school system until 1959. She was regularly interviewed by newspapers, and she had pamphlets printed with the letter and the editorial, which she mailed out to correspondents. She died in 1971.

After many years as a derelict shell, her old house was finally renovated a few years ago.

FIRST CHURCH OF CHRIST, SCIENTIST

96TH STREET AND CENTRAL PARK WEST

CHRISTIAN SCIENCE WAS ESTABLISHED BY MARY BAKER EDDY after the Civil War, emphasizing the spiritual over the material. Healing through faith was the element some nonbelievers focused on to ridicule what was widely viewed as another cult.

In the 1880s Mrs. Eddy sent Augusta Stetson to establish the church in New York City. Mrs. Stetson attracted a wide following, and in 1903 the church at the northwest corner of 96th Street and Central Park West, designed by Carrère & Hastings, was completed.

The result, which cost $1.185 million, is one of the most striking works of religious architecture in the city: a grand block of Concord granite combining elements of English classicism and mannerism. The high tiled roof (sheltering a large reading room above the auditorium), the contrast of the shadowy openings against the bright granite, the deeply rusticated base, and the granite steeple make the 2,400-seat church arresting even to the casual passerby.

Mrs. Stetson was talented at drawing members, but had a heavy hand. There were regular reports that she forbade followers from associating with members of other congregations, that she had dissenters frozen out, and that she claimed that First Church was the only true Christian Science congregation in New York. It was also contended that she threatened to usurp Mrs. Eddy's position.

Mrs. Stetson appears to have been a contentious person. When the Second Church of Christ, Scientist bought a building site at 68th and Central Park West in 1898, she tried to interfere with their purchase, and then purchased one two blocks south, to try to scare them away from what she thought was First Church's neighborhood. When Mrs. Eddy died in 1910 she left a bequest to Second Church, but not Mrs. Stetson's organization.

In 1909, while still head of First Church, Mrs. Stetson was excommunicated from the Mother Church in Boston and then left First Church. However, she remained in her house next door at 5 West 96th Street, successfully suing First Church in 1923 to prevent it from erecting a wall that would cut off her east light. She died in 1928.

First Church is still a peculiar enterprise—its huge auditorium seems to be rarely filled, especially in a period when many West Side houses of worship are bursting at the seams. But the interior is astonishing, even empty, a giant work of classical architecture on the scale of a midsized railroad station. The corner stairways are vertiginously steep, but there are also the glass caged elevators, an astonishing and miraculous survival.

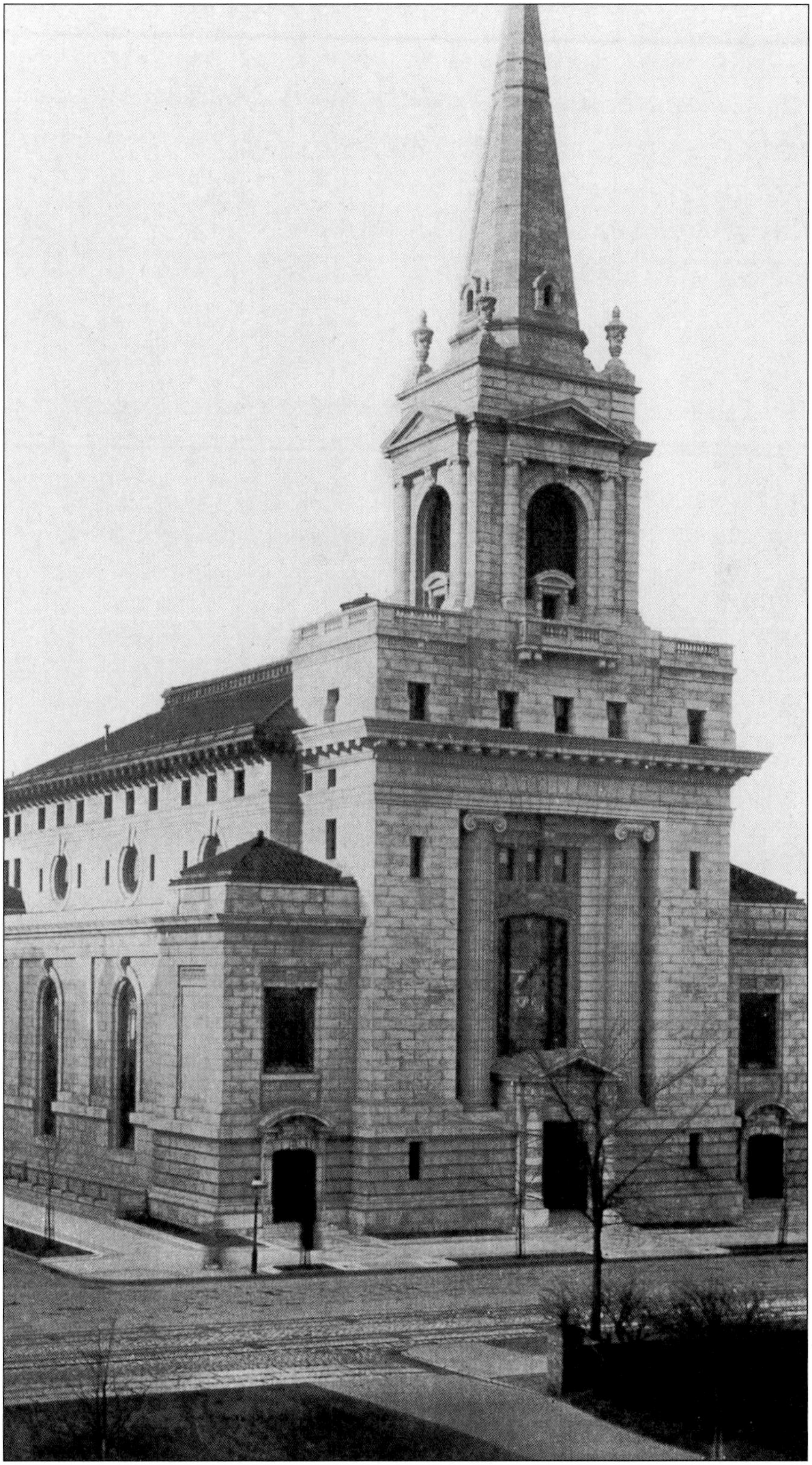

FIG 165.1

THE FIRST CHURCH OF CHRIST, SCIENTIST *at Central Park West and 96th Street in 1904.* COURTESY OFFICE FOR METROPOLITAN HISTORY

THE CLIFF DWELLING

96TH STREET AND RIVERSIDE DRIVE

AFTER 1905 RIVERSIDE DRIVE DEVELOPED as an avenue of apartment buildings, and real estate operators circled around the odd triangular plot at the northeast corner of 96th Street and Riverside Drive, only nine feet wide at one end. In 1916, when attempts failed to join it with the larger, inside lot facing 96th Street, the investor Leslie R. Palmer built a twelve-story apartment building adapted to its unlikely dimensions.

Palmer, a Westchester banker and, later, a member of the Federal Reserve Board, had already built the highly colored loft building at the southeast corner of 14th Street and Seventh Avenue, which has some of the most remarkable terra-cotta work in New York. For that building, finished in 1913, Palmer worked with the architect Herman Lee Meader, who had just started his own practice.

Meader worked out a plan for the Cliff Dwelling that made the best use of its shallow lot: he arranged that all the rooms face 96th and Riverside, and thus did not need to provide any light courts, which would eat up the plot. On the rear wall, facing east, he put the stairway, elevators, and a few secondary windows. The Cliff Dwelling was built as an apartment hotel, with five one- and two-bedroom suites per floor, served by a restaurant on the mezzanine.

On the exterior, Meader again used terra-cotta in an inventive way, worked into ornament with double-headed snakes, the skulls of cows, mountain lions, scowling mask-like faces, spears, and various Native American details. In 1916 the *New York Herald* praised the Cliff Dwelling's appearance on a lot that had been considered "only fit for a billboard" and also on its "made-in-America feeling." The newspaper suggested that its name opened up a new horizon for developers who had otherwise "exhausted the supply of names and styles from every famous palace, chateau and castle in Europe."

The lobby was furnished with Navajo rugs; tiles of tan, green, black, and blood-red; and zigzag designs on the lamps and elevator cages reminiscent of Native American designs.

It appears it was the architect rather than the client who was responsible for the building's unusual design. Meader also designed a simpler, but similar building for a different client at the southeast corner of 25th and Lexington.

Meader's niece, Madeira Meader, of Honeoye Falls, New York, says that family accounts paint Herman Meader as an "eminently fun guy." Her daughter, Jane Meader, says that a family memoir elaborates on Meader's career: he was an early adept at designing buildings, and after graduating from Harvard worked in New York for Raymond Almirall

THE CLIFF DWELLING *at the northeast corner of 96th Street and Riverside in 1916.* COURTESY THE NEW-YORK HISTORICAL SOCIETY, NEW YORK CITY

Another
"THE TRUCK OF PROVEN V
24 HOUR SERVICE 136
McFARLAN
BLUE VALLEY B
good
it's Pasteur
E VALLEY B TTER C

and Ernest Flagg, both of whom were known for terra-cotta and color effects in their architecture. He was intensely interested in Mayan and Aztec architecture, making regular expeditions to Chichén Itzá in the Yucatán and other sites.

In New York Meader also held elaborate parties at his penthouse apartment at 8 West 33rd Street, which attracted musicians, artists, writers, prizefighters, chess players, and others—at one, Meader staged a contest between a black snake and a king snake.

FIG 166.2

FIG 166.3

THE NATIVE AMERICAN–STYLE LOBBY OF THE CLIFF DWELLING IN 1916.
COURTESY CORNELL UNIVERSITY LIBRARY

FIREMEN'S MEMORIAL

100TH STREET AND RIVERSIDE DRIVE

THE FIREMEN'S MEMORIAL'S ORIGINS GO BACK TO VALENTINE'S DAY 1908, when Deputy Chief Charles W. Kruger—nicknamed "Big-Hearted Charley"—was leading the crew of Truck 8 through the cellar of 215 Canal Street to fight a fire in a picture-frame factory. In the smoky darkness, a rotten floor gave way, and Deputy Chief Kruger, fifty-four, fell into a stone cellar filled with eight feet of water and no ladder or steps. Firemen crowded around the edge, and one lowered himself down so the deputy chief could hold onto his leg. But they couldn't lift the three-hundred-pound, thirty-six-year veteran. "I'm going, boys," Kruger whispered, and slid back into the water, where he drowned before rescuers could reach him.

Deputy Chief Kruger had often risked his life for his men. The *New York Evening Post* quoted one of his crew as saying: "I knew it would happen this way. He was always in the lead. He never said, 'Boys, go into that place.' He said, 'Boys, follow me.' And that's just what he said this time."

Within a week of the deputy chief's death, the Episcopal bishop of New York, Henry Codman Potter, who lived at Riverside Drive and 89th Street opposite the 1902 Soldiers' and Sailors' Monument, conceived the idea for a memorial to the dead of the Fire Department. He formed a committee that included Andrew Carnegie and Isidor Straus, a partner at R. H. Macy and Company, who was named chairman. They hired H. Van Buren Magonigle, who also designed the 1913 Maine Memorial at Columbus Circle and, after World War I, the soaring Liberty Memorial in Kansas City, Missouri.

The committee agreed on a site in Union Square, but progress lagged, especially after many firemen objected to the location because, according to the *New York Times*, it was "where overwrought agitators may agitate to their own relief and satisfaction." The group then agreed on the site at 100th Street and Riverside Drive, and on September 5, 1913, ten thousand people assembled for the unveiling.

Four girls—Margaret Dow, ten; May Boyne, twelve; Florence Walsh, eleven; and Mary Connolly, ten—took down two large United States flags that covered the monument. All four were daughters of firemen killed in the line of duty. Because of heavy wind that day, four firemen were stationed atop the monument to hold the flags in place. When the flags were removed, all four stood at attention, silhouetted against the sky.

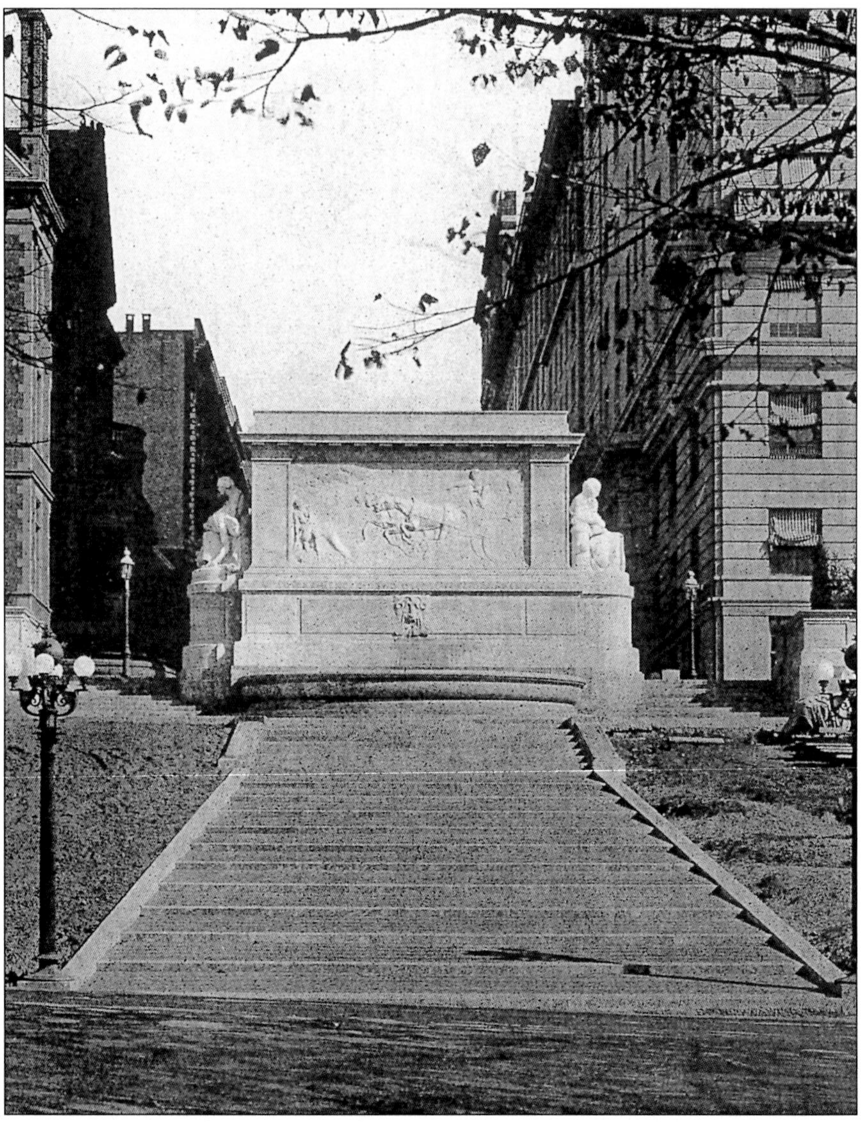

THE FIREMEN'S MEMORIAL IN 1913. COURTESY OFFICE FOR METROPOLITAN HISTORY

Magonigle designed the monument with a broad set of steps leading up from Riverside Drive to a plaza flanked by balustrades. At the center rises the monument, of Tennessee limestone, 20 feet high and 25 feet long, with a fountain at its base. At each end is a statue. One represents Duty—a mother comforting her young son; the other represents Sacrifice—a woman holding the body of her dead husband. At the center is a bronze panel of a crowd looking on while a fireman urges on his horse-drawn engine to a fire.

Around the base runs a classical wavelike form, carved in stone and woven through a background of flames. At the base of the panel are carved the words "To the Heroic Dead of the Fire Department." Isidor Straus had died in the sinking of the *Titanic* in 1912; in his place his son Jesse Isidor Straus made the opening address. "We erect monuments to our war heroes," he said, "and it is fitting that we should erect them to men who fight in the war that never ends."

THE SCHINASI MANSION

107TH STREET AND RIVERSIDE DRIVE

MORRIS SCHINASI EMIGRATED FROM TURKEY in the 1890s with his brother, Solomon. They brought Turkish cigarettes with them and popularized the much stronger tobacco here, building and cornering the market within a few years. In 1919 Solomon Schinasi's obituary in the *New York Times* said "the taste for Turkish leaf was quickly acquired by American smokers, and the sale of Schinasi brands soon became enormous."

In 1907 Solomon Schinasi, living in a row house at the northwest corner of 95th Street and Central Park West, bought and occupied the old Isaac Rice mansion at 89th Street and Riverside Drive. Morris Schinasi, then living at the original Eldorado apartments on Central Park West at 90th Street, began work on a new house a mile north, at 107th Street. Morris Schinasi retained William Tuthill, the architect for Carnegie Hall, who had a fine, light hand for detail.

The white Vermont marble blocks Tuthill selected—placed in construction in accordance with their veining—are set off by a bright green tile roof with fanciful copper cresting on the French Renaissance–style house. Schinasi had water taps distributed around the outside of the house to allow for frequent washing in New York's polluted air.

The interior Tuthill designed for Schinasi is a rich, flowing series of rooms that are generically Renaissance but also have unusual and distinctive touches. The library was decorated with East Indian teak panels (imported by the Tiffany decorating firm), Tinos marble, bronze, mosaics, and, at the ceiling, an oval dome of lacquered gold in iridescent colors. The dining room, of mahogany and Numidian marble, mixes decorations derived from both pineapples—a traditional sign of welcome—and tobacco leaves. The vestibule was of beautifully veined Greek marble with a faience tile ceiling. Most of the main rooms also carried elaborate mural decorations at the cornice level.

For such an impressive house, the principal rooms are rather small—to judge from published plans, the living room is about 15 by 18 feet—and *Architects and Builders* magazine praised this as "the Oriental idea of seclusiveness in the house." But it also felt that the interior was too opulent, and said that "the Oriental ideas of the owner have . . . overwhelmed the good taste of the designer."

But surrounded by plantings and set back from the property line on all sides, the design of the three-story-high house reproached the tall, densely built mansions going

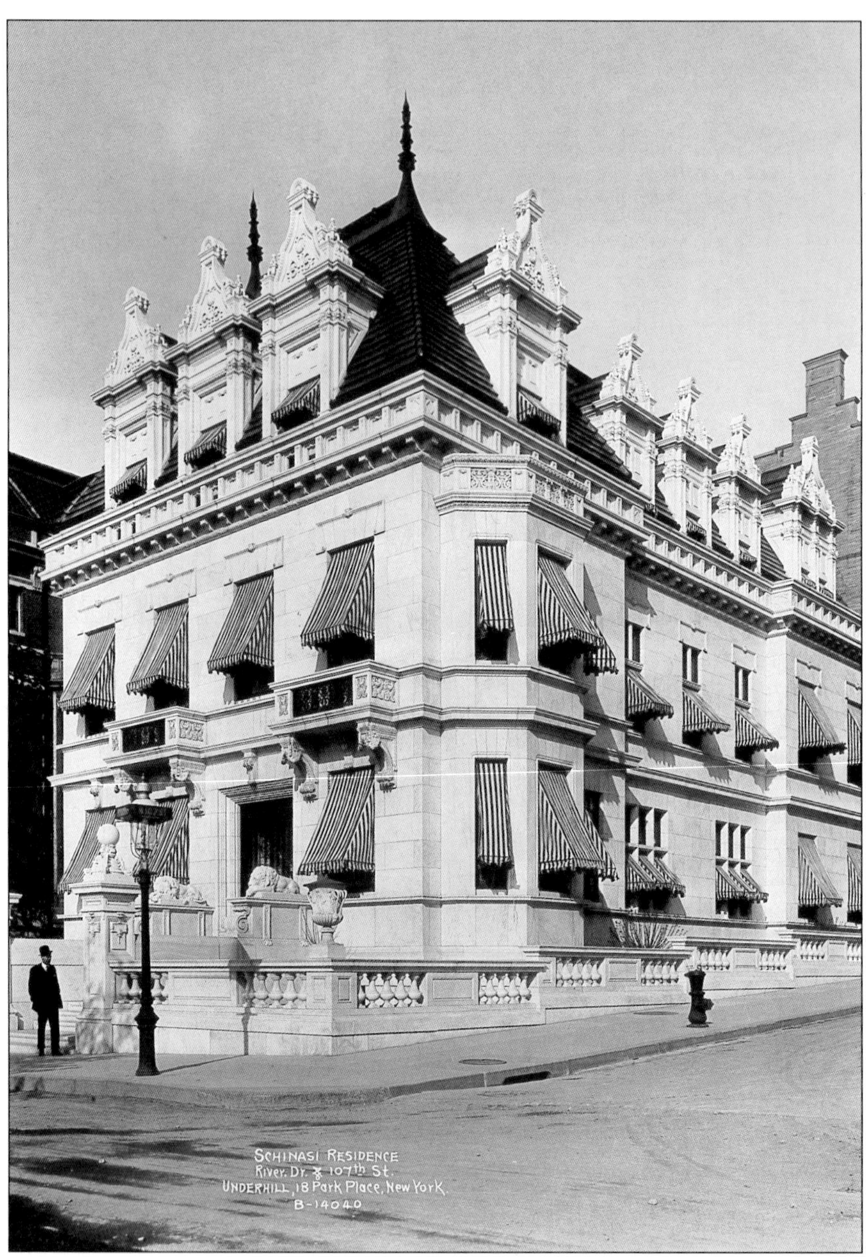

MORRIS SCHINASI'S MANSION COMPLETED IN 1909. COURTESY MUSEUM OF THE CITY OF NEW YORK

up on the East Side. When Morris Schinasi died in 1928 he left an estate of $5 million, earmarking $1 million to build and support a hospital in Magnesie, Turkey. Hans Smit, who bought the building in 1979, says that the third floor has a peculiar arrangement of small rooms leading onto a single, large room. "It was his harem floor" said Professor Smit. The third floor would typically be the servants' floor, and if Schinasi indeed kept a harem, he had catholic tastes. Census returns indicate he lived in the house with his wife, Laurette (also Turkish born), three daughters, and a changing group of household servants from England, Germany, Italy, Sweden, and other European countries.

PUBLIC SCHOOL 165

234 WEST 109TH STREET

THE LASTING IMAGE OF THE NEW YORK PUBLIC SCHOOLS built in the twentieth century is the mid-block, H-plan design of the architect Charles B. J. Snyder. It was first used in 1898 at P.S. 165 at 234 West 109th Street. These big, light, elegant buildings, often Elizabethan or French Renaissance in style, remain startling mid-block surprises wherever they appear. They elbow apart long rows of dark tenements and flats with their tall, peaked roofs, and big courtyards.

But school design—indeed most municipal construction—was widely criticized in the nineteenth century. The *Real Estate Record and Guide* in 1893 called school buildings a "civic disgrace" and said "many factories and warehouses have greater artistic value."

Outdoor privies, tiny, dark play areas, and poor light and ventilation were only part of the problem. The Board of Education's staff architect, George Debevoise, suddenly resigned in 1891 as charges developed that he had colluded with contractors to substitute cheaper materials in school projects.

His replacement, Charles B. J. Snyder, had studied at Cooper Union and made some initial changes—like forced ventilation and steel skeleton construction to permit larger

FIG 169.1

CHARLES B. J. SNYDER IN 1898. COURTESY OFFICE FOR METROPOLITAN HISTORY

P.S. 165 AT 234 WEST 109TH STREET IN 1900. COURTESY TEACHERS COLLEGE LIBRARY, COLUMBIA UNIVERSITY

windows. It is not clear how he got the job, but it must have had something to do with the banker Robert Maclay, who served as head of the school board's building committee. Snyder gave his son Robert, born about 1894, the middle name Maclay.

Snyder's earliest buildings expanded Debevoise's Romanesque style. They included Public School 23, now a community center but still at the northeast corner of Mulberry and Bayard Streets, with sinuous carving at the entranceway. Within a year or two he began experimenting with the Northern European Renaissance styles in light-colored masonry. The results included the orange brick Flemish-style school at 82nd Street and West End Avenue—now a special-programs school—and the limestone and terra-cotta Collegiate Gothic–style P.S. 166 at 132 West 89th Street.

Snyder's star rose, especially after Maclay was elected president of the Board of Education in 1895. But the architect also faced the same difficulties that Debevoise had to deal with—the corner plots favored for schools were noisy and expensive.

In late 1896, Maclay sent Snyder on a study trip to London and Paris, and the *New York Tribune* reported that the architect was particularly impressed with the late Gothic-style Hôtel de Cluny in Paris, a few blocks south of Notre-Dame. The wide courtyard facing the street gave Snyder an idea—pull back from the corners to the quiet, less expensive inside lots and build around a courtyard to ensure light and air. He expanded that idea to the through-block H-plan, which became his signature design.

The next round of school construction began in May 1897. Of the twelve structures, seven followed this pattern. The first, P.S. 165, was completed in September 1898. Six stories high, it is French Renaissance in style, with delicate dormers rising out of a sloping red tile roof, with a central copper fleche. It is miles ahead of Debevoise's utilitarian designs.

Snyder put up five, ten, sometimes fifteen buildings a year, ranging from giants like Erasmus and Morris to public schools in almost every neighborhood. More than libraries, firehouses, or police stations, these new schools symbolized the commitment of the city to care for and even uplift its citizens.

THE HENDRIK HUDSON

110TH STREET AND RIVERSIDE DRIVE

IN 1906 THE DEVELOPERS GEORGE F. JOHNSON AND LEOPOLD KAHN took an entire blockfront on Riverside Drive, from 110th to 111th Streets—a short block from the new subway station on Broadway and near the civilizing influence of Columbia's recently established campus.

They had the architects Rouse & Sloan design an eight-story building, well under the effective legal limit of about twelve stories, but still the biggest private building on the upper drive. With the broad prospect of Riverside Park and Drive before the site, the architects were able to expand a Tuscan villa design into a truly monumental work, with success practically unknown to the commercial builder.

Below the roof, the rusticated limestone and Roman brick with recessed joints is intelligent enough, with suave panels of terra-cotta with the "HH" monogram and frequent balconies. But it is at the roofline where the Hendrik Hudson rose above other efforts.

FIG 170.1

THE ENTRANCE *to the Hendrik Hudson apartments, 1907.*
COURTESY OFFICE FOR METROPOLITAN HISTORY

THE HUDSON-FULTON CELEBRATION *with the Hendrik Hudson (left rear) in 1909.* COURTESY OFFICE FOR METROPOLITAN HISTORY

Instead of the typical projecting cornice, Rouse & Sloan gave the building a wide projecting red tile roof and, above that, two massive but fanciful towers, also with tile roofs. They were connected by a broad, trellis-covered promenade for tenants' use.

The original rendering for the apartment house showed the balconies and roof trellis overflowing with greenery. No such plantings appear in photographs of the completed building, but the angled site on Riverside, twin towers, and intelligent detailing made the Hendrik Hudson one of the few apartment houses with real architectural ambition.

Architectural journals considered most apartment-house design beneath notice, but in 1909 the magazine *Architecture* interviewed William L. Rouse. He noted that the multiple dwelling demanded a "somewhat festive appearance," and although at the Hendrik Hudson "the details on the towers are somewhat heavy . . . in general the facade came up to my expectations."

The Hendrik Hudson's seventy-two apartments opened on October 1, 1907, and by January sixty-eight were rented. Most of the tenants attracted to the Hendrik Hudson were moving from other apartment houses; a few from row houses show up on the earliest lists of residents.

Marcus Loew, then in real estate but soon to establish his motion picture company, moved in from a small apartment house on West 111th Street. And Abraham Lefcourt, the clothing manufacturer who later built much of the present garment district, moved from the old Hotel Majestic, at 72nd Street and Central Park West.

Perhaps they gathered on the roof in September 1909 to watch the Hudson-Fulton Celebration, commemorating the three-hundredth anniversary of Hudson's trip up the river and the one-hundredth anniversary of Robert Fulton's demonstration of steam power for marine vessels.

Replicas of Hudson's *Half Moon* and Fulton's *Clermont* proceeded up the Hudson to two giant pylons at the foot of 110th Street, the first part of what was projected as a sweeping watergate for New York City, to serve as a greeting place for distinguished visitors and also an amphitheater. And Wilbur Wright flew from Governors Island up the Hudson and back past this point.

At some point the entire tile roof of the Hendrik Hudson was removed, and the upper section of the building has the look of a lump of bread dough dropped from a height. But with its angled site, it still presents a commanding presence.

ST. LUKE'S HOSPITAL

113TH STREET BETWEEN MORNINGSIDE DRIVE AND AMSTERDAM AVENUE

WHAT CAN YOU DO WITH PART of a historic building? That is the preservation question posed by St. Luke's Hospital on West 113th Street between Morningside Drive and Amsterdam Avenue—which has been irretrievably compromised by additions and alterations.

St. Luke's was conceived in 1846 by the Reverend Dr. William A. Muhlenberg, pastor of the Church of the Holy Communion. By the 1880s its long rectangular building on the west side of Fifth Avenue between 54th and 55th Streets was considered outmoded and the value of land on Fifth Avenue made relocation attractive.

In 1892, the trustees bought the full block bounded by 113th and 114th Streets, Amsterdam Avenue and Morningside Drive and held a closed competition for its design. None of the invited competitors was selected; to their surprise, the job went to an unknown outsider just starting out, Ernest Flagg.

Flagg, who had studied in Paris at the École des Beaux-Arts, was anything but a typical architectural student. At entry, he was already a veteran of fish importing and margarine businesses and had gone bankrupt. With his father, the Reverend Jared Flagg, he had also promoted cooperative apartment houses in the early 1880s, an endeavor with shady connotations at the time.

Mardges Bacon, author of a monograph on Flagg, said he got the commission through the influence of his cousin, Cornelius Vanderbilt II, who was on the hospital's board and who had paid Flagg's way at the École.

Flagg's design, unlike the others, did not try to complement the medieval styling of the Cathedral of St. John the Divine, then beginning to rise across 113th.

Rather, he chose what Dr. Bacon calls the form of the "classical palace hospital of the seventeenth century," like the Hôtel des Invalides in Paris. Nine five-story, mansard-roofed pavilions were planned, connected to a central building surmounted by a great

171.1

FIG

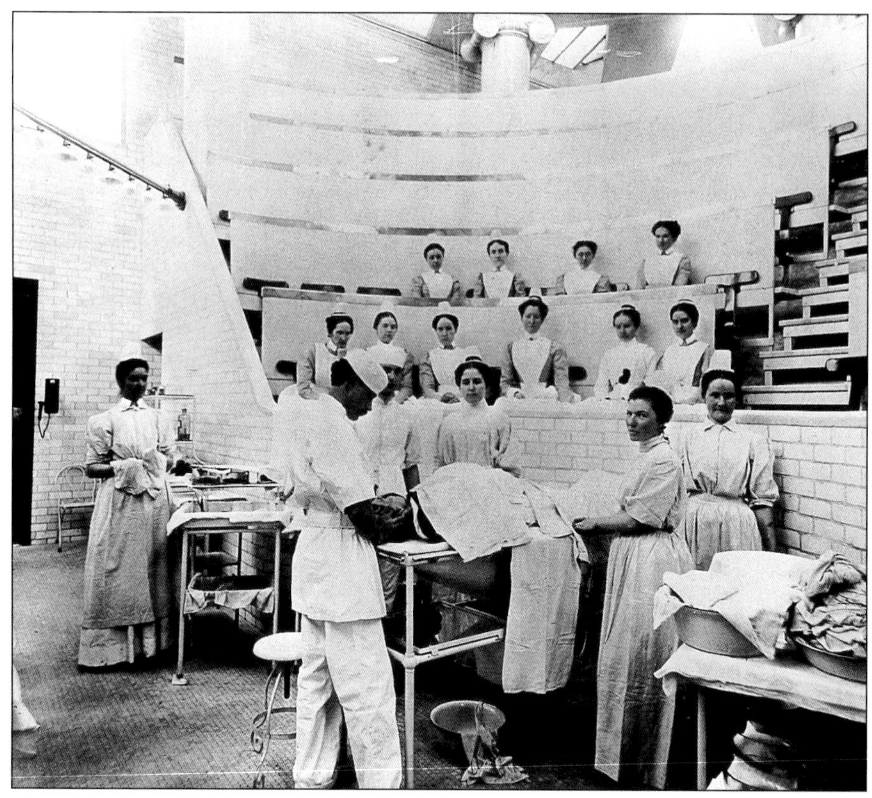

THE OPERATING THEATER AT ST. LUKE'S HOSPITAL IN 1899. COURTESY MUSEUM OF THE CITY OF NEW YORK

171.2

FIG

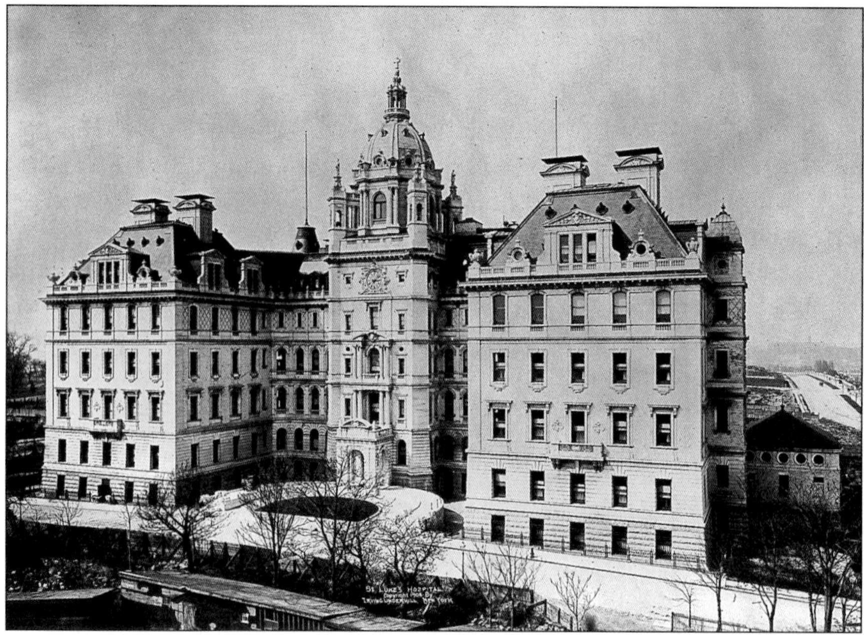

ST. LUKE'S HOSPITAL ON 113TH STREET AND AMSTERDAM AVENUE IN 1904. COURTESY MUSEUM OF THE CITY OF NEW YORK

dome. Everything was in marble or light brick except some diaper-patterned brickwork at the top floor.

The pavilion plan was adopted out of concern for patients; each ward was self-contained, connected by a narrow, windowed walkway to the main structure, which held the stairs and elevators. The walkways were to form barriers of fresh air against disease.

Harper's Weekly praised the hospital's "symmetrical perfectness so loyal to the French renaissance."

Flagg's nine-pavilion plan was carried out gradually through the 1920s except for the two pavilions on Amsterdam Avenue, which were never built. Only five pavilions survive.

The dome of the main building was demolished in the 1960s, and gradually windows have been filled in and balusters, cresting, ironwork, and other details have been removed. The elegant central building is rudely crowded on the west by the uncompromisingly modern Stuyvesant Pavilion, and the former light courts are filled in with miscellaneous structures. The brickwork and stone have been cleaned but the building is still painfully lopsided; the new construction utterly disrupts its original character, despite the present careful steps. It is both beautiful, and painful, to look at.

LOW LIBRARY, COLUMBIA UNIVERSITY

IN 1889 COLUMBIA COLLEGE WAS STRUGGLING on a cramped midtown block, struggling to attract students while New York's well-to-do sent their sons off to Harvard and Yale. It was in that year that the trustees chose Seth Low as their new head, with the promise that he would remake the institution. In 1881 Low had been elected mayor of Brooklyn on a reform program, and accomplished things like opening Brooklyn schools to black students. He soon brought this spirit to Columbia, where he made changes like ending compulsory attendance at Christian chapel services because he felt it would alienate Jews.

In 1891 the board agreed to move Columbia up to a four-square-block site, from 116th to 120th Streets, between Broadway and Amsterdam, to expand Columbia's horizons, both literal and figurative: a view of downtown Manhattan spreads out from the elevated site. Low's ambitious building plans—designed by Charles McKim of McKim, Mead & White—were soon put at risk by recalcitrant alumni. Columbia had trouble raising money for the site alone. To move the project ahead, Low announced he would give up to $1 million for the campus centerpiece, a library, in memory of his father, who ran a fleet of clipper ships.

A DISTANT VIEW OF COLUMBIA UNIVERSITY'S LOW LIBRARY, 1897. COURTESY THE NEW-YORK HISTORICAL SOCIETY, NEW YORK CITY

Set on a high terrace, the library, completed in 1897, was at the center of the campus, which then only went down to 116th Street, and faced the broad boulevard of 116th Street. Its limestone mass was more imposing than Stanford White's Gould Library for New York University, then building its own new campus in the Bronx overlooking the Harlem River. But Low and McKim were disappointed when Irish quarries could only produce two of the eighteen giant green Connemara marble columns for the interior, whereas White was able to get enough for all the narrower columns for his project.

The two Connemara marble columns inside the main entrance moved Charles H. Caffin to write in *Harper's Weekly* of "the exquisite mystery of graded greens and grays and black, their tempestuous streakings and tender veining. The most heedless visitor cannot pass them unadmired, the connoisseur will be enthusiastic." The others were made of green Vermont granite, and all were topped by gold-plated bronze capitals, a striking touch.

Low Library was based on an early-nineteenth-century French church, and the *Real Estate Record and Guide* gave an interesting perspective on contemporary design: "There is scarcely any original designing done in this city, except the vagaries of the incompetent. The rest is mostly a copybook reproduction of classical and other detail. Successful architects have too much to do to be preeminently artists—they must be first rate men of business."

Low resigned to run, successfully, as a reform candidate for mayor of New York in 1901, but he remained on the board of trustees. He must have been especially pleased in 1903, when Columbia was able to buy the plot between 114th and 116th Streets, creating a huge forecourt for the library. But he was at swords' points with his successor, Nicholas Murray Butler—who sought to restrict access for Jews to Columbia—and resigned in 1914.

In 1934 Columbia moved its books to the new, much larger Butler Library, built directly to the south. People still refer to the older building as "Low Library," and every year a few new students stumble into the grand rotunda with a confused expression on their faces: "Uh, is this the library?"

THE CASA ITALIANA

116TH STREET AND AMSTERDAM AVENUE

ACCORDING TO RESEARCH BY THE LANDMARKS PRESERVATION COMMISSION, which designated the building in 1978, Casa Italiana had its roots in an Italian club for students founded at Columbia in 1914. This was a time when Italian immigration formed a new laboring class in New York City, and Italians faced widespread discrimination. By the 1920s, the club had expanded and an entire building was proposed as a center for Italian studies.

The developers, Joseph and Michael Paterno and Anthony Campagna—who were active in building tall apartment houses on the major residential avenues—offered to erect the $250,000 building without charge, and an executive committee set out to raise support across the nation. Serving on the committee were Fiorello H. La Guardia, then a United States representative from New York City, and Otto Kahn, the banker.

The architectural firm of McKim, Mead and White was the official campus architect, and late in 1925 Burt L. Fenner, a partner, wrote Joseph Paterno offering his firm's services at cost, charging only 3 percent of the cost of construction.

But according to Daniel Gil Feuchtwanger, an expert on campus history, there was a sharp objection to the offer. In July of 1926, Teunis J. Van der Bent, another partner at the firm, wrote an interoffice memo asking "for full information as to who was responsible for our financial arrangements with reference to our commission."

He added that "we will lose a pile of money" and said, "I do not intend to stand by such an arrangement." It is not known how the matter was resolved.

At the cornerstone laying later in 1926, the university president, Nicholas Murray Butler, said "only those so fortunate as to live in a new country can know the uplifting

THE CASA ITALIANA ON COLUMBIA UNIVERSITY'S CAMPUS IN 1927.
COURTESY OFFICE FOR METROPOLITAN HISTORY

power and stimulation of a civilization that has been going on for three thousand years." The building opened the next year.

The site chosen by the university was off the main campus across Amsterdam Avenue at the northeast corner of 117th Street on a block already built up privately with row houses and flats. The architects produced a tall, Florentine palazzo with an open loggia at the top and a tiled, peaked roof. It is conventionally handsome but rather predictable, a compressed version of the firm's design for the Racquet & Tennis Club a decade before.

The interior was filled with Italian antiques, some donated by Premier Benito Mussolini. It is distinguished principally by a large library and, on the third floor, a long auditorium with rusticated plasterwork in imitation of stone and a coffered ceiling.

The original scheme was for it to serve as a cultural and educational center for Italian students and for persons interested in Italian language and culture. But by 1930 the *New York Times* described it as something of a white elephant, without clear direction. In that year a revival was undertaken with an Italian book club, chorus, and diction class.

By the 1970s, the university's new east campus project had obliterated West 117th Street and replaced it with an elevated bridge covering the old street bed and extending across Amsterdam Avenue, spoiling Casa Italiana's prospect. But a lateral addition of frankly modern design, by the architects Buttrick, White and Burtis, with the Italian architect Italo Rota, has injected some new life into this curious building, and helps it hold its own against the bridge that cramps its considerable style.

UPPER MANHATTAN

AGUILAR LIBRARY

174 EAST 110TH STREET

UNTIL THE LATE NINETEENTH CENTURY, New York had no municipally sponsored public circulating libraries. But in 1886 a new state law offered support to any charitable library with at least $20,000 in real estate and more than ten thousand volumes.

To meet that threshold two Jewish organizations, the Young Men's Hebrew Association and the Hebrew Free School, merged their small holdings and in 1886 established the Aguilar Free Library, named for Grace Aguilar (1816–1847), an English writer of Sephardic Jewish descent considered a pioneer in Jewish literature. The first two branches were at 721 Lexington Avenue, near 58th Street, and 206 East Fifth Street on the Lower East Side.

FIG 174.1

THE AGUILAR LIBRARY *at 174 East 110th Street as it was rebuilt in 1905.* COURTESY NEW YORK PUBLIC LIBRARY ARCHIVES

Aguilar trustees included established, successful Jews; according to Aimee Kaplan, who has studied the history of the Aguilar Free Library, one of their goals was to efficiently Americanize more recent Eastern European Jewish immigrants. A report by Ms. Kaplan says that the libraries stocked popular works in the hope of attracting the working class to American literature.

In 1899 the trustees put up a new building for a branch at 174 East 110th Street, in a district of tenements where many Jews from the Lower East Side were relocating. The original 110th Street branch, designed by Herts & Tallant, was a craggy rock-faced building with Art Nouveau

THE AGUILAR LIBRARY *in 1899, the year it opened.* COURTESY NEW YORK PUBLIC LIBRARY ARCHIVES

ironwork hammered out of common I-beams, of such deliciously bizarre appearance it could have been the portal for a Coney Island house of horrors.

In 1901 the industrialist Andrew Carnegie offered $5 million for a system of neighborhood libraries, and the offer created pressure for a single organization for library branches.

In 1903 the Aguilar Free Library agreed to join, although not without hesitation by the trustees, who correctly saw that their own efforts would be subsumed under a new bureaucracy. They lobbied to retain the name Aguilar on their four branches, but the central administration would agree to only one, the building on 110th Street.

The 110th Street Aguilar Library was also rebuilt in 1905, redesigned by Herts & Tallant, who by this time were riding a swell of fame with their theater designs, such as their Art Nouveau New Amsterdam, at 214 West 42nd Street, and their boldly Beaux-Arts Lyceum, at 149 West 45th Street.

They doubled the width of the library by building an addition to the west, covering the whole with a hugely scaled facade of two fluted limestone piers supporting an even bigger stretch of limestone across the top. It was all on the scale of a giant public building—except that the new Aguilar was just a single colossal bay wedged into a street of common tenements.

At your first sight of the 1905 Aguilar Library, you may stare in wonder—it's a neoclassical redwood in a forest of architectural scrub brush, surrounded by parking lots and lesser buildings.

THE HARLEM COURTHOUSE

121ST STREET AND SYLVAN PLACE

HARLEM HAD A LOCAL COURT AS EARLY as 1660, and by the 1880s what was originally a remote village was becoming a regional center. Theaters, clubs, churches, blocks of houses, and department stores sprang up, especially around Mount Morris Park and along 125th Street, which had rail stops at Park, Second, and Third Avenues.

The city's courts were divided between criminal and civil, and the Police Court and District Court shared rented quarters in the old Harlem Hall at 125 East 125th Street. In 1889, the clerk of the District Court, Thomas F. Gilroy, was appointed commissioner of Public Works. One of his first projects was a new courthouse for Harlem at the southeast corner of 121st Street and Sylvan Place.

Designed by Thom & Wilson and completed in late 1892, it gave an unmistakably civic air to tiny Sylvan Place, a little street connecting 120th and 121st Streets, between Lexington and Third Avenues. The building is symmetrically organized around a round corner tower that extends up to an octagonal belfry with four clockfaces. Gable-end bays and arch-topped windows spread out on each side. The individual elements are generally Romanesque in style, but the spiked, choppy quality of the massing contributes a Victorian air.

Gilroy officially opened the building on New Year's Day 1893 in his new capacity, as mayor.

Vehicular bays, some for arriving prisoners, occupied most of the ground floor, and the corner tower served as an entry. Several floors of bare brick jail cells in the rear survive but the principal rooms are the two courts.

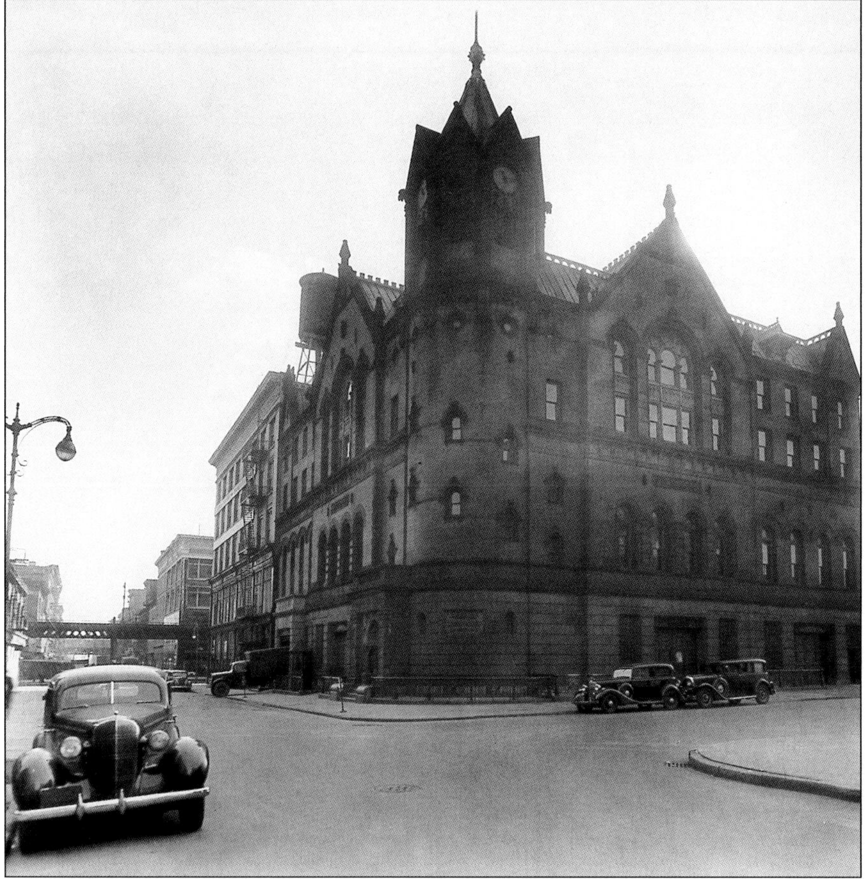

THE HARLEM COURTHOUSE *at 121st Street and Sylvan Place in 1938.* COURTESY MUNICIPAL ARCHIVES

The old Police Court, on the second floor, is a wide, grand room with oak paneling and a Renaissance revival plasterwork ceiling. The old District Court, on the third floor, has varnished oak paneling, a podium, jury box and railings, and a ceiling in a huge, three-centered curve with plaster molding, simpler and grander.

Money had been allocated for decoration but never spent, and in 1936 two Works Progress Administration murals were painted by David Karfunkle. They show an Egyptian scene with laborers and a Venetian scene of commercial trading. Their titles are uncertain, but according to Marlene Parks, an art historian, they were known as *The Exploitation of Labor* and *The Hoarding of Wealth*.

Deborah Bershad, executive director of the Art Commission, said that the National Association for the Advancement of Colored People, the Urban League, and Harlem activists protested the original designs because they depicted blacks in submissive roles. In the final painting, skin colors were changed.

The courthouse was designated a landmark in 1967, and in the 1980s the city gave it a new copper roof in the belief that the original roof was copper—even though the original elevation drawings show that the roof was tile. Because the building was so little used, there was constant vandalism, and much of the copper roof was stolen for scrap. In the early 1990s a new roof was put on—modeled after the original tile—which so far has proven to have no scrap value.

202–220 WEST 122ND STREET

AFTER 1880, THE CONSTRUCTION OF THE ELEVATED TRAINS up Eighth Avenue through West Harlem sparked development on what had been mostly open plains. In 1887 and 1889 Addison P. Smith, an inventor and developer, built two rows of houses, 202–210 and then 212–220 West 122nd Street. Smith, who was active in Harlem affairs, worked on both projects with the architect George B. Pelham, son of an English naval designer.

Pelham did the first group, completed in 1887, in an energetic Queen Anne style, except for No. 202, which resembled an unusual rock-faced castle with a square, crenellated tower of galvanized iron. The next year, Smith had him design the additional group, 212–220, but by then the craving for individual novelty and red brick had faded. The second group, completed in 1889, is composed as a single unit of what was considered the Renaissance style at the time, with brownstone at the basement and stoop level and some lighter stone, perhaps limestone, above.

In 1887 the *Real Estate Record and Guide* described the first row as having been built with "extreme care and taste." Opening the doors on the parlor floor created "a sweep of rooms 70 feet from end to end," and the houses were finished in mahogany, oak, and sycamore.

The same journal described the second row in 1889 with similar praise and took note of an unusual innovation. Smith, a former iron merchant, called for an "oxidized iron grill bearing a shield with the house number above the doorway." The *Record and Guide* said that these houses were just as good as "the Madison Avenue type" but, at $20,000 each, half the price because of the lower land costs.

The first buyers included J. Edward Cowles, the manager of the cigar department at Austin, Nichols & Company, who bought No. 208, and Michael Wineburgh, an editor turned advertising executive, who bought No. 216. Wineburgh soon controlled the advertising franchise on street-car lines and founded the Omega Oil company, whose brilliantly painted patent medicine advertisements still survive on walls in a few locations.

The row houses that blanketed Harlem were not significantly different from those put up on the east and west sides of Central Park. However, by 1920 it was clear that Harlem was losing ground to those areas as a residential area—almost no elevator apartment houses of the West End Avenue or Park Avenue type went up.

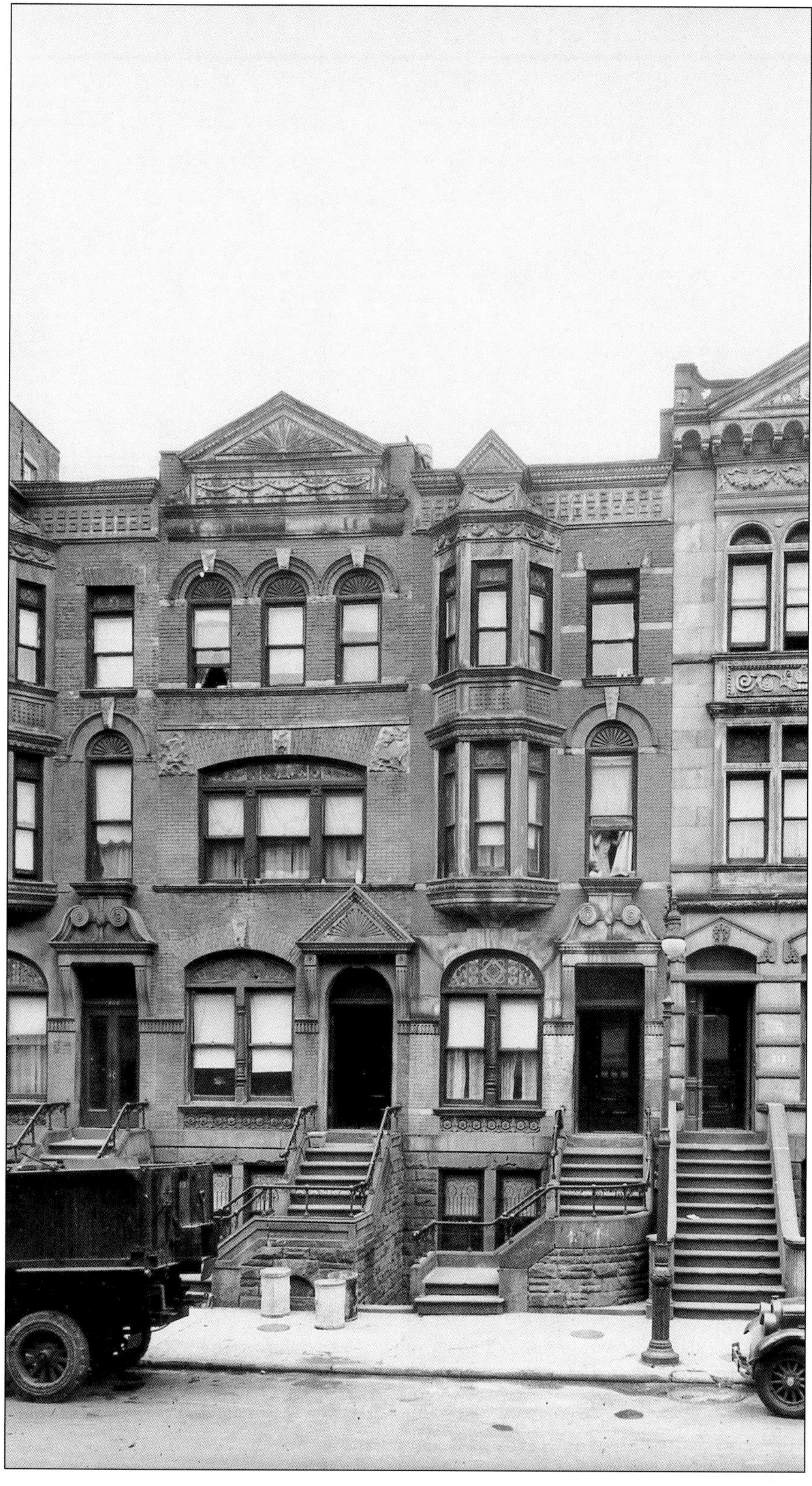

206–214 WEST 122ND STREET IN 1938. COURTESY OFFICE FOR METROPOLITAN HISTORY

RENDERING OF 212–220 WEST 122ND STREET IN 1889. COURTESY OFFICE FOR METROPOLITAN HISTORY

Blacks, long jammed into older downtown sections by nearly universal racial discrimination, had been moving into Harlem housing, starting at around 140th Street and moving south. The 1925 census documents the first black households in the row: at No. 206, Thomas Hill, fifty-four, a native of British Guiana; and at No. 220, Wilbert and Marie Given, forty-three and forty-one, both American born.

Both took in lodgers; Hill had six and the Givens had three. Most accounts of Harlem at this time indicate that blacks had to double and triple up, but the Hill and Given households had no more lodgers than their white neighbors: Adie Hakim, a twenty-seven-year-old Syrian-born bookkeeper, had three lodgers at No. 202.

The lodgers made a rich mix on the block: George Tsoukaula, a Greek-born singer, roomed at No. 212; Lionel Fribourg, a French-born silver designer, at No. 214; and George Weihl, a British West Indian court interpreter, at No. 220. But despite such variety, each rooming house observed strict racial segregation.

BLUMSTEIN'S DEPARTMENT STORE

230 WEST 125TH STREET

IN 1885 LOUIS BLUMSTEIN ARRIVED IN THE UNITED STATES from Germany. He worked as a street peddler and in 1894 opened a store on Hudson Street. In 1898 he moved the store to West 125th Street between Seventh and Eighth Avenues, already a major regional shopping center. Blumstein died in 1920, and in 1921 his family demolished the store to build a five-story building, the biggest thing on West 125th Street after the Hotel Theresa at Seventh Avenue.

The architects Robert D. Kohn and Charles Butler designed the $1 million store in an odd amalgam of late Art Nouveau and early Art Deco. It was completed in 1923.

The simple limestone facade surrounds three bays of intricately worked copper ornament with delicate top-floor balconies and slim marquees. Instead of the usual cornice at the roof, the architects installed two flagpoles on bases, reminiscent of the work of the Secession movement in Germany and Austria around 1910.

Whites resisted black migration to Harlem housing, and it was no different with jobs. In the late '20s black religious and civic leaders began pointing out that the 125th Street merchants hired only or mostly whites, and in 1929 Blumstein's did hire its first blacks—as elevator operators and porters.

In 1932, one leader, J. Dalman Steele, called for a boycott of such companies, but his call was ineffective. In the spring of 1934, as more New Yorkers lost jobs because of the depression, the Reverend John H. Johnson, vicar of the Protestant Episcopal St. Martin's Church, began a "Buy-Where-You-Can-Work" campaign. The *New York Age* newspaper backed this movement, noting that 75 percent of Blumstein's sales were to blacks but that it refused to hire black clerks or cashiers. The paper called for a boycott of Harlem's most important store.

Picketing began in the second week of June. Preaching to two thousand at his Abyssinian Baptist Church, the Reverend Adam Clayton Powell Jr.—who twelve years later was to start his long career as a congressman—supported the boycott.

The *New York Age* published names and photographs of blacks who crossed the picket line. Mr. Johnson predicted that success there would open the other stores to blacks. "As Blumstein's goes, so will go 125th Street," he said. On July 26, William Blumstein, head of the store, capitulated, promising to hire thirty-five blacks for clerical and sales

BLUMSTEIN'S DEPARTMENT STORE *on 125th Street with its mechanical Santa on the marquee in 1949.* COURTESY OFFICE FOR METROPOLITAN HISTORY positions by the end of September. Despite a heavy rain, 1,500 people marched in a victory parade.

Soon Mr. Powell organized the Greater New York Coordinating Committee for Employment and in 1938 won an agreement from Woolworth's, Kress, A. S. Beck, and other major businesses not to discriminate against blacks.

The *Christian Century* editorialized: "Here is a weapon which the American Negro is only beginning to realize he holds in his hands. It is interesting to reflect upon what would happen in the average southern city if its Negro population should determine not to patronize stores which discriminate against the Negro."

According to the *Amsterdam News*, in 1943 Blumstein's had the first black Santa Claus, was the first to use black models and mannequins, and successfully appealed to cosmetic manufacturers to produce makeup for non-white skin tones. For years its mechanical black Santa Claus was a Christmas fixture on 125th Street.

28 WEST 126TH STREET

THE BLOCK OF 126TH STREET WEST OF FIFTH AVENUE was raw country in 1871 when Edward Gleason, superintendent of the Union League Club at 26th Street and Madison Avenue, put up the three-story house at No. 28. Designed by Calvert Vaux and Frederick Withers, the house was begun that May and finished that September, at a cost of $11,000.

The top floor of the Gleason house originally had a mansard roof with a central dormer, later rebuilt as a straight wall. The deep-red Philadelphia brick contrasts markedly with the soft, light Ohio stone. This stone bears the typical incised carving of other Vaux and Withers projects, like their Jefferson Market Courthouse on lower Sixth Avenue, completed in 1877.

In 1902 a banker named Joseph G. Robin purchased the house. Robin then sold the house to his sister, Dr. Louise Robinovitch—reports indicated that he had changed his name. Directory and census records are not complete, but it appears that the two occupied the house.

After 1905 Dr. Robinovitch became widely known for experiments with electricity and anesthesia. In 1908 the *New York Times* said she had received her medical degree at twenty and described her as a small and retiring person who "lives only for her work."

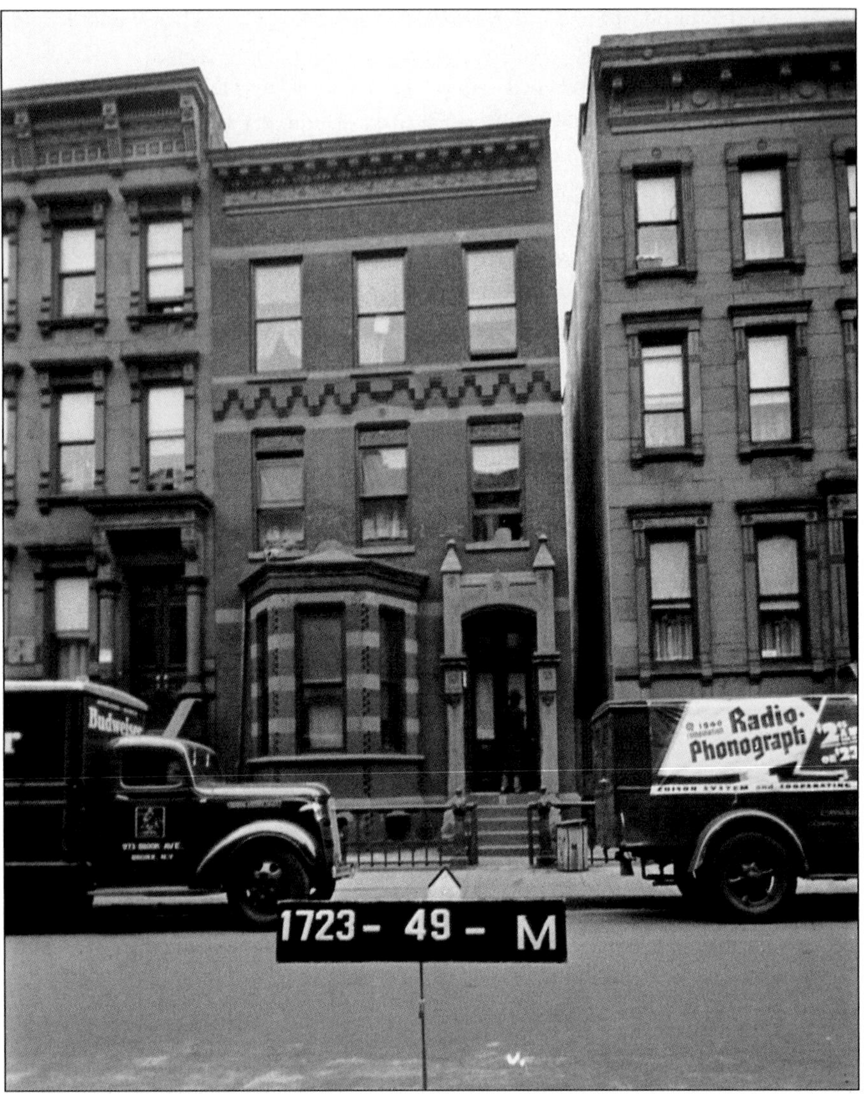

28 WEST 126TH STREET IN 1940. COURTESY MUNICIPAL ARCHIVES

Dr. Robinovitch believed that a direct current of about thirty-five volts was far better for surgical procedures than were chloroform or cocaine.

In 1909 she resuscitated a dead rabbit in the offices of the New York Edison Company on Duane Street; company officials were trying to find ways to revive employees electrocuted while on duty. In 1910 the *Times* reported that she had served as the electro-anesthesiologist at Saint Francis Hospital in Hartford during the amputation of a man's frozen toes.

Her medical career was cut short in 1910 when the Northern Bank of New York, at 215 West 125th Street, which was controlled by her brother, ran short of funds because of his misdeeds. Robin was also responsible for the failure of two other banks.

In January 1911, two aged, impoverished Brooklyn residents, Herman Robinovitch and his wife—she was unnamed in news accounts—showed up at a hearing for Robin offering to help.

According to the news accounts, the Robinovitches convincingly claimed to be the parents of Joseph and Louise—Mrs. Robinovitch cried out, "Meine kinder, meine kinder"—but the brother and sister denied the relationship, without explanation. "I do not know these old people," Robin said, while his sister kissed him and sobbed hysterically on his shoulder.

Three days later Dr. Robinovitch was indicted for perjury on her brother's behalf. Robin was convicted of larceny and spent ten months in prison, but the disposition of Dr. Robinovitch's case was not reported. The pair dropped from view after 1915 when she sold the house.

In 1922 the Finnish Progressive Society built Finnish Hall at 15 West 126th Street, and the 1925 census shows 28 West 126th Street with eight residents, most of them Finnish-born carpenters—by that time it was a boardinghouse.

12 WEST 129TH STREET

IN THE MID-NINETEENTH CENTURY, Harlem was an orderly suburban village with large, freestanding houses oriented to the street grid. Late in 1862, William Paul, a carpenter living in the West 20s, bought a 75-foot front triple lot on the south side of West 129th Street.

Paul was in business with another carpenter, Thomas Wilson, and in 1863 one or the other—or both—built a clapboard two-and-a-half-story house that was later numbered 12 West 129th Street. The two men soon listed their home addresses as "129th off Fifth," and Wilson actually acquired the house from Paul in 1865. No photographs of the house survive from that era, but later records indicate that it had a gabled roof and may have in fact been a double house.

In 1882, the estate of a subsequent owner, Martin England, leased 12 West 129th Street to John B. Simpson Jr., later head of the Estey Piano Company. In the same year, Simpson, acting as his own architect, added first a front and then a rear porch—he called both "piazzas"—screened by piers and arches of elaborately sawed wood in a Moorish pattern. He also added chalet-style wood detailing to the gabled roof, giving a picturesque exoticism to what had apparently been a fairly conventional frame building.

12 WEST 129TH STREET IN 1932. COURTESY MUSEUM OF THE CITY OF NEW YORK

Simpson occupied the house until the early 1890s. The England estate sold it to the Missionary Sisters of the Third Order of St. Francis in 1896.

A Peekskill architect, Asbury Barker, was retained to raise the house to a full three stories under a flat roof. In 1921, the sisters built a convent on the rear of the lot, at 15 West 128th Street, and perhaps it was at this time that the clapboard house went through its final metamorphosis: a coat of stucco that completely covered its original wooden sheath.

What had begun in 1863 as a frame-country house, been altered into an exotic chalet in 1882, and given a flat roof in 1896 was now a villa with a seaside air. A 1932 photograph shows that the stucco was tinted in contrasting colors, reminiscent of the style of Savannah, Georgia, or the Gulf Coast—a particularly curious, but wonderful sight in Central Harlem.

ASTOR ROW ON WEST 130TH STREET

THE ASTOR ESTATE, WORTH $80 MILLION IN THE MID-1870S, began a particularly aggressive building program in 1878, eventually putting up structures like the old Waldorf-Astoria, the St. Regis, and other big buildings. But it also built more modestly, and from 1880–1883 William Astor built twenty-eight brick row houses for investment at 8 to 62 West 130th Street, designed by Charles Buek.

In 1883 the *Real Estate Chronicle* described them as "Philadelphia-style," and they are unique in Manhattan—fourteen pairs of houses set back 20 feet from the street, three stories high, with wooden porches, and recessed light courts partly separating each pair. The intelligence and ingenuity of their planning rebukes the standard high-stoop brownstones built across the street.

In 1920 the row was still sound but buffeted by changing conditions. A real estate collapse in Harlem around 1905 had given blacks their first toehold in the neighborhood, previously almost exclusively white.

The 1920 census shows that Astor Row's tenants were all white. But in late 1920 the Astor Estate, headed by the young Vincent Astor, announced that it would open the houses to blacks, noting that the whites were on leases with ninety-day cancellation clauses.

The exact reasoning behind the decision was not reported. One typical hypothesis is that whites fled areas next to those with blacks, but the 1920 census shows no empty houses. Another is that the quality of white tenants in such areas suffered, whereas the succeeding blacks were more respectable. But there were professionals in both white and black groups, and equal numbers operated their homes as rooming houses.

A final common explanation is that blacks paid more by crowding in. The black tenants may well have paid more, but they were not materially more crowded, with 316 tenants recorded in the 1925 state census, a modest increase over the 292 white tenants in 1920.

Whatever the explanation, the 1925 census offers a picture of black life. At 12 West 130th Street, the occupants were Joseph Bushnell, a fifty-year-old minister; his wife, Effie; their five children; and three lodgers: Thelma Hatcher, a teacher; Charles Hamlet, a bellman; and his wife, Iva. All were American born.

26 WEST 130TH STREET, PART OF ASTOR ROW, IN 1939. COURTESY OFFICE FOR METROPOLITAN HISTORY

Forty-six West 130th Street was occupied by a machinist, Allen Abramson; his wife, Mary; and several roomers. Most of the occupants had come to this country from St. Kitts, St. Thomas, or Barbados starting in 1905. The youngest Astor Row inhabitant recorded in 1925 was Marion Walton at 32 West 130th Street, 106 days old, daughter of Wilbert Walton, a West Indian electrician who had been in America since 1919.

Astor Row was pretty much forgotten by 1978. Norval White and Elliot Willensky, the authors of the second edition of the *AIA Guide to New York City*, mourned the "restrained beauty which has been tarnished by years of economic distress," especially the fragile wooden porches, many of which were collapsing or had been removed. Since that time a renovation effort, spearheaded by the New York Landmarks Conservancy, has restored many of the houses.

Not many years ago there was something almost romantic for students of architecture discovering this ignored, tumbledown row. But this same romance was killing Astor Row.

13 WEST 131ST STREET

AT THE TURN OF THE TWENTIETH CENTURY, MANHATTAN'S BLACK POPULATION was spread around—in parts of Greenwich Village, the area of the future Pennsylvania Station, and the West 60s. New housing was frankly restricted to whites, and blacks typically occupied older, deteriorating buildings.

At the same time, overbuilding of row houses and medium-sized apartment houses in Harlem created first weakness and then a crash in the market, and some owners began, in a very limited way, to rent new apartments to blacks.

In 1899, Philip A. Payton Jr., was trying to break into the real estate business in New York City. His father was a barber, and Payton himself had limited schooling, although two of his brothers went to Yale. Payton first had an office on West 32nd Street near Eighth Avenue and later was quoted in *The Negro in Business* by Booker T. Washington as saying that everyone tried to convince him "that there was no show for a colored man in such a business in New York."

Nevertheless, Payton kept at it, and in 1903 opened an office at 67 West 134th Street—since demolished—as he slowly persuaded white owners to turn over their buildings to him to manage. The next year he incorporated the Afro-American Realty

181.1 FIG

PHILIP A. PAYTON JR., HIS WIFE, MAGGIE, AND THEIR HOUSE AT 13 WEST 131ST STREET IN 1903. COURTESY OFFICE FOR METROPOLITAN HISTORY

THE PAYTON HOUSE IN 1938. COURTESY OFFICE FOR METROPOLITAN HISTORY

Company. Payton's effort was commercial, but there was always the sense of mission behind his expanding operations.

A display advertisement in the *New York Age* in 1906 began: "Colored Tenants, Attention! After much effort I am now able to offer to my people for rent" several apartment houses "of a class never before rented to our people."

Payton also jousted with recalcitrant white owners. In one case, he sold some buildings to a white syndicate, which unexpectedly evicted the black tenants. Payton then bought two nearby apartment houses and filled them with blacks. In this way, block by block, Harlem became a black community.

In 1914, the *Outlook* noted that three-quarters of the black population of New York City, and all blacks of prominence, lived in Harlem. It called Payton "the father of his Negro community." The *New York Age* called him "the pioneer Negro real estate agent in New York City."

In the same year that Payton opened his 134th Street office he also bought an 1887 Victorian Gothic row house at 13 West 131st Street. It had been designed and built by John E. Darragh. Darragh's row, indeed the entire street, was all white in 1900 when Ernest Rothschild, manager of a cracker factory, lived at No. 13 with his family.

Payton moved into the house in 1903 with his wife, Maggie, and was listed there in the next issue of *Phillips's Elite Directory,* a listing of genteel householders arranged by address, although the directory soon dropped blocks with incoming blacks. By the time of the 1915 New York State census the block was almost completely inhabited by blacks born in Bermuda, Barbados, Grenada, St. Thomas, and the United States, with occupations like valet, cook, yachtsman, porter, domestic, and elevator operator.

Payton died in 1917 at his country house in Allenhurst, New Jersey, and Maggie Payton sold their house in 1919, which by the 1940s was rented as furnished rooms.

HARLEM'S LAFAYETTE THEATER

2225 ADAM CLAYTON POWELL JR. BOULEVARD

THE LAFAYETTE OPENED IN NOVEMBER 1912, a project of Meyer Jarmulowsky, a Lower East Side banker. V. Hugo Koehler, an established theater architect, designed the two-story, 1,500-seat theater in the Renaissance style, facing Seventh Avenue between 131st and 132nd Streets.

At the time, Harlem's real estate market was depressed, and many owners had begun to rent to black tenants apartments that previously had been let only to white tenants. The *Age,* a Harlem newspaper, reported that the racial character of the area was shifting, with 132nd Street recently black and 131st still white.

The Lafayette allowed blacks only in the balcony, and the bitter complaints in the *Age* and elsewhere document the state of black consciousness in New York at the time. By August 1913 blacks were allowed in the orchestra but had to pay double the white price of ten cents, five cents for children.

But the theater had trouble making money and that year became the first major theater to desegregate, according to Jervis Anderson's *When Harlem Was in Vogue*. In October 1913, a troupe called the Darktown Follies opened *My Friend from Kentucky*, and the audience was 90 percent black.

Lester Walton, drama critic for the *Age*, voiced optimism that an increase in black audiences would produce a corresponding increase in serious black productions. In

THE LAFAYETTE THEATER, WHILE MACBETH WAS IN ITS EIGHTH WEEK IN 1936.
COURTESY MUNICIPAL ARCHIVES

1914, Walton was named manager. The 1915 opening of *Darkydom* attracted Irving Berlin, John Cort, Charles Dillingham, and, reported the *Age*, a variety of "names which might be seen on the Social Register."

In 1916, the black actor Charles Gilpin established the Lafayette Players, Harlem's first black legitimate theater group, at the Lafayette, and Bessie Smith, Ethel Waters, Moms Mabley, Leadbelly, Duke Ellington, Fletcher Henderson, Earl Hines, Stepin Fetchit, and others performed there.

The theater was closed in the '30s, but John Houseman, developing the Works Progress Administration's Negro Theater Project in New York, took it over for an effort that ultimately employed two hundred black performers. In consultation with Virgil Thomson, Mr. Houseman planned two types of works: plays written, produced, and directed by blacks—like *Walk Together Chillun!* and *Conjur Man Dies*—and classical works adapted to black circumstances.

The first of this latter group, directed by the twenty-year-old Orson Welles, was *Macbeth,* set in Haiti and soon dubbed *Voodoo Macbeth*. It played to full houses for ten weeks, then moved on to Broadway and a national tour. The Negro Theater Project ended in 1939, and in 1951 the Williams Christian Methodist Episcopal Church, founded in 1919, bought the building.

While the interior was altered, the exterior had remained largely unchanged, until 1990, when the church demolished the facade—jackhammering off projecting ornament—for a new one "to make it look more like a church than a theater," according to the Reverend Dr. James Arthur Jones, the pastor. Percy Griffin, the architect, designed a new front of marble and concrete formed to imitate rock-faced stone.

Michael Adams, president of the Upper Manhattan Society for Progress Through Preservation, a new Harlem landmarks group, said: "Of course they have a legal right to do it—but not a moral right."

CITY COLLEGE

138TH TO 140TH STREETS, AMSTERDAM AVENUE TO ST. NICHOLAS TERRACE

CITY COLLEGE WAS ESTABLISHED IN 1847 and soon built a large, neo-Gothic building at the southeast corner of 23rd Street and Lexington Avenue. But by the 1890s, the city grew up around the site and enrollment increased and City College—like New York University and Columbia College—began to look for a campus farther uptown. The trustees eventually settled on a rocky plateau running from 138th to 140th Streets, from Amsterdam Avenue to St. Nicholas Terrace.

When George B. Post won the design competition he had an engineering degree, twenty-five years of experience with everything from tenements to mansions and skyscrapers, and a reputation for sober, conservative designs. He designed a group of buildings in the collegiate Gothic style of which the centerpiece was the main building, later named Shepard Hall.

In form, Shepard Hall is like a giant cathedral: a front with two towers faces the campus, behind which the "nave" is terminated by a huge, square, central tower, something like that over the crossing in a Gothic church. Two curving wings of classrooms extend out from the sides. The giant main hall on the ground floor will impress all but the most snobbish ivy-leaguer.

For the sake of economy, the buildings were faced with Manhattan schist taken from the site and trimmed with bright, white terra-cotta. The dark, rough, rocky schist and the bright, smooth, angular terra-cotta form a startling combination.

At the time of the City College commission, glazed terra-cotta had been only recently introduced and was considered a versatile material. It looked like stone, but could be mass-produced, and was light in weight.

Most of the facades at City College were bearing walls, instead of masonry veneers supported on steel framing, and Post used the terra-cotta as if it were stone, piling one block on top of another, sometimes with no real backing or other stiffener, especially in the big, square central tower.

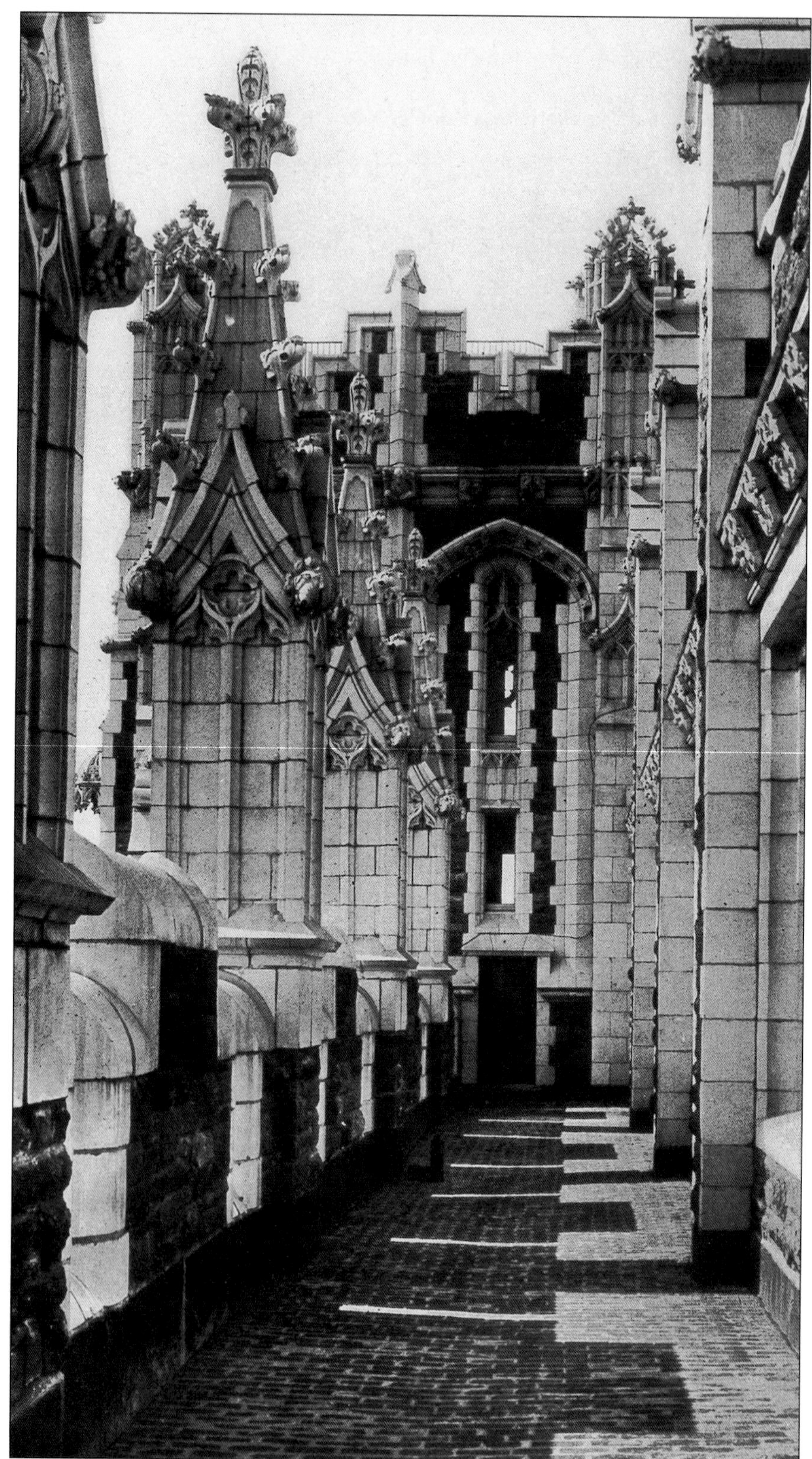

THE PARAPET AT SHEPARD HALL, CITY COLLEGE'S MAIN BUILDING, IN 1908.
COURTESY OFFICE FOR METROPOLITAN HISTORY

But terra-cotta is not like stone—it cracks easily, is not nearly as strong, and its hollows easily trap water, which can freeze and expand.

By the 1990s problems with the terra-cotta were long-standing. The main tower walls had shifted dramatically—and with no steel skeleton, the entire structure depended on their stability. At that time the Stein Partnership, an architectural firm, had to redesign the building from the inside out, install new concrete walls and floors, and replace fifty thousand terra-cotta elements.

But the case of Shepard Hall shows an experienced architect using a new material in new ways on a large scale, apparently without considering the possibility that the material might not hold up. Post left little margin for safety, or evidence of awareness that he was using a new, untested material.

HAMILTON GRANGE

141ST STREET AND CONVENT AVENUE

IN 1795, ALEXANDER HAMILTON LEFT A DISTINGUISHED CAREER in public service to make some money. None of his work as a developer of the Constitution, as George Washington's secretary of the treasury, or as a leader of the Federalist Party provided well enough for his wife and four children, so he started a private law practice.

In 1798 he conceived of "a sweet project," a country house in upper Manhattan, which he built in 1802. Probably designed by John McComb Jr., later one of the architects of City Hall, Hamilton Grange was on a woody hilltop at what later became the southwest corner of 143rd Street and Convent Avenue.

The Hamiltons occupied it in the warmer months, and Hamilton could even commute daily to his office in downtown Manhattan, a three-hour round trip by carriage. It originally was a two-story squarish structure with wide porches on each side and the chaste detailing typical of the Federal style.

His enjoyment lasted only for two years; in 1804 he was killed in a pistol duel with Aaron Burr in Weehawken, New Jersey. Mrs. Hamilton sold the house in 1833, after which it gradually declined. In 1889 Amos Cotting bought the land under it for a row house development. He heard that St. Luke's Episcopal Church, then at Hudson and Grove Streets, was looking for a new site uptown, and he gave the church the house in exchange for building a new church near his row houses, at the northeast corner of 141st Street and Convent Avenue.

The church relocated Hamilton Grange just to the north of its intended site, and used it first as a church and later as a rectory and church hall. The original main facade

HAMILTON GRANGE IN 1899, *after it was moved from 143rd Street and Convent Avenue to 141st Street and Convent Avenue.* COURTESY NATIONAL PARKS SERVICE

wound up pushed against the side of the church, and one of the side porches became the new entry. The church's massive brownstone side porch squeezes the house on the south side, and a six-story apartment house butts up against it on the north.

If you prize a varied streetscape, it's a pleasing wonder; if you prefer untouched architecture, it's a painful mutilation.

The church sold Hamilton Grange in 1924 to the American Scenic and Historic Preservation Society, which maintained it as a house museum as well as it could. But in 1962 it was acquired by the National Parks Service.

Discussions of moving the house back to a more rural setting appeared as early as 1901; few people have ever defended its jammed-in situation. Continued deterioration brought a new push for relocation and restoration in the 1950s and 1960s. Different sites have been proposed, including the City College campus, Riverside Park, vacant land on Amsterdam Avenue, and near the Cloisters.

In 1966 the Reverend David Johnson, rector of St. Luke's, opposed moving it to any location other than next to the church, although he did suggest moving it to a large vacant lot behind the church to permit the restoration to its original appearance.

But a plan to move Hamilton Grange to a nearby park was approved several years ago, although actual relocation is at least a year or two away. So at some point the advocates of a more sanitized building will have their sway.

THE JAMES A. BAILEY HOUSE

150TH STREET AND ST. NICHOLAS PLACE

JAMES A. BAILEY WAS NAMED JAMES MCGINNIS when he was born in Detroit in 1847; by the time he was nine, both his parents had died. At fourteen, he found work in a circus, taking the surname of a manager who helped him. A skilled administrator, he became a circus owner in the 1870s, going on tour through Australia and South America. When Bailey bought the Great London Circus, including a baby elephant, he went on tour in direct competition with the circus of Phineas T. Barnum, even exhibiting in Barnum's home city of Bridgeport, Connecticut.

In 1880 Barnum and Bailey reached terms on a partnership, but in the mid-1880s Bailey, suffering from overwork, retired. In 1886, he began work on what he thought

FIG 185.1

THE BAILEY HOUSE AT ST. NICHOLAS PLACE AND 150TH STREET, CIRCA 1895.
COURTESY MUSEUM OF THE CITY OF NEW YORK

JAMES A. BAILEY *(lower left) in a poster from the Barnum & Bailey Circus.*
COURTESY THE NEW-YORK HISTORICAL SOCIETY, NEW YORK CITY

would be his last residence, at 150th Street and St. Nicholas Place, which is a four-block offshoot of St. Nicholas Avenue. The architect S. B. Reed designed a turreted medieval-style house of limestone; Michael Henry Adams, a Harlem preservationist, says that the interiors were designed by Joseph Burr Tiffany, a cousin of Louis Comfort Tiffany. Joseph Tiffany designed interiors like those of Wilderstein, the Suckley family homestead on the Hudson River in Rhinebeck, New York.

An 1890 article in *Scientific American* about the Bailey house catalogued the different woods in various rooms—hazel in the parlor, quartered oak in the main hall, sycamore in the library, and black walnut in Bailey's office—and noted that the house had a billiard room and art gallery on the third floor. The article particularly praised the stained glass by Henry F. Belcher, with color and pictorial effects that changed over the course of a day "with almost perfect art and skill."

But before the house was finished in 1888, the restless Bailey came out of retirement and reactivated his partnership with Barnum. "I never knew a sharper, shrewder, bolder man than Bailey," Barnum told the *New York Times* in 1887.

When Barnum died in 1891, the *Times* called Bailey "a Caesar among showmen," describing him as "a little man, slender and wiry, a perfect bundle of nerves." The *Times* said that the publicity-shy Bailey was responsible for some things often credited to his better-known partner, and that it was Bailey who started the two-ring circus and who engineered the purchase of the elephant Jumbo from the London Zoo in 1882.

Mr. Adams said that Bailey thought that St. Nicholas Place would be lined with other mansions and would develop into a Harlem version of lower Riverside Drive. But Bailey was disappointed by apartment construction in the area in the 1890s, Mr. Adams said, and moved to Mount Vernon, New York. Bailey sold the Manhattan house in 1904, two years before his death in Mount Vernon. The *Times* reported that when news of his death reached the circus at Madison Square Garden, "one of the old clowns broke down completely and only stopped sobbing when the bell rang and he had to run into the ring to make the people laugh."

John and Alfred Ringling attended Bailey's funeral, and soon they bought out Bailey's widow, Ruth, to create the Ringling Brothers and Barnum & Bailey Circus, which still plays in New York, although in a different Madison Square Garden.

THE HARLEM SPEEDWAY

CARRIAGES WITH FAST HORSES WERE THE HOT RODS of the nineteenth century, but the cost of good animals kept trotting a sport for the elite. There was occasional pressure to build a straight, level racing course in Central Park, and in 1892 Mayor Hugh J. Grant and George Washington Plunkitt, a Tammany Hall leader, pushed a bill through the state legislature authorizing construction of a fast drive on the west side of the park.

The proponents, however, misgauged public reaction. Reformers used the issue to stir up those who opposed special-interest intrusion in the park, those who feared the advent of a low crowd of gamblers and drinkers, and those who simply hated Tammany Hall.

The Central Park plan was defeated, but in early 1893 Grant's successor, Mayor Thomas Gilroy, also a product of Tammany Hall, found a politically safer way to satisfy the trotting fraternity. He arranged to give over Manhattan's Harlem River shore from 155th to Dyckman Street to a special roadway designed as a fast trotting course.

The shoreline in this section was isolated from the rest of Manhattan by high, rocky bluffs. Even industry had not settled there. The area was part of High Bridge Park, established in the 1880s, and the park's waterfront was generally unused.

Reform organizations, relieved that the speedway would no longer threaten Central Park, did not oppose the $1 million plan for the Harlem Speedway, and dissent was restricted to lesser issues. The original plan had only one pedestrian sidewalk, on the land side of the road, so pedestrians would not cross the track—but that meant they could not get to the water. And the landscaping of the roadway was an afterthought—the Parks Department designer, Calvert Vaux, was allowed to add to the basic engineering plan but not change it.

A riverside walk was added before the speedway opened on July 2, 1898, and the *New York Tribune* praised the walkway as "a wide military boulevard, like those of Italy . . . as level as a dancing floor." The roadway was 70 to 90 feet wide, surfaced with soft loam, and flanked by planting strips. The *New York Times* noted that the projected $1 million cost had swelled to $5 million.

Pedestrians were prohibited from crossing the 2.3-mile-long roadway and had to use three underground passageways. Overpasses were not built because they could disturb the horses and because people might drop things from them.

On opening day, the *Times* reported that the hotel operator Lawson N. Fuller was the first through, in his surrey drawn by Fleetwing and Fleetwood, who shared a mile time of 2 minutes, 56.5 seconds.

Sulkies—two-wheeled, one-horse carriages for one—were thought to encourage a low element and were prohibited, along with horseback riders and bicyclists. The *Tribune* wrote, however, that spectators were disappointed with the quality of the stock, quoting one observer who said there were "too many second-hand campaigners with broken backs and one or two wooden legs."

Midway up the speedway, a stone embankment on the land side was designed to serve as a reviewing stand, and pedestrians could follow a few pathways through High Bridge Park down to the road. But vehicles could enter only from the north, at the east end of Dyckman Street, or at the principal entrance, at 155th Street and St. Nicholas Avenue, down a long stone causeway that still survives.

Almost immediately a Washington Heights jeweler, William F. Doll, created a stir by twice taking his bicycle out on the speedway, against police orders. He was fined $5 but vowed he would go to jail instead of paying, on the grounds that the speedway could not be restricted to one class of vehicle. Although the League of American Wheelmen agreed in principle, they did not back Doll up because the soft surface was not good for cycling. Doll paid and was released.

The speedway proved popular with crowds and racers. In 1900 the *New York Tribune* praised the project for promoting "a sport truly American" that attracted competitors from eastern and midwestern cities. Thousands of spectators came for the parades and planned competitions by various driving clubs and for the informal "brushes" between

THE HARLEM SPEEDWAY LOOKING NORTH TO THE WASHINGTON BRIDGE IN 1905. COURTESY LIBRARY OF CONGRESS

drivers. Occasionally they got something extra—as in 1900, when a horse driven by Mrs. George Kotch broke away and took her on a half-mile breakneck trip, ended only by daring action by two mounted policemen.

But the dedication of the Harlem Speedway to elite traffic continued to rankle some, and as early as 1909, area property owners began to try to open it up to regular traffic. The interest of the rich was waning, too, as they converted their stables to garages for a new generation of toys—motorcars. In 1916 the *Times* reported that the speedway was used by fewer than one hundred carriages a day, and in 1918 the writer Reginald Pelham Bolton reported there were fewer than twenty vehicles a day.

In 1919 the speedway was opened to auto pleasure traffic along with horse-drawn vehicles. The present cast-stone railing along the riverfront appears to have been installed around this time.

From the 1940s to the 1960s the present Harlem River Drive was gradually built, but the modest four-lane width—two north and two south—on the upper part and its northern outlet onto local streets has kept it a rather peaceful highway. It has its curves and swoops, like the East River Drive farther south, but instead of a wall of high-rises, it runs along a rocky, primeval cliff face covered in jungly growth.

Because of problems of access, the promenade along the water is almost always deserted, but it makes a much better bicycle trip than the corresponding journey along the East River Drive, where the six lanes of traffic can be deafening.

155TH STREET VIADUCT

IN 1895, WHEN THE HARLEM RIVER WAS WIDENED and cut through to the Hudson as the Harlem Ship Canal, the new waterway required more modern bridges, and the present Macombs Dam Bridge was built. Its architect Alfred P. Boller, also designed a 1,600-foot-long viaduct rising from the Manhattan end of the new bridge to meet the intersection of 155th Street and St. Nicholas Place in Manhattan, 110 feet above the level of the river.

Neighborhood boosters had long complained that the high plateau was inaccessible from surrounding areas. And in 1890 *Scientific American* had lamented that horse-drawn vehicles had to make substantial detours: "To draw a load up the hill a team has to be taken a mile or more to the south." And although the elevated train running up Eighth Avenue stopped at 155th Street, before the building of the viaduct commuters returning home by the El had to descend to the street and then climb the equivalent of eight stories to their homes. The new roadway was lionized by the *New York Times* as "A Street Built in Mid-Air—New York's Wonderful Viaduct."

The 155th Street Viaduct ran above the elevated line, connected to it by lacy stairways designed by Hecla Iron Works in Brooklyn; the firm later designed the above-

FIG 187.1

AN 1890 RENDERING *of the 155th Street Viaduct.* COURTESY CORNELL UNIVERSITY LIBRARIES ground iron and glass kiosks for the first subway line. At either end, rock-faced abutments of granite and limestone were fitted with decorative stairways and special faceted lanterns. According to research by Jay Shockley at the Landmarks Preservation Commission, the western terminus was marked by a pink granite fountain, the gift of the late businessman and philanthropist John Hooper. The fountain had a 28-foot-high column topped with a weather vane and a lantern; on one side was a wide watering trough for horses, on the other separate drinking places for dogs and humans.

Although almost an industrial structure, the viaduct was as carefully and comprehensively designed as a park boulevard. Special viewing platforms extended out at the center, although it appears that pedestrians could not glimpse much more than left field in the polo grounds just to the north, where the New York Giants played from 1891 to 1957.

After the $700,000 viaduct opened in October 1893, the journal *Engineering News* praised it as a "thoughtful creation combining fitness, stability, and beauty." Lawson Fuller, a neighborhood hotel owner and real estate investor who lived at 155th and Amsterdam Avenue, probably drove down the viaduct when the new 415-foot-long bridge opened in 1895. Fuller, a carriage enthusiast, wanted to be the first to cross—but a bicyclist sneaked in ahead of him.

Now there are only a few fragments of the original ornament, and the surface of the viaduct looks like any other urban highway, although the pronounced drop and the city views are dramatic. But it is underneath that this work is still its most majestic. At the intersection of 155th Street and Frederick Douglass Boulevard, the view west is dramatic: an airy network of rivet-spotted columns and skinny crossbars marching away into the huge, rocky stone abutment leading up to St. Nicholas Place.

MORRIS-JUMEL MANSION

160TH STREET AND JUMEL TERRACE

IN 1765 AN ADVERTISEMENT IN THE *New York Mercury* offered a river-to-river site in upper Manhattan, with oystering, clamming, and fishing; an orchard with plenty of quince trees; and "the finest prospect in the whole country," with panoramic views of Long Island, Staten Island, New Jersey, and the mainland. Roger Morris, a retired British officer who had served in Canada, and his wife, Mary, a member of the Philipse family, bought the property as a country house—they also had a city house at Broadway and Stone Street.

They built Mount Morris—what is now known as the Morris-Jumel Mansion—between 1765 and 1770, with several remarkable touches. The most obvious is the grand Doric portico—facing south over the river toward New York Bay—but the Morrises also

POSTCARD OF THE MORRIS-JUMEL MANSION ABOUT 1910. COURTESY OFFICE FOR METROPOLITAN HISTORY

used flush-boarding on the principle facades on the south and west, with less expensive shingling on the east and north. Most unusual is the plan of the house: many riverfront houses adopted the model familiar from the mansions on the James River—entering from the land side into a large hall that empties onto the water side, giving a through-building view of the water. But the Morrises ran their main hall south-to-north, terminating in an elongated octagonal room.

The house has never been firmly attributed to an architect or even a builder. Perhaps it was Morris himself, whose father, an architect, might have had a strong hand in it.

In 1775 Roger Morris went to England for unexplained reasons, leaving his wife in charge of the houses. Like her husband she was a loyal Tory, and she left the house in 1776 as American forces approached from the south. Washington used the house as his headquarters in September and October of 1776, before being forced to escape from advancing British troops.

Although the English controlled New York, neither of the Morrises ever returned to their masterpiece—during the war the house was taken over by loyalist forces and they occupied rented quarters elsewhere in New York. At the end of the war in 1783, the year the British left, the Morrises auctioned their household goods and left for England.

In 1790, when Washington returned to the house for a visit with John Adams, John Quincy Adams, Thomas Jefferson, and Alexander Hamilton, it was a tavern for travelers headed north. But in 1810 Stephen Jumel, a merchant, and his wife, Eliza, bought it for their own use. John Pintard, a prominent New Yorker, said in his letters that Eliza Jumel had been Stephen Jumel's mistress, and married him by feigning a fatal illness. A later court case offered testimony that she had been a prostitute in Rhode Island.

Constance Greiff, the architectural historian, did an extensive study of the Morris-Jumel Mansion in 1995, and she says the 1810 census records the Jumels in the house with two free African-American males and six white males, who may have been servants or farm hands.

Jumel died in 1832, and in 1833 Eliza Jumel, about fifty-eight, married Aaron Burr, seventy-seven, who had served as vice president under Thomas Jefferson. Burr had killed Alexander Hamilton in an 1804 duel, and was later tried (but acquitted) for treason. He misused Eliza Jumel's money and she sued for divorce on the grounds of adultery. Ms.

MORRIS-JUMEL MANSION ABOUT 1915. COURTESY MORRIS-JUMEL MANSION ARCHIVES

Greiff's research indicates the final decree was granted in 1836 a few hours after Burr's death, which permitted Eliza Jumel to claim she was the widow of a vice president.

Ms. Greiff says that there are reports of the aged, perhaps unbalanced Eliza Jumel riding around the property on horseback with an "army" of homeless, armed with sticks for rifles, in mock parade. After she died in 1865 there was a bitter dispute among heirs, with separate, warring factions occupying different parts of the house.

In 1894 it was purchased by the Earle family and renamed Earle Cliff; in the same year the house narrowly escaped destruction by fire. Ms. Greiff's research indicates that Ferdinand Earle promoted various patriotic projects, like a combined building for all such organizations at 77th and Central Park West (the site of the present New-York Historical Society), and around that time the Daughters of the American Revolution (DAR) began meeting in the mansion.

Earle advertised the site for sale in 1898 anticipating splitting up the land into building lots and moving the structure to another location, but that never occurred. Then in 1903 New York City purchased the house and land—now reduced to two square blocks, from 160th to 162nd Streets, Edgecombe Avenue to Jumel Terrace. In early 1904 the DAR was challenged in its quest to operate the house by the Colonial Dames of America—"Daughters in War Paint–Patriotic Blood Afire" ran the headline in the *New York Tribune*.

Finally the Department of Parks decided to retain administration of the property and eventually ringed the plot with an iron fence. The building is open to the public and is part of the Jumel Terrace Historic District. It is a peaceful place, featuring rooms with various periods of furniture—including grand Second Empire pieces from Eliza Jumel and a writing desk used by Aaron Burr—as well as the unusual plan of the house, with its wide, open hall terminating in the unusual octagonal room. From the porch the views south and west have long since been lost, but the view east over Yankee Stadium still takes in Long Island Sound.

168TH STREET IRT STATION

NEW YORK'S FIRST SUBWAY OPENED IN 1904 but reached only to 137th Street and Broadway. In the first section of the subway the work was mostly cheap cut-and-cover construction with stations close to street level. Two years later the vast stations at 168th and 181st Streets were opened. At these points the line is about 100 feet below surface, too deep for cut-and-cover construction. So the contractors blasted through rock for the tunnel—a far more expensive procedure—and enlarged it to about 50 by 300 feet for the stations.

Joseph Cunningham, a transportation writer, says the stations were designed, like the earlier stations, by Heins & Lafarge. They produced their famous system of pictorial plaques of terra-cotta—the *Santa Maria* at Columbus Circle and the steamship *Clermont*

189.1 FIG

at Fulton Street—surrounded by intricate mosaic tile work, carved marble, ironspot brick, and terra-cotta ornament. Station ironwork and other details were given varying colors to help in identification—yellow for West 66th Street, violet for West 79th, gray-blue for West 86th was a typical series. The *Real Estate Record and Guide* said on October 29, 1904: "New York can congratulate itself on one specimen of 'Civic Art' in which a useful structure has been decorated with the utmost propriety."

At the 168th Street stop, it is not so much the decoration but rather the long, vaulted station area that is astounding in a system usually marked by low ceilings and screens of columns.

At the southern end of the vault the double portal over the tracks lends railroad grandeur to what in other areas is just a utilitarian hole. Along the center line of the ceiling runs a series of terra-cotta medallions (for long-lost light fixtures), multicolored explosions of geometric meanders, and lengthy floral work. Across the tracks runs the original elevated pedestrian crossing to the original elevator shaft on the east side.

Although these spaces are among the most spectacular subterranean vistas in New York, the Landmarks Preservation Commission has designated only the earlier, 1904 stations of the IRT line. But the Transit Authority has made an attempt to recognize the 168th Street station's historic character. Strip fluorescent lighting has been replaced by reproduction torchères on the side walls and fluted, park-type lamp standards on the overpasses.

The lower walls have been given new tile, and the careless runs of conduit, piping, and other baggage have been removed or minimized. Some missing decorative tiles have been patched. The great tan brick vault has been swept of loose dirt, but not properly cleaned, and is still spotty and discolored. It is a small advance.

FIG 189.2

TWO-PART PANORAMA OF THE SUBWAY STATION AT 168TH STREET IN 1922.
COURTESY THE NEW-YORK HISTORICAL SOCIETY, NEW YORK CITY

But with all its faults, anyone who has traveled the subways of Washington, which boast many such high spaces, will wonder how different the New York system would be if every station was as grand as that at 168th Street.

HUDSON VIEW GARDENS

181ST STREET AND PINEHURST AVENUE

IN 1923 CHARLES PATERNO DECIDED TO DEVELOP the land across Cabrini Avenue from his house and hired the architect George F. Pelham Jr., who came up with an unusually inventive plan. The long, north-south site slopes steeply down to the west from Pinehurst Avenue to Cabrini, and Pelham designed two solid walls of apartment buildings facing the avenues. He made each line an irregular facade of peaked roofs and landscaped indentations, all in the Tudor style, which was then becoming popular in suburban apartment houses.

In a brilliant move, Pelham and Paterno created a secluded enclave by placing the building entrances toward the center of the lot—an area developers of other sites usually left as a barren concrete courtyard. Running a private street down the center—it is still private—they put the taller six-story elevator apartment buildings on the high side, and the lower four-story walk-up buildings on the low side, to distribute river views as widely as possible among the 354 apartments.

Because the westernmost buildings are downslope, this long central area has plenty of afternoon light. The craggy retaining walls and irregular stairways make a picturesque space, creating the feel of a medieval hill town. Because Paterno wanted to appeal to a higher economic class than that in the surrounding buildings, he built Hudson View Gardens as a co-op rather than a rental complex. In one advertisement in August 1924, the most expensive apartment was a two-bedroom for $10,000, with maintenance of $84 a month. Most apartments were one- or two-bedrooms.

For the target tenant—someone who might otherwise live in a small mid-block apartment in central Manhattan—Hudson View Gardens was out of the way. Therefore, Paterno put everything he could into providing efficient apartments in beautiful surroundings. Kitchens were carefully planned and had automatic dishwashers; living rooms had built-in Murphy beds. There was central radio service with a rooftop technician in charge of monitoring incoming signals, a post office, a child's nursery, a barber shop, community rooms, a restaurant, and a grocery.

In 1925 Pelham wrote about the difficulty of marketing new ideas. "There is little of the pioneer in the speculative builder," he declared, because "the New York renter is indeed a timorous fellow." Perhaps because of this timorousness, two hundred apartments

INTERIOR COURTYARD AND DRIVEWAY OF HUDSON VIEW GARDENS IN 1926.
COURTESY CORNELL UNIVERSITY LIBRARIES

remained vacant for a year, and Paterno increased his advertising budget from $50,000 to $400,000.

Andrew S. Dolkart, a preservationist and historian, moved into the complex a decade ago and has painstakingly collected Paterno's promotional literature. The newspapers of the day were filled with advertisements designed to look like news stories: "Fine Families Flock to Apartment Citadel" was the headline for one in the *New York Times* in 1924. Paterno even offered purchasers a money-back guarantee.

A look at the few available previous addresses of new tenants suggests that many were already living in upper Manhattan: Harry A. Kidder, an electrical engineer, moved from Wadsworth Avenue, and William Gettinger, an engraver, moved from West 160th Street. It is difficult to determine how well Paterno made out on his investment, but he did protect his cliff-top castle from undesirable neighbors.

Mr. Dolkart said that Paterno's venture had apparently not influenced other builders—the surrounding buildings are almost all standard in design.

THE REMAINS OF CHARLES PATERNO'S CASTLE

CHARLES PATERNO'S FATHER, JOHN, LEFT CASTELMEZZANO, Italy, near Naples, in the 1880s with his wife, Carolina, after an earthquake destroyed one of his building projects. He brought with him two of his sons, including Charles, born in 1876. Although real estate was the family business, Charles planned another career and graduated from Cornell Medical College in 1899.

That same year, Charles's father died, leaving a half-finished apartment building at 507 West 112th Street. To make good on their inheritance, Charles completed the building and continued in the business as other projects presented themselves. Gradually other brothers joined the firm, and what had started as John Paterno & Sons evolved into the Paterno Brothers Construction Company.

Some accounts say that Charles Paterno decided to return to medicine during the Panic of 1907, but times must not have been too bad. From 1907 to 1909 he built one of the most unusual houses in New York, a cliff-top marble fantasy that quickly became known as the Paterno Castle, on the west side of Cabrini Avenue north of 181st Street. Perhaps Paterno designed much of the building himself—the architect listed on the building permit is John C. Watson, who otherwise did only small apartments and commercial buildings for the family.

Period descriptions said it included rooms of various styles—including one in a Japanese motif, a mushroom cellar, a swimming pool surrounded by bird cages, and a 20-by-80-foot master bedroom. It was surrounded by an extensive series of greenhouses and gardens—Paterno ultimately expanded the site to seven acres—and a giant pergola-topped retaining wall, 1,000 feet long, still visible from the northbound lanes of the Henry Hudson Parkway below.

From his unusual house, Paterno expanded his real estate empire. In 1910 he built, with Joseph, the curving, near-twin buildings at 435 and 440 Riverside Drive at 116th Street. But by the mid-1910s the brothers had apparently formed separate companies. Charles Paterno built large apartment buildings with elevators on the West Side, among

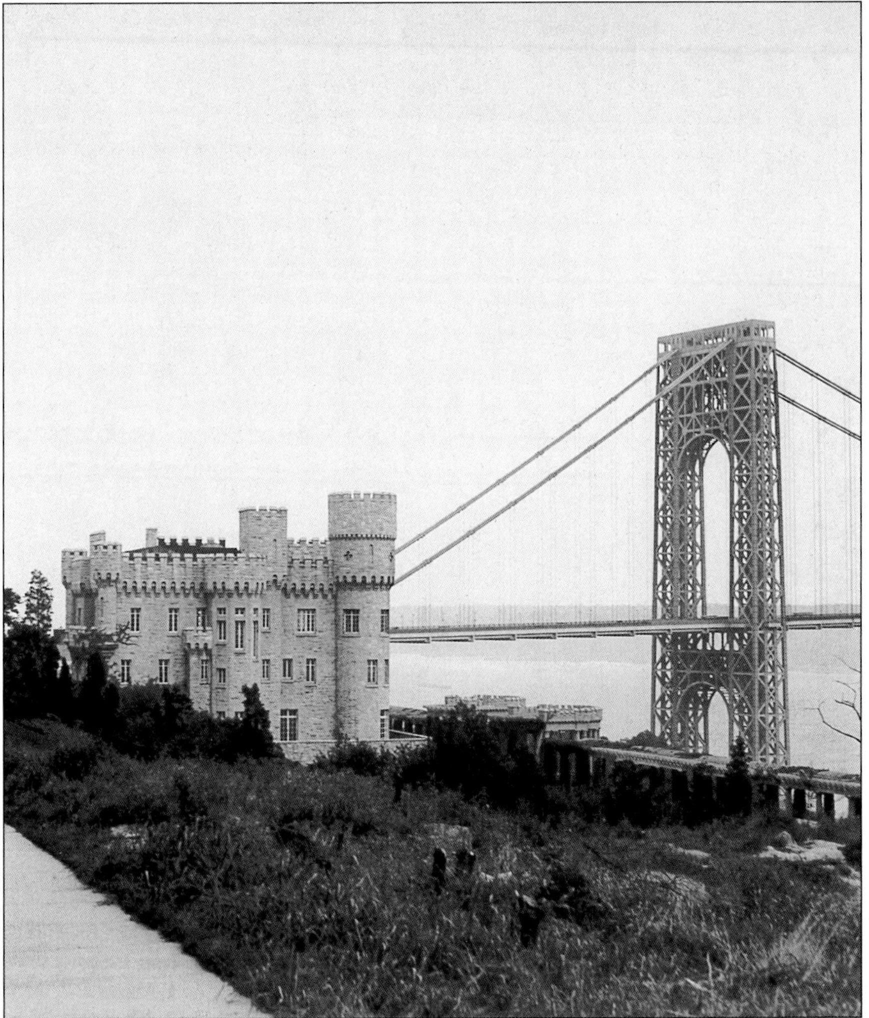

PATERNO CASTLE IN THE 1930S. COURTESY OFFICE FOR METROPOLITAN HISTORY

them 300, 575, and 885 West End Avenue and 280, 285, and 290 Riverside Drive. By 1918 he had put up about seventy-five buildings housing perhaps twenty-eight thousand people. In an interview in *American* magazine in 1918 he noted that the average apartment tenant stayed two years and would pay 30 percent more in rent to reduce the business commute by ten minutes.

In 1924 Paterno told the American Institute of Architects that "there is no progress in building; we lay bricks just as was done five hundred years ago," and he predicted the invention of mechanical bricklaying, plastering, and even painting. In the same year he built Hudson View Gardens, across from his estate, on the block between Northern (now Cabrini) Boulevard and Pinehurst Avenue. By the mid-1930s he was spending more time away from the Paterno Castle, and in 1938 he demolished the building, replacing it with the $6 million Castle Village, five thirteen-story neo-Georgian brick towers with 580 apartments sharing his large garden. The retaining wall survived as well as a few fragments of the estate, among them a single marble pillar at the entrance gate on Cabrini Avenue. But otherwise the Paterno Castle was destroyed.

191.2

FIG

THE PATERNO CASTLE ABOUT 1910. COURTESY OFFICE FOR METROPOLITAN HISTORY

192.1

FIG

BILLINGS'S HORSEBACK DINNER *for thirty-six to celebrate opening of Billings Lodge in 1903.* COURTESY MUSEUM OF THE CITY OF NEW YORK

THE C. K. G. BILLINGS ESTATE

IN 1901 CORNELIUS KINGSLEY GARRISON BILLINGS retired at age forty as president of the People's Gas, Light & Coke Company in Chicago and moved to New York. He pursued the customary interests of a millionaire—yachting, racehorses, carriage driving—and joined other sportsmen at the Harlem Speedway, a favorite resort of those with fast trotters.

Billings occupied a house at Fifth Avenue and 53rd Street and decided to build a stable and lodge near the speedway, buying what is now the lower end of Fort Tryon Park, beginning at 190th Street and Fort Washington Avenue. The architect Guy Lowell designed a 25,000-square-foot stable with quarters for entertaining guests (near the site of the present concession building in Fort Tryon Park) and, on the highest point of his land, a lodge in the form of a round tower, which offered views far up the Hudson and south to the Statue of Liberty.

When Billings completed his tower lodge in 1903, he scheduled a celebratory dinner in the stable to be catered by the elegant Sherry's restaurant, with thirty-six guests seated around a table on large hobbyhorses.

But the *New York Tribune* reported that the crowds gathered at the entrance to the estate were so large that Billings relocated the dinner to the ballroom of Sherry's itself, at 44th Street and Fifth Avenue. At Sherry's, waiters dressed as grooms served Billings's guests, who were seated around a table on real horses.

Cornelius Billings so enjoyed his hilltop retreat that he had Lowell, working with the landscape architect Charles Downing Lay, expand it into his full-time residence. Completed in 1907, it encompassed a giant, French-style house with a central two-story-high courtyard, a 75-by-30-foot swimming pool, a bowling alley, a squash court, and formal gardens.

At the same time, he altered his stable to accommodate his newest interest, a fleet of thirteen automobiles. According to a privately printed estate catalogue owned by the historian Andrew Alpern, special precautions were also taken for fire protection of the twenty-five-acre property, with a private pumping system and three standpipe outlets on each floor of the house.

The 1910 census taker found Billings in residence with his wife, two children, and twenty-three servants. He listed his occupation as "capitalist at large."

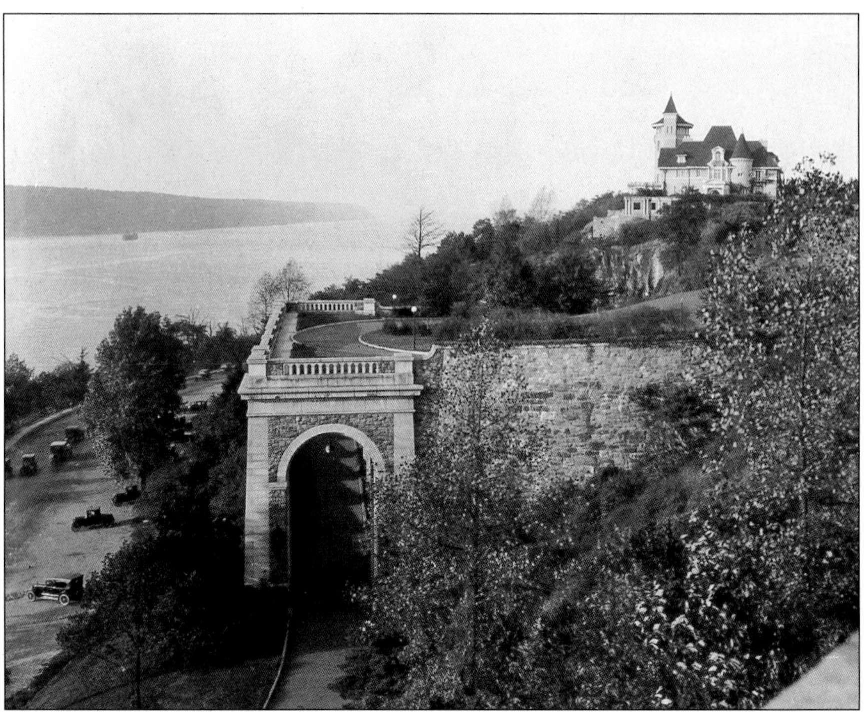

LOOKING NORTH TO THE BILLINGS HOUSE AND THE PORTE COCHERE.
COURTESY THE NEW-YORK HISTORICAL SOCIETY, NEW YORK CITY

Billings also had a yacht landing on the Hudson River—where the Dyckman marina now stands at the foot of 204th Street—but the principal access to his estate was up Fort Washington Avenue, just inside the present southern entrance of the park.

However, beginning in 1908, Riverside Drive above 135th Street was paved and improved and became a popular driving spot. Near the Billings estate, Riverside Drive followed the line of the present northbound lanes of the Henry Hudson Parkway.

The western side of the property, leading from the house down to Riverside Drive, was exceptionally steep, so the architects Buchman & Kahn devised an unusual plan for access. At the point where the drive would intersect 193rd Street (where the street cut through) they began a giant 1,600-foot S-curve rising 100 feet up to the main house, at a 6 percent grade.

At the first switchback, they had to chop a curve out of the rock wall. At the second switchback, to make the turn, the road would have had to go back out into midair. To support this upper turn, the architects designed a 50-foot-high arched gallery of Maine granite and local stone, costing $250,000, which still survives—visible to every northbound motorist on the Henry Hudson Parkway—and is also accessible from Fort Tryon Park.

The new roadway was paved with a special brick with beveled edges to give horses a foothold, and the gallery itself had large torchères and ceiling fixtures. It was, and still is, one of the sights of upper Manhattan, although few know its original purpose and history.

The toys of rich men are sometimes not of enduring interest to them. In 1916 Billings sold the entire estate to John D. Rockefeller Jr., and purchased a home in Oyster Bay, Long Island, as well as the eighth-floor apartment at 820 Fifth Avenue at 63rd Street. Rockefeller wanted to give the estate and neighboring land to the city for Fort Tryon Park, with the idea of demolishing the house.

THE PORTE COCHERE TO THE BILLINGS ESTATE ABOUT 1910. COURTESY OFFICE FOR METROPOLITAN HISTORY

But according to accounts in the *New York Times*, "protests from architects" saved the building, and it was rented out as a residence to a drug manufacturer, N. C. Partos, while Rockefeller and the city negotiated a deal. At the same time the sculptor George Grey Barnard used the stable as his studio.

In 1926 the mansion was destroyed by a spectacular fire that continued into the evening, witnessed, according to the *Times*, by hundreds of thousands. The private pumping system did not work, and city water pressure, 250 feet above the waterline, was reduced to a trickle. When the lodge's turret fell, it "spouted fire and smoke like a volcano," the *Times* reported.

Rockefeller's gift was finally accepted by the city, and the sixty-seven-acre Fort Tryon Park was completed in 1935. A map of 1936 labeled the top of Billings's gallery "overlook" and the road underneath it "pedestrian underpass," indicating that automobile access from the Henry Hudson Parkway was no longer permitted.

A complex of terraces—with dramatic views up and down the Hudson—succeeded the Billings house and were connected by a long, bowed promenade leading to the south entrance of the park. Even in cold weather the heather and winter grasses make a visit to this area a delight. Billings's double switchback driveway is still intact under a layer of asphalt, and a walk down the gentle slope is a trip back in time.

At the top is a fairly straightforward lawn, but halfway down, the path follows the dramatic curved cut in the craggy rock to a pine grove. The driveway was blacktopped long ago, but patches of the blacktop are breaking off, especially as you approach the gallery.

From the inside, the gallery is a striking vaulted space, slightly spooky because of its remove from the park. However, the brick roadway here is uncovered. At the bottom, there are the remains of a freestanding entrance gate, and you can look up the cliff and see the Billings gatehouse, another fragment that survives. Because this part of the park is so near the highway, it is a neglected jungle. If you really want to get away from New York, this is the spot.

THE SEAMAN-DRAKE ARCH

ACCOUNTS CONFLICT BUT IN THE 1850S EITHER John F. Seaman or Valentine Seaman, who were brothers, built a great marble house on the high ridge between what are now 215th and 217th Streets and Park Terrace East and Park Terrace West. Directories indicate that in 1855 John F. Seaman moved up from his house at 19 Jay Street to the new mansion, which was approached up a winding driveway leading from what is now Broadway through the 35-foot-high marble entry arch that survives at 215th Street. An account in the *New York Tribune* in 1895 said that the house took six years to build, and that John Seaman brought over "several plans from abroad" for the house, as well as Italian artists to fresco the ceilings, but it did not identify a designer.

The estate had twenty-six acres, with a chapel, greenhouses, stone stables, a trout pond, grape arbors, and extensive plantings, all overlooking both the Hudson and Harlem Rivers. When Ann Drake Seaman, John Seaman's widow, died in 1878 in her mid-eighties, she left the house and most of her money—her estate was valued at $2 million in 1900—to Lawrence Drake, variously described as her cousin or nephew. One hundred and forty-five relatives contested the will, saying that Drake had unduly influenced his aged relative. But Drake prevailed, and the place became associated with the Drake name.

Drake in turn sold the estate around 1900, and in 1906 Thomas Dwyer, a prominent builder, bought and occupied the estate, establishing his offices down the hill on Broadway in what his letterhead called "The Marble Arch Building," to which he added a mansard roof in 1910. Dwyer was the contractor for major projects like City College and the Soldiers' and Sailors' Monument at Riverside Drive and 89th Street. He sold off much of the land, and by 1920 garages and car dealerships lined the west side of Broadway at this location, engulfing the arch.

THE SEAMAN-DRAKE HOUSE ABOUT 1890. COURTESY ERIN DRAKE GRAY

THE SEAMAN-DRAKE ARCH ABOUT 1890. COURTESY ERIN DRAKE GRAY

In 1928 Dwyer sold the mansion to a developer who erected apartment buildings on top of the hill, but the Seaman-Drake Arch survived, although in increasingly ragged condition. Now commercial buildings engulf the arch about halfway up.

Sidney Horenstein, a geologist who lives nearby, recalls that the interior of the structure was badly damaged by a fire one night in the 1970s. On the upper section of the rear of the arch a half-dozen window openings, apparently original, suggest that it was once a gatekeeper's quarters. Now the arch's marble exterior is slowly sugaring into piles of dust. A drive through the arch leads to Jack Gallo's auto body shop, which has been on the site since 1960. Mr. Gallo has become the de facto curator of this peculiar monument, showing off this ancient relic, which the Landmarks Commission has declined to protect, to the occasional curious visitor—for as long as it lasts.

ACKNOWLEDGMENTS

THE LATE, GREAT MICHAEL STERNE FIRST CONCEIVED the "Streetscapes" column for the *New York Times* in 1986; his successor Michael Leahy has continued and improved it. Over the last decade at the *Times,* John Forbes, Bill Hollander, Rosalie Radomsky, Mervyn Rothstein, and the late, sorely missed Richard Roberts kept the column out of the most serious trouble. And, perhaps more importantly, there are the regular readers of my column to thank, including my mother Anna Margaret Riepma Gray (even though ours was a household where the *Tribune* was the paper of record). Every Sunday, I am writing for all of you.

The heavy lifting on the column is the arduous task of ferreting out all the census returns, building permits, newspaper articles, and directory entries. It's lucky that I don't do it, because I could never do it as well as Suzanne Braley, who not only deserves her own byline, but her own book. Perhaps someday she will write one.

The curators, administrators, and archivists who serve as gatekeepers to New York's photographic and documentary resources are vitally important. For buildings in Manhattan over the last decade or so, this list of helpful people has included at the New York City Municipal Archives, Director Kenneth Cobb, with support from Ellen Chin, Michael Lorenzini, and Leonora Gidlund; at the New York City Department of Buildings, Commissioner Patricia Lancaster, with support from Ilyse Fink and David Laws; at the Museum of the City of New York, Terry Ariano, Anne Easterling, Elizabeth Ellis, Anne Guernsey, Marguerite Lavin, Eileen Kennedy Morales, Tony Pisani, and Wendy Rogers; at the New-York Historical Society, Mary Beth Betts, Eleanor Gillers, Holly Hinman, Mary Beth Kavanagh, Valerie S. Komor, Dale Neighbors, Laird Ogden, Wendy Shadwell, Mariam Touba, and Nicole Wells; and at Columbia University's Avery Architectural and Fine Arts Library, Curator Janet Parks with support from Louis Di Gennaro, Jim Epstein, Anne-Sophie Roure, Vicki Weiner, and the awesome, please-move-back-to-New-York Dan Kany.

For various advice but not always consent I thank most deeply Andrew Alpern, Henry Barkhorn, George Beane, Paul H. Feinberg, Joan Kane, and David Marks. For some seriously good editing at Abrams, thank you Gail Mandel, and for the marvelous design, thank you Eric Strohl of Eric Baker Design Associates.

Here I would like to add a cautionary note: Some libraries, museums, and archives are beginning to hop on the "royalties bandwagon" and are using their collections to support their budgets, whereas it has heretofore been the other way round. So, with a sad irony, I see major institutions everywhere are looking with different eyes at the data they and their predecessors have developed. Instead of seeing Internet-based platforms as a way to distribute this glorious heritage with profoundly increased efficiency, they are seeing it as a way to create a new revenue stream. With some institutions, I fear that before too long, researchers will be asked to pay to get someone to pick up the phone—"Press 1, if you wish to pay by MasterCard. Press 2 for Visa...."

This "revenue approach" is becoming particularly noticeable in the area of permissions to reproduce historic photographs. The widespread dissemination of materials—whether text or photo based—is part of any cultural institution's obligation, perhaps even privilege. But researchers and writers everywhere complain about the high cost of permission fees for historic images, in many cases where the institution does not even hold the copyright but simply one of many intermediate reproductions. Such policies limit the replication of these materials significantly, whether in scholarly or "commercial" endeavors. At present, some institutions' permission fees run so high that the cost for the rights to reproduce one- to two-hundred images for a single book would cost in the tens of thousands of dollars.

If such institutions attitudes are a harbinger, then the future of widespread reproduction of historic images in books and other forms is indeed in trouble. John Kouwenhoven's masterpiece *The Columbia Historical Portrait of New York,* for instance, just could not have been published under such conditions. Someone like myself, active over twenty-five years in the field, can easily work around most of such fees, finding alternate resources. But I weep for the typical author, who has not made a life's work of dealing with photo archives, and I help them as often as possible—and without any so-called "rights" charge.

This book is dedicated with love to my wife, Erin, whom I first met in 1976 while she was courageously saving from demolition the old Towers Nursing Home on 106th and Central Park West. The building is now an empty shell, but had it not been for her, it would not be there at all.

CHRISTOPHER GRAY

INDEX

Page numbers in italics refer to illustrations.

C

D

E

F

G

H

I

J

K

L

M

N

O

P

Q

R

S

T

U

V

W

Y

Z

EDITOR: Gail Mandel
DESIGNER: Eric Janssen Strohl, Eric Baker Design Associates
PRODUCTION MANAGER: Jane Searle

Library of Congress Cataloging-in-Publication Data
Gray, Christopher, 1950-
New York streetscapes : tales of Manhattan's significant buildings and landmarks / Christopher Gray ; research by Suzanne Braley.
p. cm.
Includes index.
ISBN 0–8109–4441–3 (hardcover)
1. Architecture—New York (State)—New York. 2. Historic buildings—New York (State)—New York. 3. New York (N.Y.)—Buildings, structures, etc. 4. Manhattan (New York, N.Y.)—Buildings, structures, etc. I. Braley, Suzanne. II. Title.

NA735.N5 G733 2003
720'.9747'1—dc21 2002152032

Published in 2003 by Harry N. Abrams, Incorporated, New York.

Printed and bound in Italy
10 9 8 7 6 5 4 3 2 1

Harry N. Abrams, Inc.
100 Fifth Avenue
New York, N.Y. 10011
www.abramsbooks.com

Abrams is a subsidiary of